FAMILY DEVELOPMENT

Family

Development

Third Edition

EVELYN MILLIS DUVALL, Ph.D.

Family Life Consultant

J. B. LIPPINCOTT COMPANY

Philadelphia
New York

Preface

This book is designed to equip the preprofessional worker with conceptual tools useful in his or her work with families, and to help the experienced worker get a sharper cutting edge on the tools of his or her profession: teaching, public health work, extension work, social-agency programs, community development, social work, family life education, counseling and research, or whatever involves working with and for families and family members.

The thesis of the book is that families grow through predictable stages of development that can be understood in terms of the development of the individual family members and of the family-as-a-whole. It deals with concepts that have been in the process of formulation for many years, with hundreds of persons contributing to their development.

THE DEVELOPMENTAL TASK CONCEPT

When I returned to the University of Chicago in 1941–1942 to complete my residency for a Ph.D. in Human Development, I was fresh from seven years active community work with teenage youth and their parents. At that time "impulses" and "drives" were popular ways of interpreting adolescent behavior. Such concepts appeared to remove responsibility for their behavior from young people, and to make it seem to them and to those who worked with them, that adolescents were, as one writer in a book for youth put it, "human puppets on an invisible string." Such a point of view interpreting human behavior in terms mainly of biological drives was inacceptable to me.

Another concept that had gained considerable acceptance was that of "needs." This had the advantage of recognizing that people, like all other growing organisms have needs that must be met if they are to grow satisfactorily. It had the disadvantage of being ambiguous, and capable of being interpreted in many ways. Even more serious from my point of view was that so often "the needs of youth," were discussed in terms of the limitations and inadequacies of schools, families and community agencies in meeting these seemingly inexhaustible requirements. Youth was too often seen as an empty cup impatiently waiting for someone or something to fill it. Problems were seen as reflecting unmet needs. Growth of young people was likened to that of a tomato plant, which, given the proper amounts and kinds of nutrients, sunshine, moisture and other requirements would flower and bear fruit in due time. Again, the person himself had little responsibility for his behavior, development or destiny.

It was with this immediate background that I found members of the Committee on Human Development exploring the possibilities of the concept of the developmental task. Work in classes, seminars and professional workshops with Daniel Prescott, Director of the Division of Child Study of the Commission on Teacher Education of the American Council on Education, and a member of the faculty of the University of Chicago first introduced me to the developmental task concept. Study with Robert J. Havighurst, who had just come to the University of Chicago as Chairman of the Committee on Human Development, acquainted me with the history of the developmental task concept to that time. He credits Lawrence K. Frank with first using the term in his hearing about 1935, at one of the many meetings of the staff of the Progressive Education Association's "Adolescent Study" under the direction of Caroline Zachry.[1] It is probable that the original idea came from Frankwood Williams, who several years earlier had published essays stressing what youth must do to work through his developmental problems.[2]

Peter Blos of the Adolescent Study Staff referred briefly to adolescent adjustment problems as "tasks," in his book that appeared in 1941,[3] as one of several volumes published by members of the staff in which adolescence was increasingly recognized as a time of life in which certain essential tasks must be mastered if the young person is to emerge into effective adulthood.

The first published work giving a central place to the developmental task concept was a chapter written collaboratively by Robert J. Havighurst, Daniel Prescott, and Fritz Redl, for the North Central Association's *General Education in the American High School* in 1942.[4]

The developmental task concept satisfied my search for a frame of reference that dealt dynamically with the challenges of human development, keeping responsibility in the hands of the developing persons, and still allowing room for the helping and assisting roles that family members, school personnel and community workers might play. It satisfactorily met the objections raised in the use of "impulse," "drive," and "needs," and yet covered the realities implied in

[1] Robert J. Havighurst, *Human Development and Education* (New York: Longmans, Green and Company, 1953), p. 328.

[2] Frankwood Williams, *Adolescence-Studies in Mental Hygiene* (New York: Farrar and Rinehart, 1930).

[3] Peter Blos, *The Adolescent Personality* (New York: Appleton-Century, 1941), p. 275. (This reference was mainly illustrative, with developmental task still to be recognized as a key concept.)

[4] B. L. Johnson, ed., *General Education in the American High School* (Chicago: Scott, Foresman, 1942), Chapter 4.

each of these concepts. Further, it seemed adequate to cover not only the developmental sequence of the teen years, but appeared to be quite as effective throughout the entire life cycle.

In 1943, the American Council on Education undertook, through a committee chaired by T. R. McConnell, to prepare an outline of objectives and courses in general education that would be appropriate for members of the armed forces. Ernest W. Burgess, of the University of Chicago chaired the subcommittee, of which Reuben Hill, Oliver Ohmann, and myself were members, commissioned to draw up an outline of a course in *Marriage and Family Adjustment.*[1]

As a result of this assignment Reuben Hill and I were appointed by the United States Armed Forces Institute to prepare a workbook on marriage and the family for the use of members of the armed services. This eventuated in the text, *When You Marry,*[2] the first to be written functionally to satisfy student interests and readinesses, from "first date through last baby." It was during this collaboration that the life cycle approach well-known among sociologists, and the developmental task concept emerging in human development began to be seen as a series of developmental tasks through the life cycle.

In 1947, Reuben Hill and I were asked to work together in the preparation of background papers for the forthcoming National Conference on Family Life held in Washington in May 1948. As co-chairmen of the Committee on the Dynamics of Family Interaction, Dr. Hill and I prepared a two-dimensional outline for plotting the developmental tasks of children, and of parents, for each stage of the family life cycle with implications for services arising out of the challenges, hazards, and problems involved in the achievement of each developmental task in our culture. Eight subcommittees of specialists at the various developmental levels, were appointed by the co-chairmen to prepare reports on the various life cycle stages, as noted in the original outline, p. viii.

In referring to this committee's work, Dr. Havighurst credits it with creatively contributing to the development of the concept:

This committee made a step forward in the use of the concept by showing how each member of the younger, middle, and older generations in the family has his own developmental tasks, and how the successful achievements of one person's tasks is dependent on and contributory to the successful achievement by others in the family of their appropriate tasks.[3]

[1] American Council on Education Studies, *A Design for General Education* (Washington, D. C., 1944), pp. 74–84.

[2] Evelyn Millis Duvall, and Reuben Hill, *When You Marry* (Boston: D. C. Heath and Company, and simultaneously New York: Association Press, 1945).

[3] Robert J. Havighurst, *op. cit.,* p. 331.

The work of the Committee on the Dynamics of Family Interaction appeared in several hundred pages of mimeographed working papers used as background study for the National Conference on Family Life.[1]

STAGE IN FAMILY LIFE CYCLE	DEVELOP-MENTAL TASKS OF CHILDREN	DEVELOPMENTAL TASKS OF PARENTS MOTHER FATHER	CHALLENGES, HAZARDS, CRISES, PROBLEMS WHICH ARISE FOR EACH STAGE	IMPLICATIONS FOR SERVICES NEEDED, AIDS EDUCATION
Early Marriage and Expectant Family		Judson T. Landis, Michigan State University John F. Cuber, Ohio State University David Treat, Director, Clara Elizabeth Fund, Flint, Michigan		
Childbearing Family (Birth to 30 Months)		Loyd W. Rowland, Director, Louisiana Society for Mental Hygiene		
Preschool Family (2½ to 5 years)		Marion L. Faegre, United States Children's Bureau, Chairman James L. Hymes, New Paltz Teachers College Caroline Chandler, M.D., Johns Hopkins University Henry Work, M.D.		
School-Age Family (5 to 12 years)		Ralph Ojemann, State University of Iowa Afton Smith, Iowa Child Welfare Research Station May P. Youtz, Iowa Child Welfare Research Station		
Family with Teenagers (13 to 19 years)		Leland H. Stott, Merrill-Palmer School, Detroit, Mich., Chairman Robert G. Foster, Merrill-Palmer School Robert J. Havighurst, University of Chicago Fritz Redl, Wayne University, Detroit		
Family as Launching Center (early twenties)		Henry Bowman, Stephens College, Columbia, Missouri W. Clark Ellzey, Stephens College Homer Rainey, Stephens College		
The Aging Family		Ruth S. Cavan, Rockford College, Chairman Ernest W. Burgess, University of Chicago, Consultant Robert J. Havighurst, University of Chicago, Consultant		
Families in Crisis		Earl L. Koos, University of Rochester, Chairman David Fulcomer, Drew University, Madison, New Jersey		

Many years have come and gone since the report first appeared. In that interval, faculty members of several university centers have generously shared criticisms, questions and further elaborations of the original materials that have helped bring it to the present state of development.

[1] Evelyn Millis Duvall, and Reuben Hill, co-chairmen, *Report of the Committee on the Dynamics of Family Interaction*, National Conference on Family Life, Washington, D. C., May 1948, mimeographed materials.

FAMILY DEVELOPMENTAL TASKS

The idea of developmental tasks of the family-as-a-whole emerged out of the first interdisciplinary workshop on marriage and family research at the University of Chicago during the Summer of 1950 which, as Executive for the National Council on Family Relations, I called and directed. One of the subgroups of that workshop set itself the task of carving out a multidisciplinary way of studying families that would have creative possibilities for research in family development. The calibre of the members of the work group; the recency of Eleanor Godfrey's graduate work with Talcott Parsons; Reuben Hill's growing interest in stimulating sound family research; Dorothy Mummery's close acquaintance with the problems of rural families; Leland Stott's planning for a series of longitudinal studies of family life at Merrill-Palmer School; Richard Stewart's recent success in measuring husband-wife interaction and empathy with the Minnesota Multi-Phasic Inventory; Mildred Morgan's and Letitia Walsh's responsibility for graduate research in family living through their respective home economics departments; David Fulcomer's research in family crises; and my continuing interest in family development- -all served to make this group an outstandingly creative one.

This 1950 Work Group in Family Development research was the first to formulate the concept of family developmental tasks as such. In its report, it defined family developmental tasks as "those which must be accomplished by a family in a way that will satisfy (a) biological requirements, (b) cultural imperatives, and (c) personal aspirations and values, if the family is to continue and grow as a unit." [2] Using the structure-function approach, this work group carved out an outline of family developmental tasks for Stage I of the family life cycle. Since then, this outline has been greatly elaborated and extended to cover the entire family life cycle and developed into the present volume.

The book is in three parts, and it can be most effectively used in the given sequence. Part I, *Growing Families in Changing Times*, describes in detail the developmental task concept and its application to family developmental tasks, seen throughout the family life cycle. It then considers the characteristics of the American family life cycle in midtwentieth century, the influence of social change on family form and functions, the nature of changing patterns of family

[2] Quoted by Reuben Hill in his report of the workshop—Reuben Hill, "Interdisciplinary Workshop on Marriage and Family Research," *Marriage and Family Living*, Vol. XIII, No. 1, February 1951, pp. 21–22.

orientation and of childrearing, and how social class makes for family differences.

Part II, *Expanding Families*, takes the family from its inception at the marriage of husband and wife through the period of expansion with the coming and rearing of children until they are about to be launched into lives of their own. Part III, *Contracting Families*, starts with the launching of the first young adult "child" from the family and carries the family through its middle and later years, with a final chapter appraising the relative vulnerability of families in several areas throughout the family life cycle.

Each chapter is designed to put into the hands of the readers effective tools for a professional attitude toward families. Consequently, throughout the book, there are outlines and detailed analyses for meeting the problems that arise in the family life cycle such as: child-proofing the home for the rearing of children; checking a child's readiness for school; gathering information on how to prepare a child for a new baby brother or sister; building in safety features in the home during the middle and later years; learning to live with in-laws; adjusting to bereavement.

Readings are more extensive than is usual in a book of this kind so that they may (1) stimulate the student of the family and (2) functionally serve the professional worker who is currently concerned with the problems of families and family members.

Suggested activities are more elaborate and detailed than is traditional in order to serve the teacher, leader, or the situation in which a wide variety of dynamically effective methods of study makes the educational experience creatively satisfying. The photographs used to illustrate the book were selected from many cooperative sources, credited picture by picture throughout the text.

Considerable advance in family theory and research in recent years has made possible extensive updating and upgrading throughout this edition. I am grateful to the busy professional specialists who gave time from full schedules to read this work critically and who, in every instance, added something of their own wisdom and expert knowledge to particular chapters. It should be clear that a book such as this is the work of no single author alone; it represents the thinking of the most creative minds in professions holding central concerns in family living. It would be inadequate to merely acknowledge these contributors, but it is appropriate to recognize them as the collaborators they all are in the development of this work.

Evelyn Millis Duvall

Williams Bay, Wisconsin
September, 1966

Contents

PART 1

Growing families in changing times

Families run on bursts of emotional energy generated by the interacting personalities of their members. What are the forces that keep a family alive and growing? How do these forces operate in performing family functions? What challenges do American families face as they shift in size and nature, structure and function within our changing society?

To every thing there is a season, and a time for every purpose under the heaven:

A time to be born, and a time to die; a time to plant, and a time to pluck up that which is planted; . . .

A time to weep, and a time to laugh; a time to mourn, and a time to dance; . . .

A time to get, and a time to lose; a time to keep, and a time to cast away; . . .

ECCLESIASTES, III

CHAPTER ONE

The family life cycle

Knock on any family door, and what will you find within? No one can tell you exactly, for every family differs in many ways from any other. But generally, if you know three things about a family, you somewhat reliably can predict what you will find going on within it: (1) where a family is in time—in its life cycle, within an era of social change, and in a given season, day, and hour, (2) who lives in the family home, and (3) how the family rates in the community as seen in its social status. If you know these three things, you can tell even before you meet the family what the important elements to look for are and what forces you may find in action there.

FAMILY TEMPOS AND RHYTHMS

Families have a developmental history marked by periods of dynamic action and spelled by intervals of relative calm. This is true even within a day, a week, a season. Typically, the family day begins with the bustle of arising, washing, dressing, collecting the day's equipment, and getting into the day's activity. This first spurt of energy is followed in many homes by the midday pause with nobody home but Mom and the dog. By late afternoon there is the rush of homecoming with reports of the day, fixing equipment, cleaning up, and preparing the evening meal. In many families there is a period of eating together with family attention focused upon itself. Outside pressures then are suspended momentarily and a high degree of family interaction is possible. Between the evening meal and bedtime, activities vary by the age and interests of the family members, the stage of the family life cycle, and its orientation. Young parents may go out for the evening with a sitter in to stay with the baby. The family may spend a quiet evening at home with the peace broken by intervals of conflict over the choice of television programs, the use of the telephone, or the pressures of privacy and group demands. There may be guests in who are entertained by the whole family, by the adults only, or by the children. Retiring tends to be serially routinized, with the youngest going to bed first, and the others according to age and interest.

Weekly rhythms are fairly predictable in most families. Monday through Friday routines are built upon work and school schedules. Saturday and Sunday are the weekend intervals filled with shopping and food storage, cleaning and making ready for the coming week, in addition to individual and whole family recreation (travel, trips, picnics, hobbies, movies, entertaining, and "just being lazy"); as well as religious services for the various family members.

In most parts of the country there are seasonal variations characterized by Spring, with its housecleaning, gardening and storage of winter clothing and equipment; Summer, with more out-of-doors living, sports, and vacation activities; Autumn, with the busyness of organizational, educational and vocational life, and getting the home ready for the Fall and Winter activities in the community. Late in the Fall, there is the flurry of "getting ready for the holidays" in home, school, and community, with the bustle of seasonal entertaining, and festivities in various settings. By midwinter, families settle down to indoor activities with routines established for getting things done before Spring rolls around again.

THE FAMILY LIFE CYCLE IS COMMON TO ALL FAMILIES

There is a predictability about family development that helps us know what to expect of any family at a given stage, regardless of who or where it is. Much as an individual grows, develops, matures, and ages, undergoing the successive changes and readjustments from conception to senescence, no matter who he or she is, so families likewise have a life cycle that is seen in the universal sequence of family development.

The family life cycle, as a frame of reference, is a way of taking a long look at family life. It is based upon the recognition of the successive patterns within the continuity of family living over the years. It opens the way for study of the particular problems and potentials, rewards and hazards, vulnerabilities and strengths of each phase of family experience from beginning to end. It recognizes the peculiar rhythms and tempos that pulse through family living, now soft and sweet, now loud and tempestuous, now swift, now slow, in movements that every family everywhere knows in its harmonies and dissonances of living together through the years.

Families take form in the marriage and early establishment of the newly married couple. They develop rapidly as husband and wife assume, with the coming of their first child, additional roles as father and mother. As successive children are born, family members enlarge their roles to encompass the additional children as individuals and as members of the growing family group. Each addition to the family brings not only an increase in the number of family members, but a significant reorganization of family living, so that no two children are born in exactly the same family.

As children grow older, their parents are growing older also, changing in their needs and desires, their hopes and expectations, as well as their responses to the demands and pressures of growing children. Concurrently, the children are progressively changing in their relationship to their parents, to their brothers and sisters, and to other relatives.

Families mature as their children grow up, through childhood, into adolescence, and finally into lives and homes of their own. Families that once expanded to accommodate the requirements of growing children, later must contract as they release these same children as young adults. The big bustling years when family life runs at a hectic pace eventually give way to the long slow-moving years of the empty nest, when the middle-aged and aging parents face the later half of their marriage together as a pair. With the prolongation of life these later years present new opportunities and problems.

Each family grows through the years in its own particular way. Just as the individual person is born, grows and develops, matures, and ages, undergoing the successive changes and development from conception through senescence in his own way, so a family lives out its life cycle in its own unique fashion.

STAGES IN THE FAMILY LIFE CYCLE

The family life cycle may be divided into few or many stages, on the basis of several factors. It is possible to think of a two-stage family life cycle: (1) *the expanding family stage* taking the family from its inception to the time its children are grown and (2) *the contracting family stage* in which children are being launched by the family into lives of their own and in which the family contracts through the later years with one or both of the original pair still at home. Such a two-stage cycle delineation is usually too gross for definitive study, but the factor of shifting plurality patterns in the family was one of the first used to see stages in the family life cycle.

As early as 1931, Sorokin and others [1] discussed a four-stage family life cycle based upon the changing family member constellation within the family: (1) married couples just starting their independent economic existence, (2) couples with one or more children, (3) couples with one or more adult self-supporting children, and (4) couples growing old.

E. L. Kirkpatrick and others [2] saw the stages of the family life cycle in terms of the place of the children in the educational system in a four-stage cycle: 1) preschool family, 2) grade-school family, 3) high-school family, and 4) all adult family.

In plotting the changing income and outgo financial patterns through the family life cycle, Howard Bigelow [3] elaborated on the school placement factor in a cycle he demarked into seven periods: (1) establishment, (2) childbearing and preschool period, (3) elementary school period, (4) high-school period, (5) college, (6) period of recovery, and (7) period of retirement. The most complex breakdown of the family life cycle into stages, to date,[4] elaborates the eight-stage cycle of this text into a twenty-four-stage cycle. Following not only the predictable development of a family as the oldest child grows, this proposal also keeps the youngest child in focus. Such a delineation calls for two preschool family stages, three schoolage, four teenage, five young adult, and five launching stages. The first of these is the stage as defined on page 8. The others make provision in each family life cycle stage for a possible youngest child who theoretically plunges the family back into an

[1] P. Sorokin, C. C. Zimmerman, and C. J. Galpin, *A Systematic Source Book in Rural Sociology* (Minneapolis: University of Minnesota Press, 1931), Vol. II, p. 31.

[2] E. L. Kirkpatrick *et al.*, "The Life Cycle of the Farm Family in Relation to Its Standard of Living," *Research Bulletin #121* (Madison, Wisconsin: Agricultural Experiment Station, University of Wisconsin, 1934).

[3] Howard F. Bigelow, "Money and Marriage," Chapter XVII in *Marriage and the Family,* Becker and Hill, eds. (Boston: D. C. Heath, 1942), pp. 382–386.

[4] Roy H. Rodgers, "Proposed Modification of Duvall Family Life Cycle Stages," paper presented at the American Sociological Association meetings, New York City, August 31, 1960.

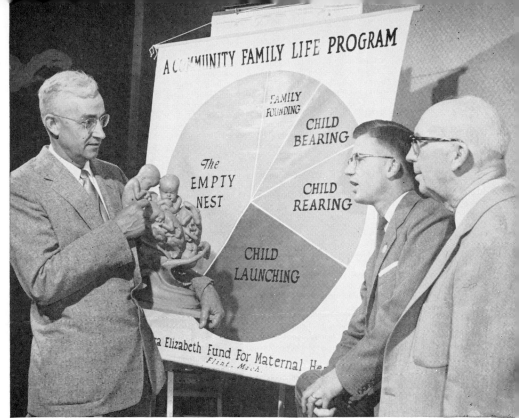

The image shows a banner reading "A COMMUNITY FAMILY LIFE PROGRAM" with a pie chart divided into segments labeled: FAMILY FOUNDING, CHILD BEARING, CHILD REARING, CHILD LAUNCHING, The EMPTY NEST. At the bottom: "Clara Elizabeth Fund For Maternal Health, Flint, Mich."

The family life cycle is one way of taking a long look at family life. Here we see David Treat (left), Director, Clara Elizabeth Fund for Maternal Health in Flint, Michigan, outlining a community family life program that takes into account the entire family life cycle.

earlier age-group interest. Such an elaboration may be helpful in research design, but is unnecessarily detailed for our use here.

The problems of delineating family life cycle stages which will hold for all families are many because families themselves are so varied. Some couples marry early and others not until much later. Some couples have their first baby in the first year of their marriage, others not until years afterwards, and still others never have children. Some babies arrive one after another in quick succession, while others are spaced by as much as a dozen years or more. Some children follow a regular progression through elementary school, high school, and college, while others cease being school children before they are scarcely in their teens. Even more difficult to take into account are the many forms of broken and rebuilt families—with all that is involved in divorce, remarriage, and the establishment of families in which "your children," "my children," and "our children," are all part of the same family. Military service but partially

Each family grows through the years in its own particular way. Rich or poor, large or small, in the city or on the farm, every family has a life cycle that is seen in the universal sequence of family development.

launches many young men from their parental families, for although they leave home, their independence is incomplete when they must return to finish their educational plans and finally get settled in lives of their own. No less indefinite is the status of the girl who may be a wife of an absent serviceman and yet still a daughter at home with her parents.

Whatever schema for defining family life cycle stages is used, it is merely a convenient division for study of something that in real life flows on from one phase to another without pause or break. The genius of the concept is the explicit awareness that each stage has its beginnings in the phases that are past and its fruition in development yet to come. Being cyclical by definition, the family life cycle and each of the stages within it has no beginning and no end. No matter where you start to study the family life cycle, there are always relevant roots in the near and distant past that must be considered. Wherever you are at the moment, you have grown out of the stage just before and are heading into the stage ahead.

This book recognizes and depicts the family life cycle as consisting of eight stages:

Stage I   Beginning Families (married couple without children)
Stage II   Childbearing Families (oldest child, birth to 30 months)
Stage III   Families with Preschool Children (oldest child 2½ to 6 years)
Stage IV   Families with School Children (oldest child 6 to 13 years)
Stage V   Families with Teenagers (oldest child 13 to 20 years)
Stage VI   Families as Launching Centers (first child gone to last child's leaving home)
Stage VII   Families in the Middle Years (empty nest to retirement)
Stage VIII Aging Families (retirement to death of one or both spouses)

The age and school placement of the oldest child are used as criteria of family cycle stage placement from arrival of the first child in the family up to the launching center stage when we shift focus to the situation facing those remaining in the original family. Families as Launching Centers (Stage VI) is the stage that begins with the leaving home of the first child and concludes with the departure of the last child into marriage, military service, work, or whatever pulls him or her as a young adult into a life of his or her own.

This treatment is organized around a modification of the seven-stage family life cycle structured by the co-chairmen for the National Conference on Family Life in 1948.[1] It represents a combination of the several factors used in determining family life cycle stages: (a) plurality patterns, (b) age of the oldest child, (c) school placement of the oldest child, and (d) functions and statuses of families before children come and after they leave. This combination of factors seems to be workable for the study of the majority of American families, and to parallel such reliable data as are available to date both from the United States Bureau of the Census and from less extensive research studies.

OVERLAPPING OF FAMILY LIFE CYCLE STAGES

In defining the stages in terms of the oldest child, the presence of other children in the family is not explicitly recognized. A clean-cut sequence of stages of the family life cycle such as that outlined above seems to occur only in the one-child family. In families with more than one child,

[1] Evelyn Duvall and Reuben Hill, co-chairmen, *Report of the Committee on the Dynamics of Family Interaction*, prepared at the request of the National Conference on Family Life, (Washington, D. C.: February 1948), mimeographed materials.

there are several years of overlap at various of the stages. The average mother of two or more children is in the period of childbearing for a longer period than Stage II indicates, she has preschool children over a longer span of time than is predicted for Stage III, she has school age children longer than is considered in designating Stage IV, she has teenagers in the home for a longer period than that covered by Stage V, see Chart 1, page 13.

There is no simple solution to the conceptual problem of overlap of stages of the family life cycle in families of more than one child. Since our thesis is that families grow and develop as their children do, our answer to the question of overlapping of stages is that a family grows through a given stage with its oldest child, and in a sense "repeats" as subsequent children come along. We see a family being pushed out into new unknowns in its experience as its oldest child becomes a preschooler, goes to school, gets into the teens, and finally leaves for a life of his own. As younger children come along, they arrive in a family already somewhat familiar with these normal events and stages of children's growth through the induction given by the eldest. Thus, while a family may be seeing its firstborn into preschool, a younger sibling arrives in a preschool family rather than a childbearing family, because of the family's involvement with the older child also. Actually that family is not solely a childbearing family, because it is already grappling with the problems and pressures of its preschooler, at the same time that it nurtures its newborn. And so it goes through the years that children are in the home. The oldest child is always taking his family with him out into the growing edges of family experience. Younger children necessarily arrive into a different family than that into which the firstborn came, if only in the degree of its experience with children of his age.

THE MARRIED COUPLE AS "FAMILY"

Three stages of the family life cycle, as we define it, deal with the husband and wife as a couple: Stage I as a married couple before children come, and Stages VII and VIII as a married couple after their children have grown and gone. It can be argued that a couple without children is not a family, but more accurately a married couple.

But, seeing the whole family in focus through the years, the newly married couple appear as "the beginning family" which develops very quickly in the majority of cases into the childbearing family. The norm is for the young married couple to be a family-in-the-making not only in that their children eventually make a family of them, but they think of themselves as potential parents long before children actually arrive. In terms of the time factor alone, many couples spend as much or more of their early married stage as expectant parents as they do as bride and groom.

The middleaged or aging couple who has already been through the childbearing, rearing, and launching stages of the family cycle is still a couple, true. But they are parents of grown children, too. They quite probably have grandchildren. They keep up the home base more often than not. They make a home for varying lengths of time for their married children and grandchildren; perhaps for their own aging parents and other older relatives. They continue to think of themselves as "family" and to function as family members long after their own children are grown and off in homes of their own. Therefore, we designate them as in the later stages of the family life cycle.

PLURALITY PATTERNS

The size of the family increases by arithmetical progression—first two persons as husband and wife marry and settle down to establish a family, then the first baby comes along, followed by the second sibling, and so on as long as the family grows in size. The complexity of family relationships increases much more rapidly. According to the Law of Family Interaction: With the addition of each person to a family or primary group, the number of persons increases in the simplest arithmetical progression in whole numbers, while the number of personal interrelationships within the group increases in the order of triangular numbers.[1]

To find the number of interpersonal relationships within a family, the following formula is used in which x equals the number of interpersonal relationships, and y equals the number of persons:

$$x = \frac{y^2 - y}{2}$$

Applying this formula to a specific family, the following series emerges:

Number of persons in the family   2 3 4   5   6   7   8   9 and so forth
Number of relationships in the family 1 3 6 10 15 21 28 36 and so forth

[1] James H. S. Bossard, "The Law of Family Interaction," *American Journal of Sociology,*" January 1945, p. 292, copyright 1945, University of Chicago.

Thus we see that a family consisting of a mother, father, and three children, has a total of five individuals, with a total of ten interpersonal relationships: father with mother, father with first child, father with second child, father with third child; mother with first child, mother with second child, mother with third child; first child with second child, first child with third child; second child with third child.

Dynamically, the number of interrelationships within that family may increase with the coalitions that form from time to time as separate units within the family. It is common, for instance, in a three-child family for two children to form a tight little dyad which functions almost as another entity within the family group. Not infrequently, the children line up as opposed to the parents in still another interrelationship along generational lines. The conclusion to be drawn is that as the family grows in size its interpersonal relationships multiply even more rapidly; and conversely, when the family contracts in size in the launching stage of the family life cycle, the number of persons leaving the home is not as large as the decrease in the number of interrelationships.

THE LENGTH OF THE STAGES

Americans usually think of a family as one in which there is a father and mother and two or three young children. Advertisements beam on such a picture of family life. Church and school materials often portray this stage of the family life cycle as though it were the only one that mattered. Commercial word pictures commonly assume that the family with young children is *the* family. Holiday sentiments and everyday assumptions put this stage of the family life cycle so much in the foreground that none other seems to exist. Such a stereotype is understandable. Certainly the childrearing and childbearing stages are highly important in family relationships, in the family's contact with school, church, and community, in the development of the personalities of the children, and for the family as a consumer with its bulging appetites for more and ever more goods. Yet this stage in the family life cycle is but a small fraction of the whole. It consists of but a few years, an average of a dozen or so, out of the total of fifty to sixty years in the life of the average family.

In marriage and family life courses, in schools and colleges, it is usual to spend the greater part of the time on the processes leading to marriage, in the adjustments of the newly married pair, and their functions

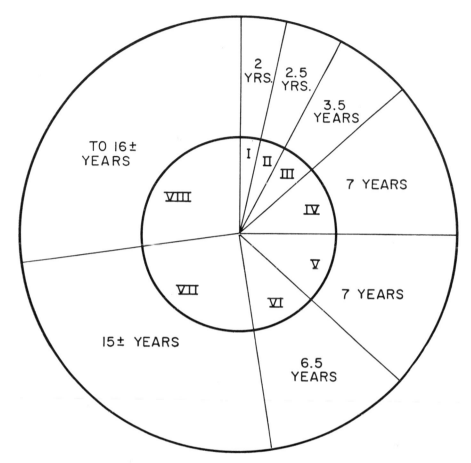

CHART 1. The Family Life Cycle by Length of Time in Each of Eight Stages [1]

- I BEGINNING FAMILIES (Married couple without children).
- II CHILDBEARING FAMILIES (Oldest child birth—30 months).
- III FAMILIES WITH PRESCHOOL CHILDREN (Oldest child 30 months—6 years).
- IV FAMILIES WITH SCHOOL CHILDREN (Oldest child 6–13 years).
- V FAMILIES WITH TEENAGERS (Oldest child 13–20 years).
- VI FAMILIES AS LAUNCHING CENTERS (First child gone to last child leaving home).
- VII FAMILIES IN THE MIDDLE YEARS (Empty nest to retirement).
- VIII AGING FAMILIES (Retirement to death of both spouses).

[1] Data from U. S. Bureau of the Census.

as expectant and actual parents. This, of course, is justifiable in that it reflects the readiness of the student, as well as the significance of the husband-wife relationship for the stability of the family. Yet at the same time such an emphasis misrepresents the time the married pair have together in the family they have established.

If they are a man and woman of the average ages the U. S. Bureau of the Census reports as typical at first marriage, birth of children, marriage of last child, and death of spouse, then the family cycle they may envisage for themselves is largely ignored in courses that focus solely on the young married couple. As is seen in Chart 1, one-half of the marriage typically is spent as a couple after the children have grown and gone.

The significance of the duration of the various stages not only for education, but for budgeting, housing, health, recreation, home management, and a host of other family resources and services excites the imagination, and will be dealt with in part in the subsequent chapters devoted to each of the stages of the family life cycle.

THE LIFE CYCLE OF THE MIDCENTURY FAMILY MEMBER

In much the same way that actuarial tables of an insurance company can predict life expectancy, so in a measure, we can plot the generalized family expectancies through which we as family members pass. Anyone may personally depart from the generalized profile of family experience at any point in the schema. Such variations do not invalidate the predictions which hold true at a given time for the population as a whole.

Using the norms of our American society, with the United States Census Bureau data, a woman's life may be outlined as follows. She comes into her family of orientation at birth, she starts school at six, enters her teens at thirteen, and marries at about twenty. At this point she leaves her family of orientation and enters her family of procreation. Her first child is born about two years later, and her last child is born when she is about 26 years of age. By the time she is twenty-eight, her first child enters school. He becomes a teenager when she is about thirty-five, and marries when she is in her early forties (42–45). Her last child marries before she is fifty (at an average of 47±, earlier for daughters, later for sons). She shares her middle age in the empty nest with her husband until his death which comes when she is well past sixty years of age. Then she is faced with nearly sixteen years of widowhood until her own death.

Of course no woman is a cold statistic, but a living person who will

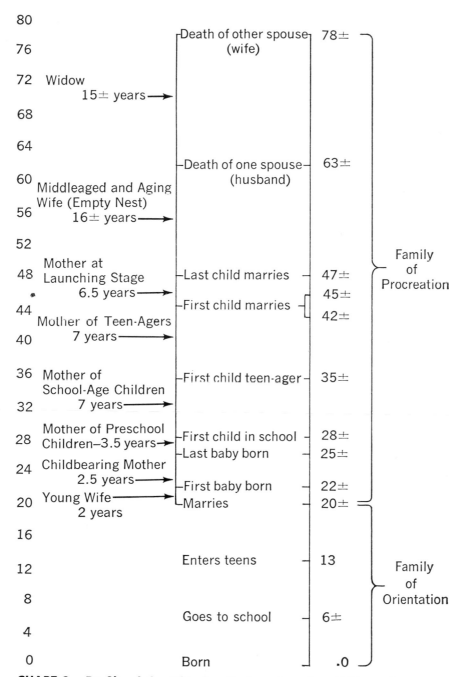

CHART 2. Profile of the Life of a Modern American Wife and Mother [1]

[1] Data from U. S. Census for 1950 and 1960; from Paul C. Glick, "The Life Cycle of the Family," *Marriage and Family Living*, Vol. XVII, No. 1, February 1955, pp. 3–9; and from Ben J. Wattenberg and Richard M. Scammon, *This U. S. A., op. cit.*, p. 42.

pass through several phases distinct from those that have gone before or those that come after in her life. These phases can be seen as a series of long and short pulsations that vary in length and intensity throughout life. She starts with the long pulsation of girlhood that lasts the first thirteen or fourteen years of life. Her career as a young woman is approximately half as long, until she marries in her very early twenties. Then come four short, intensely active phases of about equal length of seven years each: having babies and small children in the home (7 years); having school age children in the home (7 years); having teenagers in the home (7 years); and launching young adult children into lives of their own (6½ years).[1] Now life slows down a bit as she shares the empty nest with her husband for the long leisurely phase of sixteen years more or less, until she is widowed by his death when she is in her early sixties (63±). The last long slow stage of her own aging years continues for another sixteen years more or less.

A female college graduate usually marries about three years later than the average American woman. Girls with no high school education tend to marry before they are eighteen. Those who have completed their high school education usually marry by the time they are twenty.[2] Generally, women with four or more years of college enter marriage two to four years later. Because the college educated woman marries later than her less-well-educated sister, she has her first baby at a later age, and enters the next stages of the family life cycle somewhat later. However, the smaller number of children that college educated women have offsets their later age at marriage to some extent.[3] So, the life cycle profile for the college woman and the typical American woman in the United States tend to parallel each other in the latter half of life, from the launching stage onward.

The profile of life as a woman consists of three long periods of about fourteen years each: girlhood, middle years, and aging years. There are

[1] The launching center stage begins with the departure of the first child from the home for marriage, for work, for military service, or in some cases for college or other advanced training that takes him or her away from home as a young adult, and ends with the emptying nest as the last child leaves home for a life of his or her own. The figures used here, typical in midtwentieth-century United States, are not significantly different from 1960 and projections for 1980 using similar methods, see Table 2, p. 23.

[2] Population 1960 Age at First Marriage (Washington, D. C.: Bureau of the Census, U. S. Department of Commerce, 1966, Table 9, "Years of School Completed —Persons Ever Married 14 to 79 Years Old, by Age at First Marriage," p. 124.

[3] The average number of children ever born to women 45 years old and over was 1.015 for all American women, and .755 for college graduates in 1964, see Current Population Reports, Series P-20, No. 147, January 5, 1966, Table 4, p. 16.

After a woman marries, there is an intensely active phase of childbearing and rearing that lasts about twenty-five years to be followed by an equally long period that remains after the children are grown and gone. It is easy to see the woman's role in the childrearing stage above. But, can you see her just as clearly twenty-five years from now?

five short phases of approximately seven years each: life as a young woman, childbearing years, school-age children's years, teenager's years, and launching-center years. Looking at a woman purely as a reproductive being, we see that she spends the first twenty years of life growing up and getting ready to have children, the next twenty-five years bearing and rearing children, and the last thirty years or more alone or with her husband after their children have grown and gone.

Seeing oneself as a grown woman focuses attention on the fact that more than half of one's life after marriage remains after children have grown. Such a view of life through the years raises many questions about the kind of education needed not only for the immediate future but for the years ahead. What will a woman need to prepare herself for the long middle years after her parent roles are over? What will be necessary for the period of widowhood that stretches on for fully half of her later years? Does this have implications for life insurance plans? What does it say about mate selection that will not unduly prolong the period of

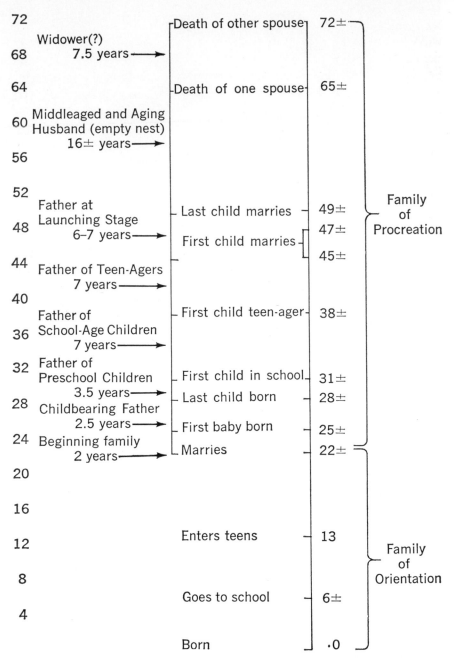

CHART 3. Profile of the Life of a Modern American Husband and Father [1]

[1] Data from U. S. Census for 1950 and 1960; from Paul C. Glick, *op. cit.;* and from Ben J. Wattenberg and Richard M. Scammon, *This U. S. A.* (Garden City, New York: Doubleday & Company, 1965), p. 42.

widowhood? What is indicated in terms of interests and activities with carry-over possibilities for the later phases of life? One's roles as a woman are played out not just in the quick-moving busy years of young woman-hood, but through the ever-changing tempos of the entire family life cycle.

Plotting a profile of the life of the man in the American family using medians and norms projected from U. S. Bureau of the Census data gives us the following outline which differs slightly from that of the American woman. Like her, the male enters his family of orientation at birth, goes to school at six, and becomes a teenager at thirteen. He marries on the average two years later than the woman, when he is 22± years of age. At this point he becomes part of his family of procreation. His first child is born a little more than two years after his marriage when he is not much over twenty-five (25±). His last child is born when he is 28± years of age, and 2½ years later his first child enters school. He becomes a father of teenagers when he is 38± years old. When he reaches his mid-forties (45± to 47± years old) he becomes the father of the bride (or groom) when his first child marries. Before he reaches fifty his last child is married (49±). By this time he probably is a grandfather. From now on he and his wife live in an empty nest, their parenting roles over, for more than fifteen years. The chances are that he retires in his mid-sixties. Characteristically then, he is the first spouse to die (65±), but if he survives beyond the average, he may or may not be widowed through his final years at the latter end of the marriage. The chief differences be-tween the length of the various phases of his life as a man and those of his wife are the slightly longer period before marriage (2± years) and the shorter middle-aged and aging period due to his shorter life span.

Of course, there is no such thing as the average man. Each man has the particular ages and stages in his life cycle which are peculiar to him. On the average, however, he can anticipate spending most of his adult life as a husband and father. He and his wife will spend the first two years or so as a couple before their first child arrives. Then, after his last child has married and left home he may expect another fourteen years (plus or minus) as a member of a couple again. His second decade of life will be spent in becoming a young man, his third in becoming a fa-ther. His forties will be characterized by children and teenagers and young adults being launched into lives of their own. His fifties and sixties, after the peak of childrearing responsibilities are over, will be relatively

1900   1910   1920   1930   1940   1950   1960   1970   1980   1990

Family of Orientation (Parents' Family)

X is Born

Family of Procreation (Own Family)

X Marries Y

Family of Gerontation[I] (Children's Families)

XY's First Child Marries

Family of Gerontation[II]
(Grandchildren's Families)
XY's First Grandchild Marries

**CHART 4. Overlapping of the Life Spans of the Families of
Association of the Individual (1950 Census
Projections for Average American Women)** [1]

quiet ones on the family scene, with just himself and his wife and their
life as grandparents. The chances are that he will leave his wife a widow,
with all the implications of life insurance, retirement plans, housing requirements, and the rest of the factors involved for them both in planning their later years.

ONE GENERATION AFTER ANOTHER

Typically a family develops through a predictable sequence of stages
following one another in reliable progression. Before one family unit has
completed its cycle, its children have been launched to start out on theirs.
Most twentieth-century American family members have the privilege
of seeing the family life cycle start a second time and sometimes a third
as children marry and rear their children who marry and have their
children while older members of the family are still living.

Chart 4 is a schematic portrayal of family development from one generation to the next. Using as a base line the length of time the original
husband and wife have been married, we see their children coming at the
usual ages, marrying at the median ages at first marriage, and having
their children at ages typical in America today. Thus we see that both

---

[1] Generations of girls are shorter than generations of boys, since girls marry at
earlier ages than do boys.

original husband and wife survive the marriage of all their children and participate in the induction of sons- and daughters-in-law into the family. Both of the original parents live to see their grandchildren born and raised and most of them married, before their lives are terminated in death. The original woman lives to see the marriage of practically all her grandchildren, and not unusually has the experience of seeing her great-grandchildren well underway before she too passes on. Thus, at midcentury, the American family typically consists of four or more generations in its extended forms. Dr. Ruth Albrecht predicts that, with increased longevity, generations will be added to the family so that five and six generation families seem likely in the future. She suggests that if a girl with two parents, three grandparents, and two great-grandparents marries the boy with two parents and four grandparents, they will have to maintain a social and affectional relationship with 13 parent figures.[1]

FAMILIES ON THE MOVE

Geographical mobility tends to separate members of the extended family, so that face to face contacts between the generations may be

TABLE 1. *Mobility of the Population of the United States* [2]

Residential Status			Per cent
Same house (non-movers in a given year)			79.9%
Different house in the United States			19.6
Same county		13.0	
Different county		6.6	
Within a state	3.3		
Between states	3.3		
Abroad			0.5

infrequent in some modern families. Table 1 shows that in a recent year nearly 20 per cent of the population moved to a new residence. Mobility rates through recent decades have been remarkably constant.

Roughly the same percentage of the population has moved every year

[1] Ruth Albrecht, "Intergeneration Parent Patterns," *Journal of Home Economics,* Vol. 46, No. 1, January 1954, p. 31.

[2] *Statistical Abstract of the United States: 1965,* p. 32; and *Mobility of the Population of the United States* (Washington, D. C.: Bureau of the Census Series P-20, No. 150, April 14, 1966), 50 pp.

since 1947. Census surveys show that men are slightly more mobile than women, and that nonwhites are more mobile than whites. The nonfarm population moves more than do farmers. The unemployed generally have a higher mobility rate than the employed, probably because many men unable to find work move to other localities in search of employment. However, professional men move more often than do other occupational groups; and men with a college education have higher migration rates than those who have not attended college. Young married couples have higher mobility rates than single young adults. In 1965, in the same age group the rate for single persons of both sexes was 22 per cent, whereas for married couples the corresponding rate was 39 per cent. The census report concludes, "It is evident that the years of early married life may involve successive moves in response to changing needs."[1]

Even though millions move from one place to another every year, this does not mean that the majority of modern families are shorn of ongoing contact with relatives. A recent study of families in the Detroit Area found only 11 per cent of the families with no relatives in the metropolitan area, and a high frequency of intra-family visiting: 29 per cent daily, 37 per cent weekly, 20 per cent monthly, and 13 per cent yearly.[2]

TWENTIETH-CENTURY CHANGES IN THE FAMILY LIFE CYCLE

Today, more children survive the early years, more mothers come through childbearing safely, and a larger percentage of men and women lives to round out the life span than did formerly. Marriage is at younger ages, and both husband and wife can anticipate considerably more years of marriage and family living now than was typical at the close of the last century.

The changes in the family life cycle since 1890 (Table 2) briefly summarized are: (1) men and women marry at younger ages, (2) the childbearing period is shorter, (3) the empty nest, characterized by the marriage of the last child comes sooner, (4) more men and women complete their life span as individuals and as a married pair, (5) there is a longer period together as a couple after the children have grown (the typical family in 1890 had no such period), and (6) each family member has a larger number of older living relatives now than formerly.

[1] *Mobility of the Population of the United States, ibid.* p. 3.
[2] Robert O. Blood, Jr., report on kinescope program "In-Laws (No. 11 in the 1956 Marriage Series) University of Michigan Television Center, Ann Arbor, Michigan, 1956.

TABLE 2. *Median Age of Husband and Wife at Selected Stages of the Life Cycle of the Family for the United States: 1890 to 1980* [1]

Stage	1890	1940	1950	1960	1980
Median Age of Wife at:					
First marriage	22.0	21.5	20.1	20.2	19.5–20.4
Birth of last child	31.9	27.1	26.1	25.8	27–28
Marriage of last child	55.3	50.0	47.6	47.1	48–49
Death of one spouse	53.3	60.9	61.4	63.6	65–66
Median Age of Husband at:					
First marriage	26.1	24.3	22.8	22.3	22–23
Birth of last child	36.0	29.9	28.8	27.9	29–30
Marriage of last child	59.4	52.8	50.3	49.2	51–52
Death of one spouse	57.4	63.6	64.1	65.7	68–69

FAMILY LIFE CYCLE ANALYSIS—PROBLEMS AND PROMISE

There are a number of unsolved problems in family life cycle study. The first is that actual families do not follow statistical models derived from census data. Some family units do not fit any system of stages thus far designed—how many will not be known until there are more longitudinal family studies. The second is that any particular schema of stages has some advantages but fails to meet other specifications adequately. The two-stage family life cycle (expanding and contracting families) is too gross for detailed analysis. The twenty-four-stage cycle suggested by Rodgers is too complex to handle with ease. The eight-stage family life cycle has the disadvantage of explicitly focusing on the oldest child with vision of the younger children in the family blurred by implication and inference. However admittedly imperfect, family life cycle analysis along these lines is a productive way of studying the complexities of contemporary American families.

The family life cycle approach emphasizes the dynamics of family interaction as shifting and changing from one period to another in family experience. It is this dynamic quality that seems best to match the active life of real families. It is the long look longitudinally through the life

---

[1] Source: Paul C. Glick, David M. Heer, and John C. Beresford, "Social Change and Family Structure: Trends and Prospects" paper delivered December 29, 1959 at the annual meetings of the American Association for the Advancement of Science. The figures for 1890, 1940, and 1950 are from Paul C. Glick, "The Life Cycle of the Family" *Marriage and Family Living*, Vol. XVII, No. 1, February 1955, Table 1. Those for 1960 and 1980 are estimates using methods similar to those used for earlier years.

history of a family that keeps in perspective each moment and each person in relationship to all others—past, present, and future. Furthermore, there is evidence that the family life cycle is superior to other variables in explaining and anticipating family behavior.[1] With further refinement, it may become a major tool in appraising and predicting many aspects of family living.

SUMMARY

Families are many and varied. They are similar in that they develop through the years in ways that are in part predictable. Every family develops through a family life cycle in which it becomes established in the marriage of the man and his wife, enters into childbearing and childrearing with the coming of children, becomes an arena of interacting family members as the children grow up, and in time launches the children into lives of their own. The middleaged and aging couple live through their remaining years in an empty nest that is, however, still a home base for their married children, their grandchildren, their other relatives, and so continues to be in fact part of the family cycle. The eight stages of the family life cycle differ in form and function, and in length of time spent in each one before the next stage comes. Each succeeding generation overlaps those that have gone before and those that come after. Millions of families move every year, decreasing their contacts with relatives, especially in the early stages of the family life cycle. Significant changes in age at marriage, birth of children, and at death, through recent decades, tend to increase the potential number of intergenerational relationships, and shift the length of time spent in family life cycle stages. These changes are part of the matrix of social change taken up in Chapter Three. Family life cycle analysis has both unsolved problems and promise as a tool in family life study.

SUGGESTED ACTIVITIES

1) Develop Roy Rodgers' thesis (page 6) that the youngest child may be quite as important in a family's development as is the oldest child. Consider for instance, the influence of the youngest child of different sex than those born previously, i.e. a boy after a number of girls. Recognize that sibling interaction, including the usual rivalrous squabbling be-

[1] John B. Lansing and Leslie Kish, "Family Life Cycle as an Independent Variable," *American Sociological Review,* Vol. 22, No. 5, October 1957, pp. 512–519.

tween children in the family is introduced by those who come after the first child. Think through what difference spacing factors make, as in the case of the baby born after a long interval, when the others are in their teens. See that it is the last child launched rather than the first that plunges the parents into an empty nest. What sequence of stages do you suggest to take care of these factors adequately?

2) List the forms of family life in America today that are not explicitly accounted for in the family life cycle stages as outlined in this chapter. Include especially (a) couples without children, (b) families broken by death, divorce, or separation, (c) remarriage of husband, wife, or both, (d) families with stepchildren, (e) unmarried parents, (f) others. Describe one such family as you have listed and indicate its possible placement in the family life cycle. Give your reasons for assigning it to the stage to which you feel it belongs.

3) Plot your expected life line following the profile for American man or woman in Charts 2 and 3, using data to date with projections into the future.

4) Prepare a biography of your family up through the present time, by stages of its development as far back as you can recall or gather from what older members of the family have told you. Include the most important events your family has experienced during the past year, with some indication of how the various situations were handled. Finally, anticipate the problems and opportunities facing your family in the immediate future. Keep this paper for review at the end of the course.

5) List the names of ten men and women of various ages, known to you, and opposite each indicate the stage of the family life cycle in which he or she now is. Give data documenting each designation.

6) Write a paper on woman's education today taking into account the competencies she will need during her career as a woman, a wife, a mother, and in the many other social roles she must face during her life time.

7) Discuss the implications of the family life cycle for courses in marriage and family in high schools, colleges, and in adult education.

8) Review in terms of family life cycle insights, *The Fourposter* by Jan de Hartog, a three-act play, Random House, 1951; and/or Thornton Wilder's one-act play, *The Long Christmas Dinner*.

READINGS

Aldous, Joan, "The Consequences of Intergenerational Continuity," *Journal of Marriage and the Family*, Vol. XXVII, No. 4, November 1965, pp. 462–468.

Aldous, Joan, and Reuben Hill, "Social Cohesion, Lineage Type, and Intergenerational Transmission," *Social Forces*, Vol. 43, No. 4, May 1965, pp. 471–482.

Bigelow, Howard, "Financing the Marriage," Chapter 13, *Family, Marriage and Parenthood* (Boston: D. C. Heath and Company, Revised Edition, 1955), by Howard Becker and Reuben Hill, eds., pp. 411–414.

Cavan, Ruth, *The American Family* (New York: Thomas Y. Crowell Company, 1953), Part Three, The Cycle of Family Life," pp. 261–612.

Clark, Lincoln, ed., *Consumer Behavior Vol. II: The Life Cycle and Consumer Behavior* (New York: New York University Press, 1955).

Dublin, Louis I., *Factbook on Man From Birth to Death* (New York: The Macmillan Company, 1965).

Duvall, Evelyn Millis, *Family Living* (New York: The Macmillan Company, Revised Edition, 1961), Chapter 18, "How Families Grow and Change."

Glick, Paul C., *American Families* (New York: John Wiley & Sons, Inc., 1957).

Hardy, James M., *Focus on the Family* (New York: Association Press, 1966).

Hill, Reuben, "Decision Making and the Family Life Cycle," Chapter 6 in Ethel Shanas and Gordon Streib, eds., *Social Structure and the Family: Generational Relations* (Englewood Cliffs, N. J.: Prentice-Hall, 1965), pp. 113–139.

Hill, Reuben, revision of Willard Waller's *The Family: A Dynamic Interpretation* (New York: The Dryden Press, 1951), Part Five, pp. 375–449.

Hurlock, Elizabeth B., *Developmental Psychology* (New York: McGraw-Hill Book Company, Second Edition, 1959).

Kenkel, William F., *The Family in Perspective* (New York: Appleton-Century-Crofts, Inc., 1960), Chapter 14, "Basic Concepts: The Family Life Cycle and Developmental Tasks."

Kirkpatrick, Clifford, *The Family as Process and Institution* (New York: The Ronald Press Company, 1963), Part III, "Life Cycle of Family Experience," pp. 175–535.

Lansing, John B., and Leslie Kish, "Family Life Cycle as an Independent Variable," *American Sociological Review*, Vol. 22, No. 5, October 1957, pp. 512–519.

Pressey, Sidney L., and Raymond G. Kuhlen, *Psychological Development through the Life Span* (New York: Harper & Brothers, 1957).

Rodgers, Roy H., *Improvements in the Construction & Analysis of Family Life Cycle Categories* (Kalamazoo, Michigan: Western Michigan University, 1962).

Stott, Leland H., "The Longitudinal Approach to the Study of Family Life," *Journal of Home Economics*, Vol. 46, February 1954, pp. 79–82.

Sussman, Marvin, "Family Continuity: Selective Factors Which Affect Relationships between Families at Generational Levels," *Marriage and Family Living*, Vol. XVI, No. 2, May, 1954, pp. 112–120.

Toman, Walter, *Family Constellation* (New York: Springer Publishing Company, Inc., 1961).

Wattenberg, Ben J., and Richard M. Scammon, *This U. S. A.* (Garden City, New York: Doubleday & Company, 1965).

Woods, Sister Frances Jerome, *The American Family System* (New York: Harper & Brothers, 1959), Chapter 8, "The Beginning Family," pp. 237–274.

The proper study of mankind is man.
ALEXANDER POPE

Growth is the only evidence of life.
JOHN HENRY, CARDINAL NEWMAN

CHAPTER TWO

Family developmental tasks

The family is a unity of interacting persons [1] related by ties of marriage, birth, or adoption, whose central purpose is to create and maintain a common culture which promotes the physical, mental, emotional, and social development of each of its members. As a social group, a family must come to terms with certain basic conditions, called *functional prerequisites*,[2] essential for its survival, continuity, and growth. The *basic tasks* of American families may be listed as: [3]

1. Physical maintenance—providing shelter, food, clothing, health care, etc.
2. Allocation of resources—meeting family needs and costs, apportioning material goods, facilities, space, authority, respect, affection, etc.
3. Division of labor—deciding who does what, assigning responsibility for procuring income, managing the houschold, caring for family members, and other specific tasks
4. Socialization of family members—guiding the internalization of increasingly mature and acceptable patterns of controlling elimination, food intake, sexual drives, sleep, aggression, and etc.

---

[1] For a fuller discussion see Ernest W. Burgess and Harvey J. Locke, *The Family* (New York: American Book Company, Second Edition, 1953), pp. 7, 8.

[2] Talcott Parsons, *Essays in Sociological Theory, Pure and Applied* (Glencoe, Illinois: The Free Press, 1949), pp. viii, 6–7, 42–51.

[3] Adapted from course outlines in family development developed by Carlfred Broderick, Pennsylvania State University; Reuben Hill, University of Minnesota; and Roy Rodgers, Western Michigan University.

5. Reproduction, recruitment, and release of family members—bearing or adopting children and rearing them for release at maturity, incorporating new members by marriage, and establishing policies for inclusion of others: in-laws, relatives, step-parents, guests, family friends, etc.
6. Maintenance of order—providing means of communication, establishing types and intensity of interaction, patterns of affection, and sexual expression—by administering sanctions insuring conformity to group norms
7. Placement of members in the larger society—fitting into the community, relating to church, school, organizational life, political and economic systems, and protecting family members from undesirable outside influences
8. Maintenance of motivation and morale—rewarding members for achievements, satisfying individual needs for acceptance, encouragement and affection, meeting personal and family crises, refining a philosophy of life and sense of family loyalty (through rituals, festivals, etc.)

These eight basic tasks confront the family as a group in all social classes and subcultures, through changing times and throughout the family life cycle. All eight basic tasks at any given stage in the family life cycle are the *family developmental tasks* of that period in its history as a family. The tasks of all families are implemented by the roles family members play in interaction.

FAMILY INTERACTION

Family interaction is the process by which a family relates to life outside itself, and through which one member's action is stimulated by the behavior of other members within the family.[1] Family interaction is the sum total of all the family roles being played within a given family. Family roles are *reciprocal*, in that the roles played by each family member are related directly to roles played by others in the family. Each of these roles is defined by *norms*[2] which both the family and the larger

[1] See Robert F. Bales, *Interaction Process Analysis* (Cambridge, Massachusetts: Addison-Wesley Press, 1950); and George C. Homans, *The Human Group* (New York: Harcourt-Brace and Company, 1950).

[2] For a discussion of the concepts norm, position, and role as they are used here, see Frederick L. Bates, "Position, Role, and Status: A Reformulation of Concepts," *Social Forces*, May 1956, Vol. 34, No. 4, pp. 313–321.

society expect of the person occupying a given position. The *position* a family member holds is a location in the family associated with a set of social norms. A family then can be seen as composed of a number of positions related to each other in dyads, i.e. paired positions of "father" and "child," "husband" and "wife." Thus one family member can occupy two (or more) positions: both husband and father (as well as son, brother, etc.).

A *role* is a part of a social position consisting of a more or less integrated or related set of social norms distinguishable from other sets of norms forming the same position. For instance, father plays many roles in the family—that of breadwinner, teacher, disciplinarian, companion, and so forth. These concurrent roles may be thought of as a *role cluster.*

Although a role is defined by the expectations the group has for it (social norms), it is rarely played in exactly the same way. The manner in which a person actually plays a given role may be termed *role behavior,* i.e. given father's actual performance as provider. When the role behavior deviates too greatly from the norms, negative *sanctions* in the form of punishment are applied to press the person to meet group expectations. A person's role behavior that conforms to the norms may bring forth positive sanctions as rewards from the group.

Throughout his life-time each person is a developing and changing organism—biologically, intellectually, and socially. As a person develops, he is expected to take on new roles and to abandon old ones. That is, the role content of the positions he holds over time changes. If the individual is to be an acceptable member of the family, he must play those roles expected of him by virtue of his position in the group. If he does not, or is incapable of doing so for one reason or another, his adjustment in the group, and hence his personal adjustment will suffer, as does also the adjustment of the family group.

Families are the nurturing centers for human personality. More than any other association in the entire society, families are held responsible for the well-being of their members. It is within the family that the child is born, nurtured, taught, socialized, matured, and released to start a family of his own. No other social group receives the child so young, relates to him so intimately, interacts with him with deeper and more lasting emotion, influences his behavior so profoundly, or has continuing contact with him over so long a period.

Although individual family members develop in unique ways, each human being grows through a life cycle which in broad outlines resembles that of all other persons. The focus of this book is on these developmental similarities. Human development is generally predictable, proceeding stage by stage through the life cycle from the cradle to the grave.

THE EIGHT STAGES IN THE LIFE CYCLE OF MAN [1]

"Personality," [2] Erikson has written, "can be said to develop according to steps predetermined in the human organism's readiness to be driven toward, to be aware of, and to interact with a widening social radius, beginning with a dim image of a mother and ending with an image of mankind. . . . "Following are the steps he has identified in man's psychosocial development, and the special crises they bring. In presenting them, he has emphasized that while the struggle between the negatives and positives in each crisis must be fought through successfully if the next developmental stage is to be reached, no victory is completely or forever won.

I. Infancy: Trust vs. Mistrust. The first "task" of the infant is to develop "the cornerstone of a healthy personality," a basic sense of trust—in himself and in his environment. This comes from a feeling of inner goodness derived from "the mutual regulation of his receptive capacities with the maternal techniques of provision."—a quality of care that transmits a sense of trustworthiness and meaning. The danger, most acute in the second half of the first year, is that discontinuities in care may increase a natural sense of loss, as the child gradually recognizes his separateness from his mother, to a basic sense of mistrust that may last through life.

II. Early Childhood: Autonomy vs. Shame and Doubt. With muscular maturation the child experiments with holding on and letting go and begins to attach enormous value to his autonomous will. The danger here is the development of a deep sense of shame and doubt if he is deprived of the opportunity to learn to develop his will as he learns his "duty," and therefore learns to expect defeat in any battle of wills with those who are bigger and stronger.

III. Play Age: Initiative vs. Guilt. In this stage the child's imagination is greatly expanded because of his increased ability to move around freely and to communicate. It is an age of intrusive activity, avid curiosity, and consuming fantasies which lead to feelings of guilt and anxiety. It is also the stage of the

[1] From "Youth and the Life Cycle," an interview with Erik H. Erikson by Kathryn Close, March-April 1960 issue of CHILDREN, interprofessional journal published by the Children's Bureau, Department of Health, Education, and Welfare.

[2] For detailed treatment see, Erik H. Erikson, "Growth and Crises of the 'Healthy Personality'," in Symposium on the Healthy Personality, Supplement II *Problems of Infancy and Childhood*, M. J. E. Senn, ed., Josiah Macy, Jr. Foundation, New York, 1950; and *Childhood and Society* (New York: W. W. Norton & Company, 1950).

establishment of conscience. If this tendency to feel guilty is "overburdened by all-too-eager adults" the child may develop a deep-seated conviction that he is essentially bad, with a resultant stifling of initiative or a conversion of his moralism to vindictiveness.

IV. School Age: Industry vs. Inferiority. The long period of sexual latency before puberty is the age when the child wants to learn how to do and make things with others. In learning to accept instruction and to win recognition by producing "things" he opens the way for the capacity of work enjoyment. The danger in this period is the development of a sense of inadequacy and inferiority in a child who does not receive recognition for his efforts.

V. Adolescence: Identity vs. Identity Diffusion. The physiological revolution that comes with puberty—rapid body growth and sexual maturity—forces the young person to question "all sameness and continuities relied on earlier" and to "refight many of the earlier battles." The developmental task is to integrate childhood identifications "with the basic biological drives, native endowment, and the opportunities offered in social roles." The danger is that identity diffusion, temporarily unavoidable in this period of physical and psychological upheaval, may result in a permanent inability to "take hold" or, because of youth's tendency to total commitment, in the fixation in the young person of a negative identity, a devoted attempt to become what parents, class, or community do not want him to be.

VI. Young Adulthood: Intimacy vs. Isolation. Only as a young person begins to feel more secure in his identity is he able to establish intimacy with himself (with his inner life) and with others, both in friendships and eventually in a love-based mutually satisfying sexual relationship with a member of the opposite sex. A person who cannot enter wholly into an intimate relationship because of the fear of losing his identity may develop a sense of isolation.

VII. Adulthood: Generativity vs. Self-absorption. Out of the intimacies of adulthood grows generativity—the mature person's interest in establishing and guiding the next generation. The lack of this results in self-absorption and frequently in a "pervading sense of stagnation and interpersonal impoverishment."

VIII. Senescence: Integrity vs. Disgust. The person who has achieved a satisfying intimacy with other human beings and who has adapted to the triumphs and disappointments of his generative activities as parent and co-worker reaches the end of life with a certain ego integrity—an acceptance of his own responsibility for what his life is and was and of its place in the flow of history. Without this "accrued ego integration" there is despair, usually marked by a display of displeasure and disgust.

THE DEVELOPMENTAL TASK CONCEPT

"A developmental task is a task which arises at or about a certain period in the life of an individual, successful achievement of which leads to his happiness and to success with later tasks, while failure leads to

unhappiness in the individual, disapproval by the society, and difficulty with later tasks." [1] So the developmental task was defined through more than a dozen years when the concept was being explored and elaborated at the University of Chicago.[2] In order to learn how to use this intellectual tool, let us look at the phrases that make up the definition, so that the meanings may become clear.

"A developmental task is a task . . ." implies that a developmental task is a job-to-be-done, something he should achieve, a responsibility the individual assumes for his development. This puts the burden of development upon the individual in tasks he himself assumes for growing up at any period in his life in his culture.

The next phrase—*". . . which arises at or about a certain period in the life of the individual—"* recognizes that at some periods of an individual's life certain developmental tasks are especially important because of what is happening in the organism, and in what his world expects of him. At other times, other facets of his personality surge ahead, and the developmental tasks associated with their emergence gain ascendency. A parallel can be drawn between the emergence of developmental tasks and the pattern of development of the physical organs of the embryo. Quoting C. H. Stockard, *The Physical Basis of Personality* (New York: W. W. Norton and Company, Inc., 1931), Erikson says,

> In this sequence of development each organ has its time of origin. This time factor is as important as the place of origin. If the eye, for example, does not arise at the appointed time, "it will never be able to express itself fully, since the moment for the rapid outgrowth of some other part will have arrived, and this will tend to dominate the less active region and suppress the belated tendency for eye expression.". . .
>
> The organ which misses its time of ascendency is not only doomed as an entity; it endangers at the same time the whole hierarchy of organs. "Not only does the arrest of a rapidly budding part, therefore, tend to suppress its development temporarily, but the premature loss of supremacy to some other organ renders it impossible for the suppressed part to come again into dominance so that it is permanently modified . . ." The result of normal development is proper relationship of size and function among the body organs: the liver adjusted in size to the stomach and intestine, the heart and lungs properly balanced, and the capacity of the vascular system accurately proportioned to the body as a whole. Through developmental arrest one or more organs may

---

[1] Robert J. Havighurst, *Human Development and Education* (Longmans, Green and Company, 1953), p. 2.
[2] *Ibid.*, pp. 328–332, and Preface of this book.

become disproportionally small: this upsets functional harmony and produces a defective person.[1]

The physiological development of the organism suggests the way in which development of the individual-as-a-whole takes place. If a developmental task is not satisfactorily accomplished at its appointed time, it may not be achieved as well later, and its failure may be reflected not only in itself, but in the incomplete fulfillment of related aspects of development.

Illustrations of developmental task failures are numerous. The adolescent who does not establish his autonomy and free himself from his childish dependence on his parents may have difficulty in his social development as a teenager, and may continue to be tied to his parents as a "Mama's boy" even as an adult. The newly wedded man or woman who fails to make an adequate adjustment as husband or wife not only fails to find happiness in the marriage, but finds difficulty also in accomplishing the developmental tasks as a parent in the years that follow.

The phrase—*"successful achievement of which leads to his happiness"*—indicates the bright side of the developmental task concept in the satisfactions which accrue to the individual when he is successful in accomplishing a developmental task. To use the illustrations above in their positive aspects: the teenager who learns to make his own decisions, to stand on his own feet and to develop more mature forms of affection for his parents finds satisfaction in becoming a man; the young married couple who succeed in achieving their developmental tasks as husband and wife find happiness in their marriage, and as parents and grandparents and as persons throughout life.

The phrase—*"and to success with later tasks"*—has been anticipated in our treatment of the ways in which failures to achieve a developmental task at its appointed time leads to difficulties later on. Conversely, successful accomplishment of a developmental task paves the way for the emergence and effective achievement of future developmental tasks. A ready example is that of the girl who learns as an adolescent how to be an autonomous person. Because she has learned to be comfortable with her parents on a mature basis, she is free to love and to be loved. She can win the affection of a suitable mate (granted that she has achieved

[1] Erik H. Erikson, *Childhood and Society* (New York: W. W. Norton and Company, Inc., 1950), pp. 61–62.

success in the other developmental tasks that are relevant), and finds fulfillment in marriage as a woman.

The phrase—*"while failure leads to unhappiness of the individual"*— may be illustrated with the plight opposite that of the above illustration. This girl, for one or more reasons, does not successfully accomplish the developmental task of freeing herself from her infantile dependence on her parents. She is unhappy because she has not found herself as a person. She feels that she does not belong to her own generation as do the other young people who achieve more success in this task.

The phrase—*"disapproval by the society"*—indicates the cultural basis of the developmental task in the rewards for success in achievement, and the penalties for failure to accomplish a given developmental task. A common example is found in the child who fails to learn to read with the others of his age and grade. Such a boy or girl feels the disapproval of his teacher, his father, mother and siblings with intensity that depends upon his cultural group. The middle-class family that makes much of educational achievement may be especially anxious about, and severe with, the child who seems to fail in such a basic intellectual accomplishment as reading. A child in such a family may feel rejected by them at this time because of the threat of the conditional love [1] (receiving love only when achieving something desired by parents) that seems to be withdrawn when he does not measure up to their expectations of him.

The meaning of the final phrase—*"and difficulty with later tasks"*— should be clear by now. If, for some reason, a developmental task is not satisfactorily achieved at its proper time, the individual presumably will have difficulty with developmental tasks later on. Let us take as an illustration the child who does not satisfactorily learn to read in the first or second grades when his peers are learning this task. Not only does he fail to learn to read competently, but also in so doing, he does not master the basic tool for accomplishing such future tasks as are involved in learning history, literature, social studies, and all such educational and personal areas of life dependent upon reading ability. Furthermore, the feeling of failure engendered in his inadequate efforts to achieve

---

[1] Carson McGuire, "Family Life in Lower and Middle Class Homes," *Marriage and Family Living*, Vol. XIV, No. 1, February 1952, says in discussing this factor, "A conditional element in giving and withholding affection seems to serve to foster striving behavior in members of middle class families . . . It is perpetuated because the 'conditional love' of the parent . . . usually reinforces learning to be responsible, to achieve . . ." (p. 3).

mastery of reading fundamentals quite likely carries over into other tasks with the unfortunate overtones of lack of self-confidence, and proneness to failure, that add further to his difficulties.

ORIGINS OF DEVELOPMENTAL TASKS

Developmental tasks have two primary origins: (1) physical maturation, and (2) cultural pressures and privileges. A secondary origin derived from the first two is found in the aspirations and values of the individual.

As the individual grows, he matures. Growth is much more than just added stature and bulk. It involves the elaboration and maturation of muscle, organ, bone, and neural systems of the organism that develop according to a predictable sequence within the individual. Certain developmental tasks come primarily from the maturation of one or more aspects of the organism. Examples are many. As the infant's leg and back muscles develop strength enough, and the neural connections mature to the place where the child has conscious control over their movement, he faces the developmental task of learning to walk. When the adolescent girl's body develops into one resembling that of a woman and she begins to menstruate, she must come to terms with her femaleness and develop a wholesome acceptance of herself as a woman. Later, when she is in her forties, menopause is a reality that must be met with the new developmental task of accepting the termination of her reproductive life and facing the challenge of aging. And so it is with many other developmental tasks throughout the life of both men and women.

Cultural pressures are seen in the many rewards and penalties the individual receives (and anticipates) for his various behaviors. Society, in the form of peers, associates, parents, teachers, and all "the significant others" of his life, expects and often puts pressures upon the person to conform to the prescribed ways of behaving within that culture. These expectations and pressures emerge at the times believed appropriate in the culture for the individual to function in the roles and statuses assigned to him. Unfortunately they may be too soon or too late for an individual.

By the time a child reaches a certain age, he is expected to eat solid foods, at another age to be toilet trained, at another to walk, at another age to talk, at another to respect property rights, at another to mingle socially with members of the other sex, at another to marry and "settle

Society in the form of peers, associates, parents, teachers, and all "the significant others" of his life, expects and often puts pressures upon the person to conform to the prescribed ways of behaving within that culture.

down," and so on through his entire life span. Regardless of what they are and when they come into effect, these expectancies exert pressures upon the individuals of the culture to behave in certain ways and so are an important origin of his developmental tasks. Examples in our society are: learning to read, learning to handle money responsibly, learning how to gain a place for oneself with one's age-mates, establishing oneself as an acceptable member of a dating crowd as a teenager, and among the young married set as a husband or wife.

Developmental tasks differ from culture to culture. Each cultural group has its own developmental definitions and expectations. They also vary from region to region in our country, even from class to class in the same area, resulting in many persistent problems among children of different ethnic and cultural backgrounds.

Encouragement and support by family and friends are often essential in achieving developmental tasks that the individual alone might find too difficult. As cultural pressures play upon the maturing organism, the emergent personality is formed with all of its idiosyncratic values and aspirations which themselves then influence greatly the direction and form of future developmental tasks. Two examples of developmental tasks derived primarily from the personal aspirations and values of the individual are choosing a vocation and achieving a personal philosophy of life, which of course are always responsive to the life around the person.

Basically, a developmental task is a thrust from within the individual to develop in such a way as to narrow the discrepancy between his present behavior and what he might achieve. The push to change usually comes from inside the person but may be evoked by others' demands and expectations. It receives its direction from the cultural definition of what is expected of such an individual at his stage of development. A developmental task, while culturally defined, is neither a chore nor a duty, in the sense that it is externally imposed. It is rather a growth responsibility the individual assumes for his own development as he relates himself to his life situation.

The individual's assumption of a given developmental task consists of at least four interrelated operations: (1) perceiving new possibilities for his behavior in what is expected of him or in what he sees others, more mature than he, accomplishing, (2) forming new conceptions of himself (identity formation), (3) coping effectively with conflicting demands upon him, and 4) wanting to achieve the next step in his development enough to work toward it (motivation). To illustrate: a small boy sees somewhat bigger boys riding their bicycles (operation 1—perception); he conceives of himself as a potential bicycle rider (operation 2—identity formation); he resolves the conflicts between his mother's protests that he might get hurt and his own fears of failure with the expectancies of his peers, and the demands of his father that he become "a big boy" (operation 3—coping with conflicting demands); and finally, he wants to learn to ride a bike enough to practice what it takes to become proficient in it (operation 4—motivation).

Most of the growth responsibilities the individual is faced with result from the combined impact of his biologic maturing, the environmental forces that play upon him, and his own personal drives, ambitions, and value orientation. Thus, being weaned results from his physiological maturation (teething, etc.), as well as from the cultural pressures in the form of maternal insistence that he take solid foods and his own desire

The child who is loved and knows it has the inner security needed to keep working on his or her developmental tasks.

to be a "big boy" and eat as the others in the family do. Teenage dating emerges partly from the biologic maturing of puberty, partly from the cultural pressures of friends and family to have a girl or boy friend and go out to young people's activities in the community, and partly from the person's own aspiration to belong, to be accepted, to be a recognized member of the younger set in the neighborhood.

THE TEACHABLE MOMENT

When the time comes that the body is ripe for, culture is pressing for, and the individual is striving for some achievement, the teachable moment has arrived. It is at the convergence of the several origins of the developmental task that its accomplishment is most highly motivated, when the individual is most truly *ready for* the next step in his development. Before that the person is not mature enough for the desired outcome, and so efforts to push him through a premature accomplishment may be largely wasted. Readiness also implies that the person has lived fully at his present stage and so is not being hurried into the next stage.

An illustration is found in the early efforts to toilet train an infant. In the 1920's and 1930's, this training was often attempted while the baby was but a few weeks old. At that age, his sphincters were not ready for such control, his neural connections were not matured enough to make possible his cooperation, and his own aspirations were in quite another direction. It is not surprising to find that these precocious demands of the parent upon the child met with failure and often created persistent conflict. Knowledge of child development has modified these expectancies, and today good practice is to wait for signs that the baby is ready for toilet training before assisting him to achieve the task. This concept of readiness is well established in the field of human development.

The concept of the teachable moment goes a bit deeper in indicating specifically the three dimensions in which readiness emerges—in the physical organism, in the social pressures, and in the personal values of the individual. It has importance for anyone responsible for the growth, development, and guidance of others: teachers, supervisors, parents, indeed anyone who works with, or cares about, other people. For it gives a gauge of what we expect of given persons and at what time we may anticipate change. This ability to predict what persons at various stages of development are, or soon will be, ready for is of paramount importance to curriculum formulators, and educators in general. If we assume that the general purpose of both family life and education is to assist the individual to grow up to his own best potential, we see that some knowledge of developmental tasks and especially of the teachable moments at which these tasks arise is highly relevant.

> *There is a tide in the affairs of men,*
> *Which, taken at the flood, leads on to fortune;*
> *Omitted, all the voyage of their life*
> *Is bound in shallows and in miseries.*
>   SHAKESPEARE, *Julius Caesar,* (IV, 3.)

Let us review quickly the concept *developmental task,* by indicating specifically just what is and what is not included. Teething is not a developmental task because it occurs automatically without the participation of the person. Learning to eat solid food *is* a developmental task, because it involves the active assumption of responsibility for eating on

	INFANCY (Birth to 1 or 2)	EARLY CHILDHOOD (2–3 to 5–6–7)	LATE CHILDHOOD (5–6–7 to pubescence)
I *Achieving an appropriate dependence-independence pattern*	1. Establishing one's self as a very dependent being 2. Beginning the establishment of self-awareness	1. Adjusting to less private attention; becoming independent physically (while remaining strongly dependent emotionally)	1. Freeing one's self from primary identification with adults
II *Achieving an appropriate giving-receiving pattern of affection*	1. Developing a feeling for affection	1. Developing the ability to give affection 2. Learning to share affection	1. Learning to give as much love as one receives; forming friendships with peers
III *Relating to changing social groups*	1. Becoming aware of the alive as against the inanimate, and the familiar as against the unfamiliar 2. Developing rudimentary social-interaction	1. Beginning to develop the ability to interact with age-mates 2. Adjusting in the family to expectations it has for the child as a member of the social unit	1. Clarifying the adult world as over against the child's world 2. Establishing peer groupness and learning to belong
IV *Developing a conscience*	1. Beginning to adjust to the expectations of others	1. Developing the ability to take directions and to be obedient in the presence of authority 2. Developing the ability to be obedient in the absence of authority where conscience substitutes for authority	1. Learning more rules and developing true morality
V *Learning one's psycho-socio-biological sex role*		1. Learning to identify with male adult and female adult roles	1. Beginning to identify with one's social contemporaries of the same sex
VI *Accepting and Adjusting to a changing body*	1. Adjusting to adult feeding demands 2. Adjusting to adult cleanliness demands 3. Adjusting to adult attitudes toward genital manipulation	1. Adjusting to expectations resulting from one's improving muscular abilities 2. Developing sex modesty	
VII *Managing a changing body and learning new motor patterns*	1. Developing physiological equilibrium 2. Developing eye-hand coordination 3. Establishing satisfactory rhythms of rest and activity	1. Developing large muscle control 2. Learning to co-ordinate large muscles and small muscles	1. Refining and elaborating skill in the use of small muscles
VIII *Learning to understand and control the physical world*	1. Exploring the physical world	1. Meeting adult expectations for restrictive exploration and manipulation of an expanding environment	1. Learning more realistic ways of studying and controlling the physical world
IX *Developing an appropriate symbol system and conceptual abilities*	1. Developing preverbal communication 2. Developing verbal communication 3. Rudimentary concept formation	1. Improving one's use of the symbol system 2. Enormous elaboration of the concept pattern	1. Learning to use language actually to exchange ideas or to influence one's hearers 2. Beginning understanding of real causal relations 3. Making finer conceptual distinctions and thinking reflectively
X *Relating one's self to the cosmos*		1. Developing a genuine, tho uncritical, notion about one's place in the cosmos	1. Developing a scientific approach

of Behavior of the Individual from Birth to Death

EARLY ADOLESCENCE (pubescence to puberty)	LATE ADOLESCENCE (puberty to early maturity)	MATURITY (early to late active adulthood)	AGING (beyond full powers of adulthood through senility)
1. Establishing one's independence from adults in all areas of behavior	1. Establishing one's self as an independent individual in an adult manner	1. Learning to be interdependent —now leaning, now succoring others as need arises. 2. Assisting one's children to become gradually independent and autonomous beings	1. Accepting graciously and comfortably the help needed from others as powers fail, and dependence becomes necessary
1. Accepting one's self as a worthwhile person really worthy of love	1. Building a strong mutual affectional bond with a (possible) marriage partner	1. Building and maintaining a strong and mutually satisfying marriage relationship 2. Establishing wholesome affectional bonds with one's children and grandchildren 3. Meeting wisely the new needs for affection of one's own aging parents 4. Cultivating meaningfully warm friendships with members of one's own generation	1. Facing loss of one's spouse, and finding some satisfactory sources of affection previously received from mate 2. Learning new affectional roles with own children, now mature adults 3. Establishing ongoing satisfying affectional patterns with grandchildren, and other members of the extended family 4. Finding and preserving mutually satisfying friendships outside the family circle
1. Behaving according to a shifting peer code	1. Adopting an adult-patterned set of social values by learning a new peer code	1. Keeping within reasonable balance activities in the various social, service, political, and community groups and causes that make demands upon mature adults 2. Establishing and maintaining mutually satisfactory relationships with the in-law families of spouse and married children	1. Choosing and maintaining ongoing social activities and functions appropriate to health, energy, and interests
	1. Learning to verbalize contradictions in moral codes, as well as discrepancies between principle and practice, and resolving these problems in a responsible manner	1. Coming to terms with the violations of moral codes in the larger as well as in the more intimate social scene, and developing some constructive philosophy and method of operation. 2. Helping children adjust to the expectations of others and to conform to the moral demands of the culture	1. Maintaining a sense of moral integrity in the face of disappointments and disillusionments in life's hopes and dreams
1. Strong identification with one's own sex mates 2. Learning one's role in heterosexual relationships	1. Exploring possibilities for a future mate and acquiring "desirability" 2. Choosing an occupation 3. Preparing to accept one's future role in manhood or womanhood as a responsible citizen of the larger community	1. Learning to be a competent husband or wife, and building a good marriage 2. Carrying a socially adequate role as citizen and worker in the community 3. Becoming a good parent and grandparent as children arrive and develop	1. Learning to live on a retirement income 2. Being a good companion to an aging spouse 3. Meeting bereavement of spouse adequately
1. Reorganizing one's thoughts and feelings about one's self in the face of significant bodily changes and their concomitants 2. Accepting the reality of one's appearance	1. Learning appropriate outlets for sexual drives	1. Making a good sex adjustment within marriage 2. Establishing healthful routines of eating, resting, working, playing within the pressures of adult world	1. Making a good adjustment to failing powers as aging diminishes strengths and abilities
1. Controlling and using a "new" body		1. Learning the new motor skills involved in housekeeping, gardening, sports, and other activities expected of adults in the community	1. Adapting interests and activities to reserves of vitality and energy of the aging body
		1. Gaining intelligent understanding of new horizons of medicine and science sufficient for personal well-being and social competence	1. Mastering new awareness and methods of dealing with physical surroundings as an individual with occasional or permanent disabilities
1. Using language to express and to clarify more complex concepts 2. Moving from the concrete to the abstract and applying general principles to the particular	1. Achieving the level of reasoning of which one is capable	1. Mastering technical symbol systems involved in income tax, social security, complex financial dealings and other contexts familiar to Western man	1. Keeping mentally alert and effective as long as is possible through the later years
	1. Formulating a workable belief and value system	1. Formulating and implementing a rational philosophy of life on the basis of adult experience 2. Cultivating a satisfactory religious climate in the home as the spiritual soil for development of family members	1. Preparing for eventual and inevitable cessation of life by building a set of beliefs that one can live and die with, in peace

Source: An elaboration of Caroline Tryon and Jesse W. Lilienthal III, "Guideposts in Child Growth and Development," *NEA Journal*, March 1950, p., 189.

the part of the child. Menstruating is a purely biological phenomenon, while learning what it means to be a woman is a developmental task. In other words, the developmental task implies the assumption of responsibility for accomplishment on the part of the person. His talents, his biologic machinery, and his inheritance, are all part of his "givens" with which he attempts to achieve the tasks of growing up.

PRINCIPLES WHICH MAY BE DERIVED FROM THE DEVELOPMENTAL TASK CONCEPT

1) Every growing person faces certain responsibilities of growing up at every stage of his life as man or woman, adult or child.
2) A person must accomplish the developmental tasks of any given period in his development if he is to grow on to the next level of his maturation.
3) Growth responsibilities are so urgent and insistent, they take precedence over outside pressures.
4) No one else can accomplish for the individual the developmental tasks that he faces.
5) Very few developmental tasks can be mastered in isolation.
6) A teacher or parent who encourages and assists a child accomplish his developmental tasks, helps to promote the child's development.

The developmental task concept is helpful in understanding a given individual's behavior by indicating fruitful aspects for investigation in his success or failure in the tasks of his developmental level, as well as the contributing factors. Furthermore, the developmental task concept enables prediction of behavior in general by foretelling the readiness of groups and of individuals of certain developmental levels living within certain cultural settings, and functioning within certain general value orientations.

DEVELOPMENTAL TASKS OF THE INDIVIDUAL THROUGH HIS LIFE HISTORY

The developmental tasks an individual faces through the years of his life from birth to death are innumerable. It would be impossible to completely list all of the growth responsibilities to be achieved by any one person. Yet, there are certain general categories of tasks that make possible a cataloging of the more common developmental tasks within our culture. Such a formulation is found on pages 40 and 41 in an elaboration of one developed originally by Caroline Tryon and Jesse W. Lilienthal III.

This outline is used as being illustrative of the kind of developmental tasks to be achieved by individuals in the various periods of the life history. It is not a catalog of those to be considered in more detail in the chapters that follow but is rather one frame of reference that may prove to be of value to those students interested in further elaborating the development of the conceptual tool. Study of this outline of the individual's developmental tasks from birth to death in ten categories of human behavior perhaps best summarizes the discussion of the nature of developmental tasks.

Such a listing of the individual's developmental tasks is not all-inclusive, nor is it universally applicable. Different cultures and subcultures make different demands upon their members. In most of the cultures of the world today, the general expectancies change from time to time, so that the developmental tasks of one generation differ somewhat from those of the preceding or of the succeeding one.

Whatever the society in which the individual grows up, he faces the developmental tasks peculiar to it at every stage of his life span. The successful achievement of his developmental tasks brings the individual from a state of helpless dependence as an infant, through varying dimensions of independence as an adolescent, to a mature level of interdependence with his fellowman that lasts through the greater part of adulthood.

INTERACTING DEVELOPMENTAL TASKS OF FAMILY MEMBERS

This progression is not regular and all-of-a-piece. At any moment, children are striving to meet their growth needs, parents to reconcile conflicting demands, and each individual to find himself within the security and threats of his world.

At times members of the family mutually support and sustain one another. During certain stages of the family life cycle, the developmental tasks of both children and parents call for the same general direction of energies, so that the family moves as a unit toward the meeting of the developmental requirements of each member. Such a time comes when the children are established in school and daily bring home to their parents the stimuli and broadened horizons that both mother and father are striving for as mature adults at the school-age stage of the family life cycle.

Just as "naturally," upon occasion, the goals, needs, strivings, and developmental tasks of family members are in conflict. If we hold the entire family in focus, we see that many of the normal tangles of members during the family's life cycle are due to incompatibility of the diverse developmental strivings of family members at critical points of growth.

From time to time the developmental tasks of the husband may conflict with those of his wife. A simple illustration is found in the young husband's developmental task of developing competency with his do-it-yourself projects that clutter up the house at the time when his wife is trying to maintain a pleasant, attractive home amid the already heavy demands of infants and small children.

Developmental tasks of children conflict with those of their parents at several stages in the family life cycle. In adolescence the young person is struggling to emancipate himself or herself from the authority of the parents, whose own developmental tasks as parents call for sustained guidance and supervision of the not-yet-adult child. At such a time, storms brew and break within the family as normally as they do in the weather, when two or more energy systems moving in opposite directions collide.

Now unified, now atomized, each family lives out its own unique history in pulsing, throbbing rhythms and everchanging tempos. Each family is an arena of interacting personalities, each trying to achieve his own developmental tasks within the pattern of family life that in turn is evolving in interaction with the larger society of which it is a part.

Most developmental tasks of most persons, as children and as adults, are worked out within the family through their lifetimes. The modern family assumes as one of its primary functions that of promoting the continuing development of each of its members throughout the entire life cycle. So families, as families, can be seen to have responsibilities, goals and developmental tasks that are specifically related to the development of their members. All these developmental tasks of both family members and families-as-a-whole shift as the family changes and are constantly being modified by the interplay of forces both within and without the family in every society, in every age.

FAMILY DEVELOPMENTAL TASKS

A family developmental task arises at a given stage in the family life cycle as the family meets the needs of its members and satisfies the requirements for its continued growth and development as a family unit.

Family developmental tasks parallel the developmental tasks of individuals and can be similarly defined: A family developmental task is a growth responsibility that arises at a certain stage in the life of a family, successful achievement of which leads to satisfaction, and success with later tasks, while failure leads to unhappiness in the family, disapproval by society, and difficulty with later family developmental tasks.

Family developmental tasks are those growth responsibilities that must be accomplished by a family at a given stage of development in a way that will satisfy its (1) biological requirements, (2) cultural imperatives, and (3) personal aspirations and values, if the family is to continue to grow as a unit.

Much as individual developmental tasks change over the years, so family developmental tasks shift with each stage of the family life cycle. Family developmental tasks cluster around the meeting of the requisites for family continuation and growth at a particular period in the life of a family. Family developmental tasks, then, are basic family tasks particularized and specified for a given stage of development in the family life cycle.

As norms are clarified, it becomes possible to locate a given family at a particular stage in the family life cycle as on schedule, ahead of schedule, or behind schedule. Child development specialists speak intelligibly of a child being "precocious," or "retarded," as "early maturing," or "late blooming." So students of family life may become professionally expert in appraising family development by progress in the accomplishment of family development tasks at any given stage of the family life cycle.

The developmental tasks of any given family are many, complex, and difficult to enumerate in detail. Families differ from one another in many, many ways. However, just as it is possible to predict, in general, the developmental tasks of an individual at any given developmental level, so too, we can describe, in general, the family developmental tasks of American families throughout the family life cycle. Through Chapters 6–14, inclusive, we follow the developmental tasks of individual family members and of the family as a whole through an eight-stage family life cycle.

Families as families, are seen to have responsibilities, goals, and developmental tasks that are specifically related to the development of their members. All these developmental tasks of both family members and families-as-a-whole shift as the family grows and changes, and are constantly being modified by the interplay of forces both within and without the family in every society, in every age.

FAMILY ASPIRATIONS, GOALS AND VALUES

Ask a family what it is trying to do at any given time, and the answer may be in terms of its aspirations as a family. One family is building a new home, another is saving up for a vacation, a third is trying to pay its bills and get out of debt, while another is attempting to put its children through school, or to nurse an ill member back to health, or to release a young adult into marriage. Family aspirations are specific to the individual family in its social setting at a particular time. They tend to shift from time to time as one objective has been met (i.e. the home has been built, or the vacation is over), and others appear (i.e. the new home must be furnished, and the family in its new setting tries to get into the circles within the community to which it wants to become related). Family aspirations, then, are the short-term tension-reducing objectives that are defined by a family and its social set as important.

Beyond the specific, temporary and individual aspirations of a given family are objectives that society as a whole has for families generally. National goals are in terms of family health, family safety, family stability, family standards of living, family levels of education and culture, and family competence in developing effective citizens for a free society. As the Report of the President's Commission on National Goals specifies in Part I, "Goals at Home":

"The status of the individual must remain our primary concern. All our institutions—political, social, and economic—must further enhance the dignity of the citizen, promote the maximum development of his capabilities, stimulate their responsible exercise, and widen the range and effectiveness of opportunies for individual choice." [1]

Family goals can be seen as lying between the short-term aspirations of a given family at a particular time and the long-term national goals for all families within the society. Family goals ideally facilitate the psychosocial development of family members step by step through life. Family goals are expressed in the contemporary processes that dominate a family's developmental tasks at any stage of the family life cycle. Thus, family goals at the establishment phase of family life, center in adjusting

[1] *Goals for Americans* (Programs for Action in the Sixties), A Spectrum Book, 1960, page 3.

to living as a married couple. When children come, family goals are in terms of providing for their care, nurture, and development. As children mature, family goals are focused upon loosening family ties and releasing young adults into homes of their own. Family goals profoundly influence family functioning and developmental tasks at every stage of the family life cycle.

Family values are the over-riding purposes that express a family's life style. They arise out of a family's orientation and reflect its social class, its mobility drives, and the family's view of itself in perspective. Family values are closely related to the family's philosophy of life at a particular time. Changing conditions, continually growing family members, and the developing family itself call for refinements in the philosophy of life from stage to stage through the family life cycle. As the philosophy of life of a given family changes to fit new conditions, family values may be expected to be somewhat modified. But since a family's life style remains relatively constant, family values tend to be more permanent than either its short-term aspirations, or the stage-oriented goals that motivate a family. Family values may be seen as giving a sense of direction to the aspirations and goals of a family.

SUCCESSFUL FAMILIES

The success of a family can be appraised in several ways. Frequently used measures of family success are: (1) how well the family is meeting its short-term aspirations, (2) how well the family is attaining the goals that society has set for it, and (3) how well the family is achieving its developmental tasks.

1) It is not unusual today to find families defining their success in terms of the things they have acquired and the status they have achieved. Such family members may compare their present status with that of a previous period and feel that they have succeeded as they have "bettered themselves," by moving up the social ladder to a higher status. They measure success by how well they are living up to their particular aspirations and ambitions.

2) The second way of appraising family success is in terms of the family's social contribution. Zimmerman and Cervantes [1] define the successful family as one that (a) avoids disruption by divorce and deser-

[1] Carle C. Zimmerman and Lucius F. Cervantes, *Successful American Families* (New York: Pageant Press, 1960), page 7.

tion, (b) avoids interference by the police; and (c) puts its children through school. In their study of 60,000 American families, they define successful families as those that meet all three of these tests. Beyond such minimal criteria are other tangible evidences of a family's producing members who make positive contributions to the larger society, or serving as a constructive example of good family living in one of many ways. The "Family of the Year" is often chosen according to one or both of these criteria.

3) Successful families in the framework of this text are defined as those that (1) encourage and assist their members in the achievement of their developmental tasks; and (2) effectively accomplish the appropriate family developmental tasks at every stage of the family life cycle to date in its history. When the basic family tasks are being accomplished effectively stage by stage through its career, a family is considered to be successful.

A family is successful, then, when its members—adult and child, male and female—are getting the support, the acceptance, and the opportunities for working through the developmental tasks they each must achieve in order to move smoothly into the next stage of their development and the family-as-a-whole is meeting effectively the developmental tasks of its present stage in the family life cycle.

Much as individuals sometimes succeed and sometimes fail to accomplish one or more of their developmental tasks, so families too at times function effectively and at other times find the going rough. Families, as do individuals, find that success leads to further success, while failure tends to increase the difficulty of the tasks that lie ahead. Difficulty in certain areas is greater at some stages of the family life cycle than at others, as is seen in the comparative overview in Chapter 15.

The successful American family today is a flexible group of persons who mean enough to each other to have the courage to innovate and the willingness to explore new possibilities in the working through of its developmental tasks and those of its members. When family goals are in terms of raising mature persons capable of withstanding the stresses and strains of modern living, and contributing creatively to society, the developmental task concept has special relevance.

SUMMARY

The basic tasks of American families are (1) physical maintenance, (2) allocation of resources, (3) division of labor, (4) socialization of family members, (5) reproduction, recruitment and release of family members, (6) maintenance of order, (7) placement of members in the larger society, and (8) maintenance of motivation and morale. Family interaction is the sum total of all the family roles being played within a given family over time.

Families are the nurturing centers for human personality. Individuals, though unique, develop through a life cycle that resembles that of all other persons. In each of the eight stages in the life cycle of man there are developmental crises that must be fought through successfully if the next developmental stage is to be reached: (1) Infancy: trust vs. mistrust, (2) Early childhood: autonomy vs. shame and doubt, (3) Play age: initiative vs. guilt, (4) School age: industry vs. inferiority, (5) Adolescence: identity vs. identity diffusion, (6) Young adulthood: intimacy vs. isolation, (7) Adulthood: Generativity vs. self-absorption, and (8) Senescence: integrity vs. disgust.

Developmental tasks originate in the biologic maturing of the individual, and the cultural pressures that are exerted upon him. As cultural pressures and opportunities play upon the maturing individual, his personality emerges with the personal aspirations and values that further influence and give direction to his developmental tasks. A developmental task is a thrust from within the individual to narrow the discrepancy between his present behavior and what he might achieve. Operationally, the individual's assumption of a given developmental task consists of (1) perception of new possibilities, (2) identity formation in the new direction, (3) coping with conflicting demands, and (4) motivation sufficient to assume the task. The developmental tasks of the individual have been outlined from birth to death in ten categories of human behavior. The developmental tasks of various members of the family interact so that sometimes they are in conflict and sometimes they mutually support each other.

A family developmental task is a growth responsibility that arises at or about a certain stage in the family life cycle, successful achievement of which leads to satisfaction and success with later tasks, while failure leads to unhappiness in the family, disapproval by society, and difficulty with later family developmental tasks. Family developmental tasks are essential for its continued growth through each stage of the family life cycle. Family developmental tasks shift as the family grows, and are modified by the interplay of forces from within and without the family throughout the family life cycle.

Family aspirations are short-term specific objectives defined by a given family as important. National standards and goals for families are those held by the society as a whole for its families. Family goals, lying between its short-term aspirations, and long-term national goals, focus upon the developmental tasks that are critical at a given stage in the family life cycle. Family values are the over-riding purposes and life-style of a family that give direction to its aspirations, goals, and developmental tasks.

Success in family life can be appraised by the way in which a family is satisfying its aspirations, by the social contribution of the family and its members, and by the extent to which it accomplishes its family developmental tasks and facilitates the accomplishment of the developmental tasks of its members.

SUGGESTED ACTIVITIES

1) Prepare a working glossary for yourself of terms and concepts used in this chapter. Using such readings (below) as Bates, Bell and Vogel, Blood and Wolfe, Farber et al., and Gross, define differentially: position, norm, role, role behavior, and role cluster. Explore the concepts of reciprocal roles, interacting roles, concurrent roles, and sequential roles. Distinguish between family aspirations, goals and values as used in this text and other sources. Relate the concept of developmental task to that of the social roles along the lines followed by Havighurst and Orr in *Adult Education and Adult Needs* (Center for the Study of Liberal Education for Adults, Chicago, Illinois, 1956).

2) Write a paper outlining several of the developmental tasks that you are attempting to accomplish at this period of your life. Document each developmental task with data relative to its origins in terms of your maturation, as well as your cultural pressures and personal aspirations. Illustrate with anecdotal material and appraise roughly the degree of success or failure you are currently finding in each of your developmental tasks at the moment.

3) Compare the concept of "the principle of readiness" with that of "the teachable moment." In what ways do the two resemble one another? What are their differences?

4) Make a chart outline of *The Fourposter* by Jan de Hartog (Random House, 1952) indicating developmental tasks of various members of the family and of the family as a whole by stages of the family life cycle depicted. Illustrate with quotations, and document when needed from primary sources.

5) Role play a situation illustrating the phrase, "Each family may be seen as an arena of interacting personalities, each trying to meet his own basic

needs within the pattern of family life," List the implications for family developmental tasks in the situation portrayed.

6) Support or refute the statement, "Parents, who themselves have urgent needs, make most of the adjustments in building complementary roles between themselves and their children." Would your conclusion be the same at the early stages of family development as for the later stages in the family life cycle? Explore and explain.

7) Defining the successful family as one that encourages its members to achieve their individual developmental tasks, and accomplishes effectively its family developmental tasks at any given stage in the family life cycle, set up criteria by which family success might be appraised objectively at each stage of the family life cycle, for each of the eight basic tasks outlined in this chapter. State each criterion as simply and as specifically as possible so that it clearly measures the degree of success or failure being experienced for each family task through each stage of the family life cycle.

READINGS

Bates, Frederick L., "Position, Role, and Status: A Reformulation of Concepts," *Social Forces,* Volume 34, Number 4, May 1956, pages 313–321.

Bell, Norman W., and Vogel, Ezra F., *A Modern Introduction to the Family* (Glencoe, Illinois: The Free Press, 1960), especially "Functions of the Nuclear Family," pages 6 ff.

Blood, Robert O. Jr., and Wolfe, Donald M., *Husbands and Wives: The Dynamics of Married Living* (Glencoe, Illinois: The Free Press, 1960), pages 10, 76, 77.

Child Study Association of America, "Living and Growing with Our Children: Impact on Parents of Children's Growth Phases," *Child Study,* Volume XXXII, Number 3, Summer 1955 issue.

Duvall, Evelyn Millis, "Changing Roles in the Family Life Cycle," *Journal of Home Economics,* Volume 42, Number 6, June 1950, pages 435–436.

Erikson, Erik H., *Childhood and Society* (New York: W. W. Norton, Inc., 1950), especially Chapter 7, "Eight Stages of Man."

Farber, Bernard; Jenne, William C., and Toigo, Romolo, *Family Crisis and the Retarded Child,* Research Monograph Series A, No. 1, The Council for Exceptional Children, 1201 16th Street, N. W., Washington 6, D. C., 1960, pages 7, 8, 9, and 10.

Geismar, L. L. and Ayres, Beverly, *Measuring Family Functioning,* Family Centered Project, Greater St. Paul Community Chest and Councils, Inc., St. Paul, Minnesota, 1960, Chapter II, "Conceptual Problems in Evaluating Family Functioning."

Gross, Neal; Mason, Ward S., and McEachern, Alexander W., *Explorations in Role Analysis* (New York: John Wiley and Sons, Inc., 1958).

Havighurst, Robert J., *Human Development and Education* (New York: Longman's, Green and Company, 1953).

Havighurst, Robert J., "Research on the Developmental-Task Concept," *The School Review,* May 1956, pages 215–223.

Hill, Reuben, "Interdisciplinary Workshop on Marriage and Family Research," *Marriage and Family Living,* Volume XIII, Number 1, February 1951, pages 13–28.

Hummel, Al J., and Smith, Clifford A., *The Task Method of Program Planning,* The Young Men's Christian Association of Omaha, Nebraska, 1959.

Pollak, Otto, "A Family Diagnosis Model," *The Social Service Review,* Volume XXXIV, Number 1, March 1960, pages 19–28.

Report of the President's Commission on National Goals, *Goals for Americans* (New York: Prentice-Hall, 1960).

Stott, Leland H., "The Problem of Evaluating Family Success," *Marriage and Family Living,* Volume XIII, Number 4, Fall 1951, pages 149–153.

Zimmerman, Carle C., and Cervantes, Lucius F., *Successful American Families* (New York: Pageant Press, 1960).

*Change doth unknit the tranquil
  strength of men.*
                    MATTHEW ARNOLD

*Since you cannot keep life
  Inside a neat fence
You will learn to lean on
  Impermanence.*
                    IRVING FINEMAN

*Remember that there is nothing
  stable in human affairs.*
                    SOCRATES

CHAPTER THREE

Families reflect social change

Families have changed more in recent generations than in any previous century in recorded history. In form and size, nature and purpose, families today are no longer what they used to be. Because the family unit is small and flexible, it can shift as society changes and adapt to new conditions with remarkable rapidity. It is this quality of adaptability that accounts for the persistence of family life through all times and climes.

TWENTIETH-CENTURY CHANGES IN AMERICAN FAMILIES

Industrialization has drastically changed American families within the memories of men now living. The world and the family life that Grandfather knew is no more. In more ways than can here be listed, family living has moved from one way of life to another.

Much as an individual family is upset when it moves, so American families today are unsettled, changing, shifting, moving from a known past to an uncertain future. This accounts for many of the modern family's paradoxes—more marriages and more divorces, more resources and greater debts, fewer farms and greater farm surpluses, more freedom and greater insecurity, to mention but a few. Here in over-all review are some of the twentieth century changes in American family life.

More men and women get married and at younger ages. In 1890, but 63.1 per cent of the population of the United States ever married. Now more than four out of five of all Americans over eighteen years of age are married and living with their spouses. At the turn of the century, a man typically waited until past his twenty-sixth birthday before asking for his wife's hand in marriage. By that time he had been out of school for a dozen years, having left at age fourteen to get work. Then when a man married he had saved up a nest-egg, he was settled vocationally, and he was ready to support a wife and family.

Today the median age at first marriage for the American man is twenty-two—before many a fellow has finished his term of military service, completed his education and settled into his life work. He marries a girl who is only recently out of school herself. One half of all American women are married by their twentieth birthday. A girl scarcely out of her teens has had little chance to find herself as a person before she faces the complex roles of today's married woman. Numerous studies indicate that the young marriage faces more problems and is less stable than that of more mature persons.[1] The trend toward marriages at younger ages has resulted from (1) general affluence and high employment levels; (2) the willingness and ability of the girl to get and keep a job after her marriage; (3) the generosity of parents in helping newlyweds get established; (4) the freedom allowed youth to make their own decisions; (5) educational assistance in the form of veterans' benefits, scholarships, student loans and housing for married students on most campuses; and (6) general attitudes of acceptance of marriage as the preferred way of life.

More families have three or four children. For two hundred and fifty years the size of American families declined. In 1700, the average mother of forty-five years of age or more had 7.4 children. By 1910 the number had dropped to 4.7, by 1940 to 2.9, and by 1950 to 2.5 children.[2] Since World War II there has been a reversal of the long-term trend toward smaller families. Today most married couples want three to four children.[3] The proportion of families with one child has decreased while two, three and four child families have increased steadily since 1948, even

[1] For a summary of studies to date see Lee G. Burchinal, "Young Marriages—What We Know about Them," Chapter 4 in Evelyn and Sylvanus Duvall, *Sex Ways in Fact and Faith* (New York: Association Press, 1961), pp. 69–83.

[2] Reuben Hill, "The American Family Today," in Eli Ginzberg, ed., *The Nation's Children, Vol. 1 The Family and Social Change* (New York: Columbia University Press, 1960), p. 88.

[3] Ronald Freedman, Pascal K. Whelpton and Arthur A. Campbell, *Family Planning, Sterility, and Population Growth* (New York: McGraw-Hill, 1959).

among college graduates.[1] At the time of the 1960 White House Conference, 58 per cent of the nation's children were in families of three or more children.[2]

The tendency now is for women to marry young and have their children within the next few years. The average mother today has her last child well before she is thirty. When she is somewhere between 45 and 50, the children have all been launched (Chapter 1), leaving her and her husband many vigorous years following the rearing of their children.

More persons live to complete their family life cycle. At the turn of the century, the years of marriage after the children had left home were beyond the reach of the average married couple.[3] Today practically half of the family life cycle remains after the last child has grown and gone. Now when more persons live out their life span, a man and wife typically see their children married, and their grandchildren off to a good start in their lives before the original marriage is broken by the death of one or both of the spouses.

There are now proportionately more children and more old people in the population than at the turn of the century. Chart 5 consists of population pyramids for 1900, 1960, and projections for 1980, showing how the population is distributed by age and sex in each of the three periods. Low birth rates during the depression of the 1930s, and sharp increases during the postwar period mean that a smaller proportion of men and women in the most productive age groups now support larger percentages of potential dependents at top and bottom of the population pyramid.

More women work outside the home. At the turn of the century practically half of the women in the United States never entered paid employment. Now, at least nine out of ten women work outside their homes sometime in the course of their lives.[4] Some of these women workers are single, widowed, divorced, or separated, as Chart 6 shows.

More married women are employed now than formerly. In 1890, seven out of every ten working women were single. Six of every ten women

[1] "Fertility of College Graduates," Population Reference Bureau, Vol. XV, No. 6, September 1959, p. 109.
[2] White House Conference on Children and Youth, *Children in a Changing World,* 1960, p. 5.
[3] Paul C. Glick, *American Families* (New York: John Wiley & Sons, 1957), p. 68.
[4] National Manpower Council, *Womanpower* (New York: Columbia University Press, 1957) p. 10.

POPULATION PATTERNS HAVE CHANGED—more children and old people

70-74 YEARS	1900		1960		1980	
65-69						
60-64						
55-59						
50-54						
45-49						
40-44						
35-39						
30-34						
25-29						
20-24						
15-19						
10-14						
5-9						
0-4						
	MALE FEMALE		MALE FEMALE		MALE FEMALE	
PERCENT	6 5 4 3 2 1 0 1 2 3 4 5 6		6 5 4 3 2 1 0 1 2 3 4 5 6		6 5 4 3 2 1 0 1 2 3 4 5 6	

CHART 5. Population Patterns Have Changed—more children and more old people [1]

now working are married, and three out of every ten married women are presently employed.[2] The general tendency is for the young wife to work for a while after she marries, until her first child comes, when she may leave employment or take a diminished schedule until her children demand less care. By the time they reach adolescence and near the launching stage, she may return to work. More married women in their forties and fifties work than at any other time in their marriages (Chart 6 above).

Whether a married woman plans to work or not depends upon many factors: (1) the age of her children, (2) her replacement in the home, (3) her husband's income, (4) her husband's attitude toward his wife working, (5) her interests and saleable skills, and (6) other personal and family factors.[3] The question of the effect of the mother's working upon her marriage, her family life, and her children has been widely studied. The evidence to date all points in the same direction—that the fact of her working is in itself not a significant factor in her marriage

[1] Source: 1960 Golden Anniversary White House Conference on Children and Youth, *Children in a Changing World,* page 4, from original data supplied by United States Bureau of the Census.

[2] *Womanpower, op. cit.,* p. 10.

[3] See, for instance, National Manpower Council, *Work in the Lives of Married Women* (New York: Columbia University Press, 1957); Robert O. Blood, Jr., and Donald Wolfe, *Husbands and Wives* (Glencoe, Illinois: The Free Press, 1960), Chapter 4; Charlotte Montgomery, "Can Working Wives Make It Pay?" *Better Homes and Gardens,* November 1957, pp. 68, 137, 138; Mildred W. Weil, "An Analysis of the Factors Influencing Married Women's Actual or Planned Work Participation," *American Sociological Review,* Vol. 26, No. 1, February 1961, pp. 91–96.

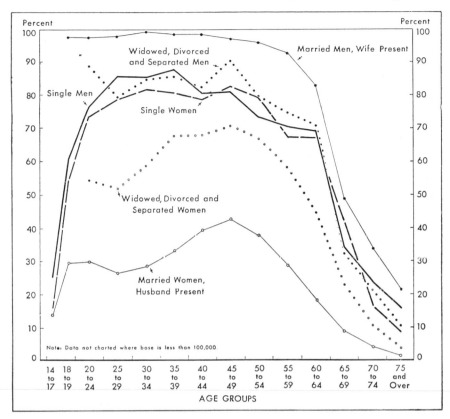

Percent

100

90

Widowed, Divorced and Separated Men

Married Men, Wife Present

Single Men

Single Women

Widowed, Divorced and Separated Women

Married Women, Husband Present

Note: Data not charted where base is less than 100,000.

| 14 to 17 | 18 to 19 | 20 to 24 | 25 to 29 | 30 to 34 | 35 to 39 | 40 to 44 | 45 to 49 | 50 to 54 | 55 to 59 | 60 to 64 | 65 to 69 | 70 to 74 | 75 and Over |

AGE GROUPS

CHART 6. Percentage of Workers in the United States by Age, Sex and Marital Status [1]

and family adjustment, or in the development of the children in the home.[2] Whether a wife's working helps or hurts appears to depend upon many personal and family factors rather than on the working itself.

Families have moved off farms and into cities and suburbs. In 1890, 64 per cent of America's families lived on farms. In the decades that followed there was a steady migration from farms to cities and suburbs, so that by 1960, only 8.7 per cent or one person in twelve was living on a

[1] Source: Jacob Schiffman, "Marital and Family Characteristics of Workers, March 1960," Special Labor Force Report, No. 13, United States Department of Labor, Bureau of Labor Statistics, from the *Monthly Labor Review*, April 1961.

[2] For a review of more than fifty studies, see Lois Meek Stolz, "Effects of Maternal Employment on Children: Evidence from Research," *Child Development*, Vol. 31, No. 4, December 1960, pp. 749–782.

farm.[1] This rapid decline of our farming population was caused by two related social forces. One was the development of industrialization that attracted men (and women) to work in the factories concentrated in and around urban areas. The second factor was the increased efficiency of the farm as it became mechanized and needed fewer and fewer workers on larger and larger acreages to support the needs of the nation. In the nineteenth century a farmer did well to support his own family. Today less than ten per cent of our entire population produces enough to care for the whole nation with enough left over to constitute a vast farm surplus.

Suburbs have grown most rapidly in recent decades. Between 1950 and 1960 suburban populations increased by 81.6 per cent, or more than three times as fast as the population of the entire United States. During the same decade cities grew only moderately, and in some areas there was an actual net loss of population in the core city.[2]

Families have shifted from production to consumption. As long as families were mainly agricultural, they raised, made, and processed most of what they needed in the home. Go back far enough, and you find the pioneer making an annual journey to the settlement to pick up his salt and coffee, all he needed to supplement what he and his family could provide for themselves. Some of us today can remember when most of the family's foods were grown, prepared, cooked and preserved at home; when the making of clothing and furnishings were home industries; when educational, religious, recreational and protective services centered in the home.

Today, the main burden of producing things has moved out of the home and into industry. The modern family is mainly a consuming unit, buying, selecting and arranging goods made in the factory for use in the home. What used to be "homemade" bread and butter, bacon, canned goods, and clothing now are mass produced in modern bakeries, dairies, packing houses, food processing plants, and factories that flood our homes with goods. Electrical mixers and grinders, ranges and roasters, refrigerators and deep-freezes, washers, dryers, and ironers, air conditioners and

---

[1] United States Bureau of the Census, *Farm Population,* Series P-27, No. 29, April 18, 1961, p. 1.
[2] *Children in a Changing World, op. cit.,* p. 8; and "The America the '60 Census Shows," U. S. News and World Report, July 3, 1961, based upon U. S. Bureau of the Census data, p. 47.

heaters, radios, record players, and television sets pour out of our factories in a tempting display to challenge the family's pocketbook.

Families have more resources. The typical American family earns more, and lives better than ever before. Families produce less and consume increasingly more goods today. There was a time when goods were so scarce that everything of any possible future use was saved in the home. Some of us remember the string pail, the grease bucket, the paper drawer, and all the rest of the devices by which a family used over and over again the little things that were hard to come by. Today we face the opposite situation in which so much floods our homes that yesterday's philosophy of "make it do" has been replaced with today's "get the new model." Our present-day economy depends upon a steady flow of goods, and an insatiable public. Advertising is designed to make our families discontent with what they have. The shift has been from the slow, painstaking fashioning of an article that would last a family for years to rapid replacement that calls for frequent selectivity rather than constant productivity on the part of the family.

The 1960 census found the median family income to be $5,620, an increase of 69.3 per cent within a single decade. Two thirds (67.2 per cent) of all families in 1960 had incomes above $4,000 a year; nearly twice the proportion in 1950 (36.8 per cent). This rise was higher than the rise in prices during the same period, giving families greater purchasing power. Home ownership is now at an all time high, as Chart 7 shows. More homes today have modern conveniences: hot and cold running water, plumbing, electrical equipment, than ever before. Cars were owned by 77 per cent of America's families in 1960, compared with 60 per cent in 1950.[1] Present-day family standards of living greatly exceed those of previous generations in our affluent society.

Family members have more leisure and better education. The working week has dropped through the twentieth century from approximately 60 to 40 hours a week. With less time on the job and more money to buy services, a great increase in the amount of leisure time has become available.[2] Family horizons are rapidly widening through travel, more

[1] *Ibid.*, pp. 46–48.
[2] For a summary of research studies on leisure and family living, see, Kenneth R. Cunningham and Theodore B. Johannis, Jr., "Research on the Family and Leisure: A Review and Critique of Selected Studies," *Family Life Coordinator*, Vol. IX, Vol, 1 and 2, September–December, 1960, pp. 25–32.

CHART 7.   Home Ownership Is at an All Time High [1]

frequent vacations, world news coverage, and increased use of magazines, books, radio, television and informal and formal education.

Public interest in education is increasing. Schools and colleges are crowded. The average adult in 1960 had 11 years of formal schooling,

TABLE 3. *More People Have More Education in the United States* [2]

Level of School Attained	1950	1960	Per Cent Increase
College graduates	5,793,000	8,100,000	39.8
College students	2,214,000	3,400,000	53.6
High school graduates	37,360,000	51,600,000	38.1
High school students	6,656,000	9,900,000	48.7

in comparison with 9.6 years in 1950. More individuals get more education at every level, as Table 3 indicates.

Higher levels of education, more leisure and greater affluence have

[1] Source: 1960 Golden Anniversary White House Conference on Children and Youth, *Children in a Changing World,* page 9, from original data supplied by Housing and Home Finance Agency, and the United States Bureau of the Census.

[2] Source: United States Bureau of the Census, from "The America the Census Shows," *op. cit.,* p. 48.

brought increased participation in a wide variety of sports, the arts, music, and community activities. Amateur dramatics, orchestras, and chamber music groups and choral societies have become increasingly popular. Civic groups and community organizations enlist the time and attention of millions of family members from Cub Scouting age upward through Senior Citizen groups. The danger is no longer social constriction but progressive proliferation of activities to the point of diminishing returns for either the individual or the family. Until a family sees its own goals clearly, it faces real hazards today in the many competing pressures for its time and resources.

Family roles have changed. There was a time when family members spent most of their time together. They worked side by side on the old home place. They played together or with their closest neighbors from nearby farms. Today family members are scattered, and their work and play activities are more individual than family based.

The roles of family members have become more complex and flexible. Men, women, and children worked hard on the old family farm in bygone years. But they knew what was expected of them, and they had been prepared rather specifically for the roles they played. A woman had to be a good cook since her family would depend upon her food throughout its lifetime. A man had to be a good steady provider before it was possible for his wife to get a job to supplement his earnings. Both men and women had learned their roles in their own homes before they married. Children had their place in the scheme of things and knew what was expected of them from the beginning. The whole neighborhood agreed on what was man's work and what was woman's work and what was to be expected of a child. The family lived according to relatively rigid rules traditionally established and maintained by social and moral pressures of the entire society.

Today both men and women expect a wide variety of roles of each other. These expectations differ from couple to couple and from family to family. In one home, a woman is expected to work outside, in another her place is seen to be in the home. In one family, a man is expected to be a companion to his wife and children, in another his roles are more traditionally defined. In general, the trend is for both husbands and wives to expect more of each other in the intangible roles of understanding companion, stimulating colleague, and loving, sympathetic parent than formerly.

The challenge of democratic interaction between family members—husband and wife, parent and child, close and extended family members—imposes new tasks and responsibilities upon all members of the family. Now that the authority of the father-head in many families has been taken over by family discussion, decisions are not as quick, nor plans as easily made. Now, when the social pressures of church and neighborhood have declined, every member of every family faces innumerable choices and possibilities.

Seeing home as a place good for people to grow up in is life at a much deeper level than seeing it as a "roof over our heads." Its potentialities are tremendous, but its problems, especially for transition generations, are felt in the very warp and woof of family living. The family, freed at last from the burden of producing things, faces as its primary task today the development of sturdy, wholesome personalities. But such a shift does not come all at once. Every step in the new direction is taken slowly, some with pain, others only after real effort as every member of the family learns its new roles, and practices the new innovations that are appropriate in today's family.

It is much harder to learn how to raise a child according to sound child development principles than it used to be when anyone with any "common sense" knew what was good for a child. Being a warmly sympathetic and companionable spouse is more difficult than baking a light biscuit or mending the harness. Such arts and skills of human interaction as are expected of family members today open new social and emotional frontiers where few have been adequately prepared by previous experience. Today's family becomes a laboratory at work on the most challenging world-wide problem—how to live together in creative peace, build harmony out of difference, and make democracy work. This is a big order in which many little families fail.

Family instability has increased. More families today are broken by separation, desertion, and divorce than formerly. There has been a marked rise in the divorce rate decade by decade in the twentieth century. Summary figures are given in Table 4.

Two facets of the trend in the rise of divorces are notable. One is that the divorce rate has risen most rapidly in the war years. The two big jumps in the number of divorces come between 1910 and 1920 (World War I) and between 1940 and 1950 (World War II). The second is that divorces decline during economic slumps. The only year in which the divorce rate was not significantly higher than that of the previous period was in 1930 at the beginning of the depression. These tendencies indicate that divorce rates and economic prosperity are closely related. When times are good, a couple who do not get along can divorce and support themselves separately. When jobs are scarce and there is little money, the married pair is forced to stay together for they cannot afford to do otherwise.

Thus far we have seen two reasons for the increased instability of American families. One, family members expect more of each other in

TABLE 4. *Divorce Rates Per 100 Marriages
the Same Year in the United States* [1]

Year		Divorces Per 100 Marriages
1900		7.9
1910		8.8
1920		13.4
1930		17.4
1940		16.5
1950		23.1
1960		25.8
1965	(provisional)	26.8

terms of personal, intangible qualities that are harder to deliver than were the simpler definite roles more easily learned in former times. Two, divorce is more possible as a solution to discord when neither man nor woman is so completely dependent upon each other for economic support. Other factors related to divorce are seen in the differential rates among segments of our population outlined below.

The evidence is that divorce is more frequent among some groups than others in America today. In general, the data point in these directions.[2]

[1] SOURCE: *Vital Statistics, Special Reports, Summary of Marriage and Divorce Statistics, United States,* 1949, Vol. 36, No. 2, Federal Security Agency, June 5, 1951; and recent figures from the National Center for Health Statistics, personal communication, July 27, 1966.

[2] Paul H. Jacobson, *American Marriage and Divorce* (New York: Rinehart & Co., Inc., 1959); and summary of research findings in Jessie Bernard, "Divorce and Remarriage—Research Related to Policy," Chapter 6 in Evelyn and Sylvanus Duvall, eds., *Sex Ways in Fact and Faith* (New York: Association Press, 1961), pp. 93–111.

Divorces More Frequent	*Divorces Less Frequent*
Among city families	Among farm families
In states with lenient divorce laws	In states with strict divorce laws
In inter-faith marriages	In marriages within same faith
In Protestant marriages	In Roman Catholic marriages
Among working class families	Among professional families
Among less educated people	Among better educated men and women
Among teenage marriages	Among those who marry at more mature ages
In first years of marriage	In later years of marriage
In childless marriages	In marriages with children

The reasons for the increase in family instability are many. The factors involved in understanding who gets divorced and why are complex. There is no question but what the revolutionary social changes of recent decades have blasted relatively stable families out of their old ways that had persisted for many hundreds of years, into new forms and functions with far reaching repercussions. The eminent historian Arnold Toynbee feels that, "The vital revolution of our time is the emancipation of women, workingmen, and "natives". . . . The women are the most important contingent of the three because, in the long run, their emancipation is going to affect everybody's life. Above all, it is going to demand an immense and disturbing psychological adjustment on the part of the men, because it implies a revolutionary change in the traditional relations between the sexes." [1]

Individual family members have more freedom. Traditionally, each family member was subordinate to the group. The very survival of the family and its members depended upon family and community solidarity. With the greater resources of our modern way of life has come an increase in individuation. The individual man, woman, and child today expects to be happy. He is encouraged to develop himself, and to work out his own problems in his own way. If his marriage is not happy, he can dissolve it. Or, better still, he is encouraged to select the kind of partner whom he can love, who will be good for him to live with, and to prepare with her for their life together from early in their courtship. Children now exist not for what they can do to help the family, but rather for themselves as growing persons with rights, privileges, and values recognized as uniquely theirs. A child no longer is expected to

[1] Arnold J. Toynbee, "We Must Pay for Freedom," *Woman's Home Companion,* March 1955, pp. 52, 53, 133–136.

follow in his father's footsteps, but rather to find his own interests and talents and choose a vocation that is meaningful to him.

Even the nature of the family is chosen today by its individual members. A couple may or may not have children. They may live much as their grandparents did, or they may establish their own unique family patterns. They may make the old rambling family homestead their home, or more likely, they may choose compact efficiency in a new little suburban dwelling or a city apartment. They may remain close to the place where they grew up, or set out into the world calling any number of places "home" for a while. Both may work and jointly run the household, or he may be the sole breadwinner, or she may support them both during intervals of his military training or further education. They may live for a while with his parents, or with her parents. They may share their home with relatives. Or, they may live by themselves while institutions care for their dependent relatives.

They may pour everything they have into living it up as they go along, or save all they can spare for the future; or they may budget for satisfactions both in the present and the near and distant future. They may bring up their children in traditional ways, or according to any of the fads or fancies proposed in our age, or try to gear into the developmental patterns that are emerging for child-rearing. Any of these, and numerous other possibilities are open to families today. They may choose what they will, both as families and as persons, and few there are who will either reward or punish them for their choices.

With so much freedom, is it any wonder today's families are confused and bewildered? When family tasks change so rapidly, it takes time and effort to become familiar with new expectations, and to assume appropriate new roles. For members of transition generations this means a period of uneasiness and instability, of innovations and exploration of new possibilities, until we can become more completely at home in these new families of ours.

THE CHANGING IMAGE OF AMERICAN FAMILIES

Families change as their world changes. The most vivid truth of today's world is that "No one will live all his life in the world into which he was born, and no one will die in the world in which he worked during his maturity." [1]

[1] Margaret Mead, "A Redefinition of Education," *NEA Journal*. October 1959.

Change in itself is neither good nor bad, but makes new demands upon persons and families. Social changes through the twentieth century require families to respond to new needs, conditions, and challenges, as well as to create fresh images of who they are and what they must do to adapt creatively in today's world.

The modern family "is more specialized than before, but not in a general sense less important, because the society is dependent *more* exclusively for the performance of *certain* of its vital functions," says Talcott Parsons.[1] The new image of family life is that of the nurturing center for human development.

Men and women as fathers and mothers today are engaged in child bearing and rearing with conscious intent upon socializing the child, transforming him or her from an immature human organism into a participating member of society, capable of creative contribution and personal integrity in a complicated explosive world situation. Parents themselves recognize that they too must continue to develop if they are to find personal happiness and be of some good to others. The garden for human development, both child and adult, continues to be the family in which the emotional soil and the spiritual climate for human growth originates.

A family is, therefore, the matrix of personality which emerges as the idiomatic patterns of functioning, of habits, ideas, beliefs, values, assumptions, and above all of emotional reactions and persistent feelings, as each child learns to live within his particular family in his or her own individual way.

Families are still the primary agents for health: in the selection and preparation of food for adequate nutrition in family meals; in the establishment of attitudes conducive to healthful eating, eliminating, resting, working, and being, as well as in the endless tasks of housecleaning, laundering, dishwashing and all the other functions that cannot be performed by doctors or outside medical agencies, but must be provided for in the home.

Families are the primary agents for basic mental health which cannot be brought about solely by psychiatrists, psychologists, or social workers. Only the family can protect and conserve the mental health of individuals through the quality of interpersonal relationships, the provision of re-

[1] Talcott Parsons and Robert F. Bales, *Family Socialization and Interaction Process* (Glencoe, Illinois: The Free Press, 1955), pp. 9 and 10.

assurance and comfort, the release and encouragement that each person needs to keep on striving for fulfillment. Love itself, the prime necessity for mental health, has its genesis in the intimate everyday warmth that husbands and wives, and parents and children find in and with each other.

Present-day American families face a level of conscious aspiration unknown to other places and times. The big change in family life in recent decades is in our aspirations as families. It is no longer enough to make ends meet, or to feed and clothe a child. Today's families in ever increasing numbers are seeking a quality of life for all their members that is truly something new in the history of mankind.

SUMMARY

Families respond with resilience to changing social conditions. Rapid industrialization through the twentieth century has been accompanied by many changes in American family life: (1) more men and women get married and at younger ages; (2) more families have three or four children; (3) more persons live to complete their family life cycle; (4) more women work outside the home; (5) families have moved off farms and into cities and suburbs; (6) families have shifted from production to consumption; (7) families have more resources; (8) family members have more leisure and better education; (9) family roles have changed; (10) family instability has increased; and (11) individual family members have more freedom. The image of family life has changed as families reflect social change. Now, freed from traditional drudgeries, today's family is more specialized than ever before as it focuses upon the development of its members as its central goal.

SUGGESTED ACTIVITIES

1) Write a paper on family living in today's suburbs, using materials from such studies as:

> Gordon, Richard E., and Katherine K., and Gunther, Max, *The Split-Level Trap* (New York: Bernard Geis Associates, 1960).
>
> Keats, John, *The Crack in the Picture Window* (Boston: Houghton Mifflin Co., 1957).
>
> Seeley, John R.; Sim, R. Alexander; Loosley, E. W., *Crestwood Heights: A Study of the Culture of Suburban Life* (New York: Basic Books, 1956).

2) Develop Toynbee's thesis (Woman's Home Companion, March 1955, "We Must Pay for Freedom") in an essay dealing with the strains and stresses in the relationships between men and women, between the generations, and between the family and the larger community, that come with emancipation.

3) View the film *Our Changing Family Life* (McGraw-Hill Book Company, New York, 22 minutes, sound) contrasting a three-generation farm family of the 1880s with today's urban family. List the explicit and implied changes in family living over the decades.

4) Select situations from Clarence Day's *Life with Father* portraying interaction between father and mother, and parents and children, as it was at the turn of the century. Role-play parallel current family situations known to you in a series of impromptu "Then and Now" skits. Discuss the reasons why family interaction has changed in the evident directions through the twentieth century.

5) Document Peter Drucker's articles "America's Next Twenty Years," *Harper's Magazine,* March, April, May and June, 1955, with current data from primary sources, and discuss how the trends he predicted have, have not, and may or may not continue, and why.

6) Collect evidence on the effect of a mother's employment outside the home on her family life, using such research reports as those listed in your *Readings* by the National Manpower Council, Lois Meek Stolz, and Mildred W. Weil. Develop into a carefully documented summary of what is known about the problems and promises of working wives and mothers in the modern scene.

READINGS

Allen, Frederick Lewis, *Only Yesterday* (New York: Harper & Brothers, 1931).

———, *Since Yesterday* (New York: Harper & Brothers, 1939).

———, *The Big Change* (New York: Harper & Brothers, 1952).

———, "The Big Change: The Coming—and Disciplining—of Industrialism," *Harper's Magazine,* October 1950, pp. 145–160.

Burgess, Ernest W., and Locke, Harvey J., *The Family from Institution to Companionship* (New York: American Book Company, 1953), Chapter 16, "The Family in Transition," pp. 447–82.

Calhoun, Arthur W., *A Social History of the American Family from Colonial Times to the Present* (Cleveland: Arthur H. Clark Company, 1917–1919).

Cavan, Ruth Shonle, ed., *Marriage and Family in the Modern World: A Book of Readings* (New York: Thomas Y. Crowell Co., 1960), Chapter 3, "From Colonial Family to the Family of the Future," pp. 58–89.

Compton, Arthur, "Effect of the New Scientific Age on Family Life," *Journal of Home Economics,* September 1947, pp. 387–390.

Drucker, Peter L., "America's Next Twenty Years," *Harper's Magazine*, March 1955, pp. 27–32; April 1955, pp. 42–47; May 1955, pp. 39–44; June 1955, pp. 52–59.

Duvall, Evelyn Millis, and Hill, Reuben, *When You Marry* (Boston: D. C. Heath and Company, Revised Edition, 1953), Chapter 20, "Marriage Isn't What It Used to Be," pp. 405–427.

Ginzberg, Eli, ed., *The Nation's Children, Vol. 1: The Family and Social Change* (New York: Columbia University Press, 1960).

Kirkpatrick, Clifford, *The Family as Process and Institution* (New York: The Ronald Press Company, 1963), Part II, "Social Changes and the Family," pp. 99–174.

Kyrk, Hazel, "Economic Responsibilities of Families—Increasing or Diminishing?" *Journal of Home Economics*, Vol. 44, No. 8, October 1952, pp. 616–619.

LeMasters, E. E., *Modern Courtship and Marriage* (New York; Macmillan Company, 1957), Chapters 21, "Wives Who Work," pp. 455–483; and 25, "Childrearing in Modern Society," pp. 535–562.

National Manpower Council, *Womanpower* (New York: Columbia University Press, 1957).

————, *Work in the Lives of Married Women* (New York: Columbia University Press, 1958).

Nye, F. Ivan, and Lois W. Hoffman, *The Employed Mother in America* (Chicago: Rand McNally & Company, 1963).

Ogburn, William Fielding, and Nimkoff, Meyer, *Technology and the Changing Family* (New York: Houghton Mifflin Company, 1955).

Sirjamaki, John, *The American Family in the Twentieth Century* (Cambridge: Harvard University Press, 1953).

Stolz, Lois Meek, "Effects of Maternal Employment on Children: Evidence from Research," *Child Development*, Vol. 31, No. 4, December 1960, pp. 749–782.

Wattenberg, Ben J., and Richard M. Scammon, *This U. S. A.* (Garden City, New York: Doubleday & Company, 1965).

Weil, Mildred W., "An Analysis of the Factors Influencing Married Woman's Actual or Planned Work Participation," *American Sociological Review*, Vol. 26, No. 1, February 1961, pp. 91–96.

Whitney, Vincent Heath, "Changes in the Rural-Nonfarm Populations, 1930–1950," *American Sociological Review*, Vol. 25, No. 3, June 1960, pp. 363–368.

Yinger, J. Milton, "The Changing Family in a Changing Society," *Journal of Social Case Work*, Vol. 40, No. 8, October 1959, pp. 419–428.

*Inferiors revolt in order that they
    may be equal, and equals that
    they may be superior.*
                    ARISTOTLE

*I have to live for others
    and not for myself:
That's middle-class morality.*
            GEORGE BERNARD SHAW

CHAPTER FOUR

Family status and social class

A child at birth is placed within society according to the social status of his parents. He may live out his life within the family status into which he was born. Or, he may move up or down the social ladder as he "betters himself" or "is no credit to his family." Such things are generally recognized; in recent years they have been studied intensively.[1]

A family generally is aware of its status within the community. Others are seen as "our kind of folks," or "better than we are," or "not the kind of people we want to associate with," as families identify those of similar status, those of higher and those of lower status respectively. Families who have social access to each other are generally considered to be of the same general social class.

A community may be predominately of one social class, or it may consist of several discernible status groups. A factory town may be made up of working-class families; a suburban community of middle-class people; while the wealthy upper class tend to cluster in the exurban areas that ring the great metropolitan areas.[2] Most modern communities have

[1] See for instance such comprehensive volumes as: Pitirim A. Sorokin, *Social and Cultural Mobility* (Glencoe, Illinois: The Free Press, 1959); Leonard Reissman, *Class in American Society* (Glencoe, Illinois: The Free Press, 1959); Reinhard Bendix and Seymour Martin Lipset, eds., *Class, Status and Power: A Reader in Social Stratification* (Glencoe, Illinois: The Free Press, 1959); and, W. Lloyd Warner and Paul S. Lunt, *The Social Life of a Modern Community*, Vol. 1 Yankee City Series (New Haven: Yale University Press, 1941; and other references in the chapter end *Readings*.

[2] A. C. Spectorsky, *The Exurbanites* (Philadelphia: J. B. Lippincott Company, 1955).

several social classes that range all the way from the families "across the tracks," to those who live in mansions "on the hill." Although definitions of, and patterns of, social stratification differ, studies of many kinds and sizes of communities, in various parts of the country find at least six social classes that may be seen as a continuum from top to bottom of the social ladder.

THE SIX SOCIAL CLASSES

The United States as a whole has six well-defined social classes that may be characterized as follows. The *upper-upper* class consists of the established old families who live in the most exclusive sections of the community in homes built by their ancestors. Upper-upper families live upon inherited wealth and upon the income of the heads of the household who are usually professional men or business executives. Members of upper-upper families tend to associate with each other in exclusive clubs, to send their children to private schools, to marry within their social class, and to maintain a strong feeling of family solidarity.

The *lower-upper* class is made up of the well-to-do families whose wealth has been too recently acquired for them to be completely accepted socially by the old established families in the best sections of town. Members of the lower-upper classes belong to the less exclusive "good" clubs, send their children to the best colleges, and live as much as they can like the upper-uppers.

The *upper-middle* class consists of the families who are "the backbone of the community." These families live in the better, but not the most exclusive sections of the community. They earn a comfortable living by professional service or business activity. They send their children to college and encourage them to make friends with "nice people" (of their own or higher status), and make a "good marriage" preferably with a member of the upper class. Upper-middle class families are active in social service organizations, churches, and do what they can to improve standards of living for themselves and others.

The *lower-middle* class is made up of skilled workmen, clerks, small shopkeepers, and some professional men and women who live in respectable sections of town in nice comfortable homes. Lower-middle class parents try to give their children a good education and some of the advantages of life that they may have lacked. They work hard, and put great stress on honesty, fair-dealing, and decency.

The *upper-lower* class with the lower-middle class just described is "the level of the common man." Families in the upper-lower class live in rented houses or apartments or simple, family dwellings not very far from the slums. The father and sometimes the mother and/or grown children earn the family income as semiskilled workers in factories, mills, mines, or in civil service jobs. These families work hard to keep up a respectable, independent life that is not to be confused with those at the bottom of the social ladder.

The *lower-lower* class is made up of families who live in the least desirable parts of town, in slums or slum-like dwellings. The family income comes from wages earned by the father, and usually the mother, at unskilled jobs that alternate with unemployment and being on relief. There is not always enough money to go around, and the family lives from day to day. Children of lower-lower class families drop out of school earlier than do members of other classes and are sooner in the labor force.

There are differences in the proportions of the various social classes by communities and by regions in this country. In general, the number and percentage of families in the middle classes are increasing rapidly with the higher levels of income and education that American families enjoy today.

HOW A FAMILY'S SOCIAL CLASS IS DETERMINED

Research studies tell us that a family's social class is determined by a number of factors: occupation, source of income, neighborhood, and type of house lived in. The *Index of Status Characteristics*, popularly known as the I.S.C., has been developed as a way of objectively deter-

TABLE 5. *Chart for Determining Social Class* [1]

Characteristics	Score
OCCUPATION	
Professionals and proprietors of large businesses (such as doctors and factory owners)	4
Semiprofessionals and smaller officials of large businesses (such as lab technicians or managers)	8
Clerks and similar workers (secretaries, bookkeepers, etc.)	12

[1] From W. Lloyd and Mildred Hall Warner, *What You Should Know about Social Class* (Chicago: Science Research Associates, 1953), pp. 22, 25.

Characteristics (Continued)   *Score*

Skilled workers (bakers, carpenters, etc.)   16
Proprietors of small businesses (owners of small groceries, restaurants, etc.)   20
Semiskilled workers (bus drivers, cannery workers, etc.)   24
Unskilled workers (such as warehousemen or ditch diggers)   28

SOURCE OF INCOME
Inherited wealth   3
Earned wealth   6
Profits and fees   9
Salary   12
Wages   15
Private relief   18
Public relief and "nonrespectable" incomes (e.g., gambling)   21

HOUSE TYPE
Large houses in good condition   3
Large houses in medium condition; medium-sized houses in good condition   6
Large houses in bad condition   9
Medium-sized houses in medium condition; apartments in regular apartment
  buildings   12
Small houses in good condition; small houses in medium condition; dwellings
  over stores   15
Medium-sized houses in bad condition; small houses in bad condition   18
All houses in very bad condition; dwellings in structures not originally in-
  intended for homes   21

AREA LIVED IN
Very exclusive; Gold Coast, etc.   2
The better suburbs and apartment house areas, houses with spacious
  yards, etc.   4
Above average; areas all residential, larger than average space around house;
  apartment areas in good condition, etc.   6
Average; residential neighborhoods, no deterioration in the area   8
Below average; area not quite holding its own, beginning to deteriorate,
  business entering, etc.   10
Low; considerably deteriorated, run-down, and semislum   12
Very low; slum   14

SCORING

Social Class	*Total Score*
Upper class	12–17
Upper class probably, with some possibility of upper-middle class	18–22
Indeterminate: either upper or upper-middle class	23–24
Upper-middle class	25–33
Indeterminate: either upper-middle or lower-middle class	34–37
Lower-middle class	38–50
Indeterminate: either lower-middle or upper-lower class	51–53
Upper-lower class	54–62
Indeterminate: either upper-lower or lower-lower class	63–66
Lower-lower class probably, with some possibility of upper-lower class	67–69
Lower-lower class	70–84

mining the social class of a given family. The ratings have been derived from social science research findings of actual families in a number of communities. The simplified version in Table 5 generally applies.

Putting the scoring device for determining social class into practice, let us take family A as an example. Mr. A manages the local plant (score 8), and has earned his present wealth (score 6). The A's live in a medium-sized house in good condition (score 6), in an above average residential community (score 6). The total I.S.C. score is 26, which puts the A family into the upper part of the upper-middle class. Family B, on the other hand lives in an apartment building (score 12) in an area that is rapidly changing and not quite holding its own (score 10). The B's income is derived entirely from profits (score 9) from their fruit store (score 20). Totaling their score, we get 51, an indeterminate score between lower-middle and upper-lower social classes, which means the B's could be either depending upon how their neighbors rate them.

Social status is on a continuum. The indeterminate scores between each of the six social classes indicates that there are no rigid categories into which all families must fit. But rather, as Cuber and Kenkel[1] suggest, we have a continuum of social status from the bottom to the top of the social ladder. In this continuum, some characteristics loom larger than others in the minds of people. Among the items used in the I.S.C. scale, occupation is felt to be most important by the people studied. Source of income and type of house lived in rank second in people's thinking, with the area of the community lived in falling into fourth place. Other factors such as the amount and type of education, church attended, style of clothing worn, clubs belonged to, and activities participated in, are all part of the status reputation a family member enjoys. This multiplicity of factors determining one's social status is related to the ease with which one can move up and down the social ladder.

SOCIAL MOBILITY

The family determines the social class into which one is born. But whether or not a person remains in the social class of his family of orientation depends on many factors. A person may conform to his or her family standards and patterns and be "a chip off the old block," remaining static in the same social status all his life. Or, he or she may,

[1] John F. Cuber and William F. Kenkel, *Social Stratification in the United States*, (New York: Appleton-Century-Crofts, Inc., 1954).

Middle-class families live in the better, but not the most exclusive, sections of the community, in good-sized homes that are in good condition.

by any of many available means (education, occupational success, sports, beauty, "a good marriage," fortunate investment of earned or inherited money, special talent, etc.) move up out of the social status in which he or she was born, so that his (her) family of procreation established upon marriage is a notch or so higher than the family of orientation in which he or she was brought up. This is called upward mobility. Downward mobility occurs when the person slides down the social ladder by lack of education, dissipation, ill-fortune, delinquency, incompetence, or whatever—losing his place in the social scene for one farther down the social scale.

Generally speaking, one of every four or five persons moves upward at least one social class level during his lifetime in the United States today.[1] The greatest amount of upward mobility occurs in the lower-middle and the upper-lower class levels, with nearly 30 per cent mobility from the status below reported at these levels. The lowest percentage of upward mobility is found at the upper-class levels, in which there is less than 8 per cent of mobility from the class below. The great American

[1] Carson McGuire, "Social Stratification and Mobility Patterns," *American Sociological Review*, Vol. 15, No. 2, April, 1950, pp. 195–204.

Lower-class families live in the less desirable parts of town, in simple family dwellings or slum-like apartments that are apt to be crowded.

Dream of "doing better than your parents did" is possible for the boy or girl from a lower-class family who gets an education, learns a salable skill, makes a good marriage, and establishes a nice home in a good neighborhood. The part of the promise that says "there is plenty of room at the top" is realized by few of those who strive for upper-class status. It takes time to accumulate the necessary wealth, to gain acceptance into upper-class circles, and gain the reputation needed for upper-class placement, as many a social climber has learned the hard way. Families oriented toward upward mobility tend to carry their children along with them and to encourage their young people to climb.[1] While more static families in which mother and father accept the way of life that is theirs tend to have nonmobile children (85 per cent).[2]

Women generally tend to rise in social status, more than do men, especially in the later decades of life.[3] A person of either sex who spends his teens in a large community is more apt to be upward mobile than is an individual who grows up in a small community.[4] The rising stand-

[1] Carson McGuire, "Conforming, Mobile, and Divergent Families," *Marriage and Family Living,* Vol. XIV, No. 2, May 1952, pp. 109–115.

[2] *Ibid.,* p. 113.

[3] Robert J. Havighurst and Ruth Albrecht, *Older People* (New York: Longmans Green and Company, 1953), Chap. 19.

[4] Seymour Martin Lipset, "Social Mobility and Urbanization," *Rural Sociology,* Vol. 20, Nos. 3 and 4, September–December, 1955, pp. 220–228.

ard of living, the increase in the assimilation of ethnic groups, the differential birth rate that creates a middle-class vacuum to be filled with lower-class children, the high valuation of education, the growth of labor unions—all seem to be associated with upward social mobility in the United States generally. A study of adults between the ages of 40 and 60 in Kansas City, Missouri, reveals more than a third as upwardly mobile (33.6 per cent), and 12.5 per cent downwardly mobile, yielding a net upward mobility of 21.1 per cent.[1]

Here then, we have a picture of the open social class system in the United States: a pyramid of status levels with the lower classes claiming the greatest number of families, with a large and growing middle class, and a small but influential upper class. Each social class has distinguishing characteristics that tend to be general for the families within it. Whatever a family's social class and its mobility pattern, they greatly affect the life of every member of the family and determine in large measure the strivings and values, routines and rituals, practices and policies of the family itself.

CLASS DIFFERENTIALS IN FAMILY ROUTINES AND RITUALS

Social class differences in the routines and rituals of family living around the clock and through the calendar, are to be found in everyday and special family celebrations of upper-, middle-, and lower-class families.[2] Daily routines from awakening, through bathroom procedures, mealtime practices, and the ways in which the day is spent and ended, differ from class to class. The lower-class family, crowded for space scatters into the neighborhood and makes out as best it can on a hand-to-mouth basis. The middle-class family tends to do more together as a family unit through the day and so establishes relatively rigid routines for getting things done efficiently. The upper class offers more privacy and physical resources to the members of the family and at the same time it demands a greater loyalty to family tradition and custom than do either of the other classes. All these tend to make for characteristic ways of living among families within the three major classes.

[1] Richard Coleman, Research paper on Social Mobility for the Committee on Human Development, University of Chicago, May 1956, unpublished material, p. 2.

[2] James H. S. Bossard and Eleanor S. Boll, *Ritual in Family Living* (Philadelphia: University of Pennsylvania Press, 1950), Chap. 6, "Class Differentials in Family Rituals," pp. 105–134.

Religious practices differ among the families of upper, middle, and lower classes; in church affiliation, church attendance, religious rituals within the home, and in use of the church for christenings, confirmation, weddings, funerals, and other rites.

The money habits of families of different classes differ widely. Allowances are not expected by lower-class children as they are in both middle- and upper-class families. Neither upper- nor lower-class children participate in family councils on budgeting of family expenditures as is common in middle-class families. Contributing to the family income, expected of lower-class children, is rare in middle-class families and found not at all among upper-class families.

The giving of presents for a wide variety of reasons and occasions is more frequent among middle-class family members than in the other social classes. Upper-class families tend to treasure and build rituals around their family heirlooms. Generally lower-class families do not value their past and have few valuable heirlooms to treasure.

Family pictures may be works of art in an upper-class family, objects of fond amusement among middle-class family members, and rare within the lower-class home. Special occasions like christenings, graduation, and weddings are usually photographed by middle- and upper-class families. A recent custom of sending a family picture on a Christmas card to friends and relatives has become established among middle-class families. Lower-class families occasionally take pictures of their babies. Their teenagers often get snapshots of themselves and their friends. But they rarely treasure old family photographs as do higher placed families who are proud of their background and antecedents.

Upper-class families tend to remain rooted on the old family place through the years from generation to generation. Their financial interests, their friends, their family traditions—all make staying on the thing to do. The lower-class family has little to keep it from moving on as soon as a more attractive possibility opens up somewhere else. When times are bad, streams of "Okies" flee the drought-hit areas for more promising possibilities on the coast. When times are good (during World War II, for instance), and good jobs open up in the metropolitan areas, workers migrate from South to North, from farm to city, and to both coasts in search of "good money." With expanding industrialization, professional and business men follow openings across the country and around the world taking their families with them to make a new life in a new place with astonishing frequency. Even more amazing is the way in which these millions of families tend to retain their social class patterns as they move from place to place: in the ways in which they work and play, make love, marry, bear and rear and educate their children, and weather or go down under the crises that hit them from time to time.

CLASS PATTERNS IN FAMILY WORK AND PLAY

The husband-father of the upper-class family goes regularly to his office, where he oversees the family investments, carries on the family business, or pursues his profession. His wife customarily is not gainfully employed, but is active socially,[1] serves the charities, and pursues the hobbies traditional in her family and among upper-class people in her area. The children, away at private schools or busy at home with their lessons in school and cultural subjects (music, art, dancing, etc.), are not expected to get or hold a job until they are adult. The young women "come out" as debutantes and, soon after, marry, leaving the protection of the father's home for that of the husband. These young women have little or no work experience save that gained as a volunteer or possibly a part-time position in some temporary connection. The young men may work in the family business or as interns in the profession they have chosen with the active assistance of the elder members of the family. Like their fathers, they tend to vote conservatively, and to affiliate with the Republican party.[2]

Some of the work in the upper-class home is done by servants under the supervision of the wife and mother, who may perform certain tasks as her privilege as lady of the house. The family assembles for family celebrations, visits to grandparents, regular opera-going, and (depending upon the area) for participation in horse shows, theatre, orchestral concerts, high status sports events, charity bazaars, and balls. The upper-class family "summers" in the same place year after year, to which many of their family friends traditionally go, for pleasant climate, change of pace, and a variety of exclusive activities.[3]

[1] James H. Williams, "Close Friendship Relations of Housewives Residing in the Urban Community," *Social Forces*, Vol. 36, No. 4, May 1958, pp. 358–362; and Zena Smith Blau, "Structural Constraints on Friendship in Old Age," *American Sociological Review*, Vol. 26, No. 3, June 1961, pp. 429–439.

[2] Raymond J. Murphy and Richard T. Morris, "Occupational Situs, Subjective Class Identification, and Political Affiliation," *American Sociological Review*, Vol. 26, No. 3, June 1961, pp. 383–392.

[3] Cleveland Amory, "Newport: There She Sits," *Harper's Magazine*, February 1948.

In the middle-class family, the husband-father works hard at his business or profession, for which he has prepared himself, with the encouragement of his parents, but without their rigid expectation that he will follow in his father's footsteps, a pattern more characteristic of the upper-class family. The wife and mother of the middle-class family may or may not be gainfully employed, depending upon the age of the children, her husband's attitudes, her abilities, and other personal and family considerations. There are few employed helpers in the middle-class home today—a cleaning woman by the day or a handy man by the hour for the heavier menial tasks of washing floors and windows is about all that is usual. Middle-class families pride themselves on their do-it-yourself skills and accomplishments, and get together for all sorts of family work projects—from the regular daily dishwashing, through weekly car washing, house cleaning and marketing, to the special building of a barbecue, or the finishing of an extra room in basement or attic.

Middle-class families enjoy a wide variety of vacations and are not bound to return to the same summer spot year after year. They may tour as a family to visit places of interest in their car; they may go to a summer cottage for the season with father commuting out for weekends; they may decide to stay home and complete some family project with only occasional excursions to the library,[1] the beach, or the country. Through the year Saturday and Sunday are special days in the middle-class home with Saturdays given over to trips into town for shopping, lunch, and a show; Sunday the day for going to church and being together as a family with a Sunday afternoon ride, on pleasant days, or the TV set or favorite games in inclement weather.

The lower-class family encourages its members to work as soon as they are able to supplement the family income. The earnings of children (paper routes, house or yard work for more affluent neighbors, work by the hour as errand boy, babysitter, etc.) are considered primarily the property of the family. The woman of the house works as she can around her responsibilities of bearing and rearing the children. The lower-class family is too busy making ends meet to have much time, money, or energy for whole family activities in either work or play. Even church attendance is on an individual basis, with some members of the family needed to care for the too young and too old or ailing family members at home,

---

[1] R. Clyde White, "Social Class Differences in the Uses of Leisure," *The American Journal of Sociology*, Vol. LXI, No. 2, September 1955, pp. 145–150.

while others go off one by one or two by two to Mass and other church functions.

In summertime, lower-class parents can rarely get away except possibly for a few days to visit relatives or attend a workers' camp. The children may get a week or two at a low-cost or free camp or may participate in the stay-at-home-camp programs available in many communities. Teenagers as well as adults slip off to the local hangout, tavern, and other commercial amusement whenever time and money allow. Parks, playground, community chest agencies, and museums are all more frequently used by members of lower-class families than by those higher in social status.[1] Home is too crowded and too noisy for games, entertainment, or even favorite radio programs for the rank and file of lower-class family members studied.[2]

SOCIAL CLASS DIFFERENCES IN EDUCATION

There are striking differences according to social level in both the type and the amount of schooling among America's children.[3] These differences are due to a complex of factors in which the family's financial circumstances, customs, beliefs, values, and attitudes are significant. The child of the working-class family receives little encouragement in his studies from home; at the same time, he feels rejected by his teacher who, being middle class, may not understand the behavior of the lower-class child.

In the words of Dr. Allison Davis, who has spent many years of work on this problem,

The slum child, whose own parents curse as a routine method of communication, fight, and consider the school unimportant in their futures, lives in a physical, economic, and cultural reality basically unlike that in which the middle-class child is trained. Therefore, if the slum child is to be realistic, many of the habits and attitudes which he learns will inevitably differ from those of the more sheltered, intimidated, and highly supervised middle-class child . . .

On the other hand, the middle-class . . . family's insistent pressure upon them for early and rapid attainment, and for conscientious work habits, makes middle-class children work much harder in school. Thus they please the teacher much more than do lower-class children . . .[4]

[1] *Ibid.*
[2] Bossard and Boll, *op. cit.*, p. 119.
[3] James S. Davie, "Social Class Factors and School Attendance," *Harvard Educational Review*, Vol. 23, 1953, pp. 175–185.
[4] Allison Davis, "Socio-Economic Influences upon Children's Learning," *School Life*, Vol. 33, No. 6, March 1951, p. 87.

Still another factor that Dr. Davis and his colleagues have found discriminating against the lower-class child's progress in school is the culturally biased "standard" intelligence test using middle-class ideologies and experiences. The lower-class child does not speak the language (literally) of the test and so rates significantly lower than his native capacity warrants. This means that he is often placed in so-called "slow" groups and given inferior equipment and curricula where his achievement remains low, quite understandably. The emergence of culturally fair tests is one practical result of these studies through the years.

A child's reputation and acceptance among his classmates in school is strongly influenced by the status level of his family. Children from lower-class families are less often wanted as friends (even by other children of their own social class), while children of middle-class families are desired as friends by children of all social levels represented in the fifth and sixth grades of a school studied.[1] The same study tells us that children from middle-class homes are considered by fifth and sixth grade children to be better looking than their lower-class classmates, in significant percentages. The lower-class child feels that school is not for him, and often drops out as soon as the law allows.

Schooling is directly related to social class, with children of the higher classes getting more years of formal education than do the lower-class children. Social class differences in school attendance are apparent from the beginning. Children from the lower social classes attend preschool in significantly smaller percentages than do those from the middle and upper social classes: A study of parents of five social classes (Warner, Meeker and Eels classification) whose children were in school or were to enter first grade in the fall shows marked differences by social class in the preschool attendance of the children:

Results showed that a child's chances of attending preschool decrease as one goes down the social ladder; almost 100 per cent of uppers and upper-middles send their children to preschool, while only 14 per cent of lower-lowers send theirs. Results cannot be explained solely in terms of the economic factor but may be due to differences in the way in which different social classes regard the school.[2]

---

[1] Bernice L. Neugarten, "The Relation between Family Social Position and the Social Development of the Child," Doctoral dissertation, University of Chicago, 1943.

[2] Celia Burns Stendler, "Social Class Differences in Parental Attitude toward School at Grade I Level," *Child Development*, Vol. 22, No. 1, March 1951, p. 45.

School drop-outs during the elementary and high school years show sharp social class differences. An extensive study of the social class system in one midwestern community [1] through the 1940's, found that three-fourths of the children at the lowest social class level, and more than half of the upper-lower class did not finish the ninth grade. Poor family heritage in terms of slum neighborhoods, broken homes, low and sporadic family income, are causes cited in that many lower-class children never finish high school.

College doors open to many students willing to work their way through to more education than their parents ever had in their time. Whereas in the 1930's colleges were made up largely of upper-middle class students, now less than a third of college students are from upper-middle class families. With increasing numbers of local community colleges, more and more students from working-class families go to college. Extensive studies in one midwestern city found more lower-middle class students than any other going to college. The greater size of the working-class population means that about 20 per cent of its students go to college, while 75 per cent of the high status students do, even though the numbers of students from the two social classes are similar. The lower-lower class family sends no girls to college and almost no boys. [2]

Studies of able young people who do not go to college find that they are disproportionately from families of lower social status, did less well in high school, have lower achievement drive, and lower scores on personality adjustment tests. Even though they rank in the upper quarter of their class in intellectual ability, their low family status proves to be a disadvantage in providing the incentives and the resources for going on with their education. [3]

FAMILY HEALTH DIFFERENTIALS BY SOCIAL CLASS

An intensive study of the 2,168 illnesses reported by 1,256 individuals in a community in the hill country of New York State, [4] indicates that members of the lower classes have a higher percentage of both disabling

---

[1] August B. Hollingshead, *Elmtown's Youth* (New York: John Wiley & Sons, Inc., 1949).

[2] Robert J. Havighurst, Paul H. Bowman, Gordon P. Liddle, Charles V. Matthews and James V. Pierce, *Growing Up in River City* (New York: John Wiley & Sons, Inc., 1962), Chap. 8.

[3] *Ibid.*

[4] Earl Lomon Koos, *The Health of Regionville* (New York: Columbia University Press, 1954).

p 83

and nondisabling illnesses and lose significantly more time from the job, especially in illnesses costing more than twenty days of time lost, than do members of the middle and upper social classes. A significantly smaller percentage of lower-class families in this study have a family doctor, and a higher percentage are dissatisfied with the medical care they receive for reasons that range from: "doctor prescribed too-expensive drugs," to "doctor not interested in caring for us."

Dental attention in terms of prophylaxis and emergency repair among members of the lower classes is considerably less than that received by persons who are better off in the community studied. This is reflected vividly in the percentage of extractions due to neglect: none at the top social class studied, 8.8 per cent of the social class members in the middle of the population studied, and 57.1 per cent of the lowest class placement. The reasons for such a high percentage of teeth lost through neglect in the lower classes are suggested by a public health worker in the community who says,

That percentage may seem high, but most of the poor grown-ups—especially those who live away from the towns and cities—let their teeth go until there isn't anything to do but have them pulled. I wonder sometimes how they can have any teeth left in their heads. Oil of cloves or some other pain killer is used in almost every low-class home in my district. So far as I am concerned, this is the biggest single over-all health problem there is.[1]

Preventive health examinations are practically nonexistent and health insurance significantly less in the lower social classes than among the middle and upper social classes. Lower-class families rely on the druggist for their health needs and stock an exceptional quantity of "kidney pills," "stomach medicines," and "liver pills" in an effort to ease discomfort and to keep well through self-medication. As several lower-class interviews report,

"My husband and I take C—— Liver Pills regular. We get to feeling stuffy if we don't, and keeping your liver flushed out gets rid of the stuffiness . . . Once in a while I take S—— Kidney Pills too. It's good to flush out your kidneys once in a while . . . If I do this, I don't get sick."

"I always take S—— Compound every fall. It thickens my blood, and gets me ready for cold weather."

[1] *Ibid.*, p. 122.

"We take H——— Tonic (alcohol 16 per cent) all the time during the winter when we aren't outdoors much. It keeps us fit; we don't have hardly any sickness since we've been doing this for three years now." [1]

This and other studies point to markedly different patterns of health and sickness, health care, and use of medical facilities among the social classes in a given community. The members of the middle and upper classes know more of the dynamics of illness and health and are more aware of the resources to be tapped for prevention and treatment of sickness. They live in a climate of social acceptance of the services of physicians, specialists (gynecologists, obstetricians, pediatricians, psychiatrists, and the rest), dentists, orthodontists, plastic surgeons, and the other professions whose services make life safer and more pleasant for human beings. The men and women of the lower classes, on the contrary, are not as aware of the nature of sickness and health. They do not feel that the health resources and facilities of a community are for "our kind of folks," so they tend to live in a heritage of bravely "getting along and making do." Self-medication and the use of nonmedical personnel are patterns that are transmitted to the children as the thing to do in everyday family living.

SOCIAL CLASS FACTORS IN DATING AND COURTSHIP

"Birds of a feather flock together" in the adolescent clique as in the adult community. This is clearly seen in examining the findings of studies of dating and courtship behavior among young people. Hollingshead's classic study of the high school students of one community reveals the fact that from 49 to 70 per cent of all clique ties are with those of the same social class. [2] The one-third of the boys and girls who associate closely in a clique with a member of another social class do so with a member of the class adjacent to his or her own. When a member of the highest social class associates with someone other than his own, it is with the next below; the lowest social class member establishes close associations within his own group, or more rarely the social class next higher in the social ladder. Bridging over more than one social class position is infrequent both in cliquing and in dating; the social distance is just too great.

Table 6 is an actual representation of the dating partner patterns of

[1] *Ibid.*, pp. 89 and 90.
[2] Hollingshead, *op. cit.*, p. 213.

the high school students of Elmtown by social classes. In this study Classes I and II are at the highest social class level, roughly equivalent to upper and upper-middle classes in other studies. Class V is the lowest social class level, roughly similar to lower-lower social class, while Classes III and IV approximate lower-middle and upper-lower class levels. There are interesting sex differences in interclass dating: when a boy crosses a class line, the chances are two to one that he dates a girl from a class below himself, while a girl, conversely, usually dates above herself when she leaves her own social class.

TABLE 6. *Intra- and Interclass Dating Patterns of High School Students* [1]

Social Class of Person Dated	Boys				Girls			
	I and II	III	IV	V	I and II	III	IV	V
Classes I and II	54%	38%	8%	——	50%	35%	15%	——
Class III	18%	53%	27%	2%	15%	58%	27%	——
Class IV	3%	11%	79%	7%	4%	16%	74%	6%
Class V	——	2%	28%	70%	——	9%	33%	58%

Boys and girls at the higher social class levels report more dates with more persons than do teenagers at the other social class levels. Higher placed girls are considered popular because of the number of dates they have and the number of boys they date. Going steady in this community tends to be frowned upon by many parents and teachers because of the emotional and sexual involvements that often result for members of the pair.

Young people from working-class families are more direct in expressing

TABLE 7. *Pre-Marital Sex Relations by Educational Level Experienced by Girls and Boys in Age Group 16–20* [2]

Educational Level	Girls	Boys
Grade School	38%	85%
High School	32%	76%
College and Graduate	17–19%	42%

[1] Data drawn with permission from A. B. Hollingshead, *Elmtown's Youth*, copyright 1949 John Wiley & Sons, Inc., page 231, excerpts from Chart I.

[2] Alfred C. Kinsey *et al.*, *Sexual Behavior in the Human Female* (Philadelphia: Saunders, 1953), p. 331.

sex interest and response and indulge less in extended petting than do young people from middle-class families.[1] The better educated the young person is, the less premarital sex experience he or she has. This association of educational level achieved to incidence of premarital sex is in a straight-line relationship age for age and grade for grade with the greater incidence at the lower educational levels, and the smallest percentages at the higher educational levels (see in Table 7).

MARRIAGE PATTERNS IN THE SOCIAL CLASSES

Young people tend to marry within their own social class. This holds generally true of men and women of all status groups, and is known as the principle of *homogamy*, the tendency for like to marry like. Over the past twenty-five years or more, when members of both sexes have enjoyed greater mobility than formerly, a recent survey finds that most of them continued to select their mates from within their own social class.[2]

Those who plan to marry either during or very soon after high school are predominantly from low-income and low-education level homes. These young people see themselves as leaving school and going to work, into military service (boys) or into homemaking (girls) immediately following graduation.[3]

More young people of lower-class families marry earlier than do those from families of higher status. Lower-class students are usually out of school in their middle teens, and so miss out on what family life education is offered in their high schools.[4] Members of lower-class families are more active in direct sex expression, are burdened less with social pressures for supporting the sex code and by urgent reasons for postponing pregnancy and marriage such as restrain more members of the middle-class families. Aspirations and achievement drives are weak in lower-class youth. Their homes are crowded, their parents are tired of trying

[1] Alfred C. Kinsey *et al., Sexual Behavior in the Human Male* (Philadelphia: Saunders, 1948); and *Sexual Behavior in the Human Female* (Philadelphia: Saunders, 1953), p. 368.

[2] Simon Dinitz, Franklin Banks and Benjamin Pasamanick, "Mate Selection and Social Class: Changes During the Past Quarter Century," *Marriage and Family Living,* Vol. XXII, No. 4, November 1960, pp. 348–351.

[3] Harold Christensen, "Lifetime Family and Occupational Role Projections of High School Students," *Marriage and Family Living*, Vol. XXIII, No. 2, May 1961, pp. 181–183.

[4] Robert J. Havighurst, "Social Class Differences and Family Life Education at the Secondary Level," *Marriage and Family Living*, Vol. XII, No. 4, Fall 1950, pp. 133–135.

TABLE 8. *Social Class and Age at Marriage* [1]

Age at Marriage	Social Class									
	Girls					Boys				
	A	B	C	D	Total	A	B	C	D	Total
Under 16	0	0	2	4	6	0	0	0	0	0
16	1	2	7	10	20	0	0	0	1	1
17	0	6	12	10	28	0	1	3	1	5
18	2	9	18	9	38	0	4	12	4	20
19	3	12	6	5	26	1	6	7	11	25
20	0	5	10	3	18	2	3	7	7	19
21–22	0	0	0	1	1	0	0	5	1	6
Total Number	6	34	55	42	137	3	14	34	25	76
Per Cent of Social Class Group	27	55	59	72	58	14	22	37	37	32

NOTE: The entire cohort was 19 or more by December 1960, the time for which these data apply. Therefore the only ages that can receive later additions are those from 20 on.

to make ends meet. Early marriage follows as the inevitable next step for the majority of lower-class youth.

Data on the young people in one typical community were collected from the time they were in sixth grade (1951–1952) until they reached adulthood. Four social class groups were recognized: upper-middle and upper-class combined (A), lower-middle (B), upper-lower (C), and lower-lower class (D). Table 8 shows clearly that those who married early tended strongly to come from lower status homes.

FAMILY CRISES ARE MORE SEVERE IN LOWER STATUS LEVELS

Young people of the lower classes are more frequently from broken homes than are the more privileged young men and women of the higher social class levels. There are many factors related to this tendency for greater instability of family life at the lower levels than among the higher social classes. Age at marriage is related to success in marriage, with the teen-age marriages significantly more risky than those of more mature persons. Educational level is related to stability of the family, with the better educated men and women making the more stable unions. Occu-

[1] Robert J. Havighurst, "Early Marriage and the Schools," *School Review*, Vol. 69, No. 1, Spring 1961, pp. 36–47.

pation is significantly related to proneness to divorce, as seen in a scholarly analysis of census data on divorce in America today, Table 9.

The lower income levels and less skilled occupational groupings have the highest proneness to divorce; while significantly less proneness to divorce is found among the skilled workers and professional and proprietary occupations and at the higher income levels. The reasons for these tendencies are complex and challenging to the serious student of family stability.[1]

TABLE 9. *Occupational Groupings in the United States by "Proneness to Divorce" Indices* [2]

Occupational Group	Proneness to Divorce Index *
Professional, semiprofessional	67.7
Proprietors, managers, officials	68.6
Clerical, sales	71.8
Craftsmen, foremen	86.6
Operatives (semiskilled)	94.5
Laborers (except farm and mine)	180.3
Service workers	254.7

* The proneness to divorce index expresses the relationship between the proportion or percentage of "Other Marital Status" (than single or married) in any given occupational category, to the proportion of "Married, Wife Present" in that same category. The index is a way of stating whether the number of broken homes in any given group is as much as, or more than, expected, in view of the proportion which that group is of the total population which could divorce (*i.e.*, the married). For the data from which these calculations were made see *Current Population Reports, Labor Force*, Series, P-50, No. 22, April 19, 1950, Table 5.

Families differ by the social class level they occupy in the number of crises they go through, what they consider a family crisis, the severity of their reaction to family troubles, and in the ways in which they weather family crises. In his review of his own and others' investigations of family crises, Earl Koos concluded that "middle-class families more often react more severely to crisis than do low-income families, but they recover their earlier interaction patterns more readily, and . . . they are more likely to come out of the crisis with some benefit to themselves . . . the middle-class family has far more to lose in the way of morals than does its coun-

---

[1] A provocative summary is found in August B. Hollingshead, "Class Differences in Family Stability," *The Annals of the American Academy of Political and Social Science*, Vol. 272, November 1950, pp. 39–46; as well as in the Goode study.

[2] William J. Goode, *After Divorce* (Glencoe, Illinois: The Free Press, 1956), p. 46.

terpart in the low-income group; in general, too, it has much more opportunity, and much more with which to re-establish itself after the crisis is over." [1]

SOCIAL CLASS DIFFERENTIALS IN CHILDREARING

Social scientists for several decades have studied how parental attitudes and behavior differ by family social class level. Frazier in 1939 [2] found that middle-class families of both white and Negro races had shifted to equalitarianism with respect to family dominance; while working-class families continue to adhere to the tradition and display of matriarchal dominance in the case of Negroes and patriarchal dominance in the case of whites.

COURTESY OF DOROTHEA LANGE:
"FAMILY OF MAN"

The lower-class family has few resources for meeting its crises and often suffers permanent damage as each recurring trouble leaves the family unit more vulnerable and less well integrated.

Working-class fathers tend to feel that childrearing is the mother's responsibility, while middle-class fathers and mothers agree that fathers should share equally with mothers in raising their children. [3] Middle-class fathers assume more responsibility for a wide variety of family tasks than do either husbands of either high or low status families. The upper-class mother has some hired help to assist her; the lower-class mother does the best she can by herself. It is in the middle classes where husband and wife tend to jointly share homemaking and childcare responsibilities. [4]

Planning for children declines with social class level. In a study of 1,805 upstate New York mothers with infants, 39 per cent of the upper-middle and upper-class mothers, 36 per cent of the lower-middle class,

---

[1] Earl L. Koos, "Class Differences in Family Reactions to Crisis," *Marriage and Family Living,* Vol. XII, No. 3, Spring 1950, p. 78.

[2] E. Franklin Frazier, *The Negro Family in the United States* (Chicago: University of Chicago Press, 1939), p. 439.

[3] Melvin L. Kohn, and Eleanor E. Carroll, "Social Class and the Allocation of Parental Responsibilities," *Sociometry,* Vol. 23, 1960, pp. 372–392.

[4] Marvin E. Olsen, "Distribution of Family Responsibilities and Social Stratification," *Marriage and Family Living,* Vol. XXII, No. 1, February 1960, pp. 60–65.

34 per cent of the upper-lower class, and 27 per cent of the lower-lower class mothers had planned for their babies.[1] Rainwater's intensive study of family planning in working-class families concludes, "The lack of effective contraception so common in this group is not due simply to ignorance or misunderstanding; *it is embodied in particular personalities, world views, and ways of life which have consistency and stability and which do not readily admit such foreign elements as conscious planning and emotion-laden contraceptive practices.*"[2]

Very large families tend to have smaller incomes and lower social status than do medium sized ones. In 1957, over 39 million children were in families with incomes of $4,000 or more, an increase of 11 million children in this income group between 1954 and 1957. But more than 13 million children that year were still in families with less than $3,000 income.[3]

Middle-class mothers tend to have their babies in a hospital, while women in the lower social strata may be delivered at home:

" 'My babies wuz all borned at home.'

'All my babies but one was born at home.'

'Ma was here and helped when the first two came. My sister, sister-in-law, and neighbors helped when the others were delivered.'

'There's nothing like a good mid-wife to "catch" the babies when they come.' "[4]

Mothers who read books or pamphlets that might be helpful during pregnancy or after their children are born tend significantly to be those of higher social status. In upstate New York, where such materials are distributed free to mothers, 14 per cent of the upper and upper-middle class mothers, 16 per cent of the lower-middle class, 22 per cent of the upper-lower class, and 39 per cent of the lower-lower class mothers listed *no reading* in connection with having their babies.[5] Breast-feeding was most likely at the upper levels, declining by status to 21 per cent of the mothers of the two lower classes.[6]

[1] Walter E. Boek, Marvin B. Sussman, Alfred Yankauer, "Social Class and Child Care Practices," *Marriage and Family Living*, Vol. XX, No. 4, November 1958, pp. 326–333.

[2] Lee Rainwater, *And the Poor Get Children* (Chicago: Quadrangle Books, 1960), pp. 167–168.

[3] White House Conference on Children and Youth, *Children in a Changing World,* 1960, p. 14.

[4] Carson McGuire, "Family Life in Lower and Middle Class Homes," *Marriage and Family Living*, Vol. XIV, No. 1, February 1952, p. 4.

[5] Boek, Sussman and Yankauer, *op. cit.* p. 330.

[6] *Ibid.,* p. 330.

A mother's aspirations for her children reflect her social class status. When 1,433 mothers of babies were asked how much education they would like their children to get when they grew up, 89 per cent of the highest ranking mothers in contrast to 57 per cent of the mothers in the lowest social class level said they would like their children to have a college education. An encouraging 86 per cent of the lower-middle class, and 69 per cent of the upper-lower class mothers had college aspirations for their children, reflecting perhaps today's greater opportunities for more lower status children to attend college.[1]

Working-class parents value the qualities in their children that assure respectability, in which desirable behavior consists essentially of not violating proscriptions and pleasing adults. Middle-class parents tend to value the child's development of internalized standards of conduct, in which desirable behavior consists essentially of acting according to the kind of person the child is growing to be, according to widely separated studies.[2]

Punishment of children differs from class to class in form, amount, offenses dealt with and in the person responsible for punishing children for misbehavior. In the words of one research report,

"Punishment in the lower class home tends to be inconsistent, at least from the field workers' points of view. One group of observers has included this summary, 'For a thing that is funny one time, the lower-class child may be whipped the next. They are whipped so much, they lose their fear of it and come to expect it for almost anything . . .'

"Alternate loving and 'fazing,' that is, petting and then slapping a child 'to toughen him up,' are not infrequent mechanisms which go along with shaming, ridiculing, and whipping in the lower class home. Passages such as the following are to be found in lower class interviews.

"'I whup 'em with a belt when they git out of hand.'

"'Whipping's the best way. I usually save up until they need it bad and then give 'em a good one.' 'They usually build up to one.' 'I jest got through whippin' that one. She jest needed a good strapping.'"[3]

Middle-class mothers are more frequently opposed to physical punishment, and so they use a variety of methods of control including disapproval, deprivation of some privilege, isolation from other members of the

---

[1] *Ibid.*, p. 332.

[2] Evelyn Millis Duvall, "Conceptions of Parenthood," *American Journal of Sociology*, Vol. LII, No. 3, November 1946, pp. 193–203; and Melvin L. Kohn, "Social Class and the Exericse of Parental Authority," *American Sociological Review*, Vol. 24, No. 3, June 1959, pp. 352–366.

[3] Carson McGuire, *op. cit.*, p. 5.

family by being sent to one's room, and "talking to the child," in an effort to explain why what he has done is wrong, and discussing better ways of behaving. Consequently, the middle-class child's, "If I do that so-and-so will happen," is quite different in orientation than the lower class youngster's, "I wanted to do it, so I did it." Lower-class children learn that gratifications and deprivations are immediate, or unpredictable if postponed. Most middle-class children learn that approval and disapproval extend over a longer period of time and that consequences have to be taken into account.[1]

Intensive studies of social class differences in childrearing practices have been conducted in various sections of the United States at intervals through the past thirty years or more. There were differences in the samples of children and families studied, in the methods employed, in the items explored, and in the findings of the many research studies. Bronfenbrenner's comparative analysis of the results of fifteen research studies from 1932 through 1957 involving a total of 9,242 cases, finds consistent current differences between middle-class and working-class childrearing patterns that may be summarized as follows: [2] Since World War II, middle-class—more than working-class—childrearing tends to be permissive in infant care. Middle-class mothers are more likely than working-class mothers to breast-feed, follow a self-demand schedule, wean the child later from both breast and bottle, begin and complete toilet training at a later age, and follow recommendations of the experts through books, physicians, and other authoritative resources. Middle-class families more than working-class families are permissive toward the child's expressed needs and wishes in such areas as oral behavior, toilet accidents, dependency, sex, aggressiveness, and freedom of movement outside the home. Middle-class youngsters are expected to learn to take care of themselves earlier, to accept more responsibilities about the home, and to go further in school. Middle-class parents rely more on reasoning, isolation, appeals to guilt, and methods other than direct physical punishment which is consistently more the working-class pattern of discipline. Middle-class families use methods designed to bring about the development of internalized values and controls in contrast to working-class methods which rely more on external pressures. Middle-class families are consistently more acceptant and equalitarian whereas working-class childrearing is di-

[1] *Ibid.*, p. 6.
[2] Urie Bronfenbrenner, "Socialization and Social Class through Time and Space," published as a specially written chapter in E. E. Maccoby, T. M. Newcomb, and E. L. Hartley, *Readings in Social Psychology* (New York: Henry Holt and Co., 1958).

rected toward maintaining order and obedience, and "pleasing adults." [1]

A number of studies concur that middle-class children have fewer personality problems and better personality adjustment than do children from lower-class families.[2] Sewell and Haller offer the following explanation for the lower-class child's greater handicap in personality qualities: (1) The lower-class child learns early the lower-class ways of the family. (2) He encounters in the larger social scene many values and behavior expectations that are quite different from those he learned at home. (3) He is made to feel that these more widely accepted patterns are more acceptable than those of his family, so he tries to adopt them. (4) Since there is a conflict between what he learned at home and what is expected of him outside, he experiences tension which may be manifested in (a) concern about the status of his family; (b) concern over his ability to perform up to expected levels, particularly in school; (c) rejection of family; and, (d) nervous behaviors indicative of general anxiety.[3]

Much more study is needed on the way families differ in their child-rearing practices by their social class placement. The subject has been briefly introduced in this chapter to be continued in the discussions that follow. Family status within the social class structure of our changing American society is only one of several factors influencing the ways in which children are reared. A family's social class placement is part of its total orientation as a family. What some of these basic orientations are, how they are related to family value systems, as well as to families' social status in the patterns of childrearing that are emerging is the burden of the next chapter.

SUMMARY

This chapter does not attempt to exhaust the vast amount of original research and social theory on the effect of social class upon family life. Rather, an effort has been made to introduce some of the highlights

---

[1] See for instance, Evelyn Millis Duvall, "Conceptions of Parenthood," *American Journal of Sociology*, Vol. LII, No. 3, November 1946, the first study to point such class differences in childrearing attitudes and practices.

[2] Summaries of several are found in F. Auld, Jr., "Influence of Social Class on Personality Test Responses," *Psychological Bulletin*, Vol. 49, 1952, pp. 318–332; William H. Sewell and Archie O. Haller, "Social Status and the Personality Adjustment of the Child," *Sociometry*, Vol. 19, No. 2, June 1926, pp. 114–125; and William H. Sewell and A. O. Haller, "Factors in the Relationship between Social Status and the Personality Adjustment of the Child," *American Sociological Review*, Vol. 24, No. 4, August 1959, pp. 511–520.

[3] Sewell and Haller, *ibid.*, p. 519.

and the dark shadows that are to be seen in the ways families differ by their social class placement. These differences are to be found in the everyday patterns of living within the family—in rituals and routines, work and play, education, health, dating and courtship, marriage and divorce, childbearing and rearing, as well as in family troubles and crises.

Looking at this chapter in relationship to those that have gone before, we recognize that social class is an important factor to be taken into account in understanding family life and intra-family interaction at every stage of the family life cycle, and in seeing family life through history. We turn next to trace the ways in which the philosophy of family relationships and child nurture and training are changing within our dynamic culture. Social class variables have been summarized early in this volume so that they may be seen in all that is yet to come, as significant in flesh and blood family living at every stage of the family life cycle.

SUGGESTED ACTIVITIES

1) Write a paper of the effect of a family's social class status and the personality adjustment of its children. Reconcile, to your satisfaction, conflicting findings of such studies as those by Auld; Davis and Havighurst; Duvall; McGuire; Sears, Maccoby and Levin; as well as Sewell and Haller (footnoted through your chapter) which compare middle-class with working-class childrearing patterns and their effects upon the personality development of the child.

2) Review one of the following works of fiction, identifying (1) the social class level of the principal family portrayed, (2) the extent of the social mobility exhibited by the main character, (3) the stage(s) of the family life cycle in which the action takes place. Document your decisions on all three points with direct quotations from the book, and primary research sources for the criteria you employ.

   Farrell, James T., *Father and Son* (New York: Vanguard Press, 1940).

   Fitzgerald, F. Scott, *The Great Gatsby* (New York: Charles Scribner's Sons, 1925).

   Gilbreth, Frank B. and Carey, Ernestine, *Cheaper by the Dozen* (New York: Thomas Y. Crowell Company, 1948).

   Lewis, Sinclair, *Babbitt* (New York: Harcourt, Brace and Co., 1922).

   MacDonald, Betty, *Onions in the Stew* (Philadelphia: J. B. Lippincott Company, 1954).

   Marquand, John P., *The Late George Apley* (New York: P. F. Collier and Son, 1936).

   McConnell, Raymond A., Jr., *Trampled Terraces* (Lincoln: University of Nebraska Press, 1950).

Morley, Christopher, *Kitty Foyle* (Philadelphia: J. B. Lippincott Company, 1939).

Schulberg, Budd, *What Makes Sammy Run?* (New York: Random House, 1941).

Smith, Betty, *A Tree Grows in Brooklyn* (New York: Harper & Brothers, 1943).

Streeter, Edward, *Father of the Bride* (New York: Simon and Schuster, Inc., 1948).

Wouk, Herman, *Marjorie Morningstar* (New York: Doubleday and Company, Inc., 1955).

3) Plot on an area map of your locality, the residences of the families mentioned in the society columns of one of your local papers for the period of one week. Discuss your findings in the light of what you know about social class and membership of families in the "social set."

4) Using the simplified version of the Index of Status Characteristics (Table 5) given early in this chapter, determine your own social class placement as seen in your family of orientation, and in your plans for your family of procreation. Discuss the mobility evidences apparent in any discrepancies between the two scores, with indications of their possible sources in your developmental experience.

5) Write a paper on the social class origins of the men who are the controlling voices in large industrial organizations in contemporary America using as your primary source the material found in the analysis by W. Lloyd Warner and James Abegglen in *Big Business Leaders in America* (New York: Harper & Brothers, 1955).

6) Make a simple survey of the school drop-outs in your community for the past year. Try to find out from the school authorities which children dropped out (in terms of occupation and income of the father, area lived in, probable social class placement, etc.), percentages of children leaving school by grade levels, and attitudes of representative teachers toward the boys and girls who have left school.

7) Graph the divorces granted in your area during the past year by income and occupation of the man, and by the section of the community the couples had lived in just prior to the granting of their divorce. To what extent do these findings corroborate those on the national level that divorce is more frequent among the unskilled and low income families than among the more privileged and skilled?

8) Review Moss Hart, *Act One: An Autobiography* (New York: Random House, 1959), emphasizing particularly the social class placement of Mr. Hart's family of orientation as compared with his family of procreation. Discuss the means by which his mobility was achieved step by step through his career. Conclude with your appraisal of how typical this mobility pattern is in modern American life, and the other ways by which a young person can improve his family's status today.

READINGS

Bernard, Jessie, *Marriage and Family Among Negroes* (Englewood Cliffs, New Jersey: Prentice-Hall, Inc. 1966).

Boek, Walter; Sussman, Marvin; and Yankauer, Alfred, "Social Class and Child Care Practices," *Marriage and Family Living*, Vol. XX, No. 4, November 1958, pp. 326–333.

Bossard, James H. S., *Ritual in Family Living* (Philadelphia: University of Pennsylvania Press, 1950), Chapter 6, "Class Differentials in Family Rituals," pp. 105–185.

Cavan, Ruth Shonle, "Subcultural Variations and Mobility," Chapter 14 in Harold T. Christensen, ed., *Handbook of Marriage and the Family* (Chicago: Rand McNally & Company, 1964), pp. 535–581.

Chilman, Catherine S., *Growing Up Poor* (Washington, D. C.: U. S. Department of Health, Education, and Welfare, 1966).

Cuber, John F., and Peggy B. Harroff, *The Significant Americans* (New York: Appleton-Century-Crofts, 1965).

Cuber, John and Kenkel, William, *Social Stratification in the United States* (New York: Appleton-Century-Crofts, Inc., 1954).

Davis, Allison, "Socio-Economic Influences upon Children's Learning," *School Life*, Vol. 33, No. 6, March 1951, pp. 87, 93, 94.

Dinitz, Simon; Banks, Franklin; and Pasamanick, Benjamin, "Mate Selection and Social Class: Changes During the Past Quarter Century," *Marriage and Family Living*, Vol. XXII, No. 4, November 1960, pp. 348–351.

Eshleman, J. Ross, and Chester L. Hunt, Social Class Factors in the College Adjustment of Married Students (Kalamazoo, Michigan: Western Michigan University, 1965).

Federal Extension Service, *Low Income Families* (Washington, D. C.: United States Department of Agriculture, 1963).

Goode, William J., *After Divorce* (Glencoe, Illinois: The Free Press, 1956).

Havighurst, Robert J.; Bowman, Paul; Liddle, Gordon; Matthews, Charles; and Pierce, James, *Growing Up in River City* (New York: John Wiley & Sons, Inc., 1962).

Havighurst, Robert J.; and Davis, Allison, "A Comparison of the Chicago and Harvard Studies of Social Class Differences in Child Rearing," *American Sociological Review*, Vol. 20, No. 4, August 1955, pp. 438–442.

Herzog, Elizabeth, "Is There a 'Breakdown' of the Negro Family?," *Social Work*, Vol. II, No. 1, January 1966.

Hollingshead, August B., *Elmtown's Youth* (New York: John Wiley & Sons, Inc., 1949).

Johnson, Kathryn P., and Gerald R. Leslie, "Methodological Notes on Research in Childrearing and Social Class," *Merrill-Palmer Quarterly*, Vol. II, No. 4, October 1965, pp. 345–358.

Kaplan, Max, *Leisure in America: A Social Inquiry* (New York: John Wiley & Sons, Inc., 1960).

Kohn, Melvin L., "Social Class and Parental Authority," *American Sociological Review*, Vol. 24, No. 3, June 1959, pp. 352–366.

Kohn, Melvin L., "Social Class and Parent-Child Relationships: An Interpretation," *The American Journal of Sociology*, Vol. LXVIII, No. 4, January 1963, pp. 471–480.

Komarovsky, Mirra, *Blue-Collar Marriage* (New York: Random House, 1964).

Koos, Earl L., "Class Differences in Family Reactions to Crisis," *Marriage and Family Living*, Vol. XII, No. 3, Summer 1950, pp. 77, 78, 99.

Koos, Earl L., *The Health of Regionville* (New York: Columbia University Press, 1954).

Maas, Henry S., "Some Social Class Differences in the Family Systems and Group Relations of Pre- and Early Adolescents," *Child Development*, Vol. 22, No. 2, June 1951, pp. 145–152.

McGuire, Carson, "Family Life in Lower and Middle Class Homes," *Marriage and Family Living*, Vol. XIV, No. 1, February 1952, pp. 1–6.

Mayer, John E., *The Disclosure of Marital Problems: An Exploratory Study of Lower and Middle Class Wives* (New York: Community Service Society of New York, 1966).

Moynihan, Daniel P., *The Negro Family* (Washington, D. C.: U. S. Department of Labor, Office of Policy Planning and Research, 1965).

Olsen, Marvin E., "Distribution of Family Responsibilities and Social Stratification," *Marriage and Family Living*, Vol. XXII, No. 1, February 1960, pp. 60–65.

Rainwater, Lee, *And the Poor Get Children* (Chicago, Illinois: Quadrangle Books, 1960).

Sears, Robert; Maccoby, Eleanor; and Levin, Harry, *Patterns of Child Rearing* (Evanston, Illinois: Row, Peterson and Company, 1957).

Seeley, John; Sim, R. Alexander; and Loosley, Elizabeth, *Crestwood Heights* (New York: Basic Books, Inc., 1956).

Shoemaker, Louise Proehl, *Parent and Family Life Education for Low-Income Families* (Washington, D. C.: Children's Bureau Publication No. 434, 1965).

Sorokin, Pitirim, A., *Social and Cultural Mobility* (Glencoe, Illinois: The Free Press, 1959).

Steinbeck, John, "America and the Americans," *The Saturday Evening Post*, July 2, 1966, pp. 32–47.

Stendler, Celia Burns, "Social Class Differences in Parental Attitudes toward School at Grade I Level," *Child Development*, Vol. 22, No. 1, March 1951, pp. 37–46.

Warner, W. Lloyd, *American Life: Dream and Reality* (Chicago: University of Chicago Press, 1953).

Waters, Elinor, and Vaughn J. Crandall, "Social Class and Observed Maternal Behavior from 1940 to 1960," *Child Development*, Vol. 35, 1964, pp. 1021–1032.

West, James, *Plainville, U.S.A.* (New York: Columbia University Press, 1945).

The hickory stick is obsolete
Discipline has long been on the
skids
Everything in the modern home
Is controlled by a switch—but the
kids!
AUTHOR UNKNOWN

He who stops being better
stops being good.
OLIVER CROMWELL

CHAPTER FIVE

Trends in family orientation and childrearing

F amily orientation may be thought of as the basic attitude toward life that a family assumes. Out of its family orientation emerge the direction, the form, and the type of behavior that characterize a given family. Family values, ambitions, aspirations and philosophy of life are all rooted in family orientation. A family's orientation emerges from the family heritage and individual self-conceptions that a man and woman bring to their marriage and redefine throughout their family life. In essence, family orientation is the image of itself by which a family lives.

TYPES OF FAMILY ORIENTATION

Child-, home-, and parent-oriented families. In studying families of mentally-retarded children, Farber finds three types of family orientation: [1] (1) *child-oriented* in which both parents structure their family life around the needs and demands of the children. In the child-oriented family husband-wife roles are sharply defined, economic security is highly valued, and community participation is very important; (2) *home-oriented*, in which both parents concentrate on congenial interpersonal relations in the home, the husband-wife roles tend to overlap, and com-

[1] Bernard Farber, *Family Organization and Crisis: Maintenance of Integration in Families with a Severely Mentally Retarded Child*, Monograph Serial No. 75, Vol. 25, No. 1, *Society* for Research in Child Development, 1960, pp. 39–63.

munity participation is of little importance; and (3) *parent-oriented*, in which husband and wife concentrate on his career advancement, and their family life is built around achievement, personal development and the acquisition of social skills in their children and themselves.

Past, present, and future orientation. Another type of family orientation is that described by Godfrey [1] as three types of families by ways of meeting their basic family tasks: (1) *past-oriented families*, (2) *present-oriented families*, or (3) *future-oriented families*. In the family that is geared to the past, family standards are rigidly upheld, with the major sanctions being religion and the mores. The immediate family is recognized as part of the larger extended family, with each individual subordinated to the group as a whole. Family government is patriarchal. Children are trained by strict traditional methods. Women's spheres of activity are limited and subordinate to those of the men of the household. The father directs the economic affairs of the family in which economic interdependence is emphasized. Family solidarity is largely work-oriented, with farming seen as a family occupation. There are close ties with the church, but few active connections with the school or other social and civic organizations.

The family geared to the present views individual welfare as more important than group preservation. The immediate family is separated from the larger kinship group. Public approval is the major sanction with methods of control derived from current practice and standards that are contemporary. Family government is equalitarian. Children are trained under the careful supervision of the mother according to currently popular methods. There is a well-defined division of labor between the sexes, but both men's and women's work are considered equally important. Husband and wife jointly control the money of the family and emphasize mature children's economic independence. Family solidarity is based largely on recreational ties. Farming as such is seen as a profitable business. There is little recreation with relatives, and individual family members are encouraged to be active in numerous organizations in the community.

The family geared to the future sees the needs of the individual and the group as equally important. The immediate family is most impor-

---

[1] Eleanor Powell Godfrey, "A Construction of Family Types and Their Initial Empirical Validation," Unpublished Ph.D. Study, Radcliffe College, Cambridge, Mass., 1951.

tant, although past and future generations are considered. Standards are set by individual capacity with methods derived freely from any source. The family is governed by group consensus. Child training is permissive and in terms of the nature of the individual child. The division of labor is functional, along personal lines of feasibility. Mutual economic responsibility is emphasized, with money allocated by the whole family. Family solidarity is based upon both work and play, with farming seen as a way of life. There is a considerable amount of both family and organizational activity, with relationships with relatives along lines of personal friendship.

Although these three time-geared types of family orientation were found in corn-belt families, they can be recognized too in the larger society. The past-oriented family is the traditional family found as typical of the family systems of old China, Japan, Germany, Poland and Ireland, with vestiges still present in many communities throughout the United States. The present-oriented family appears similar to the new middle-class family in transition, broken away from old family ties, and highly individualistic. The future-oriented family seems to be emerging in twentieth century America as the family that is focused upon the development of its members as its primary goal.

Variations in family themes. Analyzing the psychological and social processes in family interaction, Hess and Handel [1] find a variety of family themes which express the dominant concerns of individual family members. A family theme arises out of some significant issue in the life of one or more family members and has consequences for the personalities of all the members of a given family. A parent's unresolved psychological issue thus becomes a concern for the children as well. For instance, the family theme of one family, seen to be avoidance of emotional and economic catastrophe, is understood to arise from the lack of stability in the childhood experience of the parents. In another family the dominant theme is desire for companionship and cooperation in family interaction, which is seen to help meet the parents' need for warding off feelings of incompetence. Such family themes are idiosyncratic, highly individual, and helpful in understanding the dynamics of interaction within a given family.

Families vary by the amount of connectedness and separateness char-

[1] Robert D. Hess and Gerald Handel, *Family Worlds* (Chicago: University of Chicago Press, 1959).

acterizing their basic family patterns. This dimension is seen in what they do together, and how they feel about their family ties. Connectedness has both binding and constraining dangers. There is a certain mistrust and vulnerability of closeness, and emotional interaction poses a threat to the self-image of the individual family member. On the other hand, separateness, sacrificing the warmth and emotional security of close family ties for autonomy and individual identity, threatens apprehension about the pain of separation. How a given family resolves these basic conflicts in ways that meet or frustrate the needs of the individual family members is that family's theme in the dimension of intimacy.

Family boundaries vary greatly. Each family is seen as staking out its own "world" in which it lives. This may be narrow, restricted to the house, yard, or immediate neighborhood, as it is in some families. Or the family may be at home in many lands and climes with genuine interest in the entire world. The intensity of emotional experience that a family defines as appropriate may be constricted or permissive. Affection and hostility are expressed according to the internal boundaries set by a given family. A child is allowed to "talk back" or not, in line with the limits established by his parents. Such variations in family themes give each family its own unique characteristics which both express and set limits for each member of the family.

TRENDS IN FAMILY ORIENTATION

There have been marked changes in the basic orientation of families generally, through recent decades. These shifts in stance are ways in which families adapt to new conditions, and take on the new tasks and roles required by social change and social status mobility. It is this ability to adjust itself to changing social, economic and political situations that has made it possible for families to survive through the centuries. Throughout the twentieth century there has been a particularly marked trend toward increasing adaptability as a basic type of family orientation.

From rigidity to flexibility in family roles and patterns. Up to the turn of the century, family roles were rigidly defined in most American families. Father was the unquestioned head of the house. Mother's roles revolved around her homemaking and childcare activities. Children "knew their place," and behaved themselves in ways becoming to little ladies and gentlemen. Since then families have departed from the old world patterns of family living that they brought from Europe and Asia in the waves of migration that swept into the United States. Industrialization, increasing affluence and democratization have removed many of the old rigid class lines, until, as Kenneth Boulding suggests, the twentieth century may go down in history as the "great age of integration," in which for the first time in history "a classless society was created by everybody becoming middle-class." [1]

Whether any man now living will see the disappearance of social class differentiations among American families is debatable. There is no question that both individuals and families now have greater freedom to live as they wish than was possible until recent decades. Many men and women now living have seen tremendous changes in the basic orientation of American families: from autocratic to democratic in their authority patterns; from differentiated to overlapping roles of family members as pertain both to the husband-wife and the parent-child relationships; from formal reserved ways of behaving to informal expressive forms of interaction between the sexes and between the generations. Some complain that children no longer "respect" their elders, that the age of chivalry has passed in relations between the sexes, and that men now do "women's work" while their wives "gallivant all around the town." Others applaud the greater freedom enjoyed by all family members to express themselves, and play the roles they find most meaningful in today's world. Whether one regrets or welcomes such changes, the fact remains that they are real as families have moved from rigid to flexible patterns of interaction.

From institution to companionship. Burgess and Locke [2] first advanced the thesis that American families have been in transition from an institution in which family behavior was controlled by the mores, public opinion and law, to a companionship in which family interaction arises out of the mutual affection and consensus of the family members. They see the old patriarchal family giving way, under the advance of industrialization, to modern democratic family life in which a number of trends are notable: (1) from family-arranged marriage to freedom of choice of a mate on the basis of romance, compatibility and companionship;

---

[1] Kenneth Boulding in *American Perspective: The National Self-Image in the Twentieth Century* edited by Robert E. Spiller and Eric Larrabee (Cambridge: Harvard University Press, 1961).

[2] Ernest W. Burgess and Harvey J. Locke, *The Family from Institution to Companionship* (New York: American Book Company, 1945).

(2) from high intergenerational interdependence, often in a common household in the traditional extended family to independence from parents by young people after marriage (and by older family members from their children in the later years of life); (3) from male-dominated household to increasing equality of the husband and wife; (4) from authority of the father-head to decisions made by husband and wife with the children's participation as they become old enough; (5) from individuals subordinated to the family-as-a-whole to increasing freedom of its members as one of the modern family's objectives. The type of family life that is emerging under the new social, economic and cultural conditions is described as a companionship of husband and wife and of parents and children bound together by mutual affection and concensus, as a unity of interacting personalities.

From inner-directedness to other-directedness. David Riesman [1] describes a basic change in the personality orientation of the typical American man, woman and child from being inner-directed to other-directed in recent decades. With the decline in the size of the working-class and the increase in the numbers of persons in the "new middle-class" has come a new emphasis in the kind of person one should be. The typical member of the "old middle-class" (banker, tradesman or small entrepreneur) grew up with a strong inner sense of direction that was implanted early by the elders and directed toward inescapably destined goals of a generalized type. The new other-directed person looks to his contemporaries for direction. Depending upon others for guidance in life is internalized early, and the process of striving and paying close attention to others' signals carries through life, in an insatiable need for approval. The older family was production-oriented and postponed enjoyment until the work was done. Today's family is consumption-oriented stressing having fun and enjoying things here and now for their own sake. Other-directed persons make their choices in terms of what will please and satisfy their fellows, rather than by standards they impose upon their world as does the inner-directed individual. How all this looks to a particularly perceptive man is seen in what Franz Alexander calls "the natural history of an inner-directed person." [2]

Trends in family orientation necessarily involve changes in childrear-

[1] David Riesman and others, *The Lonely Crowd: A Study of the Changing American Character* (New Haven: Yale University Press, 1950).

[2] Franz Alexander, *The Western Mind in Transition* (New York: Random House, 1960).

ing. As families shift their stance with changing times, they inevitably develop new and different images of themselves, their children and their childrearing practices. Childrearing reflects family orientation and can be expected to follow parallel trends in a changing society.

TRENDS IN CHILDREARING

Basic changes in point of view are evident in the trends in childrearing concepts and practices in recent decades. In the old-fashioned farm family children were expected to obey and honor their parents, hold their tongues, and respect their elders. The youngster who did not conform to these expectations was promptly punished. Through the years, ways of raising children have changed rapidly toward more flexible methods. These newer approaches are related to shifts in the larger culture, in several discernible ways.

From entrepreneurial to bureaucratic parents. Miller and Swanson's study of 582 mothers with one or more children under nineteen in the Detroit area[1] found the Riesman dichotomy in evidence in the two types of middle-class families: (1) entrepreneurial "older" middle-class families; and (2) bureaucratic "newer" middle-class families. They classified entrepreneurial families as those having, (a) husband self-employed, (b) husband getting at least one-half of his income in profits, fees or commissions, (c) husband working in a small-scale organization (only two levels of supervision), (d) husband or wife was born on a farm, and (e) husband or wife was born outside the United States. Bureaucratic families were classified as having none of these five characteristics; and the husband works for someone else in an organization of at least moderate complexity.

Entrepreneurial and bureaucratic families were found to use significantly different childrearing methods of which the following is a general summary.

Entrepreneurial	*Bureaucratic*
Stress self-control and internalization in control of impulses	Child is taught to fit in with others, to be a "nice guy," affable, un-
Train child to change the situation	threatening, adaptive, and to seek
Stress activity and independence	direction
Encourage mastery	Child learns to go to parents for wis-

[1] Daniel R. Miller and Guy E. Swanson, *The Changing American Parent* (New York: John Wiley & Sons, Inc., 1958).

Prefer sharp differences between sex roles

More likely to:

    Feed babies on schedule

    Begin toilet training early

    Use symbolic punishment

    Let babies cry

Training is by suppression of impulsive drives

Egocentricity and hostility are more frequent

dom in social skills, even as adults

Person is trained to be cautious, precise, rational, secure, and unaggressive

New levels of comfort and security with lessening psychic pressures are sought

New sense of participation in a responsible, moral community is emerging

Loyalty to the group is central

Child and adult are free to enjoy themselves and to express their feelings

Individual should be warm, friendly, supportive of others

With the increase in the size and complexity of large corporations, has come an increase in the number of bureaucratically oriented families which encourage their children to be accommodative, to express their feelings freely, and to seek direction from the organizational programs in which they find themselves. The entrepreneurial family orientation at the present time is seen as a kind of anachronism, gaining less and less support from the values and institutions of the larger society. The bureaucratic family is an emergent type of family with childrearing patterns compatible with contemporary values in American life.[1]

From strict to permissive childrearing. Analyzing more than a score of studies of childrearing practices over the past twenty-five years, Bronfenbrenner reports [2] a clear trend away from strict, rigid methods of child care toward flexible, permissive ways with children. American mothers of both the lower- and middle-classes have become more flexible in caring for their infants. They are more likely now than previously to feed their babies on demand, and to wean them later from both breast and bottle. They are more likely to be permissive in toilet training, beginning and completing bowel and bladder training at later ages. Those who are in touch with what the experts say in books, pamphlets and in

[1] *Ibid.*, p. 193.

[2] Urie Bronfenbrenner, "Socialization and Social Class through Time and Space," published as a specially written chapter in E. E. Maccoby, T. M. Newcomb and E. L. Hartley, *Readings in Social Psychology* (New York: Henry Holt and Co., 1958), pp. 400–425.

direct contact are changing more rapidly than those with little access to such sources.

Middle-class mothers in the period following World War II have become increasingly more permissive toward the expressed needs and wishes of children in such specific areas as dependency, sex, aggressiveness, oral behavior, toilet accidents and freedom of movement outside the home. Middle-class children are expected to take care of themselves earlier, to accept more responsibilities at home, and to go further in school. Successive generations of parents are becoming progressively more permissive, affectionate, and likely to use psychological techniques of discipline. There is evidence from several sources that the gap between the social classes is narrowing in their patterns of childrearing which move steadily toward greater permissiveness.[1]

Parent-child relationships are consistently reported as becoming more acceptant and equalitarian with greater tolerance of the child's impulses and desires evident in recent years. Fathers are assuming more intimate roles in nurturing their children, at the same time that the focus of parental authority shifts from husband to wife in the modern family.[2]

Sibylle Escalona contrasts former with more recent thinking about young children thus:

> Ten years ago and less, authoritative public opinion subscribed to sentiments and rules which may be characterized as follows: Bodily and mental health is based upon an orderly, strictly scheduled existence from early childhood onwards. Prescribed formulae are superior to breast feeding, chiefly because the ingredients are known and nutrition becomes therefore, a controlled process. When babies or children cry without recognized legitimate cause it is best to let them cry it out. It is the responsibility of adults to teach children what is "right" and what is "wrong" in regard to meal times, sleeping hours, play interests and most other activities.

> It is now thought that it is up to us as adults to meet the needs of the younger child, rather than to expect early adaptation from him. To wit, self-demand schedules and all that goes with them. Among the needs of the young child we recognize the need for affection and for an intimate relationship with the mother as of very great importance, tending to evaluate it as more crucial

---

[1] Leone Kell and Joan Aldous, "Trends in Child Care over Three Generations," *Marriage and Family Living,* Vol. XXII, No. 2, May 1960, pp. 176–177.

[2] Urie Bronfenbrenner, "The Changing American Child—A Speculative Analysis," *Merrill-Palmer Quarterly,* Vol. 7, No. 2, April 1961, pp. 73–84; and Wanda C. Bronson, Edith Katten, and Norman Livson, "Patterns of Authority and Affection in Two Generations," *The Journal of Abnormal and Social Psychology,* Vol. 58, No. 2, March 1959, pp. 143–152.

CHART 8.   Childrearing Changes from the 1880's to the 1960's [1]

1880's—Discipline was based upon authority with instant, unquestioning obedience expected.

Training was directed toward "uprooting the evil in human nature"
when widespread belief was that children are "conceived in sin and
born in iniquity," and the clear duty of parents was to "whale the
devil out of them."

Society for the Prevention of Cruelty to Children was organized "to
resolutely and persistently attack cruel ways of treating children."
Articles on prevention of cruelty to children mention: "whippings
until bruised and sore," "shutting in dark closets until ill with
fright," and "depriving of food until emaciated and feeble."

Frances Parker, G. Stanley Hall, William James, and Felix Adler
started respectively the Cook County Normal School, studies on
child development, psychology based upon experience at Harvard,
and Society for the Study of Child Nature in New York.

1890's—Authority is still basic point of view. Larkin Donton, of the Boston
Normal School expected "instantaneous obedience, with no sulkers,
no laggards, no guerrillas, no independents, and the movement of
all uniformly, quietly and instantly."

John Dewey founded Laboratory School, and Frances Parker founded
an independent institute which was to become the School of Education, both at the University of Chicago.

The National Congress of Parents and Teachers was founded in 1897.

1900's—Discipline is a major issue. Sixteen out of eighteen schools report corporal punishment in use, one in primary grades only, another "seldom" and others "good as a last resort," "cannot be dispensed with
but might be reduced."

Guidance begins to replace "training" in the literature. G. Stanley
Hall published *Adolescence* (1904), the first work on the older
child. William James, *Talks to Teachers* set the theme for the decade
in stressing the importance of habits.

1910's—William Bagley, *School Discipline* (1915) admonished never to punish in anger, to use switch on legs or ruler on palm of hands but
never to box the ears.

First Edition of *Infant Care* published by the Children's Bureau, established in 1912, recommended to stop thumb-sucking, pinning
sleeve of baby's jacket down over "fingers of offending hand for
several days and nights."

Freud, Montesorri, John Dewey and William H. Kilpatrick men-

[1] Adapted freely from Grace Langdon and Irving Stout, *The Discipline of Well-
Adjusted Children* (New York: John Day Company, 1952), Chap. 1; "Parents Wel-
come New Edition of Infant Care," *The Child,* Children's Bureau, Washington, D. C.,
January 1952, pp. 66, 67, 76; and Golden Anniversary White House Conference on
Children and Youth, Recommendations, 1960.

tioned frequently in popular literature. The Progressive Education Association founded in 1918–1919 with emphasis on "freedom for children to develop."

1920's—John B. Watson's *Behaviorism,* and *Psychological Care of Infant and Young Child* widely followed, recommended kissing child on the forehead if at all, shaking hands with the child in the morning, never hug, kiss or let child sit on your lap. The conditioned reflex, stimulus-response bonds, and laws of learning concepts current.

Child Development Institutes established in several universities, and the National Council on Parent Education founded, all with Laura Spelman Rockefeller Memorial grants.

Teachers College, Columbia University announced a new course, "Training for Leadership in Education of Parents" in cooperation with the Child Study Association. "The child" and "child-centered" appear often in the literature.

1930's Objectivity at its zenith with great emphasis on the importance of routine, habit formation—i.e. "adhere without deviation to regular habits for sleeping, eating, and toileting beginning in early infancy." The parent is advised to be cool, detached, and unperturbed. High interest in specifics: sex education, allowances, and toilet training.

National Council on Family Relations established 1938 as national clearing house of persons with professional interests in family living. Research in family life, child and adolescent development increases markedly. Corporal punishment rare in schools that are now more relaxed. Discussion of spanking as discipline continues among parents.

1940's—Family-centered approach to children seen in first National Conference on Family Life held at the White House in May 1948. Gesell and staff at Yale, Redl, Baruch, Hymes, and Spock advise accepting the child and his feelings without shame and gearing guidance to the readiness of the child. Spock's *The Common Sense Book of Baby and Child Care* becomes mothers' "bible" as permissive, "enjoy your youngster" attitude toward children becomes widely accepted.

1950's—Midcentury White House Conference on Children and Youth considered the role of the home, school, church, leisure-time agency, as well as vocational guidance, health, social services and law enforcement, in healthy personality development.

The developmental task concept, formulated earlier, widely used through this decade in the literature that discussed "the teachable moment," "developmental level," etc.

1960's—Golden Anniversary White House Conference on Children and Youth made recommendations for family life education at every age level, both in public schools and under private auspices. Research in family life and childrearing steadily increases the quantity and quality of authoritative literature for professional and functional use.

than the need for good physical care. We prize self-expression, sincerity of feeling and spontaneous interest above good manners, self restraint or intellectual accomplishment.[1]

From traditional to developmental conceptions of parents and children. The first formulation of the traditional-developmental dichotomy of conceptions of family members came out of the author's original study of differential conceptions of parenthood.[2] The data were the verbatim responses of 433 mothers to the questions of "What are five things a good mother does?" (2,010 responses), and "What are five things a good child does?" (1,847 responses). Keeping the original working used by the subjects, the responses were grouped into categories that distinguished traditional from developmental conceptions of both parents and children.

Traditional conceptions of motherhood were seen to be those having to do with what a mother expects herself to do *to* and *for* her home and children, i.e. keep house, make the child behave, etc. Traditional conceptions of childhood centered around the child's behaving in ways that please adults, i.e. obeys, respects property, runs errands willingly, etc. Traditional conceptions of both motherhood and childhood tend to be static, rigid, specific behavioral expectancies in line with former child-rearing orientations.

Developmental conceptions of motherhood emphasize a mother's encouraging her children to develop, enjoying and loving them, and viewing herself as a growing person, i.e. gives child freedom to grow, shares with the child, and gets enough recreation. Developmental conceptions of childhood center in his being a happy, healthy, growing person, i.e. is developing socially, enjoys growing up, etc. Developmental conceptions are recognized as dynamic, flexible and growth-promoting. They emphasize encouraging development of the person rather than any specific form of discipline, or type of behavior.

Parallel contrasts in traditionally and developmentally oriented fathers were found in Elder's[3] exploration of fathers' conceptions of parenthood and childhood, following the Duvall methods. Traditional fathers

[1] Sibylle Escalona, "A Commentary upon Some Recent Changes in Child-Rearing Practices," *Child Development*, Vol. 20, No. 3, September 1949, pp. 157–162.

[2] Evelyn Millis Duvall, "Conceptions of Parenthood," *The American Journal of Sociology*, Vol. LII, No. 3, November 1946, pp. 193–203.

[3] Rachel Ann Elder, *Traditional and Developmental Conceptions of Fatherhood*, Iowa State College Master's thesis, Ames, Iowa, 1947, and "Traditional and Developmental Conceptions of Fatherhood," *Marriage and Family Living*, Vol. XI, No. 3, Summer 1949, pp. 98, 99, 100, 106.

disciplined their children for more reasons and with fewer methods. Developmental fathers were more interested in children's maturation, believed more in parent guidance literature and PTA meetings, and were more apt to help in childrearing, and to find parenthood enjoyable.

Using the traditional-developmental conceptions approach and methods developed earlier, a Florida State University team replicated the previous studies with university students and their parents, with remarkably similar results:

> Generally speaking, the traditional type of good father was defined in terms of providing for the family financially, disciplining and advising the children, and setting a good example . . . the traditional good mother as one who cares for the home and cooks, teaches religious values, and is a good example. The traditional good child is one who respects and obeys parents . . .
>
> The developmental good father fosters the growth and development of the child and other family members, including himself in the home situation. The respondents viewed the developmental mother in much the same way as they saw the developmental father but added the concept of having outside interests such as the PTA. The developmental child responses centered about growing in all areas of personality and social development.[1]

Traditional conceptions are significantly more frequent among working-class than middle-class parents, and among mothers of children over five years of age than among mothers of younger children. Developmental conceptions of both the good mother and the good child are significantly more frequent among middle-class than lower-class mothers, and among white than Negro mothers, at both lower- and middle-class levels.[2] Developmental fathers tend to be skilled rather than semiskilled or unskilled workers who are more likely to be traditional in their conceptions of motherhood, fatherhood and childhood.[3] These consistent tendencies are interpreted as follows:

> In its transition from the traditional institution type of family to the person-centered unit of companionship that it is becoming, conceptions of the role of the parent and the child are shifting. These changes do not appear all at once and with equal force throughout the total society, but are evidenced first in little islands of the new that break off from the mass of tradition and become established in subgroups within the culture. These developmental islands are

[1] Ruth Connor, Theodore B. Johannis, Jr., and James Walters, "Intra-familial Conceptions of the Good Father, Good Mother, and Good Child," *Journal of Home Economics*, Vol. 46, No. 3, March 1954, pp. 187–191.

[2] Duvall, *op. cit.*

[3] Elder, *op. cit.*

Traditional and Developmental Conceptions [1]

Traditional Conceptions
A good child:

Keeps clean and neat, is orderly, is clean, keeps himself neat, etc.

Obeys and respects adults, minds his parents, no back talk, respect teachers, etc.

Pleases adults, has good character traits, is honest, truthful, polite, kind, fair, etc.

Respects property, takes care of his things, is not destructive, hangs up his clothes, etc.

Is religious, goes to Sunday School, loves God, prays, follows Jesus, etc.

Works well, studies, goes to school, is dependable, takes responsibility, etc.

Fits into the family program, has an interest in his home, does his share, helps out, etc.

Developmental Conceptions
A good child:

Is healthy and well, eats and sleeps well, grows a good body, has good health habits, etc.

Shares and cooperates with others, gets along with people, is developing socially, etc.

Is happy and contented, is a cheerful child, is emotionally well-adjusted, etc.

Loves and confides in his parents, responds with affection, has confidence, etc.

Is eager to learn, shows initiative, asks questions, expresses himself, accepts help, etc.

Grows as a person, progresses in his ability to handle himself, enjoys growing up, etc.

A good mother:

Keeps house, washes, cooks, cleans, mends, sews, manages the household, etc.

Takes care of the child physically, feeds, clothes, bathes him, guards child safety, etc.

Trains the child to regularity, establishes regular habits, provides a schedule, etc.

Disciplines, corrects child, demands obedience, rewards good behavior, is firm, etc.

A good mother:

Trains for self-reliance, encourages independence, teaches how to adjust to life, etc.

Sees to emotional well-being, keeps child happy and contented, helps child feel secure, etc.

Helps child develop socially, provides toys and companions, supervises child's play, etc.

Provides for child's mental growth, reads to child, provides stimulation, educates, etc.

---

[1] Traditional and developmental conceptions of a good child and a good mother are categories of verbatim responses of 433 mothers in Duvall's research, *op. cit.*, pp. 195–196; traditional and developmental conceptions of a good father are derived from constructed father types emerging from Elder study, *op. cit.*, p. 21.

Makes the child good, instructs in morals, builds character, prays for, sees to religion, etc.

Guides with understanding, gears life to child's level, interprets, answers questions, etc.

Relates lovingly to child, enjoys and shares with child, is interested in what child says, etc.

Is a calm, cheerful, growing person oneself, has a sense of humor, smiles, keeps rested, etc.

A good father:

Is a strong individual, always right, and the child is his ward

"Knows" what the child "should" be so does not seek to understand child as an individual

Is interested only in activities which he determines are his responsibility for child's "good"

Places emphasis on giving things to and doing things for the child

Is interested in child's accepting and attaining goals set by the father

Finds satisfaction in child's owing father a debt which can be repaid by child's obedience

Feels parenthood is a duty which the church, and/or society expect him to discharge

A good father:

Is an individual, as is his child

Seeks to understand the child and himself

Places emphasis on the growth of the child and himself

Is interested in child's determining and attaining child's own goals

Finds satisfaction in child's becoming a mature individual

Feels that parenthood is a privilege which he has chosen to assume

characterized by such concepts as respect for the person (both child and adult), satisfaction in personal interaction, pride in growth and development, and a permissive, growth-promoting type of guidance as opposed to the more traditional attempts to "make" children conform to patterns of being neat and clean, obedient and respectful, polite and socially acceptable.

Traditional conceptions of parenthood remain in the lower-middle and upper-lower class levels, where recent migration, household drudgery, cramped living, and infrequency of opportunity to meet with other modes of adjustment keep both parents and children in line with traditional conceptions of role. The effort to achieve respectability so evident in the two lower class levels and among the minority racial group tends further to perpetuate conformity.

The tendency for mothers of younger children toward more developmental replies may be interpreted in a number of ways. The evidence points to the possibility that conformity is demanded of families with children old enough to have some life outside the family circle. As children become old enough to go to school and to range further afield in the community, the social pressures toward conformity are felt both by them and by their mothers.

Thus, we hypothesize a seesaw progress even within the more advanced groups. Some inexperienced mothers view their roles along new lines and break with the past in their efforts to make a more adequate adjustment to a changed social situation. As their children grow older and begin to represent them in the larger world, the earlier flexibility is modified by the demands of the more traditional mass.[1]

SOME CONSEQUENCES OF THE NEWER CHILDREARING PRACTICES

A study of parents with preschool children living in a university community confirms the general observation that parents with a developmental ideology are more permissive with their children than are parents holding traditional conceptions of what constitutes a good child. Using parents' "pick-up policy" regarding children's clutter allowed in the living room, and the number of types of children's activities permitted indoors, Blood[2] found that permissive parents as compared with restrictive parents reported (1) parents' lives more disrupted by children's behavior, (2) parents' activities more often disturbed by children's noisiness, (3) parents' privacy more difficult to achieve, (4) parents have greater difficulty controlling children's activities, (5) living room furnishings more often damaged by children, and (6) living rooms more frequently cluttered with children's things.

Developmentally oriented parents appear able to pay the price their permissiveness costs them as adults. They apparently can take the immediate consequences of their childrearing practices, because they put their children's developmental progress high in their value orientation, because they do not expect to have a model picture-book home while their children are small, because they "child-proof" the house by adapting to what reasonably can be expected of little children, because they realize that the sacrifice of some of their adult values (for neatness, quiet, etc.) is only for a while, and that as children grow older there will be less of a discrepancy between the interests and values of the two generations.

[1] Duvall, *op. cit.*, pp. 202–203.
[2] Robert O. Blood, Jr., "Consequences of Permissiveness for Parents of Young Children," *Marriage and Family Living*, Vol. XV, No. 3, August 1953, pp. 209–212.

Restrictive fathers are found to be [1] constricted, submissive, suggestible individuals with little self-assurance. Permissive fathers, in contrast, tend to be self-reliant, ascendent, and functionally effective. These findings are in line with what is known about the authoritarian personality [2] who tends to be the kind of person most comfortable with traditional childrearing practices.

Fundamentally, developmental parents appear to be the kind of men and women who by personality, life history and family orientation are inclined to accept the growing body of evidence (from child development research, nursery school experience, and clinical findings) that supports their inner predispositions to encourage and enjoy the development in their children and in themselves.

Effects of childrearing practices on the child's personality. These have been explored widely in recent years, by many investigators. The studies vary widely and their findings have yet to be brought together in a clear complete picture of how childrearing policies and methods affect the growing child's personality. Since there are so many other factors besides childrearing practices influencing child development, it may be impossible ever to say with assurance that one particular method will surely produce any predictable consequence in the growing child's personality. There are, however, findings in recent research that suggest significant relationships between parent-child interaction, childrearing practices, and the emerging personality of the child. The following are representative.

Relating children's behavior in nursery school to the atmosphere within their homes, Baldwin found a number of related factors.[3] Family climates of warmth, activity, and democracy produce more curious, emotional, nonconforming, and competitive children in the nursery school than do cold, authoritarian and low activity families.

Longitudinal records of the complete childhood of 140 children studied at the Fels Research Institute provide extensive data for such relationships as are pertinent here. Among the conclusions of this investigation

---

[1] Jack Block, "Personality Characteristics Associated with Fathers' Attitudes toward Childrearing," *Child Development*, Vol. 26, No. 1, 1955, pp. 41–48.

[2] T. W. Adorno, *The Authoritarian Personality* (New York: Harper & Brothers, 1950).

[3] Alfred L. Baldwin, "Socialization and the Parent-Child Relationship," *Child Development*, Vol. 19, No. 3, September 1948, pp. 127–136.

is that a child's need for achievement (which is related to accelerated rates of mental growth) develops in a family situation in which the mother uses democratic principles in disciplining the child, and, at least in the case of boys, tends to stress independent achievement at an early age.[1]

Studies of 261 boys and girls between 5 and 21 years of age, selected as well-adjusted by their teachers, found many types of discipline used in their homes, but a common core of factors by which parents accounted for their children's favorable adjustment. The parents said they enjoyed being parents, they believed in having fun together with their children, they appreciated their children and trusted them, and most important of all, they rated "loving the children and letting them know it." [2]

Extensive studies at Harvard University find that children of warm mothers mature more rapidly socially, and that "the unhappy effects of punishment have run like a dismal thread through our findings." Mothers who punished their children's toilet accidents ended up with bedwetting children. Mothers who punished aggressive behavior severely had more aggressive children than did mothers whose punishment for aggression was light. In the long run punishment was found to be ineffectual as a technique for eliminating the kind of behavior toward which it was directed.[3]

Tests of the abilities and aptitudes of 450,000 students in 1,357 high schools across the country being analyzed at the University of Pittsburgh, find that although most high school students cannot write a five-minute theme without making some kind of error, they have a better grasp of world affairs than their parents had when they were enmeshed in school books.[4] Newer emphases in teaching as well as family-based childrearing may account for these trends in today's youth.

Recent trends toward the pursuit of excellence, and the thrust for achievement in both home and school, as well as evidence pointing up the dangers of too much permissiveness, may already be at work in a

[1] Lester W. Sontag, Charles T. Baker and Virginia L. Nelson, *Mental Growth and Personality Development: A Longitudinal Study,* Monograph of the Society for Research in Child Development, Vol. XXIII, Serial No. 68, No. 2, 1958, p. 139.

[2] Grace Langdon and Irving Stout, *These Well-Adjusted Children* (New York: John Day Company, 1951).

[3] Robert R. Sears, Eleanor E. Maccoby and Harry Levin, *Patterns of Child Rearing* (Evanston, Illinois: Row, Peterson and Company, 1957), p. 484.

[4] AP release, Pittsburgh, Pa., November 21, 1960, "Johnny Can't Spell, But He Knows World Affairs."

swing toward setting controls and limits to the freedom allowed a child. As Nye finds, "a middle way giving major responsibility but not discontinuing supervision and guidance entirely appears to be associated with least delinquent behavior." [1]

Developmentalism is increasing. Concern for wholesome development of the human personality has increased in recent years. Developmentalism does not imply unrestrained permissiveness, but rather the kind of setting that is conducive to optimal development, with the freedom, and the controls that are good to grow in, both as parents and as children. College students are found to be more developmental than are their parents as Table 10 shows.

TABLE 10. *Mean Developmental Scores of Conceptions of Good Father, Good Mother, and Good Child by Fathers, Mothers and Adolescents* [2]

Respondent	Good Father	Good Mother	Good Child
Father	51.2	39.6	20.6
Mother	51.1	31.5	24.5
Adolescent	65.1	62.8	34.6

Grandmothers are significantly more authoritarian and less permissive than are the mothers of the same children. [3] This study of grandmother-mother pairs in the same urban community elaborates and extends earlier findings that developmentalism is found more among young than older mothers, and bears a positive relationship to the amount of their formal education. [4] Today's college girls are significantly more developmental than their mothers, who were in turn more likely to have permissive values than were the students' grandmothers, showing a trend over the past three generations toward increasing developmentalism. [5] Continuing studies of three-generational families find the grandparent generation more traditional, fatalistic and past-oriented, in contrast to the young couples who are more adaptable. Young husbands and wives have

[1] F. Ivan Nye, *Family Relationships and Delinquent Behavior* (New York: John Wiley & Sons, Inc., 1958), p. 100.

[2] Connor, *et al., op. cit.,* p. 190.

[3] Ruth Staples and June Warden Smith, "Attitudes of Grandmothers and Mothers toward Childrearing Practices," *Child Development,* Vol. 25, 1954, pp. 91–97.

[4] Evelyn Millis Duvall, *op. cit.,* p. 202.

[5] Leone Kell and Joan Aldous, "Trends in Child Care Over Three Generations," *Marriage and Family Living,* Vol. XXII, No. 2, May 1960, pp. 176–177.

more flexibility, are more companionable and communicative. Hill reports that the young couple today appear better able to meet new and unusual problems because they have a sense of common direction, superior ability to communicate and greater adaptability.[1]

Since developmentalism is associated with education and comfortable levels of living, it can be expected to increase. Improved standards of living, general education as well as specific family life education for more of the population, may in time be expected to narrow the gap between the haves and have-nots and to make the developmental "traditional" in times to come. As the 1950 White House Conference on Children and Youth predicted, ". . . Within another generation the new ways of bringing up children may themselves become traditional . . . If this happens, young parents' confidence should increase, since they will not feel so alone and so much in disagreement with the older generation."[2]

SUMMARY

Types of family orientation can be seen in Farber's child-oriented, home-oriented and parent-oriented schema; in Godfrey's past-oriented, present-oriented and future-oriented families; and in the variations in family themes explored by Hess and Handel, as ways in which families vary by their basic stance toward life. Trends in family orientation are seen as: (1) from rigidity to flexibility in family roles, (2) from institution to companionship, and (3) from inner-directedness to other-directedness. Trends in childrearing in recent decades, paralleling those in family orientation are described as (1) from entrepreneurial to bureaucratic, (2) from strict to permissive, and (3) from traditional to developmental. Developmental parents pay a price for the freedom they allow their children which their value orientation helps them bear, as the kind of persons they are. Children who grow up in warm, democratic families are found to have more initiative, higher achievement drives and accelerated rates of mental growth. Well-adjusted children are loved and know it, and those of warm mothers mature socially more rapidly than do those in cold, punitive families. Responsibility with freedom and guidance is seen as a combination good for development. Increasing developmentalism is apparent in significantly more developmental conceptions

[1] Reuben Hill, "Transmission of Conceptions of Parenthood by Generations," Twin City Study, in progress.
[2] Helen Witmer and Ruth Kotinsky, *Personality in the Making* (New York: Harper & Brothers, 1952), p. 102.

and patterns among young than older family members in recent three-generation studies. In time as affluence and education spread, what now is developmental may become traditional as a basic pattern of family orientation.

SUGGESTED ACTIVITIES

1) Write a term paper reviewing Robert W. White, *Lives in Progress: A Study of the Natural Growth of Personality* (New York: The Dryden Press, 1958), with particular stress on the family orientation and childrearing practices that seem related to the development of Hartley Hale, Joseph Kidd and Joyce Kingsley. Document your comments from both the White book, and the references in this chapter of your text.

2) Review Lorraine Hansberry's play, *A Raisin in the Sun* in terms of the family themes that the Younger family seem to represent. Illustrate with quotes from the drama.

3) Conduct a study of the ideologies of the members of your class and their parents, by providing each of them with cards on which to write, a) five things a good mother does, b) five things a good father does, and c) five things a good child does. Tabulate the statements as developmental or traditional according to the criteria in this chapter. Compare the developmental and traditional scores of males and females in the class, and of student and parent generations. Report your findings to the class with your interpretations of the data.

4) Plan a symposium of members of at least three generations—a student, a parent, a grandparent—on childrearing practices as they remember them when they were young. Try to match the participants for social class and educational backgrounds as closely as possible.

5) Write a letter to yourself as a parent (actual or potential), reminding yourself of the policies and practices that you feel are best in childrearing. Summarize briefly at the close the ways in which your recommendations for the rearing of your children differ from the ways in which you yourself were reared. In what ways are they similar?

6) Outline procedures for "child-proofing" the home of a young couple who want to be flexible with their young children and who are comfortable in the developmental point of view both for themselves and for their children. Itemize in detail the changes that should be made in every room of the home in order to meet the child's needs and still maintain comfort and pleasure for the parents.

7) Review Dr. Brim's study (See *Readings,* below), and write a reaction paper of your own on the major points that are covered in this research.

READINGS

Adorno, T. W., and others, *The Authoritarian Personality* (New York: Harper & Brothers, 1950).

Baldwin, Alfred L., "Socialization and the Parent-Child Relationship," *Child Development*, Vol. 19, No. 3, September 1948, pp. 127–136.

Brim, Orville G., Jr., *Education for Child Rearing* (New York: Russell Sage Foundation, 1959).

Bronfenbrenner, Urie, "Socialization and Social Class through Time and Space," published as a specially written chapter in Maccoby, E. E.; Newcomb, T. M.; and Hartley, E. L., *Readings in Social Psychology* (New York: Henry Holt and Co., 1958), pp. 400–425.

Bronfenbrenner, Urie, "The Changing American Child—A Speculative Analysis," *Merrill-Palmer Quarterly*, Vol. 7, No. 2, April 1961, pp. 73–84.

Bronson, Wanda C.; Katten, Edith S.; and Livson, Norman, "Patterns of Authority and Affection in Two Generations," *Journal of Abnormal and Social Psychology*, Vol. 58, No. 2, March 1959, pp. 143–152.

Duvall, Evelyn Millis, "Conceptions of Parenthood," *American Journal of Sociology*, Vol. LII, No. 3, November 1946, pp. 193–203.

Burgess, Ernest W.; and Locke, Harvey J., *The Family from Institution to Companionship* (New York: American Book Company, 1953).

Farber, Bernard, *Family Organization and Crisis: Maintenance of Integration in Families with a Severely Mentally Retarded Child*, Monograph for the Society of Research in Child Development, Vol. 25, No. 1, 1960, pp. 39 ff.

Hess, Robert D.; and Handel, Gerald, *Family Worlds: A Psychosocial Approach to Family Life* (Chicago: University of Chicago Press, 1959).

Kell, Leone; and Aldous, Joan, "The Relation between Mothers' Child-Rearing Ideologies and Their Children's Perceptions of Maternal Control," *Child Development*, Vol. 31, No. 1, March 1960, pp. 145–156.

Langdon, Grace; and Stout, Irving, *These Well-Adjusted Children* (New York: John Day Company, 1951).

Miller, Daniel R.; and Swanson, Guy E., *The Changing American Parent* (New York: John Wiley & Sons, Inc., 1958).

Riesman, David, *The Lonely Crowd: A Study of the Changing American Character* (New Haven: Yale University Press, 1950).

Sears, Robert R.; Maccoby, Eleanor E.; and Levin, Harry, *Patterns of Child Rearing* (Evanston, Illinois: Row, Peterson and Company, 1957).

Sewell, William; Mussen, Paul; and Harris, Chester, "Relationships among Child Training Practices," *American Sociological Review*, Vol. 20, No. 2, April 1955, pp. 137–148.

Sontag, Lester; Baker, Charles; and Nelson, Virginia, *Mental Growth and Personality Development: A Longitudinal Study*, Monograph of the Society for Research in Child Development, Vol. XXIII, Serial No. 68, No. 2, 1958.

Stendler, Celia B., "Sixty Years of Child Training Practices," *Journal of Pediatrics*, Vol. 36, 1950, pp. 122–134.

Vincent, Clark E., "Trends in Infant Care Ideas," *Child Development*, Vol. 22, No. 3, September 1951, pp. 199–209.

Wolfenstein, Martha, "Trends in Infant Care," *American Journal of Orthopsychiatry*, Vol. 33, 1953, pp. 120–130.

PART 2

Expanding families

Families begin at marriage and with the coming of children, families grow both in size and in complexity of interaction. What are children trying to accomplish—as infants, as preschoolers, as schoolagers, and as teenagers? How do families change as children grow up? And, in what ways do family members sometimes complement and sometimes conflict with each other in what they are trying to become?

To have and to hold from this day
    forward,
For better, for worse, for richer,
    for poorer,
In sickness, and in health, to love
    and to cherish,
Till death us do part.
        BOOK OF COMMON PRAYER

CHAPTER SIX

Beginning families: establish-
ment phase

The establishment phase of the family life cycle begins with the couple at marriage, and continues until they become aware of the fact
that the wife is pregnant. Usually lasting about one year, this may be a period of a few months or many years. It may last for the duration of the
marriage as in the homes of childless couples. It may be a brief phase of
only a few weeks.

Typically, there are two members in the family at the establishment
phase: husband and wife. The man is about 22 and the woman about 20,
median ages for first marriage currently. As a two-person group they
maintain one interpersonal relationship—that of husband—wife. They
each confront individual developmental tasks as young adults, with
developmental crises in terms of intimacy vs. isolation. The major family
goal at this stage is adjusting to living as a married pair.

Marriage marks a drastic role shift from the parent-child relationship
in the family of orientation to the husband-wife relationship within the
marriage. Marriage and family may be seen as two separate social systems with different purposes and tasks within a given household. The
family system ministers primarily to the needs of the children, the marriage primarily to the needs of husband and wife.[1]

[1] Floyd M. Martinson, *Marriage and the American Ideal* (New York: Dodd, Mead
and Company, 1960), page 343.

ORIGINS OF DEVELOPMENTAL TASKS
OF THE EARLY-MARRIED COUPLE

The developmental tasks of the newly married couple arise in both the husband and wife first out of their physiological maturation, with its adult drives for ongoing sexual fulfillment. The second origin of the developmental tasks of the newly married couple is found in the cultural expectations and pressures for the married pair to settle down and behave as married couples are supposed to in the given community. Thirdly, the man and woman are moved by their own personal aspirations to establish their marriage according to the dreams that both of them have built through the years.

The multiple nature of the origins of the developmental tasks at this stage makes for some difficulties in itself. What the culture expects and what the young couple want do not always coincide, especially in this day and age. What the realities of the situation are and what the married pair dream of as right for them are rarely identical. The young woman who has built up extravagant ideas of what she must have at the time she marries may be disappointed when hers does not turn out to be a fashionable wedding or a modern home correct to the latest detail. The dreams of the husband and wife may mesh in many respects, but be miles apart in others. Being married first of all involves coming to terms with what is expected—by one's culture, by one's mate, by oneself, and as a couple.

COMPLEMENTARY AND CONFLICTING DEVELOPMENTAL
TASKS OF HUSBAND AND WIFE

At the time of their marriage, the husband is attempting to achieve his developmental tasks as a young adult male, while his wife is concurrently working out her growth responsibilities as a young adult female. The young man must learn what it means to be a young adult, with young adult responsibilities in his home and community. He must learn what is expected of him as a husband, and what it means to be a married man. By the time his first baby is on the way, he is faced with the task of defining his role as a father and of becoming a parent. Simultaneously, the young wife is learning what it means to be a wife, a young married woman both in her home and in the community, and what becoming a mother involves. Sometimes the developmental tasks of husband and wife complement and mutually support each other. At other times the efforts

The bride and groom each have personal aspirations to establish their marriage according to the dreams that both of them have built through the years.

of one conflict with those of the other. This is the nature of the dynamics of interaction in marriage and family living, as is suggested in the following items.

Some Contemporary Developmental Tasks of the Young Husband	*Some Contemporary Developmental Tasks of the Young Wife*	*Complementary and Conflicting Possibilities*
Becoming established in an occupation	Making a home and managing the household	Complementary (Shared responsibility in homemaking)
Getting specialized training	Getting settled in a home	Conflicting (Husband engrossed in work away from home, while wife tries to elicit his active cooperation in homemaking)
Assuming responsibility for getting and holding a job.	Establishing and maintaining household routines	
Working toward security and advancement in his work	Learning the many skills of homemaking and housework	

Some Contemporary Developmental Tasks of the Young Husband	*Some Contemporary Developmental Tasks of the Young Wife*	*Complementary and Conflicting Possibilities*
Assuming responsibility for the support of his family Earning the family income Planning for the long pull of family support through the years	Becoming a financial helpmate in establishing the home Working until her husband is established Seeing her work as secondary and temporary	Complementary (Both are economic partners through establishment phase) Conflicting (Her work threatens his status as bread winner)
Fulfilling his military service requirements Choosing the time for service Juggling educational, marital, occupational plans with the demands of military service Absenting himself from home for the duration of his service	Maintaining a home base with her husband in service Deciding where and how to live while he is away Keeping a sense of being married during her husband's absence Continuing educational, vocational, and family activities after her marriage	Conflicting (Husband is pulled away from home, while wife's efforts are in maintaining unity and integrity of home through their separation)
Establishing mutually satisfying sex relationships Awakening his wife sexually Developing competency as a husband	Becoming a satisfactory sex partner Learning her sex role as wife Responding effectively and participating in their mutual fulfillment	Complementary (Each has the task of communicating intimately with the other)
Becoming "domesticated" as a married man Sharing leisure time with his wife Developing mutual interests Cultivating joint activities Getting into the young married set	Assuming hostess and companionship roles as a married woman Planning for recreational activities as a couple Accepting and refusing social invitations Entertaining their friends and associates	Complementary (Both husband and wife are learning to move in tandem in their social life as a couple)

The distinction should be made between the conflict of developmental tasks of the husband and wife and conflict arising out of the couple's difficulties in accomplishing their tasks. The young wife may be ineffectual as a sex partner at first, experiencing some degree of sex conflict with her husband. But, in such a case, it is not the developmental tasks of the husband and wife that conflict. It is rather the husband's inexpertness or the wife's difficulties in working through the complementarity of sex roles that result in their conflict as sex partners. The husband may find it hard to become socially "domesticated," involving some marital conflict, but his task in this direction complements his wife's.

There are some complementary and some conflicting aspects in many of the developmental tasks of husband and wife. When the two people are drawn together in mutually supportive ways as they work on their individual developmental tasks, we see those tasks as complementary. When the working through of their tasks as husband and wife tend to pull the couple in opposite directions, the tasks are conflicting. The difference is in the lines of force, in the pull toward or away from the other. In conflicting developmental tasks the lines of force between the pair oppose and repel. In complementary tasks the lines of force pull the two together and operate toward unity, as we see in Chart 9.

Conflicting developmental tasks:

Complementary developmental tasks:

Developmental tasks with both conflicting and complementary aspects:

CHART 9. Conflicting and Complementary Developmental Tasks

The two persons who come together in marriage have much to learn about each other, and about what it means to be married. It takes conscientious effort and a great deal of interpersonal perception to become aware of one another as distinct individuals with preferences, interests, values, and predispositions firmly rooted in each personality. Differences emerge to be recognized and evaluated. Some are simple idiosyncrasies that can be modified for the good of the union. Others are so important that ways must be found of coping with conflicts between the partners.

Being married involves a new way of life for both the new husband and his bride. Somehow they must develop together the patterns of daily living that express and satisfy them both. Every day brings decisions that must be made, problems to be solved, and plans to be laid for the development of the home they are establishing together. Some of these ongoing interdependencies are filled with mutual satisfaction. Others are burdensome to one or both members of the pair. Each couple approaches their husband-wife-couple roles with varying degrees of readiness, flexibility and indecision. At first this all may be done in a spirit of playing at being married, until one day they begin to feel that they are really established in a going marriage.

THE DEVELOPMENTAL TASKS OF THE ESTABLISHMENT PHASE

The developmental tasks of beginning families are basic for the establishment of the family. Although they differ from family to family, from class to class, and from culture to culture, they may be listed in their more general aspects as follows:

1) establishing a home base in a place to call their own
2) establishing mutually satisfactory systems for getting and spending money
3) establishing mutually acceptable patterns of who does what and who is accountable to whom
4) establishing a continuity of mutually satisfying sex relationships
5) establishing systems of intellectual and emotional communication
6) establishing workable relationships with relatives
7) establishing ways of interacting with friends, associates, and community organizations
8) facing the possibility of children and planning for their coming
9) establishing a workable philosophy of life as a couple.

How couples go about accomplishing these developmental tasks is a long and interesting story that never can be completely told. Some of the variables in our society, found in working through the developmental tasks of the establishment phase, are discussed in the sections that follow.

ESTABLISHING A HOME BASE TO CALL THEIR OWN

One of the first questions a couple considering the possibilities of marriage faces is, "Where will we live?" If they are still in school or college, they may explore the resources for married students living near the campus. If the boy is soon to leave for military service, they consider where the wife will live while the husband puts in his time for Uncle Sam. The girl may remain at home with her parents, seeing her service-bound husband only on furloughs and leaves. She may make her home with his parents. She may follow her man, going from camp community to camp community and making a home base as best she can close to her husband for as long as she can. "Home" may be a dozen different spots in the first year or two of marriage, in any of the places they call their own during the period.

Couples with both schooling and military service out of the way find more stability in their home base as they choose the place where they can settle down and invest themselves and their resources in making a real home. At first this probably will be a rented place near their work and possibly near friends and family. It may be a furnished room or two for the couple marrying "on a shoe string," or a commodious house or apartment for the more affluent. Newly married members of the upper class sometimes move into a new house completely furnished for them by one or both of their families, but this is rare. Most couples must together puzzle out their homemaking plans from the possibilities at hand and the promises ahead.

ESTABLISHING MUTUALLY SATISFACTORY SYSTEMS FOR GETTING AND SPENDING MONEY

At the time of first marriage, the husband is usually young, inexperienced, and so relatively poorly paid. Yet the needs and wants and dreams of the young couple call for more money than will be available to them for some time. A successful family in the eyes of the midtwentieth century man or woman, is one able to buy not only the necessities of life in terms of shelter, food, and clothing but also such important "extras" as education, preventive medical care, leisure time activities, and cultural opportunities. The source of much of the trouble in "making ends meet" among young married couples stems from the incongruity between the sales pressures they are under and the realities in the nature of things. Few newly married couples can meet the magazine advertisement standards for the modern American kitchen, living room, or neighborhood. Today's high-priced household equipment is either inaccessible to the vast majority of young married couples or can be made available only at the sacrifice of more children, future financial security, and peace of mind.

Everybody accuses everybody else of "keeping up with the Joneses," but despite protestations almost no one wholly escapes it. For the young married pair in America most financial problems do not involve a struggle to secure the bare biological essentials of life or even the conventional comforts. The "squeeze" comes in trying to get those things which one is almost forced to want, not to meet his own needs but to meet those superimposed desires related to what is usually called one's "social position." Husband and wife feel they *need* a car, club membership, or a home in the "better part" of town, not so much because they need these things intrinsically, but rather that they are under pressure to display evidence of their success to their friends, business associates, and in-laws, who may be better established or simply more lucky.

Trouble arises from the tempting expedients the family is induced to use in its sometimes frantic efforts "to live beyond its means." Radio, newspapers, television, and neon signs remind one hourly that everything he wants can be bought for a fraction down and a ridiculously small amount per week. There are no singing commercials to remind the family novitiate that these ridiculously small weekly payments on home, car, dental fees, fur coat, radio, bedroom suite, and dream kitchen quickly add up to what the hard-headed New England forefather would call "paying for a dead horse."

To be sure, some people do escape the "rat race" of pecuniary rivalry, whether the majority or the minority is difficult to say. Some couples endure their privations with grace and the determination to "put first things first." Others develop skills for home production of goods and services, new ways for noncommercial leisure, and cooperative purchasing in order to make savings by quantity orders. Their inventiveness is impressive.

The young husband and wife may augment their income in a number of ways. Some couples accept financial help from their parents in any of the various forms of subsidy current today. This is not unusual, especially among those who marry before they have completed their educational plans in which the parents already have an investment. Many parents would rather help out the young married couple for awhile, than have their son or daughter drop out of school upon marriage. This is not always an easy arrangement, and many couples avoid it if at all possible. Some young husbands carry a part-time job in addition to their full-time employment or school load. This makes strains in the establishment phase when relaxed time together is so important for the building of the marriage.

The most frequent solution is found in the wife's ability and willingness to work during the establishment phase of the marriage. During the first year of marriage some 40 per cent of all wives work outside the home.[1] Unforeseen problems often arise in this connection. Not all women have the salable skills that will net them enough to be worthwhile. Not all women have health and energy enough to handle both a job and a home, however abbreviated the latter may be. Not all men either know how or feel constrained to share the household responsibilities with their working wives.

The more optimistic side of the picture is found in the many men and women who are learning the new roles required for a real partnership in getting and spending the family income. As more and more married women enter the working force and bring home their pay checks, decisions about the spending of the family income tend to become cooperative, democratic, and based on joint planning of husband and wife.

One study of married students indicates that an overwhelming majority (86.8 per cent) of the couples made their financial plans jointly. Some 84.1 per cent of them budgeted their money, and nearly three-fourths of the couples who used financial plans (74.2 per cent), kept records of their expenditures.[2] This is in sharp contrast to older patterns of handling money where the woman often did not know how much income there was or how it was spent, but like Vinnie Day[3] cajoled what sums she could from her reluctant mate who held the purse strings with a firm hand.

With both husband and wife increasingly responsible for getting and

[1] Paul C. Glick, "The Life Cycle of the Family," *Marriage and Family Living,* February 1955, Vol. XVII, No. 1, p. 8.
[2] Alice C. Thorpe, "How Married Students Manage," *Marriage and Family Living,* Vol. XIII, No. 3, Summer 1951, pp. 104–105, 130.
[3] Clarence Day, *Life with Father* (New York: Alfred A. Knopf, 1935).

By reading labels and intelligently comparing values, young married couples stretch their money as far as it will go.

spending the family income, there arises more consideration of the principles of wise purchasing. When both have planned for the purchase of some new item, they both are concerned with "getting the best buy." Courses, classes, units, and single lectures in consumer buying; and subscriptions to such guides as *Consumer Reports* and *Consumers' Research Bulletins* have greatly increased in recent years. Today one sees an occasional young couple reading labels on packaged products and intelligently comparing the values of competing commodities. With a limited amount of money and a large number of needs, today's early married couple wants to know how to stretch the family dollars as far as they will go.

Establishing mutually satisfactory systems for getting and spending money as a developmental task involves at least four specific challenges: 1) coming to terms with the realities of one's own financial situation in the face of the appealing claims of modern advertising, high pressure salesmanship, and "keeping up with the Joneses" pressures, 2) finding mutually comfortable sources of income for the immediate and the distant future, 3) establishing ways of deciding how the money will be spent, for what and by whom, and 4) developing sound financial plans and buying methods. These challenges must be met in some way during the early days of the marriage. Successful methods express the values of the couple (see section "Establishing a Workable Philosophy of Life as a Couple"), and are based upon the realities of their situation. Upon the successful accomplishment of this developmental task rests the future financial health of the family.

ESTABLISHING MUTUALLY ACCEPTABLE PATTERNS OF WHO DOES WHAT AND WHO IS ACCOUNTABLE TO WHOM

Traditionally the roles of husband and wife were rigidly defined and underwent little variation by the individual couple. There was man's work and woman's work, and each knew which was which. The man was the head of the house, and his wife and children respected his authority and bowed to it. Today's newly married couples have no such definite outlines to follow in the division of responsibilities and the assignment of the roles within the union. They must work them out for themselves within the new patterns of freedom characteristic of the modern age.

Couples are free to define their interlocking roles as husband and wife along traditional lines if they wish. But, the trend is toward more democratic, flexible roles [1] (Chapters Two and Three).

Nowadays more women find a place for themselves outside the home in remunerative work and volunteer service within the larger community. Concurrently men are becoming increasingly familiar with the household and its operation. Thus we find that among the married students already cited,[2] most of the husbands regularly help with the housework (77.2 per cent). Husbands as well as wives are found taking the laundry to the nearby laundromat and casually enjoying menu-planning as foods are bought for the week ahead. Men as well as women today engage in meal preparation with the help of packaged products, quick-frozen foods, modern kitchen equipment, and outdoor grills and barbeques. Merchandising that directly appeals to the male food handler (men's aprons, chef-outfits, etc.) both represents and facilitates this trend.

[1] Debi D. Lovejoy, "College Student Conceptions of the Roles of the Husband and Wife in Family Decision-Making," *The Family Life Coordinator*, Vol. IX, Nos. 3–4, March–June, 1961.
[2] Alice C. Thorpe, *op. cit.*, pp. 104–105.

The young couple today continues the mutual exploration of each other's interests and skills begun during the courtship and engagement periods, in the experimentation that becomes a major challenge in early marriage. Together they work out their own system of who will do what on the basis of individual preference, work schedules, time and strength, and a sense of fairness. One young husband says, "Sure I mop the kitchen floor and help clean house on Saturdays. It's the least I can do when she has so many other things to do all week."

Accountability in terms of who checks up on whom works itself out either along the older lines of male domination and authority, or along the newer approaches of the authority resting in the one who is taking the more responsibility for the activity, with each accountable to the other for his stewardship. The first pattern is familiar. The wife accounts to her husband of what she did with her time and their money during the day. He approves or corrects as he deems wise, and the household runs along on the principle of coming up to the expectations of the man of the house. The current trend is in the direction of responsibility for a project being assumed by the one who does the work on it, with joint consultation and planning as the source of general direction. Thus, the couple together decides to paint the kitchen, what color to use, and when it can best be done. Either the man or the woman, or both of them together may do the actual painting with its related decisions, problems, and rewards accruing to the worker(s). Both are accountable to their common budget and to each other in their decision-making and performance.

Modern equalitarian principles do not always work out happily in the new marriage. Both husband and wife bring to their marriage not only their desires to be flexible and intelligent about these things, but also their previous conditionings and emotional sets that are very much a part of the picture. A man may agree intellectually that he should carry some of the load of work around the house while his wife is working quite as hard as is he at remunerative work. But, if he has been brought up by a mother who has dominated the household with her efficiency, driving her sons from the kitchen with her insistence that they wait until they are called to dinner, he may find it hard to know how to start being helpful, what to do as his part of the responsibility, or even to accept emotionally the idea that he too is a partner in the housekeeping.

Similarly, if the wife has grown accustomed to seeing her mother ac-

Young couples today work out their own systems of who does what; they enjoy joint planning, consultation, and working together on mutually agreed projects.

count to her father in all things, she may *need* to report to her young husband many a detail that neither he nor she intellectually accept as necessary in their relationship. These things have to be worked out in the day by day association of the married pair in the many varied situations that make up their life together.

ESTABLISHING A CONTINUITY OF MUTUALLY SATISFYING SEX RELATIONSHIPS

Part of the enigma of marriage stems from the fact that American codes have not yet reached agreement concerning the eternally troublesome questions of sex and love.[1] Being in love is presumed by most people to be a sufficient answer in itself to any questioning of an adequate reason for a marriage. Elders, generally speaking, think that love is not enough to marry on and they make a good case for their point of view. But to Joe and Jane in their teens or early twenties, the principal and impelling fact which stimulates them to marry, and to marry each other, is the unanswerable imperative that "it *is* love."

[1] See Sylvanus M. Duvall, *Men, Women, and Morals* (New York: Association Press, 1952). For abundant statistical data see Alfred C. Kinsey, Wardell B. Pomeroy, and Clyde E. Martin, *Sexual Behavior in the Human Male* (Philadelphia: W. B. Saunders, 1948); and Kinsey *et al., Sexual Behavior in the Human Female* (Philadelphia: W. B. Saunders, 1953).

Probably most people assume that sex is, at its best, one of life's great fulfillments, and there is evidence in many marriages that the assumption is a sound one. But it is not always fully recognized that this blessing is unequally distributed among married couples in America and that frustration is experienced by many in their search for such fulfillment.

Sexual maladjustments of one sort or another are confusing and irksome to many couples, especially during the first few years of marriage. Generally speaking, much of the trouble stems from the contradictions between the couple's expectations for pleasant experience, on the one hand, and the inaccuracy of their knowledge regarding the subtleties of "the facts of life." [1] The problem is not, of course, wholly a matter of knowledge and intent. It is greatly complicated by the fact that husbands and wives both bring to marriage numerous and significant unconscious needs and wants.[2] At best we perceive our true selves only dimly, as if through a dense mist into which we can occasionally peer, with distortions and mirages common. But the illusion persists that we really know ourselves, our needs, our desires, and also those of our mates.

Individual needs growing out of different hereditary makeup, different background of experience, and differing conceptions of the purpose of sex, create barriers to mutual gratification. Accumulating frustrations bring forth angered epithets like "prude," "cold," "sensual," "beastly," "oversexed," and the like. It requires time,[3] more patience than some people have, more information than many can get, and skills of a specific nature to find mutual fulfillment. The almost innumerable avenues of sex satisfaction present further difficulties. Intimate personal acts which embellish the sexual experience for one mate may offend the fastidiousness of the other. Guilt, shame, indecision, and, many times, deep and abiding hostility become ingrained in the very fabric of sex in marriage. More than that, hostilities which were unnecessary in the first place, may over a long time grow and fester into an impairment of the whole marital structure.

---

[1] Inadequacies in knowledge in this area may be met in part by reading such books as Eustace Chesser, *Love Without Fear* (New York: Signet Books, 1949); Evelyn Duvall and Reuben Hill, *When You Marry* (New York: Association Press, 1953 edition); and Hannah and Abraham Stone, *A Marriage Manual* (New York: Simon and Schuster, 1952 edition).

[2] John Levy and Ruth Monroe, *The Happy Family* (New York: Alfred A. Knopf, 1938).

[3] Judson T. Landis, "Length of Time Required to Achieve Adjustment in Marriage," *American Sociological Review*, Vol. 11, No. 6, December 1946, pp. 666–677.

There are often painful discoveries such as lack of sexual response of the wife, the "insatiability" of the husband, jealousies with or without foundation in fact, or inabilities to forgive indiscretions in the past. These may have been confessed by the spouse in the frantic attempt to relieve guilt feelings, only to find his or her marriage bond threatened by candor.

In time, sexual difficulties like other conflicts and disappointments work out one way or another. The nature of this accomplishment is indeed varied. Failure is seen in resignation to one's fate, chronic frustration concealed (or ill-concealed), overt hostility to the mate, or generalized irritability. Progress is found in discovery of unexpected strength in self or mate, realization that success is worth working for and that the race for it can be fun, selective forgetting of earlier frustrated goals, and learning the knowledges, skills, and attitudes that make for mutual fulfillment.

The husband and wife who work out together a continuity of mutually satisfying sex relationships early in their marriage not only find a source of deep satisfaction for the present, but they also have established a firm foundation upon which other tasks can be undertaken, and future happiness built.

ESTABLISHING SYSTEMS OF INTELLECTUAL AND EMOTIONAL COMMUNICATION

One of the biggest jobs facing the recently married couple is that of communicating with each other. Two people may live in the same house, they may share the same bed and board, but unless they establish effective systems of communication between them, they might as well be miles apart. She may live through the days in tight-lipped silence, he may pout and mope through the evenings, with no awareness of what "is eating" either of them, unless and until they have developed the signs and signals, the words and the gestures that keep the state of affairs open to them both.

Human beings do not live in emotional vacuums, but in a climate of feeling that changes quite as often as the weather. Each of us as men and as women at times feel loving and at times feel hateful; at times are high and at other times low; are sometimes mad and sometimes sad. Mental hygiene findings have indicated without question that the healthful way to live is to recognize emotional states for what they are, as they arise, and to deal with them realistically. Pretending that all is well while one seethes inside is hypocrisy, and it is corrosive if it becomes habitual.

If two people are to live intimately together in marriage, they must learn to express their feelings in acceptable and healthful ways. They must develop ways of communicating for the mutual planning and furtherance of mutual services; and for the necessity of sharing the meanings of a moment in true companionship—understanding and being understood in a system of satisfying mutual identification.

In a study of the development of the relationship of recently married couples Bolton finds that some couples discover an immediate ability to communicate freely with one another. One young wife reports, "We communicated right away. We spoke the same language. There was a mutual understanding of feelings about things without having to go into detail." A young husband says, "I can tell by the kind of tenseness in her body whether she wants to be kissed or not. There's a lot of things like that by which I can tell her mood—whether she's quiet, the way she curls her lip, whether she looks up when I talk to her."

Couples reporting an awareness of spontaneous empathy describe it as some feeling of homogamy, and of responsiveness. They seem to feel an immediate meshing of behavior without resorting to words. But the development of lasting communication appears to depend more upon the use of words or upon gestural cues translated into verbal intentions.

Most couples are found to develop a private vocabulary consisting of terms of endearment, special names, and unique symbolic meanings attached to jokes, rituals, or events shared in the relationship. Some couples work out special techniques for facilitating communication under tension. As a whole the form of communication remains relatively stable throughout the relationship. The evolution of the relation occurs more in the content than in the form of communication. Indeed, the conclusion is that "the mode of communication is one of the most stable and fundamental personality characteristics."[1]

Communication is an intricate complex of words, gestures, signs, and symbolic actions that have meanings to the communicating people. Some of these words and meanings are universal. Some are peculiar to the language and cultural group. More subtle systems are highly individ-

---

[1] Charles D. Bolton, "The Development Process in Love Relationships," Ph.D. Dissertation, University of Chicago, Department of Sociology, August 1959, pp. 242–243.

ual and must be built up within the new relationship. One of the joys of courtship, engagement, and the honeymoon is found in the development and the practice of intimate, personal gestures and symbols that have meaning only for the two persons. They identify "our song," they walk by "our house" through "our park," and they repeat little ceremonies that convey more than words could the special significance each has for the other. Special gestures of affection become their own language of love that channel love feelings and add immeasurably to the satisfaction they get in each other's company.

It may be relatively easy to get through to each other with love and affection. But learning how to handle the inevitable negative feelings that arise from time to time is a difficult assignment for many couples. No two people see eye to eye about all things. No two people feel the same way about everything they share in life together. So some conflict is to be expected in marriage, especially during the establishment phase when the two people are learning to mesh their former ways of living into a unity of habits, aspirations, and values.

The romantic illusion prevalent in America calls for two people in love living "happily ever after" in a state of perpetual bliss that offers no room for the disagreements and differences that two normal people inevitably find cropping up between them. So, when the first quarrels occur, one or both of the pair mistakenly may feel that the marriage is failing, their love is not lasting, or they were not "made for each other" after all. The couple that is able to see conflict as a part of the close, intimate marriage relationship, accepts its reality and assumes the responsibility for meeting constructively the differences that arise.

One of the critical tests of the adequacy of the communication established within a marriage is found in the way in which the two people meet a conflict situation. As long as they keep silent and pretend that they have no problems, little progress can be made in getting through to each other. When one person leaves the conflict situation in anger or in tears, or in patient martyrdom, communication between the partners is poor. As the husband and wife make a real effort to share their true feelings and to accept without anxiety or fear the fact that their feelings and values do differ, they are able to learn to bridge their differences.

The outline, "A Pattern for Problem Solving" has evolved in family life education classes at Oklahoma A & M College as a guide for the development of skills in solving interpersonal problems.

A PATTERN FOR PROBLEM SOLVING *

Stillwater, Oklahoma

Oklahoma A & M College

Division of Home Economics

By permission, Department of Family Relations and Child Development,

Girdie Ware

STEPS	KEY QUESTIONS	PURPOSE
1. FACE THE PROBLEM	What is the matter? Why do I/we think it is a problem?	To get problem into words. To uncover the fear involved.
2. LOOK AT THE CAUSES	What has been happening? What has made it a problem now?	To get the build-up of the problem. To get a clear statement of what is bringing it to a head.
3. SET SOME GOALS	What do I want to accomplish for myself? For the other person? What do we/I want the situation to be?	To be sure of desires for self. To be sure that decisions will benefit others as well as self. To set a definite change to work toward.
4. GET MORE KNOWLEDGE AND UNDERSTANDING	What knowledge from the biological, psychological and social sciences are applicable? Have I found all the available material in technical and popular literature? What has been the experience of other people in similar situations?	To increase understanding. To gain insight.
5. BE THE OTHER PERSON (Try to be each of the other persons or groups of persons involved in the problem)	Just how would I, as this other person, think about it? And as this other person what does he or she feel?	To get the other person's point of view and emotional slant. To allow thinking and feelings of others be a framework for the next step.
6. CONSIDER WHAT TO DO	What could we/I do about it? Will that bring me to my goals? Will it fit the thoughts and feelings of the other person?	To get a list of possible actions. To be sure they lead to the goals To be sure they will be acceptable to other person.
7. MAKE A PLAN OF ACTION	Just how can this be done? Who will do each part? How will I do it? Who will help me?	To plan how to do it. To develop a 1, 2, 3, plan. To select the person to help at each point if needed.
8. CHECK THE PLAN WITH THE GOALS	Will this plan lead you to your goals? Does it provide for each goal?	To be sure the plan is really directed at the desired solution. To be sure it covers all the goals set.
9. PLAN THE FOLLOW-UP	What shall I/we watch for to be sure the plan is working?	To encourage watchfulness in using the plan. To encourage abandonment if it seems to be failing.

* An adaption of "A Pattern for Counseling" by L. A. Lynde, Extension Specialist in Parent Education, Jan. 30, 1947.

It takes time to learn to live constructively with differences in ways that increase the harmony of the marriage and the understanding of each other. It may not be fully accomplished during the first establishment phase of the marriage, but it should be begun well enough so that further tasks will not be rendered more complicated by failure to communicate effectively in moments of strain and tension. The husband and wife who establish good systems of communication for handling the hot spot areas of their relationship find real satisfaction in knowing "if we can handle this, we can weather anything that comes."

Unity as a couple is established by the network of bonds that weave the two into two-in-one. The bonds are not ties in the sense of fetters. There are open systems of communication through which each gets across to the other for the comfort, the love, the understanding, the sympathy, the loyalty and the sense of purpose a man or woman needs to feel truly married. Without such communication a person may ache with loneliness even while beside the mate. With a well-established communication system, the husband and wife feel united even though they may be separated by many months and miles.

ESTABLISHING WORKABLE RELATIONSHIPS WITH RELATIVES

The man and woman marrying for the first time undergo a basic role shift from their parental homes to their own home-in-the-making. Simultaneously they find themselves in three families: her family of orientation, his family of orientation, and the family they are founding together as their family of procreation. The success of the marriage depends in part upon how competently both husband and wife 'forsake all others and cleave only to each other as long as they both shall live' to paraphrase the biblical injunction. For twenty years, more or less, the woman has been a daughter in her parents' home; now suddenly her husband must come first. For years, the young man has been a free agent, accountable only to his parents; now he is expected to be devoted exclusively to his wife. Difficulties in making these role shifts are seen in in-law problems through the early years of marriage.

Relationships with in-laws are generally dreaded before marriage, and avoided as much as possible thereafter, in the stereotyped fear of intrusion that forms the basis of the universal mother-in-law joke and general mother-in-law avoidance. Yet actual investigation of in-law relationships turns up many satisfactory, mutually helpful in-law relationships. Kinfolk are often counted on as friendly allies by the young married pair and become even more appreciated as the years roll by.[1]

A Cornell University study of recently married couples finds their parents making tangible contributions to the new households. Some of this help is in cash, some in food, clothing, furnishings, household equipment, and furniture, and the rest in services such as baby-sitting, lodging, use of equipment, and household help. "This study indicates that parents do assist their newly married children with contributions of both goods and services. There is no evidence of the young family being isolated from the parental family."[2]

Sussman and others find mutual help between the generations widespread among both middle- and working-class families. They find that couples receive financial aid from parents most often 1) during the early years of marriage, 2) when the parents approve the marriage, and 3) when the young people marry while still in school. Beyond the giving of tangible gifts to the young couple, there is a service network in families in which such assistance as help during illness, child care, visiting, escorting, shopping, and advice flow between parents and married children, in both directions as voluntary mutual kin responsibilities through the years. Turning to relatives when trouble comes, rather than going first to community agencies set up for such service, is a common practice among the families studied.[3]

It is clear that few young married couples live to themselves alone, but rather within a total joint family of his relatives and hers. One of their tasks early in marriage is to establish those mutually satisfying relationships that it takes to thrive as members of the larger family. These interactions, most intense with parents of the pair, also branch out to siblings and other relatives.

Although it is the members of the immediate family that most often have to be dealt with in the establishment phase of marriage, there are many others who may affect the lives of the young adult today,

[1] Evelyn Millis Duvall, *In-Laws: Pro and Con* (New York: Association Press, 1954).

[2] Alma Beth Clark and Jean Warren, *Economic Contributions Made to Newly Married Couples by Their Parents* (Ithaca, New York: Cornell University, May 1963), p. 5.

[3] Marvin B. Sussman and Lee Burchinal, "Kin Family Network: Unheralded Structure in Current Conceptualizations of Family Functioning," *Marriage and Family Living*, Vol. XXIV, No. 3, August 1962, pp. 231–240.

as Dr. Albrecht points out (see Chapter One). A relative may need a home for awhile. A younger sister or brother may call upon the young couple for help. An accident may befall a cousin or an aunt or uncle rallying the whole family and its resources to the assistance of the stricken ones. Disgrace can hit the young couple through a relative, as can sudden wealth or any public notice. One never can completely cut off one's roots. The larger family circle surrounds each newly married couple and some sort of relationship must be established that will carry through the years.

ESTABLISHING WAYS OF INTERACTING WITH FRIENDS, ASSOCIATES, AND COMMUNITY ORGANIZATIONS

"With someone like you, a pal so good and true, I'd like to leave it all behind, and go and find, someplace that's known to God alone, just a spot to call our own . . . and let the rest of the World go by," are words of a popular song that are often repeated in one way or another by the newly married pair desiring nothing so much as to be let alone. Being alone together is expected during the engagement and the honeymoon periods. But there comes a time when the married pair is ready for social activities. Friends, associates, and the larger community expect the couple to be active as a young married pair in the married set.

Getting into the young married set of the neighborhood is a developmental task that comes easily to the couple that settles down in the home community. It may pose problems for large numbers of young husbands and wives who move into a new area where they know no one and must find for themselves the companions and the social activities that interest both of them.[1] The mixed marriage may require redefinitions of who is considered a pleasant companion and what is an acceptable social activity. Different experiences bring different definitions of how home is used. Jane, a minister's daughter, sees her home almost as a social center and expects neighbors and friends to drop in unannounced; while Jane's Joe sees their home as a refuge with privacy and undisturbed quiet as prime values.

The demands upon the married couple made by the husband's job

---

[1] "About four-fifths of the persons who marry change residences at the time of marriage or within the ensuing year." Paul C. Glick, "The Life Cycle of the Family," *Marriage and Family Living*, February 1955, Vol. XVII, No. 1, p. 8.

vary from the annual picnic of the plant to which workers and their families are invited, to the exacting pressures made upon the corporation wife by the young executive's boss. The amount of business entertaining a young couple is expected to do depends upon his job, their social standing, and their social mobility. "Having the boss to dinner" has become a stereotyped problem situation in popular thinking that not incorrectly describes the anxiety and effort involved in becoming established as a socially acceptable married pair.

The extent to which the young husband and wife participate in community organizations depends on their previous involvements, on their social status, and on the length of time married. Lower-class families tend to be much less active in community work than are members of the middle and upper classes. Young married couples are not as active in the community as are families established a number of years. The young husband and wife are highly mobile and busy getting themselves established, a task already achieved by longer married couples. The children of the established family bring father and mother out to participate in neighborhood, school, church, and political projects that do not appeal as personally to the couple without children. The previous involvements of the young man or woman in union affairs, social activities, political campaigns, or church functions may continue to absorb the individual, especially if these interests are shared with the mate.

There may be some problems over the religious affiliations of the couple, especially if theirs is an interfaith marriage. Generally, there is more instability in mixed marriages than in those within the same faith. Three studies in various regions of the country (populations totaling 24,184) agree in finding significantly higher percentages of mixed marriages ending in divorce than do those in which the husband and wife share the same religious faith, as is summarized in Table 11.

Sylvanus M. Duvall suggests several questions to be examined by two people attempting to establish a mixed marriage:

1) How intense is the loyalty of each to his own religious group?
2) How many complicating factors are there, such as relatives and influential friends?
3) What aspects of religion does each feel most strongly about?
4) Is there danger that religious differences will be used as a means by which one can dominate the other?
5) Are there other strong bonds to compensate for the religious differences?
6) What compromises are both willing to make to solve the problem?

7) What specific decisions can be made in regard to:
   a) Who, if either, will change his church relationship?
   b) If each retains his separate faith, where will they attend church, if at all?
   c) In what faith, if any, will the children be brought up? [1]

TABLE 11. *Percentage of Marriages of Mixed and Non-Mixed Religious Faiths Ending in Divorce or Separation as Revealed by Studies of Marriages in Michigan, Maryland, and Washington* [2]

Religious Categories	*Landis Study* * in Michigan (N = 4,108)	*Bell Study* † in Maryland (N = 13,528)	*Weeks Study* § in Washington (N = 6,548)
	Per cent	Per cent	Per cent
Both Catholic	4.4	6.4	3.8
Both Jewish	5.2	4.6	—
Both Protestant	6.0	6.8	10.0
Mixed, Catholic-Protestant	14.1	15.2	17.4

* Judson T. Landis, "Marriages of Mixed and Non-Mixed Religious Faith," *American Sociological Review*, Vol. 14, No. 3, 1949, pp. 401–407.
† Howard M. Bell, *Youth Tell Their Story* (Washington, D. C.: American Council on Education, 1938), p. 21.
§ H. Ashley Weeks, "Differential Divorce Rates by Occupation," *Social Forces*, Vol. 21, No. 3, March 1943, p. 336.

Even in marriages within the same faith there often are difficulties over the degree of interest in religious activities. A common conflict occurs when the wife wants to go to church regularly with her husband, while he prefers to sleep late on the one morning of the week when that is possible. The patterns a couple develops for resolving such differences and expressing their own wishes, desires, values, and beliefs take time to work out. These accomplishments are greatly aided by discussing the possible problems and their solutions in the premarital period, and then being willing to rethink and rework the tentative working agreements as needed during the establishment phase of the marriage.

FACING THE POSSIBILITY OF CHILDREN AND PLANNING FOR THEIR COMING

The modern American couple marry with the anticipation of having children. Many of them have their first baby within the first year, some

[1] Evelyn M. Duvall and Reuben Hill with chapters in collaboration with Sylvanus M. Duvall, *When You Marry* (Boston, D. C. Heath and Company, Revised 1953), pp. 391–394.
[2] Data excerpted from Judson T. Landis, "Marriages of Mixed and Non-Mixed Religious Faith," *American Sociological Review*, Vol. 14, No. 3, June 1949, p. 403.

within the first nine months. Cross-cultural studies indicate that about one-fifth of all first births in the United States were conceived before marriage.[1] When marriage occurs after the first pregnancy has already begun, the couple faces the developmental tasks of both the establishment and the expectant phases of Stage I of the family life cycle concurrently.

The overwhelming majority of Americans believe in planned parenthood. On the basis of intensive interviews with a nation-wide sample of white couples with wife under 40, researchers found attempts to avoid conception at some time virtually universal (94 per cent) among couples with no fecundity impairment. Among fecund Catholic wives, 70 per cent were past users and an additional 10 per cent were acknowledged future users of both artificial and rhythm methods of family limitation.[2] However, many first babies are unplanned. One study of 424 married college students found that only slightly more than one-third had definitely planned their first child.[3]

Unplanned pregnancies may be a crisis for the couple, for either member of the pair, as well as for the child-to-be. Coming within the establishment phase of the newly founded family, a pregnancy may make it difficult if not impossible for the wife to go with her husband as he completes his military service; it may necessitate the wife's cutting short her educational plans; it may pull the young husband from long-range professional plans, and into some vocation where money is quicker and advancement sooner; it may mean the bringing in of one or both sets of parents for financial and personal help; or it may, if the couple is ready for a child, cement the marriage as nothing else can do.

Inability to conceive a child is another challenge to be faced. Infertility is encountered by something less than fifteen per cent of all married couples. During Bible days when a married woman did not become pregnant she was considered "barren." This term is no longer used by informed people for two reasons. First, because the condition is often caused by some inadequacy in the male, most frequently in-

---

[1] Harold T. Christensen, "Studies in Child-Spacing: I—Premarital Pregnancy as Measured by the Spacing of the First Birth from Marriage," *American Sociological Review*, Vol. 18. No. 1, February 1953, pp. 53–59.

[2] Ronald Freedman, P. K. Whelpton, and Arthur Campbell, *Family Planning, Sterility and Population Growth* (New York: McGraw-Hill, 1959), pp. 61 and 104.

[3] Shirley Poffenberger, Thomas Poffenberger, and Judson T. Landis, "Intent Toward Conception and the Pregnancy Experience," *American Sociological Review*, Vol. 17, October 1952, pp. 616–620.

sufficiently motile sperm; and, second, because the inability to have a child is frequently a temporary condition that responds well to treatment, or even to time. Infertility clinics in connection with hospitals in many communities, as well as private physicians in recent years, have increased the fecundity of many young married couples who want to become parents. Couples who have been married more than one year without conceiving a child are wise to go for examinations of both husband and wife and to accept treatment as indicated before becoming discouraged or jumping to the conclusion that theirs is a sterile union.

Nine out of ten couples who are childless from choice, have no interest in children.[1] The wife's participation in activities outside the home is directly related to her interest in and liking for children, as well as to the effectiveness of her family planning.[2] The more education a woman has the less likely she is to want either no children at all or a very large family. The married college woman tends to prefer two, three, or four children, according to a number of studies.[3]

Marital dissatisfaction tends to discourage the usual preference for three or four children.[4] Well adjusted married pairs tend to want children and to have the size family they prefer.[5]

More first-born babies arrive during the first year of marriage than at any other time. By the end of the second year of marriage two-thirds of the white mothers (66.2 per cent), and three-fourths of all nonwhite mothers (75.7 per cent) in the population have had their first baby.[6]

ESTABLISHING A WORKABLE PHILOSOPHY OF LIFE AS A COUPLE

Presumably the young adult has some kind of philosophy of life by the time he or she is old enough to marry. Yet with marriage comes the weaving of one's own convictions and values with those of the partner

---

[1] Lois Pratt and P. K. Whelpton, "Social and Psychological Factors Affecting Fertility," *The Milbank Memorial Fund Quarterly,* Vol. XXXIII, No. 4, October 1955, page 1243.

[2] *Ibid.,* Vol. XXXIV, No. 1, January 1956, page 1271.

[3] See above, and Robert O. Blood, Jr. and Donald M. Wolfe, *Husbands and Wives* (Glencoe, Illinois: The Free Press, 1960), pp. 122–123.

[4] *Ibid.,* p. 123.

[5] Robert B. Reed, "Sociological and Psychological Factors Affecting Fertility: The Interrelationship of Marital Adjustment, Fertility Control, and Size of Family," *The Milbank Memorial Fund Quarterly,* Vol. XXV, October 1947, p. 383.

[6] Bureau of the Census, *Population Characteristics,* Series P-120, No. 108, July 12, 1961, p. 51.

into a philosophical whole that gives unity to the marriage. Marriage provides for the young husband and wife many opportunities for testing previous orientations and situations that challenge former conclusions. Together the two people in marriage must choose those alternatives that best represent their present positions. Together over a period of time they develop a philosophy of life by which they can live.

Pressures during the early establishment phase of marriage push the young married couple into taking one stand or another on a good many issues. As a married pair they must decide what church they will attend, or if they will affiliate with any religious group. As a married couple they face the current political situation with either indifference or with dedicating loyalties. As soon as they are married they meet the question of the filing of joint or individual income tax returns with temptations for "saving" as much as they can on their tax, on the one hand, or submitting a completely honest statement on the other. These are the decisions that reflect and refine a philosophy-of-life.

As a newly established unit of society they find themselves forced to take some kind of position—in their social groups, in the neighborhood, at work, as they read the daily paper, listen to the news reports over the radio, and fall into casual conversations—on the widely discussed issues of the day. In a hundred different weekly situations they are testing and establishing the philosophy by which they are to live—in the attitudes they take toward the new family, from another ethnic background, recently moved into the neighborhood; in the way they feel and talk about an incident of aggression in the central square; in the position they take on the new zoning law that is being voted upon; in the way they behave when given too much change for a purchase; in the way they act toward the man who carries away their trash, or the deference they show the people above them in the community; in the degree of perfection they expect of themselves, of each other, and of others. In all these situations, and more, they are weaving the philosophy of life by which they as a couple are to live.

Establishing a philosophy of life for the average couple does not involve writing out a personal family creed. Few families come to that degree of explicit awareness of the philosophies by which they live. But whether it becomes explicit or not, the philosophy of life is there, worked out in everyday life together.

This does not imply that the couple must come to exactly the same stand on every issue of life. In some areas they may agree to disagree, each recognizing the other's right to feel as he or she must, believe what makes sense, and act according to his or her own convictions. But over and beyond the personal philosophy that moves each person to be himself is the philosophy of life-as-a-couple that must be established explicitly or implicitly in early marriage.

CHALLENGES AND HAZARDS OF THE ESTABLISHMENT PHASE

The likelihood of divorce rises rapidly after the first few months of marriage, reaches a peak in the third year, and steadily declines through the rest of the marriage.[1] Few couples realize how vulnerable marriage is during the establishment phase. The tendency to think that marriage solves all problems is one real hazard facing the romantic couple who expect to find immediate and unending bliss as soon as they are married.

Some couples do work out mutually satisfactory adjustments from the beginning. But a sizeable percentage never do, and others work at their developmental tasks for several months to many years before they agree that all is well. Chart 10 summarizes the time couples happily married for twenty years or more reported it took them to make their marriage adjustments in six areas of their lives together.

Young people lacking the maturity to enjoy the responsibilities and privileges of marriage are especially ill-prepared for the many concurrent roles they must play as husband and wife. When the marriage is combined with continuing education, military service, vocational establishment, high mobility, and/or dependence upon parents, it is filled with hazards for the young pair.

Financial strain is particularly great during the early years of marriage. Then a couple face the high costs of getting and furnishing a place to call their own in line with advertising pressures and their efforts to impress their friends. At that time when their costs may be greater than they ever will be again, the husband's income as a new worker is at a low point in his career. In order to start out in the style to which they would like to become accustomed, many a newly married couple go into debt or buy more on the installment plan than they can afford.

The wife's working to help out during the establishment phase can itself create problems that must be solved. Unless the couple learn to live

[1] Paul H. Jacobson, *American Marriage and Divorce* (New York: Rinehart & Company, Inc., 1959), pp. 144–149.

CHART 10.   Percentage of 409 Couples Reporting Various Periods of Time after Marriage to Achieve Adjustments.[1]

on the husband's income, they face additional adjustments when the wife drops out of work to have the first baby. Fitting homemaking tasks into the residue of time left after a full working day can be overtiring. Expecting a husband's help at home when he is swamped with his job, his further education, and his anxiety about military service may be more than he can measure up to.

Fallacious stereotypes about in-laws increase the difficulties the young couple have in accepting proffered help from one or both sets of parents, and can make for unnecessary strain between the young husband and wife and their relatives on both sides of the family.[2] Taboos, misconceptions, and fictions about love, sex, and marriage are disruptive, especially during the early years of marriage.[3] Yet they are rampant still in the culture and continue to be reinforced through the mass media.

[1] Judson T. Landis, "Adjustments After Marriage," *Marriage and Family Living*, Vol. IX, No. 2, May 1947, p. 33.

[2] Evelyn Millis Duvall, *In-Laws: Pro and Con* (Association Press, 1954).

[3] *Ibid.*, and E. E. LeMasters, *Modern Courtship and Marriage* (New York: The Macmillan Company, 1957), Chapter 3, "Folklore about Marriage in Our Society," pp. 48–65.

Effective premarital and marriage counseling help a couple meet many challenges in the establishment phase of their marriage.

RESOURCES FOR ESTABLISHING THE MARRIAGE

The honeymoon as a period of privacy during which the couple may explore the intimate personal side of marriage is an important resource for the newly married couple. Making good use of the honeymoon depends upon the attitudes the couple [1] have as they embark upon it. One study found 57 per cent of the women saying they felt happy and expectant, and 28 per cent confident and calm. But 21 per cent also reported they were fatigued and exhausted, 16 per cent felt apprehensive and fearful, and 20 per cent were overstimulated and tense.[2] In time, resentments and disappointments drain off in socially accepted

[1] Lee G. Burchinal, Glenn R. Hawkes and Bruce Gardner, "Personality Characteristics and Marital Satisfaction," *Social Forces,* Vol. 35, No. 3, March 1957, pp. 218–222.

[2] Betty Hannah Hoffman, "Are Honeymoons Happy?" *Ladies Home Journal,* June 1961, pp. 36, 37, 104.

ways. While through it all, the two are thrown together with the expectation of success by all who know them.

Some tasks of the honeymoon period are *intrapersonal*. Rhona and Robert Rapoport [1] list these as 1) developing competence to participate in an appropriate sexual relationship with one's marital partner; and 2) developing competence to live in close association with the marital partner. They find in their exploratory studies that young couples are often concerned about their sexual competence. Brides tend to be anxious about the possible pain of intercourse, whether their husbands will be patient and gentle with them, and whether they will be able to satisfy their husbands. Bridegrooms' fears center in their possible inability to be potent with their wives. Both members of the pair may be concerned about whether their autonomy will be threatened by the intimacy of marriage.

The honeymoon usually is the first experience of living intimately with a person of the other sex. It is then that feelings about sharing the same bed, about undressing in front of one another, about using the bathroom and other such homely details of interaction come to the fore.

Other tasks of the honeymoon are *interpersonal*: 1) developing the basis for a mutually satisfactory sexual relationship, and 2) having a mutually satisfactory shared experience as a basis for developing a continuing husband-wife relationship. The couple learn to cooperate and to sense their ability to work together. Getting married and establishing a marriage is a critical role transition for which many young people are often inadequately prepared.

Churches, YMCA's, YWCA's, and other youth and family serving agencies have established themselves in most communities as agencies interested in helping young men and women get a good start in marriage. Their services often include classes for engaged couples and young married couples, premarital and marital counseling services, special consultants in various aspects of marriage, films, books, pamphlets, and not infrequently some types of group discussion and therapy.

Schools and colleges in rapidly increasing numbers offer courses in family life education and related subjects designed to acquaint the student with the knowledges, skills, attitudes, and values that make for success in marriage.

[1] Rhona Rapoport and Robert N. Rapoport, "New Light on the Honeymoon," *Human Relations*, Vol. 17, No. 1, 1964, pp. 33–56.

Colleges and university centers in recent decades have greatly increased their research studies in marriage and family life. The implications of marriage research findings and clinical evidence are a substantial part of the many marriage texts now available for the young husband, wife, or couple interested in becoming informed in any of the various areas involved in the establishment of their marriage.

SUMMARY

The establishment phase of the beginning family takes the couple from their marriage to the time when they become aware of the wife's pregnancy. The period is one full of developmental tasks of great importance as the couple satisfy their need for ongoing adult sex fulfillment within marriage (biologic origin), as they attempt to measure up to what is expected of them as a young married couple (origin in cultural pressures), and as they try to make their dreams come true in the merging of their aspirations and values as a couple (origin in personal aspirations).

The developmental tasks of this phase of the family life cycle may be summarized as (1) establishing a home base in a place they can call their own, (2) establishing mutually satisfying systems for getting and spending money, (3) establishing mutually acceptable patterns of who does what and who is accountable to whom, (4) establishing a continuity of mutually satisfying sex relationships, (5) establishing systems of intellectual and emotional communication, (6) establishing workable relationships with relatives, (7) establishing ways of interacting with friends, associates, and community organizations, (8) facing the possibility of children and planning for their coming, and (9) establishing a workable philosophy of life as a couple.

Each of the developmental tasks involved in establishing a marriage has hazards and challenges that must be met successfully if the couple is to develop and grow satisfactorily. Success in developmental tasks does not come all at once but must be achieved if the couple is to find happiness together. Upon the accomplishment of the developmental tasks of the establishment phase rests the future success of the developmental tasks still to come in the stages ahead for the couple in the family life cycle.

Resources available to help couples satisfactorily achieve the developmental tasks of the establishment phase are: the honeymoon period that protects the young couple in a circle of privacy in which the first intimate, personal adjustments to married living may be made; the encouragement and support from family, friends, and community in becoming a married couple and learning to live as a married pair; family life education in schools, churches, and community settings that prepare young people for marriage responsibilities ahead; premarital counseling; marriage and family research with its implications for mate selection and preparation for marriage; marriage and family books that translate research and clinical evidence into discussions and recommendations that are functionally most relevant for the couple.

SUGGESTED ACTIVITIES

1) Review any five of the marriage texts listed in the *Readings* with special attention to the amount of space given the various tasks of the establishment phase of the beginning family. Count the number of pages in each text devoted to each of the developmental tasks (as described in this chapter) and make a chart by texts and tasks of the coverage of each. Discuss your findings.

2) Write a letter to your sister who is to be married soon, suggesting the resources she may want to avail herself of as her wedding date approaches, as well as after the ceremony. Tell her why you recommend the services you do.

3) Investigate the living units available in your community for a young married couple by answering a representative sampling of the advertisements in your local paper for rooms, apartments, and homes available for rent. How much rent will a young married couple have to pay for various types of housing in your area? In what condition are the available places?

4) Survey the married students in your area in terms of (a) working wives, (b) part-time employment of student-husbands, (c) other sources of income, and (d) use of budgets or other financial plans by the couple. Write up your findings in a report on "How Married Students Get and Spend Their Money."

5) Explore the factors discussed in the literature on sex adjustments in marriage for possible reasons why the task of achieving a mutually satisfying sex relationship is less often accomplished from the beginning than other aspects in building a marriage. Review your findings with an experienced physician, marriage counselor, or worker in a marriage counseling service in your community for further interpretation of the nature of this developmental task. Summarize your material in a short report.

6) Find out what research studies have to say about which in-law is the most difficult, what husbands and wives report as objectionable behavior on

the part of in-laws, and what makes for good in-law relationships. *In-Laws: Pro and Con* in your *Readings* may be a helpful resource in this assignment.

7) View the kinescope "In-Laws" (No. 11 in the 1956 Marriage Series), produced by and available from The University of Michigan Television Center, Ann Arbor, Michigan, in which Robert O. Blood, Jr. and Evelyn Millis Duvall discuss in-law relationships in marriage. Discuss.

8) Consider the importance of emotional maturity in the accomplishment of the developmental tasks of early marriage in a series of psychodramas illustrating immature and relatively mature ways of meeting one or more of the usual early marriage challenges.

9) Practice problem solving approaches to husband-wife differences in a series of "talk-out" sessions as developed by Dr. Hazel Ingersoll, Department of Home Life, Oklahoma A&M College, Stillwater, Oklahoma. She divides the class into couples (man and woman preferably, or a pair of men or of women). Each pair takes roles of husband and wife, chooses a problem from such a list as is given below, and practices talking out differences. Stress is placed on considering feelings and attitudes of individuals as well as the facts of the case. Talk-out sessions go on simultaneously for a while, then volunteer pairs do spontaneous demonstration "talk-outs" before the entire group. Problem situations such as the following are suggested:

    a) Who will manage the money—husband or wife?

    b) Working wife versus wife as a fulltime homemaker?

    c) Simple small town life versus living in a large city?

    d) He thinks entertaining is a waste of money. She thinks it is important.

    e) She wants a large church wedding but he wants a simple family ceremony.

    f) He wants to accept a job in a foreign country; she wants to stay close home.

    g) She insists on going to church and Sunday school; he likes to stay home and sleep late on Sunday.

    h) He expects her to move into a large ranch house with his father; she objects.

READINGS

Becker, Howard, and Hill, Reuben, eds., *Family, Marriage and Parenthood* (Boston: D. C. Heath and Company, 1955), Part Three, "Marriage Interaction."

Bigelow, Howard F., *Family Finance* (Philadelphia: J. B. Lippincott Company, Revised 1953).

Blood, Robert O., Jr., and Wolfe, Donald M., *Husbands and Wives* (Glencoe, Illinois: The Free Press, 1960).

Bowman, Henry, *Marriage for Moderns* (New York: McGraw-Hill Book Company, Revised Edition, 1965).

Burgess, Ernest W., and Wallin, Paul, with Shultz, Gladys Denny, *Courtship, Engagement and Marriage* (Philadelphia: J. B. Lippincott Company, 1954).

Christensen, Harold T., *Marriage Analysis* (New York: The Ronald Press, Co., 1958 Revision).

Clark, Alma Beth, and Jean Warren, *Economic Contributions Made to Newly Married Couples by Their Parents* (Ithaca, New York: Cornell University, May 1963).

Duvall, Evelyn Millis, *In-Laws: Pro and Con* (New York: Association Press, 1954).

Duvall, Evelyn Millis and Hill, Reuben, *Being Married* (Boston: D. C. Heath and Company, 1960).

Havighurst, Robert J., *Human Development and Education* (New York: Longmans, Green and Co., 1953), Chapter 16, "Developmental Tasks of Early Adulthood."

Jacobson, Paul H., *American Marriage and Divorce* (New York: Rinehart & Company, Inc., 1959).

Laing, Ronald D., H. Phillipson, and Russell A. Lee, *Interpersonal Perception* (New York: Springer Publishing Company, 1965).

Levy, John, and Munroe, Ruth, *The Happy Family* (New York: Alfred A. Knopf, 1962 Revision).

Lovejoy, Debi D., "College Student Conceptions of the Roles of the Husband and Wife in Family Decision-Making," *The Family Life Coordinator*, Vol. IX, Nos. 3–4, March–June, 1961, pp. 43–46.

Margolius, Sidney, "Why Young Couples Spend More than They Earn," *Redbook Magazine*, February 1966, pp. 56, 57, 104–107.

Martinson, Floyd M., *Marriage and the American Ideal* (New York: Dodd, Mead & Company, 1960), Part 3, "Marriage."

Pike, James A., *If You Marry Outside Your Faith* (New York: Harper & Brothers, 1954).

Rainer, Jerome and Julia, *Sexual Pleasure in Marriage* (New York: Julian Messner, Inc., 1959).

Rapoport, Rhona, "The Transition from Engagement to Marriage," *Acta Sociologica*, Vol. 8, Fasc. 1–2, 1964, pp. 36–55.

Sussman, Marvin B., and Lee Burchinal, "Kin Family Network: Unheralded Structure in Current Conceptualizations of Family Functioning," *Marriage and Family Living*, Vol. XXIV, No. 3, August 1962, pp. 231–240.

Vincent, Elizabeth Lee, and Martin, Phyllis C., *Human Psychological Development* (New York: The Ronald Press, 1961), Chapter 11, "Early Adulthood"; and Chapter 12, "Courtship, Marriage and Family Life."

Womble, Dale L., *Foundations for Marriage and Family Relations* (New York: The Macmillan Company, 1966).

Age is not all decay, it is the ripen-
ing, the swelling of fresh life
within, that withers and bursts
the husks.
GEORGE MACDONALD

CHAPTER SEVEN

Beginning families: expectant phase

T he expectant phase of the beginning family starts with the awareness that the wife is pregnant and continues until the birth of the first child. This phase is no longer than nine months, and may be considerably shorter if the woman is already pregnant at marriage. Although short in length the expectant family phase is long on tasks and responsibilities as the married pair concurrently develop their marriage relationship and their roles as parents-to-be.

There are two positions in the beginning family—that of husband and of wife, both maintaining a single basic relationship as a married couple. They are usually in their early twenties, facing the developmental tasks of early adulthood along with those of the family-in-the-making. The developmental crises of this phase are both those involved in intimacy patterns with the spouse, and those inherent in bearing children, which Erikson calls "generativity," (Chapter 2). The major family goal of this phase is adjusting to pregnancy. How husband and wife feel about their new roles as parents-to-be varies greatly.

There is no one pattern of response when she misses her first menstrual period. Rather there are four possible reactions: (1) they both accept the fact that they have become an expectant family, (2) they both reject the baby months before he/she is due, (3) the husband accepts the pregnancy while the wife does not, and (4) she is delighted but he grouses about it. The first reaction is most typical today, but the other three reactions are not uncommon.

COMPLEMENTARY AND CONFLICTING DEVELOPMENTAL TASKS DURING PREGNANCY

As the young couple go through the first pregnancy, there are times when their individual tasks complement each other in shared accomplishment as parents-to-be. Just as naturally, there are times when their individual developmental tasks conflict and husband and wife are pulled in opposite directions. Illustrative instances are:

Some Contemporary Developmental Tasks of the Expectant Father	Some Contemporary Developmental Tasks of the Expectant Mother	Complementary and Conflicting Possibilities

Starting a family.
  Planning the first child's arrival.
  Learning what it means to become a father.
  Giving his wife his support through her pregnancy and childbirth.
	Starting a family.
	  Planning the first child's arrival.
	  Learning what it means to be a mother.
	  Proceeding successfully through the pregnancy and childbirth experience.
		Complementary (both work together in the common task of becoming parents for the first time).

Becoming a man in a man's world.
  Finding himself among his fellow workers and male colleagues.
  Taking jeers and taunts of other men good naturedly as his wife's condition becomes apparent.
  Continuing some activities with "the boys" that do not include their wives necessarily.
	Becoming a woman in a woman's world.
	  Identifying with her women friends and neighbors in personal special female ways.
	  Participating in baby showers and other "women only" affairs.
	  Borrowing and lending, sharing and being shared within the feminine fellowship of her relationship with "the girls."
		Conflicting (the husband is pulled into male circles and his wife is being absorbed in feminine interests and functions).

Being responsible as the main support of the family.
  Getting to work on time.
  Carrying a full load as a breadwinner.
	Seeing her chief jobs as mother-to-be as well as wife.
	  Letting up on her outside interests as the pregnancy advances.
	  Becoming content to be wife and mother primarily.
		Complementary (common task of nest-building).
		
		Conflicting (he is pulled outward, and she is pulled inward in her childbearing.

DEVELOPMENTAL TASKS OF THE EXPECTANT FAMILY

The developmental tasks of the expectant family arise in the biological reality of gestation, the cultural images of appropriate parenting roles, and the individual aspirations that both father-to-be and mother-to-be bring to their first experience in parenthood. The developmental tasks of this period in the family life cycle cannot be denied. They are peculiarly urgent and insistent. Whether the potential mother and father are ready or not, the pregnancy will come to term in the usual nine months. If the married couple is to make a comfortable adjustment to pregnancy, and to have their first baby with more of a sense of fulfillment than of distress, they must accomplish a number of developmental tasks that are particularly relevant to this stage in the family life cycle. These are in brief summary:

1) arranging for the physical care of the expected baby
2) developing new patterns for getting and spending income
3) revaluating procedures for determining who does what and where authority rests
4) adapting patterns of sexual relationships to pregnancy
5) expanding communication systems for present and anticipated emotional needs
6) reorienting relationships with relatives
7) adapting relationships with friends, associates, and community activities to the realities of pregnancy
8) acquiring knowledge about and planning for the specifics of pregnancy, childbirth, and parenthood
9) maintaining morale and a workable philosophy of life

ARRANGING FOR THE PHYSICAL CARE OF THE EXPECTED BABY

No one has to teach birds their nesting rites and responsibilities. Their instincts guide them through the whole process. Not so with humans. They must learn their nesting tasks, step by step through the expectant phase.

Some husbands and wives take the coming of their first baby casually and do very little in providing a place for it before its arrival. The story is told of the young parents who simply dumped the contents of a dresser drawer in a box and plopped the new baby in the drawer which served as a bed until the infant was big enough to sleep with its brothers. A maternity hospital reports that occasionally a baby arrives with no clothes to wear, no blankets, and no home to go to. But this is not the usual story, especially for the first baby. Later siblings may "make do" with provisions dating back to the arrival of their elder brothers and sisters. But some special provision is usually made for the first baby.

There are young couples who must make drastic shifts in their housing in order to make way for the expected first baby. Many modern apartment houses rule against children. A married couple whose first home has been in such a building must search out a more hospitable home base before their baby arrives. The husband and wife who have been floating from place to place in a series of rented rooms now want to settle down in something more permanent because of the expected arrival of their first baby. The couple who has found satisfaction in living with one set of parents, quite likely now desire to find a place of their own when they expect to become three. There are couples who must find something less expensive than they have been enjoying in housing as soon as a baby is expected. Even more numerous are the young families-in-the-making who move to more desirable neighborhoods, sensing the importance of suitable neighbors, congenial companions, adequate play space, and good schools.

The husband and wife who stay on where they have been living make some rearrangements in their living space when a baby is expected. Room is cleared and provided for the baby's sleeping, eating, bathing, and playing. This may be a separate nursery complete with new baby furniture and sundry equipment. Or it may be a corner that is equipped for baby care, away from the main household traffic. The differences in spatial arrangements are not important as long as husband and wife see eye to eye on them. Trouble comes when the definition of the demands of expectant parenthood differs greatly between the husband and wife.

The most frequent problem arising in reorganizing the household for the first baby is that of the wife wanting more elaborate preparations and expensive rearrangements than the husband deems necessary. The wife who wants to move to a new place that she considers much more suitable for them now that the baby is on the way may be distressed that her husband flatly balks or obviously does not share her enthusiasm for the shift. When her husband fails to back up her plans for the new family home, she may feel that he is rejecting not only her ideas, but her and the baby as well. The man defines the situation from his point of view as husband quite differently at times. As a man, he may tend to feel that his wife's plans are so much feminine falderal. As the principal breadwinner, he is aware of the new responsibilities that will fall on him as father and so is reluctant to undertake any unnecessary expenditures. How the two resolve their dilemma is dependent in part upon how well they achieve the other developmental tasks they face as expectant parents.

DEVELOPING NEW PATTERNS FOR GETTING AND SPENDING INCOME

"It isn't the initial cost, it's the upkeep" that mounts in having a baby. The cost of having a baby was relatively low in the days when a family's children were born in the master bedroom with only the family doctor, midwife, neighbor, or female member of the family in attendance. Today most babies are born in hospitals where the initial costs necessarily are higher, even for low-income families. The cost of rearing a child to maturity was relatively low in the days when the family home was on the farm where food and clothing were made or raised and one more mouth to feed made little economic difference. In contrast, since the Industrial Revolution, rearing a child has become a costly investment for a family. One careful study shows clearly that in families with annual incomes averaging $2,500, the cost of raising a child to maturity was $7,766 in 1935–36 price levels. Families with annual incomes in the $5,000 to $10,000 bracket spent on the average $16,337 on each child raised to 18 years of age.[1] In present-day figures these amounts would be considerably greater, as of course would be the family incomes. Proportionally, the cost of having a child now is a considerable investment by the family —not only for the bare essentials but also for what is involved in education, recreation, transportation, culture, medical care, and all the "sundries" purchased over the years.

The costs of rearing a child do not descend upon the new family all at once, but their anticipation may. Many a young wife makes her first visit to the physician to ascertain whether or not she is pregnant. She returns not only with the happy news that a baby is on the way but also with the dismaying array of costs that have been outlined for her: the doctor, the use of the delivery room, the bed she will occupy for

[1] Louis I. Dublin, and Alfred J. Lotka, *The Money Value of Man* (New York: The Ronald Press Company, Revised Edition, 1946), page 55.

her lying-in period, recommended nursing service, and all the rest. She may stop in at a baby shop on her way home and be further impressed with the amount of money charged for the tiny garments that go into making up the layette. Not knowing whether hers will be a girl or a boy, she fingers little dresses and is startled to realize they cost almost as much as a dress for herself, while clothing for little boys is priced nearly as high as her husband's items. By the time she and her husband get their pencils out to figure what it will cost to have the baby, they are sobered by the realization that family expenses from now on will be higher.

Actually costs of having a baby differ widely. Therefore, it is wise to ascertain exactly what financial responsibility the couple is assuming for the various services for which they are contracting. During the first or second visit, the expectant mother may discuss with the doctor his fee for seeing her through pregnancy and the birth of the baby. Specific arrangements should be made with the hospital to take care of the minimal costs of the delivery, as well as the probable "extras" that may be needed. Inquiries may be made as to the need for nursing service beyond what the hospital normally provides. Help for the new mother and baby upon their return from the hospital may be provided by one of the new grandmothers, or by hiring a practical nurse for awhile. The total anticipated sum may be apportioned into a monthly baby fund that assures the new family of "cash on delivery."

Something of a jolt comes when the couple realizes that with the coming of the first baby, the wife's income will stop and the family will have to live on the husband's income alone. Today, many young wives work[1] until the first baby is about to arrive and then drop out of gainful employment until the children are old enough so that fulltime mothering is no longer necessary. Some couples are smart enough to anticipate the decrease in the family income when the wife no longer contributes her earnings to it. These couples live on the husband's income from the beginning, saving wife's earnings against the time when there will be need for special outlay for a baby, a car, a down payment on a home, furniture, and other equipment. The husband and wife who have been living up all their joint income while both were working get

[1] Betty S. Martin, *Working Wives . . . Who Are They?* New York: Women's Division, Institute of Life Insurance, January, 1962, p. 1; Lois Meek Stolz, "Effects of Maternal Employment on Children: Evidence from Research," *Child Development,* Vol. 31, 1960, pp. 749–782; and National Manpower Commission, *Work in the Lives of Married Women.* New York: Columbia University Press, 1958.

a shock, when suddenly, with the coming of the first baby, they must live on only one set of earnings at the very time that they face big increases in their expenditures.

Difficult too are the tasks of the young couple facing pregnancy early in the marriage, before there has been time to accumulate a backlog of savings or even to meet the initial costs of being married.

Insurance plans help defray the initial costs of childbirth. David Treat reports that in Flint, Michigan, Blue Cross pays for three-fourths of all births.[1] Life insurance now becomes a necessity as never before. As long as both the husband and wife were working and able to work, life insurance might or might not have been an item to consider. Now, with a baby on the way, a woman needs and will continue to need the protection of life insurance on the husband until the childrearing period is over.

Savings take on more meaning when children appear in the family. Starting a savings account for the children's education, for the medical expenses, and for the other needs that are inevitable in the expanding stage of the family life cycle makes sense to young husband and wife as never before.

Where is all the money coming from for initial costs of having the baby, its upkeep through the years, the many new needs as a family, the insurance, the savings, and all the rest at the very time that the wife stops work to give her time entirely to having and raising children? The answer varies from couple to couple, from social class to social class.

Depending upon its orientation, resources, and values, the young family may decide from among a variety of solutions to their financial problems. The young family may float a loan, or dip into savings, or look to their parents for help, or go into debt or into an orgy of installment buying. But whatever it does, the decision is there to be made in the beginning stage of the family life cycle.

REVALUATING PROCEDURES FOR DETERMINING WHO DOES WHAT AND WHERE AUTHORITY RESTS

Today's young mother-to-be assumes a multiplicity of roles. She carries on the responsibilities of her household; she works as long as her physician allows throughout the pregnancy; she is at home in classroom and

[1] David B. Treat, Director, The Clara Elizabeth Fund for Maternal Health, Flint, Michigan, personal communication, June 27, 1956.

laboratory as she tries to finish her education before maternity is upon her; she is found in her smart maternity garments as hostess or playmate along with her husband at neighborhood gatherings in the companionship roles so important today. Any one of these roles has been a full-time job for some woman in the past—housewife, worker, mother-to-be, school-girl, hostess-companion. The modern young woman carries them all, with the help of her husband.

Now that men have a reasonably short working week (as compared with the 60 or more hours in the nineteenth-century work week), they have more time at home. Household tasks in the modern home, with its electrified equipment and packaged goods, are less arduous, more fun, and require less technical knowledge. Any man who wants to can whip up a tasty meal in today's kitchen. And many of them do. Now with wives out of the home carrying the variety of roles characteristic of modern woman, husbands are finding a new place for themselves in the family.

During the first trimester of pregnancy when many expectant mothers feel nauseated upon awakening in the morning, a husband may get breakfast and bring his wife something to eat that will ease the discomfort of her arising, before he leaves for work. During pregnancy, heavy mopping and cleaning may be forbidden the pregnant woman by her doctor; her figure enlarges making stooping over uncomfortable and so other tasks may be reassigned the husband. By the time the first baby is born many couples have rearranged their previous definitions of who does what to make way for the new roles and realities of parenthood.

Outsiders become a new source of authority in many an expectant family's home. What the doctor has prescribed or proscribed is taken as law, more conscientiously now than it will be for further pregnancies, in many homes. The elder women of the family may come into the picture in many ways that are threatening to the authority of the young husband. One of the hazards of this phase of family living lies in the ego-shattering experience he goes through in being low man in the hierarchy of influence in his own home:

It's foolish I know, but I'm jealous of my own obstetrician.

I hate to admit that I don't know all there is to know, but frankly, I'm lost with all this gobbledegook the wife talks over with the Doc.

Many young couples make their first trip to the obstetrician or family doctor together. There they bring up as a couple the questions they want answered and together establish the relationship with the doctor that makes carrying out the prescribed regimen of pregnancy and birth a cooperative enterprise in which doctor, wife, and husband participate. Such a mutual assumption of responsibility provides effective ways of achieving the developmental tasks involved for the couple and is to be recommended wherever possible.

ADAPTING PATTERNS OF SEXUAL RELATIONSHIPS TO PREGNANCY

When a woman becomes pregnant there are obvious changes in her body that remind both her and her husband that she is something much more than just a sexual being for the pleasures of marriage. One of the first of these changes is the filling out of her breasts early in pregnancy. In recent generations, a woman's breasts have become powerful sex symbols, almost to the point of fetishism.[1] In premarital petting, as well as during the foreplay in marriage, love-play involving the breasts is prominent in heterosexual lovemaking. But with the rounding out of the mammary glands in pregnancy, comes the realization that these organs are soon to be shared with the little newcomer already on the way. For some husbands this means an abrupt change in types of sex play. As the pregnancy progresses, both husband and wife shift earlier patterns of sexual relationships to accommodate to the realities of the physical situation. They may or may not adversely effect the sexual relationship of the marriage.

One study of married college students indicates that for the majority, pregnancy has no effect on the sexual relationship, about one in four report unfavorable effects, and nearly one in every five husbands and wives find pregnancy effecting their sex adjustment for the better, as is shown in Table 13.

Wives generally report that their husbands are more thoughtful and considerate during pregnancy than they were before with such comments as these usual:

He became more affectionate and closer to me.

More gentle in manner and speech.

[1] Betsy Marvin McKinney, "The Sexual Aspects of Breast Feeding," *Child-Family Digest*, 5320 Danneel Street, New Orleans, La., December 1955, pp. 45–57.

He babied me a lot especially towards the last part of pregnancy.

He thought and acted as if I were now a woman, no longer a child.[1]

TABLE 12. *Percentages of Husbands and Wives Reporting How First Pregnancy Affected Their Sexual Adjustment* [2]

Reported Effect	Per cent of Husbands Reporting	Per cent of Wives Reporting
No effect	58	58
Unfavorable	23	25
Favorable	19	17
	100	100

Both husband and wife tend to report decreasing sexual desire as the pregnancy progresses, suggesting that both men and women are influenced by psychological as well as physiological factors during the expectant period, at least among married college students. There is a strong tendency for husbands to identify with their wives during the first pregnancy. Such a spirit is evident in the young father-to-be who says, "We are pregnant at our house." When both husband and wife can jointly accept the pregnancy in this way, the husband suffers less of the sense of deprivation of sexual response from and access to his wife when it becomes indicated as the pregnancy progresses. Reasons for stopping sexual intercourse during pregnancy are several, with physician's advice against it most common (usually in the last six weeks of pregnancy—see Table 13).

In general, couples who have a mutually satisfying sex life before pregnancy make a good sex adjustment during pregnancy.

EXPANDING COMMUNICATION SYSTEMS FOR PRESENT AND ANTICIPATED EMOTIONAL CONSTELLATIONS

Pregnancy is an emotional adventure for most couples. Long before the baby actually arrives fantasy makes him a member of the family.

[1] Adapted from Judson T. Landis, Thomas Poffenberger and Shirley Poffenberger, "The Effects of First Pregnancy upon the Sexual Adjustment of 212 Couples," *American Sociological Review,* Vol. 15, No. 6, December 1950, pp. 767–772.
[2] *Ibid.* p. 770.

TABLE 13. *Percentages of Husbands and Wives Giving Reasons for Cessation of Sexual Intercourse during Pregnancy* [1]

Reasons	Wives (N = 184) *	Husbands (N = 191) †
Doctor ordered it	38.0%	29.9%
Painful for wife	16.5	18.3
Fear of hurting baby	15.6	18.8
I didn't enjoy it	14.6	3.2
Fear of miscarriage	5.4	9.9
Nauseated wife	4.4	2.6
It didn't seem right	3.3	6.8
Spouse didn't enjoy it	2.2	10.5

* Wives, 28 no response.
† Husbands, 21 no response (some gave multiple responses).

One young husband set a place at the table for the baby: cup, plate, spoon, and high chair, as soon as the doctor confirmed the pregnancy. His wife interpreted, "He's crazy just a little, but you see we've waited for seven long years. I've dreamt about his sitting there at the table too."

Fears of "going through the shadow of death" still haunt an occasional expectant mother. Although the dangers of childbearing are dramatically less now than a generation or two ago, the memory lingers on. As one experienced gynecologist observes:

Young people still reflect the association of childbearing with illness: the doctor, the nurse, many days of hospitalization, infants in the sterile nursery —all fear-inducing thoughts.

. . . The morbidity which resulted from the poor obstetrics of years ago was very real. There was reason enough for fear. Lacerations which were unrepaired from one pregnancy to another resulted in cystoceles, prolapse, and relaxed vaginal canals. Intercourse was painful when the tears were left to heal spontaneously. The profuse leucorrheal discharges from lacerated or infected cervices overlubricated the vaginal canal. In many, repeated deliveries occurring so rapidly that the patient hadn't recovered from one before the next pregnancy was started, resulted in very flabby, large vaginal canals. All these factors prevented many husbands and wives from enjoying intercourse after the first pregnancy. In addition to the poor approximation of the sex organs, the wife lacked desire for coitus. She was either pregnant, nursing, or in pain.[2]

[1] *Ibid.* p. 771.
[2] Nadina R. Kavinoky, "Marital Adjustments During Pregnancy and the Year After," *Medical Woman's Journal*, October 1949, pp. 1–2.

The expectant fathers' pacing room in today's maternity hospital occasionally reflects many second-hand memories locked in the minds of impressionable boys until the time when they become fathers themselves. These hand-me-down memories are prime forces in making a man feel guilty about his wife's pregnancy and childbirth. As one young expectant father put it, "If she comes through this OK, I swear, I'll never get her pregnant again." Even before the actual birth a man may be haunted by anxieties, uncertainties, and guilts:

I feel so guilty seeing her so miserable mornings, and knowing that I got her into this, and that the worst is yet to come too.

Is it normal to be so blamed scared? I get so worried about what might happen that I'm not even pleasant around the house . . . what if she has a miscarriage? what if she has the baby before I can get her to the hospital? what if she has to have a Caesarean?

Pride over his proven virility, satisfaction in his wife's prenatal care and progress, plans for his child's future, and the sense of fulfillment as fatherhood approaches are but a few of the positive emotions that the expectant father needs to learn to express. One of his developmental tasks involves developing the channels for communicating both the negative and the positive feelings that have their genesis in his first experience as a father-to-be.

Some men and women learn to express their feelings about the pregnancy, about the birth experience, and about their forthcoming relationship with their first child relatively easily. These are usually the persons whose positive acceptance of their roles as men and women overweighs their negative feelings. An investigation of the way new mothers feel about menstruation, pregnancy, childbirth, breast feeding, rooming-in, and satisfaction with woman's role in life, indicates that women who complain about pregnancy, childbirth, and breast feeding tend to be those who find it hard to accept their feminine role in life.[1]

Now, when many women attempt to carry a number of responsibilities concurrently (home, school, work, etc.), problems over conflicting roles may be expected. A study of young wives of married students reports,

Those wives who were enrolled in school or employed outside the home were to a greater extent represented among those wives who had tried to

---

[1] Niles Newton, *Maternal Emotions* (Philadelphia: Paul Hoeber, 1955).

avoid pregnancy than were those wives whose role was confined to home-making alone. The latter were more represented among the wives who planned their pregnancies. This relationship suggests that scholarly pursuits or a vocation outside the home may influence plans for children in the early period of marriage. The comments of wives whose pregnancies interrupted the completion of a college degree were more often indicative of deep regret than were those of working wives whose remarks for the most part reflected their willingness to quit wage-earning and be full-time homemakers.[1]

Clinical as well as statistical evidence indicates that those young wives and husbands who most comfortably achieve the developmental task of getting through to each other on the decisional and emotional realities of pregnancy and childbirth are those who have already accomplished previous developmental tasks of accepting feminine or masculine sex roles and so are ready for the experience of parenthood.

When the multiple roles of the sexes are as flexible as they are today, some problems in defining them are inevitable. To the extent to which the two people can learn to establish the communication systems necessary for making the decisions and handling the feelings involved in having a baby, and learning to be parents, to that extent will they find their new roles with confidence.

REORIENTING RELATIONSHIPS WITH RELATIVES

For every new baby born there is not only a new mother and a new father, but also new grandparents, new aunts and uncles, and many other new constellations in the family circle. Mothers and mothers-in-law who have been relatively successful in "keeping hands off" the new couple during their honeymoon and establishment periods feel more closely involved with the new household as soon as a baby is expected.

Relatives sometimes vie with each other in showering gifts for the new baby upon the expectant parents. These often reflect their own unfulfilled desires rather than the needs of the baby. Even more hazardous are the tales of their own experiences in childbearing with the well-meaning advice that too often is in conflict with that of the attending physician.

There is a positive side to the picture. Nowadays when nurses are hard to come by, and the new mother and tiny baby return from the

[1] Shirley Poffenberger, Thomas Poffenberger, and Judson T. Landis, "Intent Toward Conception and the Pregnancy Experience," *American Sociological Review*, Vol. 17, No. 5, October 1952, p. 617.

The expectant husband and wife who learn to establish good communication systems for making the decisions and handling the feelings involved in becoming parents, find their new roles with confidence.

hospital soon after the birth, a young couple is fortunate in having the willing hands of a mother or mother-in-law to help them through the lying-in period until the young mother can fully take over. A recent study turned up many appreciative comments:

When our daughter was born, who but Mom-in-law would have come and stayed to cook, clean, care for a baby and mother, keep a household running smoothly, and yet have unbounded love and sheer joy in doing all this? (*Mrs. M., Indiana.*)

Last month we added a daughter to our family and we asked Tom's Mom to lend us a helping hand for a while. She immediately took a month's leave of absence from her work and home duties, to give us her time during the busiest of everyone's life—the Holiday Season. (*Mrs. T., Indiana.*)

When my child was born my own mother could not be with me and although my mother-in-law, who is in business for herself and finds it hard to get away, was at time needed at home, she came to me and saw me through it all. (*Mrs. J., Illinois.*)

My husband and I have been married five and a half years. At first I resented my mother-in-law. Our first baby was born a year after we were married. She came five hundred miles to help care for me and the baby. (*Mrs. L., Kansas.*) [1]

Reorienting relationships with relatives of both sides of the family is an important developmental task during the expectant phase. Its success contributes a sense of accord and belonging to the parents-to-be, and paves the way for many helpful mutually supportive relationships in the years to come. Grandparents and other relatives can be liabilities or assets to the young family, depending in large part upon the accomplishment of this developmental task before the first child arrives.

ADAPTING RELATIONSHIPS WITH FRIENDS, ASSOCIATES, AND COMMUNITY ACTIVITIES TO THE REALITIES OF PREGNANCY

As the pregnancy progresses the recreational and social life of the couple has to be readapted to the realities of the situation. Some activities are sharply curtailed, and others stop altogether, while a regimen more suitable for the expectant mother is put into effect. Instead of gay nights out on the town, the couple may find more of their evenings given to a game of cards with old friends, or taking walks together, or reading aloud some of the current literature on bringing up Baby.

Some couples find such adaptive procedures difficult. This one did, who says, "He just does not dare go north fishing while I'm carrying this baby for him. If he does, I'll—I'll leave him and he knows I'm not fooling." Or this one, a young veteran reflects, "You have to grow up fast when you get out of the Army and your wife is pregnant, and you aren't through school yet. I almost lost my wife in the process. She went back home to her mother and our son was two months old before I even saw him. We finally got together as a family again, but we almost didn't make it."

If the wife's insecurity in her pregnancy makes her jealous of her husband's night out with the boys, or his bowling league, or his educational and vocational projects, or any of his leisure-time pursuits that are not specifically related to the pregnancy, something will have to give. The husband may give in and defer to his wife through the period. Or, the wife may weather it on her own with either immature resentment or determination to grow up and be a woman through it all. Usu-

[1] Evelyn Millis Duvall, *In-Laws: Pro and Con* (New York: Association Press, 1954), pp. 94–95.

ally outside loyalties and involvements with friends, and associates, tend to drop off in importance as the pregnancy progresses. They possibly will never return to their former state. For with parenthood comes even more confining days and nights.

New associations become a part of the expectant phase as the young mother-to-be is inducted into the women's clubs and organizations for which her new status makes her eligible. She may attend expectant mothers' classes or join a sewing circle where she will have congenial companionship while she makes maternity clothes and the wee garments for the layette. In general, she is now drawn more into feminine association than before. And if she has learned to enjoy being a woman, she will like the new woman's world that her baby and she enter together.

The hazard lies in the husband's being left out of it all as the pregnancy continues. His wife, who before shared everything with him, now shares her physical problems with the doctor and her practical plans for the baby with friends whose personal experience parallels hers. Baby showers are given for HER to which HE is not invited. If he puts on his hat and coat and goes out for the evening, it is understandable. It takes a wise young husband and wife to work out a mutually acceptable social life that gives each of them freedom for the associations that are most personally meaningful, at the same time that they pursue enough joint activities to continue to enjoy life as a couple. A comfortable balance of their individual autonomy and integration as a couple forms a basis for their life together for the years ahead.

ACQUIRING KNOWLEDGE ABOUT AND PLANNING FOR THE SPECIFICS OF PREGNANCY, CHILDBIRTH, AND PARENTHOOD

The old taboos about refusing to talk about sex and reproduction have broken down in recent decades. Today a husband and wife facing their first pregnancy want to know what is happening, and they both are learning to put their questions into words. This is harder for some than for others; more difficult for men than for women, perhaps, but it is being done.

One of the reasons why men find their wife's first pregnancy difficult is that in the areas of sex and reproduction a man hates to admit that he doesn't know all there is to be known. Up to now we have been rearing our sons that way. Parents tell sons less about reproduction than they tell daughters. The earthy and vulgar jokes about sex and

The Men's Forum of the Clara Elizabeth Fund for Maternal Health in Flint, Michigan, considers expectant fathers' questions under the professional leadership of William Genné.

pregnancy of locker room and tavern are difficult to reconcile with the tenderness a man feels for his wife when she feels miserable in her pregnancy. Didn't he "get her that way?" Along with the pride he feels over his proven virility is more than a little guilt that he is causing her distress.

Recent advances in genetics, with the unraveling of the mystery of life programmed into the DNA and RNA molecules of the genes of living cells, make inheritance a personal mystery story that expectant fathers and mothers can read and discuss.[1] Men as well as women find such materials fascinating especially as they follow the development of their own first child. In many a modern community, classes are available for parents-to-be interested in getting valid answers to their questions. Here are representative expectant fathers' queries:

[1] See Amram Scheinfeld, *Your Heredity and Environment* (Philadelphia: J. B. Lippincott Company, 1965).

Who is responsible for the sex of our baby?

How is the baby fed before he's born?

Is my reproductive system as complicated as my wife's?

Why are some babies marked?

Can childbirth be easier because there isn't fear and tension?

Are twins hereditary?

What is the rabbit test?

When can there be sexual relations during pregnancy?

Why are doctors letting women get up so early after childbirth?

How long does a woman have to be in labor?

What does it cost in dollars to have a baby?[1]

Meanwhile, an expectant mother is getting answers to her questions from her doctor, the prenatal clinic, or the preparation for motherhood classes she attends. She wants to understand the normal process of bearing and giving birth to a child. She wants to know how she can best cooperate in what she eats, what she does, and how she feels about it.

Social class differences in the expectant phase are many. In general, members of the middle and upper classes seek out more earnestly, take more seriously, and follow more conscientiously the advice of physicians and other experts than do members of the lower class, for whom childbearing tends to be taken for granted as another part of life to be endured. A recent comparative study of 401 women pregnant for the first time concludes that women of higher intelligence and higher social status tend to (1) be more careful in planning their first pregnancy and adjusting to it, (2) have better diet, (3) be more eager to breast-feed the baby, and (4) use birth control more effectively than do mothers of the lower classes. [2]

The middle- or upper-class woman may bombard her doctor with questions about his plans for her delivery, his preference for anesthetic, his opinion of "natural childbirth," rooming-in, and breast-feeding. She

[1] David Treat in "Preliminary Report, Committee on Dynamics of Family Interaction," Evelyn Duvall and Reuben Hill, eds., Washington, D. C., National Conference on Family Life, 1948, p. 18.

[2] D. Baird and Eileen Scott, "Intelligence and Childbearing," *Eugenic Review*, Vol. 45, 1953, pp. 139–154.

Expectant mothers get answers to their questions from the preparation for motherhood classes they attend, sometimes in the hospital where the deliveries will take place.

may need to be reassured about the possibilities of birth anomalies, or the incidence of trouble with incompatability of *Rh* blood types in pregnancy, or any of the other difficulties with which she has had some personal or vicarious experience.

If anything happens and she loses this first baby, she needs more help than ever. Disappointed potential motherhood can be a terrifying thing, even if she is assured that she can have another baby someday. If the couple faces the possibility of remaining childless, they must come to terms with what they are going to do about it.

Adoption is a possibility some husbands and wives consider if they find that they cannot have children of their own. One study indicates that 89 per cent of a college population (93.7 per cent of the women, and 84.7 per cent of the men) would be willing to adopt a child if they could have none of their own.[1] Child-placing agencies have re-

[1] Lemo D. Rockwood and Mary E. N. Ford, *Youth, Marriage and Parenthood* (New York: John Wiley and Sons, Inc., 1945), p. 156.

quirements that protect the baby, its mother, and its adoptive parents. Between 90,000 and 100,000 children are adopted annually in the United States. The majority are adopted by persons not related to them, Table 14.

TABLE 14. *How America's Children Are Adopted—*
By Percentage of Placements

Adopted by relatives		48%
Adopted by non-relatives		52%
Placed by social agencies	61%	
Placed independently	39%	

SOURCE: 1960 White House Conference on Children and Youth, *Children in a Changing World*, Chart 40, "Social Agencies Protect Children Who Are Being Adopted," page 46.

Communities provide a variety of services for adopting children. Medical, legal, and social services to the natural parents, especially the unmarried mother, the adoptive parents, and the child himself, as well as legislation specifying procedures for adopting children are included.[1]

MAINTAINING MORALE AND A WORKABLE PHILOSOPHY OF LIFE

Husband and wife expectant for the first time face the developmental task of rewarding each other for their achievements, and satisfying critical needs for acceptance, encouragement and affection during the pregnancy period. The expectant mother may wake up miserable through the first trimester, and feel big and misshapen during the latter part of her pregnancy. Then she has especial need for her husband's reassurance of his devotion and of his eagerness for the baby. As the father-to-be feels pushed out and yet terribly responsible for her condition and for the support of the family in the making, he too requires understanding and emotional support.

At few other times in the whole life cycle do men and women become more self-conscious about such questions as: Who are we? What is our way of life? Is this the kind of life we want to bring our children up in? What kind of parents will we be? What can we do to make ourselves the persons our children can be proud of? In this sense the expectant phase is a critical period in the life of the couple. For it means that the life style is now seen not only through the eyes of each of the pair as persons or from the point of view of the couple, but also from the viewpoint of the unborn generation, their children. This testing, evaluating, and maintaining of a workable philosophy of life runs through all other decisions and developmental tasks of the period. The beginning family successful in achieving this task is well on the way to family integration and a sense of identity upon which future periods and stages may be built.

HAZARDS AND DIFFICULTIES FACING THE FAMILY IN THE EXPECTANT PHASE

The danger of losing the wife and mother in childbirth is now dramatically less than it has been in earlier decades as we see clearly in Chart 11. Former hazards in childbearing have been greatly reduced by the increase in the number of births in hospitals, advances in medical knowledge and maternal care, as well as increases in prenatal services.

Despite the great decline in maternal mortality there still remain

CHART 11. Decrease in Maternal Mortality 1930–1965 [1]
(Maternal Deaths per 10,000 Live Births)

[1] Compiled from Metropolitan Life Insurance Company, *Statistical Bulletin*, June 1947, p. 5; July 1951, p. 2; and February 1954, pp. 8, 9; and National Center for Health Statistics, Washington, D. C., personal communication, July 28, 1966.

difficulties and problems of the expectant family that may be summarized briefly as follows:

PRESENT-DAY DIFFICULTIES OF THE EXPECTANT FAMILY

1) Modern housing must be drastically adapted for the coming of the first baby. Many places do not allow children, others have inadequate facilities for babies and so major rearrangements for coming of children must be made.

2) Double family income shrinks to one at a time when costs balloon. Wife drops out of work to have and raise her baby at a time when expenditures rise rapidly, putting strains on the family budget, and necessitating careful financial and family planning.

3) Husband or wife is not ready to assume new role as parent-to-be. Immature husband cannot accept sharing wife or adapt to changes in schedule too well. Infantile wife is not ready to settle down and have a family.

4) There is an increase in emotional instability in early pregnancy. ". . . wives as a whole experienced some heightened emotional tension in the early part of pregnancy as compared with their previous emotional stability." [1]

5) Married couples often are isolated from the supporting help of parental families. Modern marriages are often established far from families of orientation making it more difficult for members of the family to rally their resources and services to aid the new family at the birth of the baby.

6) Ignorance and superstition increase the difficulties of being expectant parents. Fallacies and current fictions about pregnancy, reproduction, and childbirth confuse the husband and wife and make their following healthful regimens more difficult.

7) There is fear of labor and childbirth experience. "Some anxiety is generally experienced" is the conclusion of one study of married college students in which 63.2 per cent of the wives studied indicated they feared the labor and childbirth. [2]

8) The pregnancy is unplanned and the baby unwanted. Difficulties occur in working through the developmental tasks of the period and accepting the baby when it comes.

[1] Shirley Poffenberger et al., op. cit., p. 618.
[2] Ibid., p. 620.

RESOURCES AND SERVICES FOR EXPECTANT FAMILIES

Preparation for parenthood begins in childhood. As boys and girls are brought up by parents who want children, who love them, and who let them know it, they get a good feeling about having children that strongly influences their own attitudes toward parenthood. As children have their questions answered by their parents, teachers, and leaders in an ongoing integrated program of sex education, they are not as influenced by unfounded fears, superstitions, and ignorance and are better prepared for pregnancy, childbirth, and parenthood. Classes in preparation for marriage give both man and woman some idea of what to expect in marriage and family life as well as a chance to clarify their values and develop the positive attitudes that go a long way toward paving the way for the realities of living together as a family.

As the period of expectant parenthood approaches there are specific services available in some communities that help beginning families accomplish their developmental tasks. In Flint, Michigan, where series of classes for expectant parents (both husbands and wives) have been held continuously since January 1939, records show that women are now seeking medical care earlier in their pregnancies than was formerly the case. The emphasis of the classes ("You need early, regular, and complete obstetrical care") frequently sends a pregnant woman to her doctor much earlier than she would otherwise have gone. Once she is under professional guidance, and in the classes for expectant mothers, her emotional health as well as her physical condition improves.

It is easier to accept the physical inconveniences that go with pregnancy if there are from a dozen to fifty others in class in various stages of expectancy who have, or will have experiences paralleling one's own. Just to see that many women together who are listening to an explanation of childbirth, makes childbearing seem to be the very normal experience it is.

Many a man enjoys the celebration with cigars that accompanies the announcement, "It's a boy! Hey, Fellows! He's a boy!" And he may be quite as proud of being responsible for the pregnancy. Privately he confides to her, "By golly, Sweetheart, I am all right, I can start a baby." Even while publicly he shuns the kidding of his fellow office workers or the men on the assembly line at the plant.

The expectant father goes to Fathers' Forum a bit sheepishly and finds to his surprise that there are more than thirty-five other men there. Perhaps the fellow in the shop with whom he eats lunch is also "expecting." The informal discussion that starts out about understanding a wife's tears and occasional temper outbursts leads the fellow in the seat ahead of him to exclaim, "Tell you what I do when my wife blows her top—I just keep my hat near the door." Whereupon another fellow blurts out, "Keep your hat near the door? Hell! I keep mine on my head." The roar of understanding laughter rips the last shred of tension away as three dozen men realize that they individually are going through some of the same experiences in trying to understand the emotional disturbances that often accompany pregnancy. So it goes, too, for answering their inevitable questions about what is happening in pregnancy and what their roles as husbands and fathers are.[1]

Modern obstetrics, nursing, and hospital care now more frequently take into account the emotional and familial factors of having a baby that, in older more rigid systems, unnecessarily increased the woman's panic in childbirth. Her physician now wins her confidence not only in his skill, but also in herself as a woman who understands what is happening. He instructs her on how to cooperate in a comfortable pregnancy and a good delivery.[2] The nurse who sees her patient not just as another light to be answered, but as a flesh-and-blood person with feelings to be considered and new responsibilities to learn, can be very helpful in giving the support that is needed during labor. She offers instruction that may be needed to get breast-feeding off to a good start and baby and mother comfortable in each other's company.

Films on the progress of pregnancy, prenatal development and care, the nature of labor, the birth of a baby, and postnatal care are used widely by many agencies, i.e., the Louisiana Association for Mental Health, and the American Institute of Family Relations' series on Parentcraft (for Husbands and Wives Who Are Expecting). The Dickinson-Belskie models of prenatal development and childbirth are extensively used, as are also a wide assortment of books and pamphlets on marriage, family relations, and the specific aspects of beginning families of greatest interest to parents-to-be.

Young couples themselves are ingenious in innovating ways of helping each other through expectant parenthood. One consumers' cooperative

[1] David Treat, op. cit., pp. 16–18.
[2] Nadina R. Kavinoky, op. cit., p. 5.

The Dickinson-Belskie models of prenatal development and childbirth are effectively used in classes for expectant parents.

has a clearing house for the exchange of maternity garments and infant furnishings by which these expensive items can be loaned from one expectant family to another with only the repair, cleaning, and replenishing costs involved for any one family. Other neighbors get together in their planning of social activities that fit the needs of young families. Potluck suppers, beach parties, community sings, and evenings around a campfire take the place of the dancing and night-clubbing that once occupied the same younger set in their courting and early marriage days. Now they are "settling down" to equally enjoyable activities that can carry through the expectant family phase into the childbearing periods just ahead.

We need have no fear that young couples are floored by the developmental tasks and hazards of childbearing. More families are having babies (two or three) today than ever before. Couples expecting their first baby are at the threshold of a great adventure. As they move from being a married couple to becoming a family "with baby makes three," they find new joys and satisfactions out of the successful accomplishment of the new tasks and responsibilities that are inherent in being in the expectant phase of family living.

SUMMARY

The expectant phase of the beginning family stage covers the period of the first pregnancy. It begins with the first awareness that a baby is on the way and carries through to the birth of the first child. There are four possible responses to the knowledge that husband and wife have become an expectant family: (1) they both accept their new status, (2) both reject the pregnancy and the unborn child, (3) he is pleased while she is unhappy about it, and (4) she is delighted but he grouses about it.

Developmental tasks of the expectant family are (1) reorganizing housing arrangements to provide for the expected baby, (2) developing new patterns for getting and spending income, (3) evaluating procedures for determining who does what and where authority rests, (4) adapting patterns of sexual relationships to pregnancy, (5) expanding communication systems for present and anticipated emotional constellations, (6) reorienting relationships with relatives, (7) adapting relationships with friends, associates, and community activities to the realities of pregnancy, (8) acquiring knowledge about and planning for the specifics of pregnancy, childbirth, and parenthood, and (9) testing and maintaining a workable philosophy of life.

In our present-day society the expectant family faces a number of difficulties in the successful accomplishment of its various developmental tasks. Promising new services and greatly improved established resources increase the chances of the survival of mother and baby in childbirth and the neonatal period and of the effective achievement of the family developmental tasks during the expectant phase.

SUGGESTED ACTIVITIES

1) Compute the costs of having a baby in your neighborhood on the basis of prevailing rates for the doctor's services, hospital costs, basic layette, infant furnishings, etc.

2) Interview a practicing obstetrician in your community on the common complaints of pregnant women and of women in labor and childbirth, with special emphasis on the kinds of supportive therapy he finds most generally helpful. Relate his experience to what you now know about the developmental tasks of women in first pregnancy and childbirth.

3) Write a paper on "How Well Are We Preparing Youth for Parenthood?" using as references one or more of the following research reports:

   1. Duvall, Evelyn Millis, "What Kind of Parents Will Today's Teen-Agers Be?" *National Parent-Teacher,* Vol. 54, No. 1, September 1959, pp. 4, 5, 6, 36.

   2. English, O. Spurgeon, Max Katz, Albert E. Scheflen, Elliot R. Danzig, and Jeanne B. Speiser, "Preparedness of High School and College Seniors for Parenthood," *A. M. A. Archives of Neurology & Psychiatry,* Vol. 81, No. 4, April 1959, pp. 85/469–96/480.

   3. Remmers, H. H., "Future Parents' Views on Child Management," *Report of Poll No. 53, The Purdue Opinion Panel* (Lafayette, Indiana: Purdue University, 1959).

   4. Walters, James, and Clara Fisher, "Changes in the Attitudes of Young Women Toward Child Guidance over a Two-Year Period," *Journal of Educational Research,* Vol. 52, No. 3, November 1958, pp. 115–118.

4) Review the series of *Pierre the Pelican* bulletins sent to expectant mothers by the Louisiana Association for Mental Health, 1528 Jackson Avenue, New Orleans, 13, Louisiana, on the explicit and implicit hazards and challenges of each trimester of pregnancy.

5) Go through Dickinson and Belskie's *Birth Atlas* (available through the Maternity Center Association, 48 East 92nd Street, New York 28), of photographs of the growth of the fetus and the birth of a baby with an expectant couple with whom you have offered to share the pictures in exchange for the privilege of recording verbatim their questions, page by page. Discuss these questions in terms of what is revealed in the interest in and knowledge about pregnancy, fetal growth, and birth by married men and women typical of the couple you studied.

6) Visit the library of your county medical association or local maternity hospital and list the films, pamphlets, and books available for expectant parents. According to their records, how many individuals availed themselves of these services during the current year? From what social class levels did these expectant parents come? Write an interpretive comment on your findings.

7) Send for *Natural Childbirth* a documentary recording (LP, 53 min.) of childbirth, available from Westminister Recording Sales Corp., 275 Seventh Ave., New York 1, N. Y. The recording was supervised by Dr. Grantly Dick Read, author of *Childbirth Without Fear.* Prepare your group for listening to this record by reading aloud the commentary provided with the recording and written by Aileen Hogan, Consultant in Maternity Nursing, The Maternity Center Association, New York, N. Y. Then, play the recording and allow time for comments and questions. Request papers to be written on reactions to the recording, describing feelings experi-

enced upon hearing the recording and subsequent feelings upon thinking about the recording.

READINGS

Bernstein, Rose, "Unmarried Parents and Their Families," *Child Welfare,* Vol. 45, No. 4, April 1966, pp. 185–193.

Bigelow, Howard F., *Family Finance* (Philadelphia: J. B. Lippincott Company, 1953 Revision), Chap. 16.

Blood, Robert O., Jr., *Anticipating Your Marriage* (Glencoe, Illinois: The Free Press, 1955), Chaps. 15 and 16.

Brown, F. G., and others, *Adoption Principles and Services* (New York: Family Services Association, 1952).

Cady, Ernest and Frances, *How to Adopt a Child* (New York: William Morrow & Co., 1956).

Davis, M. Edward, *Natural Child Spacing* (Garden City, New York: Hanover House, 1953).

Duvall, Evelyn Millis, *In-Laws: Pro and Con* (New York: Association Press, 1954), Chaps. 6 and 16.

Duvall, Evelyn Millis, and Hill, Reuben, *Being Married* (Boston: D. C. Heath and Company, 1960), Chaps. 18 and 19.

Fishbein, Morris, and Burgess, Ernest, eds., *Successful Marriage* (Garden City, New York: Doubleday and Company, Inc., 1955 Revision), Part Three.

Genné, William, *Husbands and Pregnancy: The Handbook for Expectant Fathers* (New York: Association Press, 1956).

Guttmacher, Alan F., *Babies by Choice or by Chance* (Garden City, New York: Doubleday & Company, Inc., 1959).

Herzog, Elizabeth, "Some Notes about Unmarried Fathers," *Child Welfare,* Vol. 45, No. 4, April 1966, pp. 194–197, 235.

Herzog, Elizabeth, "The Chronic Revolution: Births Out of Wedlock," *Clinical Pediatrics,* Vol. 5, No. 2, February 1966, pp. 130–135.

Himes, Norman, and Taylor, Donald, *Your Marriage* (New York: Rinehart & Company, 1955 Revision), Chaps. 20, 21, 22.

Jackson, Edith B., and Trainham, Genevieve, eds., *Family Centered Maternity and Infant Care* (New York: Josiah Macy, Jr., Foundation, 1950).

Landis, Judson T.; Poffenberger, Thomas; and Poffenberger, Shirley, "The Effects of First Pregnancy upon the Sexual Adjustment of 212 Couples," *American Sociological Review,* Vol. 15, December 1950, pp. 767–772.

Lewis, Abigail, *An Interesting Condition: The Diary of a Pregnant Woman* (Garden City, New York: Doubleday and Company, 1950).

Louisiana Association for Mental Health, *Pierre the Pelican, Prenatal Series* (New Orleans: Louisiana Association for Mental Health).

Maternity Center Association, *A Baby Is Born: The Picture Story of Everyman's Beginning* (48 East 92nd Street, New York City 28, N. Y., 1957).

Martin, Phyllis C., and Vincent, Elizabeth L., *Human Biological Development* (New York: The Ronald Press, 1960), Section on "The Perpetuation of Mankind: The Reproductive Apparatus."

Newton, Niles, *Maternal Emotions* (New York: Paul Hoeber, 1955).

Poffenberger, Shirley; Poffenberger, Thomas; and Landis, Judson T., "Intent toward Conception and the Pregnancy Experience," *American Sociological Review,* Vol. 15, December 1950, pp. 767–772.

Potter, Edith L., *Fundamentals of Human Reproduction* (New York: McGraw-Hill Book Company, Inc., 1948).

Rainwater, Lee, *And the Poor Get Children* (Sex, Contraception and Family Planning in the Working Class) (Chicago: Quadrangle Books, 1960).

Raymond, Louise, *Adoption and After* (New York: Harpers, 1955).

Rock, John, M.D., "We Can End the Battle Over Birth Control," *Good Housekeeping,* July 1961, pp. 44, 45, 107–110.

Scheinfeld, Amram, *Your Heredity and Environment* (Philadelphia: J. B. Lippincott Company, 1965).

Smart, Mollie S., and Russell C. Smart, *Children, Development, and Relationships* (New York: The Macmillan Company, 1967). Chaps. 2 and 3.

Van Blarcom, Carolyn, and Corbin, Hazel, *Getting Ready to Be a Mother* (New York: Macmillan, 1940).

Waller, Willard, and Hill, Reuben, *The Family: A Dynamic Interpretation* (New York: The Dryden Press, 1951), Chap. 18.

*You are the bows from which your
children as living arrows are
sent forth*
                    KAHLIL GIBRAN

CHAPTER EIGHT

Childbearing families

The childbearing stage of the family life cycle begins with the birth of the first baby and continues until the firstborn is thirty months of age. During this period the husband and wife have their first experience as parents. They enter the stage as a married couple and leave it as established parents with one or more children. This stage of family life proceeds at a rapid pace through a series of overlapping phases. These involve the changing nature of the parents' roles and tasks of settling down as parents, the child's developmental progress, and the parade of family developmental tasks that appear, are satisfied or left incomplete, and are replaced by other urgencies that demand the attention of the young family.

THREE PHASES IN SETTLING DOWN AS A FAMILY

The first phase of the childbearing family is one of exaltation and rejoicing. The man has come through the crisis of the birth of his first child with a sense of relief and satisfaction. He throws out his chest as he passes cigars and announces the coming of his firstborn. The woman emerges from the first fatigue of childbirth with a glorious sense of accomplishment, a sensation of being in on the process of creation itself. She puts a ribbon in her hair and relaxes in the luxury of bedcare and postpartum attention, replete with telephone calls from wellwishers, congratulations from her friends, beaming pride of her parents, and her husband's family. There is a new tenderness from her mate. There are flowers, gifts for the baby, and a general spirit of celebration.

By the end of the first week mother and baby have made their first efforts to learn to live together. The mother has already taken the step that leads her into, or away from, active nursing of her baby. The baby has made his first adjustment to nursing and is either succeeding well or having trouble at his mother's breast. The new father's visits to the hospital are full of detailed accounts of what the baby is doing, how the nurses love him, how much handsomer, or brighter, or bigger, or quieter he is than the others in the nursery, and speculations as to which relative he resembles most closely. While mother and baby have been confined at the hospital through the lying-in period, the young father has been "baching it" alone at home or has been "farmed out" for his meals among neighbors and relatives. In the relatively few families where the first baby is delivered at home (see Chart 12), parents and baby are hosts to visitors who drop in to see the new baby, and perhaps to lend a hand with the housework until the young mother is again able to take over completely.

CHART 12.   Percentage of All Births in Hospitals in the United States 1935–1964 [1]

[1] Compiled from various issues of *Statistical Bulletin* (New York: Metropolitan Life Insurance Company, December 1947, July 1951, and February 1954); *Natality Statistics Analysis*, United States, 1963, Public Health Service, March 1966, p. vi; and *Monthly Vital Statistics Report*, Final Natality Statistics, 1965.

With the homecoming of mother and baby from the hospital comes the end of the first flush of elation and the realization that parenthood is a strenuous responsibility. Now the care of the newborn is no longer in the capable hands of the nursing staff, but becomes a round-the-clock task of the young family. Baby's feeding schedule has to be worked out in ways that satisfy him and make sense in terms of the household. His bath-time at first is marked by the nervous fumbles of the new mother whose experiences in handling a tiny baby are limited, especially now when families are small and a girl has little opportunity to practice on younger brothers and sisters who used to keep on arriving until she had a baby herself. Keeping the baby clean and dry seems to be an everpresent challenge at first, and the diaper pail fills up at an alarming rate, or so it seems to the young mother who assumes as one of her responsibilities the daily laundry connected with infant care. Discouragement is so common at this time that it is generally known popularly as "postpartum blues." Even in her weakened condition, she might manage all this if only she could get a good night's sleep. But many a newborn takes time to adjust to day and night schedules at home, and his howls between 2:00 and 4:00 A.M. not only rob his parents of sleep, but also increase their insecurity about their competence in caring for him.

The coming of the first child is indeed a crisis, in that it calls for a reorganization of the family. Roles must be reassigned, new needs must be met in new ways, and family values have to be reoriented. The parents may want babies, but be dismayed to discover what they are like. One study finds thirty-eight out of forty-six (83 per cent) couples reporting extensive or severe crisis in adjusting to the first child.[1] The interpretation is that the first child forces the young parents to take the last major step into the adult world, as they encounter the developmental tasks of being responsible for another human being. Thus it is parenthood even more than marriage that demands maturity in both husband and wife.

There usually is some much-needed assistance at this stage to help the young couple through these first hectic days of establishing the new baby in the family. A nurse for the baby in the upper-class family takes over the care of the infant and keeps him from disturbing the rest of the household. In the middle-class and lower-class home, some female rela-

---

[1] E. E. LeMasters, "Parenthood as Crisis," *Marriage and Family Living*, Vol. XIX, No. 4, November 1957, pp. 352–355.

**When the baby becomes stabilized, and the mother's strength returns, the daily outing be-
comes a satisfying experience for both of them.**

tive, generally one of the baby's grandmothers, comes in for awhile and
does the housework and the baby's laundry, gets the meals, and tries to
keep things together until the mother regains her strength and has made
some progress in caring for her baby.

Where such a willing relative cannot be drafted, the young husband
may bear the brunt of the new burden, hurrying home from work to
pitch in and help his wife with all she couldn't accomplish around the
edges of baby care through the day. The strain of double duty for them
both on a day and night basis may take its toll in frayed nerves and a
kind of chronic fatigue that is characteristic of the period in many a
young family.

After a while, the baby becomes stabilized around a predictable schedule and sleeps through the night most of the time. The mother's strength
returns, and she becomes more skilled in caring for the baby as a normal
part of her day's work. Now bathtime is fun for both. The daily outing
becomes a lark and shopping an outing. The outsiders who have helped

out during the baby's first days at home have departed and father, mother, and baby settle down to the sweet peace of domesticity. Thus begins the long pull of parenthood, with its alternating phases of pride, pressure, and enjoyment.

Throughout the childbearing stage of the family life cycle, the infant is attempting to achieve his developmental tasks, the father and the mother are trying to accomplish their developmental tasks as mates, as parents, as persons, and the family is facing a series of developmental tasks characteristic of the stage that must be accomplished if the family is to move successfully into its next stage of development. What these various developmental tasks are for each member of the family and for the family as a whole, and how these individual developmental tasks fuse and fractionate the family, meeting in complementary or conflicting ways within the dynamics of the family interaction, is a story that varies from family to family, from class to class, and from culture to culture, and yet can be reliably predicted in their universal aspects.

DEVELOPMENTAL TASKS OF INFANCY AND EARLY CHILDHOOD (BIRTH TO THIRTY MONTHS) [1]

This first period of life takes the infant from birth, when he emerges as a helpless bundle of potentials, to the place where he is somewhat independent of others. At the end of this period, the child has acquired a measure of autonomy, is taking solid foods, has achieved independent locomotion, and has mastered the first steps in a complex system of communication. Each of these accomplishments represents many hours of practice in real efforts on the part of the child to achieve the developmental tasks involved. These developmental tasks can be summarized as follows:

1) *Achieving physiological equilibrium following birth:*
    Learning to sleep at appropriate times.
    Maintaining a healthful balance of rest and activity.
2) *Learning to take food satisfactorily:*
    Developing ability to nurse—to suck, swallow, and adjust to nipple comfortably.

[1] Freely adapted from Loyd W. Rowland, "II. Child Bearing Family Stage," Evelyn Millis Duvall and Reuben Hill, co-chairmen, Report of the Committee on the Dynamics of Family Interaction, the National Conference on Family Life, Washington, D. C., 1948, and the University of Chicago workshop materials through several years.

Learning to take solid foods, to enjoy new textures, tastes, and temperatures, to use cup, spoon, and dishes competently in ways appropriate to his age.

3) *Learning the know-how and the where-when of elimination:*
Finding satisfaction in early eliminative processes.
Wanting to adapt to expectations of time and place of functioning as developmental readiness and parental pressures indicate.
Participating cooperatively and effectively as ready in the training program.

4) *Learning to manage one's body effectively:*
Developing coordination (eye-hand, hand-mouth, reach, grasp, handle, manipulate, put and take).
Acquiring skills in locomotion through kicking, creeping, walking, and running.
Gaining assurance and competence in handling oneself in a variety of situations.

5) *Learning to adjust to other people:*
Responding discriminatingly to others' expectations.
Recognizing parental authority and controls.
Learning the dos and the don'ts of his world.
Reacting positively to both familiar and strange persons within his orbit.

6) *Learning to love and be loved:*
Responding affectionally to others through cuddling, smiling, loving.
Meeting emotional needs through widening spheres and varieties of contact.
Beginning to give self spontaneously and trustfully to others.

7) *Developing systems of communication:*
Learning patterns of recognition and response.
Establishing nonverbal, preverbal and verbal communicative systems.
Acquiring basic concepts ("Yes," "No," "Up," "Down," "Come," "Go," "Hot," etc.).
Mastering basic language fundamentals in interaction with others.

8) *Learning to express and control feelings:*
Managing feelings of fear and anxiety in healthful ways.

Developing a sense of trust and confidence in one's world.

Handling feelings of frustration, disappointment and anger effectively in accordance with his development.

Moderating demanding attitudes as time goes on.

9) *Laying foundations for self-awareness:*

Seeing oneself as a separate entity.

Exploring rights and privileges of being a person.

Finding personal fulfillment with and without others.

THUS A CHILD LEARNS

Thus a child learns: by wiggling skills through his fingers and toes into himself, by soaking up habits and attitudes of those around him, by pushing and pulling his own world.

Thus a child learns: More through trial than error, more through pleasure than pain, more through experience than suggestion, more through suggestion than direction.

Thus a child learns: through affection, through love, through patience, through understanding, through belonging, through doing, through being.

Day by day the child comes to know a little bit of what you know, to think a little bit of what you think, to understand your understanding. That which you dream and believe and are, in truth, becomes the child.

As you perceive clearly or dully, as you think fuzzily or sharply, as you believe foolishly or wisely, as you dream drably or goldenly, as you are unworthy or sincere—thus a child learns.

FREDERICK J. MOFFITT
Associate Commissioner for
Elementary, Secondary and Adult Education
New York State Education Department

DEVELOPMENTAL TASKS OF THE MOTHER OF THE INFANT AND YOUNG CHILD

The first baby arrives in most families when the husband and wife are still working to establish their relationship as a married couple. Therefore, there is an inevitable overlapping of the developmental tasks of the young wife with those of the young mother during the baby's infancy. The young woman carries concurrently the unfinished business of being a competent and happy wife with that of becoming an effective and fulfilled mother. She masters many new skills during the infancy of her firstborn as she adjusts to the realities of motherhood and comes eventually toward the end of the period to a feeling of being established as a mother and settled as a family. At the end of this stage of the family life cycle, the young mother has begun to discover her own strengths and weaknesses and to establish the attitudes, values, and procedures that make sense for her as wife, mother, and a person. This progress is successful to the extent to which she has effectively achieved the developmental tasks of this stage in her development which, outlined in summary form, include:

1) *Reconciling conflicting conceptions of roles:*

Clarifying her role as a wife-mother-person.

Reconciling differences in conceptions of roles held by herself, her husband, and the various relatives, friends, and significant others.

Developing a sound workable conception of what she expects of her child.

Coming to comfortable understanding of her husband's role as a young father.

2) *Accepting and adjusting to the strains and pressures of young motherhood:*

Gearing activity to the lessened physical vigor in the periods of involution and lactation.

Cooperating in the processes involved in effective infant feeding.

Balancing the demands of the child, the expectations of the husband, and her commitments as a person with the limits of her abilities.

3) *Learning how to care for her infant with competence and assurance:*

Assuming responsibility for the care of the child.

Mastering the skills of feeding, bathing, protecting, and maintaining a healthy happy baby.

Learning how to anticipate and to recognize the needs of the baby.

Becoming increasingly able to enjoy caring for the young child.

4) *Establishing and maintaining healthful routines for the young family:*

Learning how to choose, prepare, and serve nutritious foods for both adult and infant needs.

Reorganizing family routines to meet the changing needs of the growing child within the family context.

Assuring a sufficiency of rest, relaxation, and sleep for the baby, the young husband, and herself.

Readjusting time schedules to make way for the necessities and for some purely pleasurable activities within the young family.

5) *Providing full opportunities for the child's development:*

Enriching the physical situation within the limits of family resources.

Providing plentiful varieties of experiences in exploring, manipulating, and learning for the infant and small child.

Protecting the furnishings and equipment in ways that keep to a minimum the physical restraint of the growing child (child-proofing the home).

Learning to enjoy and to wholeheartedly encourage the child's development and progress.

Accepting the child as himself without undue pressure, disappointment, or comparison.

6) *Sharing the responsibilities of parenthood with her husband:*

Recognizing the importance of the father-child relationship from the beginning.

Encouraging the participation of the young father in the care of the baby and small child in appropriate ways.

Bringing the young father into the planning, decision-making, evaluating processes that make him feel that his wishes and values are being respected and appreciated.

Establishing the habits of thinking of the child as "ours" rather than "mine".

7) *Maintaining a satisfying relationship with her husband:*

Protecting her husband's values as a person through the demanding pressures of young parenthood.

Reestablishing ways of being a couple with the unique values of husband-wife companionship throughout the infancy of first child.

Maintaining the joys of being a wife in the sexual, recreational, emotional, intellectual, and spiritual aspects of married living.

8) *Making satisfactory adjustments to the practical realities of life:*

Assisting her husband in the financial and housing planning for the family.

Adapting happily to the limitations of space and resources of the family.

Innovating ways of enriching the family experience by new use of available facilities and resources.

Supplementing the family income when it seems wise or necessary in ways that safeguard the well-being of all members of the family.

9) *Keeping alive some sense of personal autonomy through young motherhood:*

Retaining some satisfying contacts with personal interests and stimuli.

Continuing some aspect of personal development that is especially meaningful within the realities of the present family situation.

Utilizing the unique experiences of young motherhood for the fulfillment inherent within it.

Following her child's growth experiences out into new horizons of personal insight and growth.

10) *Exploring and developing the satisfying sense of being a family:*

Initiating family recreation in which the whole family may participate with pleasure—picnics, trips to zoo and beach, music, automobile trips, etc.

Participating with other young families in community functions.

Joining with other young wives and mothers in cooperative endeavors.

Providing for whole-family participation in church, neighborhood, and community activities suitable to this stage in family development.

Maintaining mutually supportive contacts with parental families.

This is quite an assignment for the young wife and mother. No wonder so many young women feel so overwhelmed during this phase of their lives. In the big, old-fashioned family (in which the young couple lived near, or sometimes with, their parental families), there was a sharing of functions and responsibilities of childbearing and rearing with the support of other members of the extended family that lessened the burden on the young mother. In the simple folk-society, infants and young children are cooperatively cared for by any conveniently located adult.

Young families today are usually removed from former day-to-day supportive relationships of the extended family. The inexperienced mother is alone with her baby for most of the waking day, and shares with her mate the child's care around the clock and calendar. In addition to caring for the baby and providing opportunities for his development, the young mother does the shopping, prepares food for the family, washes the dishes, cleans the house, washes, irons, and puts away the clothes, assumes responsibility for the family's social life, tries to be a good wife for her husband, and picks up the ever-present litter that goes with infancy. One investigation found nearly 70 per cent of tired home-makers had an infant-toddler—significantly more than mothers of older children.[1]

The developmental tasks of the young mother are many and demand-ing. She must achieve them, but she can be helped by a variety of resources that communities are developing to ease the burden on the young mother. She succeeds in the urgent tasks of young motherhood as she acquires the knowledge, skill, and attitudes conducive to compe-tence in her multiple roles.

DEVELOPMENTAL TASKS OF THE FATHER OF THE INFANT AND YOUNG CHILD

The young father is not as directly responsible for his baby as is his wife, and yet he faces certain inevitable developmental tasks arising di-rectly out of his new status as father. The very fact that it is his wife rather than himself who is most intimately related to the child's birth, nursing, and early care, gives rise to some unique developmental tasks. Of course, it is humanly possible, as it is among other species, for the father to escape entirely the experiences of living intimately with his own young offspring. There are men, especially among the lower classes, who take little or no responsibility for the bearing and rearing of the child. In earlier times, a man left the care of the young child to the women of the household almost entirely. A father began his active role when his youngster could handle himself well enough to go along on hunting, fish-ing, or short treks near home. Until then, or at least until the child was "housebroken," Father's life was relatively undisturbed by baby.

---

[1] Elizabeth Wiegand and Irma H. Gross, *Fatigue of Homemakers with Young Children* (East Lansing, Michigan: Agricultural Experiment Station Technical Bulle-tin No. 265, March 1958).

Today's pattern is for the young husband-father to assume jointly the responsibilities and privileges of parenthood with his wife. These expectations are in conflict with the more traditional system in which the children were told, "Hush now, here comes Father," in the wife's sincere effort to protect the man from any noise or disturbance normal to young children. Modern fathers no longer can make all the rules, and only occasionally sit in judgment on wife and children as was once the case. Nowadays, a man improvises along with his wife as both of them attempt to live with the disturbing little newcomer in ways that will be mutually

COURTESY OF THE LIBRARY OF CONGRESS

Nowadays, the young husband-father assumes the responsibilities and privileges of parenthood along with his wife.

pleasant and satisfying. Now as always, a man is expected to be the primary breadwinner and set up his little family in the style to which he wants them to become accustomed. But here too, there are puzzling variations from the older norms. All in all, the young husband-father has quite a surprising number of developmental tasks during the childbearing stage of the family life cycle, as we see in the summary of them here:

1) *Reconciling conflicting conceptions of role:*

Settling upon a satisfactory role for himself as father out of the many conflicting possibilities in conceptions in himself, his wife, both families, friends, and others of influence.

Coming to terms with what he expects of his wife, now mother of his child, out of the conflicting expectations in each of them and in their significant other responsibilities.

Reconciling conflicting conceptions of childhood to a point of assurance in what to expect in his own child.

2) *Making way for the new pressures made upon him as young father:*

Accepting a reasonable share of responsibility for the care of the child, compatible with the realities of the situation at home and on his job.

Being willing to accept without undue stress, or complaint, his wife's increased emotional and physical need of him during the time when she is not yet functioning at peak effectiveness.

Assuming his share of responsibilities in representing the new family in the community in appropriate ways.

3) *Learning the basic essentials of baby and child care:*

Acquiring enough of the knowledges and skills of early child care to be able to function effectively in the baby's personal life, as indicated.

Practicing the fundamentals required in caring for a tiny baby and small child to serve as first lieutenant both alone and with the mother present.

Learning enough about early child development to know what to expect and understand what is relatively normal at a given stage of development.

Becoming increasingly able to enjoy intimate personal interaction with the baby.

4) *Conforming to the new regimens designed as most healthful for the young family:*

Adapting his eating habits to facilitate the new food intake patterns of mother, baby, and young family as a whole.

Working out ways of getting enough sleep and rest around the edges of the young child's needs and disturbances.

Designing new approaches in recreation that will fit in with the needs and limitations now operating in the family.

Being willing to experiment with any promising possibilities that seem worth trying, rather than insisting that "life go on as usual" in all instances.

5) *Encouraging the child's full development:*

Investing in the equipment and resources that will be most helpful and useful.

Cooperating in child-proofing the home for the period of young childhood.

Planning with his wife for the enriching experiences that will

provide opportunities for the child's well-rounded development.
Encouraging the child as it is, or may become, rather than as a
"chip off the old block" or a vessel for unfulfilled personal ambitions and dreams.

6) *Maintaining a mutually satisfying companionship with his wife:*
Wooing her back into tender sweetheart and intense lover roles
as she recovers from childbirth and the arduousness of the first
mothering responsibilities.

Seeing to it that the husband-wife relationship is neither chronically nor critically submerged beneath new parenting responsibilities.

Taking the initiative, when necessary, in renewing satisfying activities as a couple that may have been suspended during the pregnancy, childbirth and lying-in periods.

7) *Assuming the major responsibility for earning the family income:*
Carrying breadwinner responsibilities willingly.

Augmenting the family income, in ways that are appropriate, as
may become necessary.

Being willing to accept assistance, as it may be required, from either set of parents, from the wife's supplemental earnings, from
savings, from loans or other mortgages on the future, at this time
of relatively high needs and low income.

Assisting in financial planning that will keep expenditures within
available resources.

8) *Maintaining a satisfying sense of self as a man:*
Continuing personal interests and pursuits compatible with childbearing responsibilities and limitations.

Finding new levels of fulfillment in the new experiences of fatherhood.

Growing as a person in the maturing experiences of sharing fully
with his developing baby and with the full-bloom of woman-
hood in his wife.

Mastering the infantile, jealousy-provoking impulses that might
alienate him from his little family at the very times when they
need each other most.

9) *Representing the family within the wider community:*
Serving as chief representative of his family in the workaday
world.

Recognizing that he is the one to whom his wife looks for adult stimulus, interest, and activities while she is confined with baby care.

Bringing home the ideas, the people, the projects that will keep the young family in touch with the larger community during childbearing days.

Carrying on the community participation compatible with the pressures at home and on the job.

10) *Becoming a family man in the fullest sense of the term:*

` Finding satisfactions in whole family activities.

Cooperating with his wife and baby in the new pursuits that appeal to them.

Initiating experiences for the whole family that will broaden horizons and enrich their life together as a family unit.

Enjoying the new dimensions of life with other relatives now rekindled with the new roles as aunts, uncles, cousins, and grandparents of the new baby.

Needless to say, all this is more than the average man bargained for when he fell in love and got married. As Frederick Lewis Allen used to say, "Everything is easier to get into than out of." And parenthood is surely a good example. It is so easy for most people to conceive, and so hard to deliver, so easy to dream of settling down and having a family, and so hard to meet the realities of family life when they flood in upon one.

Few men have been adequately prepared for what to expect when children come. They only rarely go through schools where boys as well as girls receive an educational program in preparation for marriage and family life. They come up in homes where little has been expected of them in direct child care. Until a man's first child appears, he usually has had very little first-hand experience with a baby. He doesn't know what to expect. He finds that his fingers are all thumbs in his first attempts to change or bathe or dress a baby. He tenses in fear that he will drop the baby or that it will be hurt while in his care.

Most difficult of all may be the intimate sharing of his wife with the intrusive little rival that now claims so much of her attention. The husband has had his wife all to himself during their courting and honeymoon days and has learned to take her for granted as his partner and companion during the establishment phase of marriage. He now must see her time, energy, and love directed to the demanding baby in ways that may fill him with intense feelings of being left out and neglected. It is a mature husband indeed who can early feel enough centrally involved in the new relationships to get the deep sense of belonging necessary for his security as a husband and father. One of the usual to-be-expected hazards in this stage of the family life cycle is for the mother to devote herself disproportionally to the new baby, and for the young father to retreat emotionally to a doghouse of his own making. Until he can share his wife maturely and participate with her in the experiences of parenthood he may feel like little more than a fifth wheel around the place.

How well the young husband juggles the conflicting loyalties and expectations and manages the multiplicity of roles opening up to him depends in large measure on how ready he is for fatherhood and how successful he is in accomplishing the developmental tasks inherent in the childbearing stage of family life. As he succeeds in achieving his own developmental tasks, he will be able to participate effectively in working through the family developmental tasks necessary for the survival, continuation, and growth of the family as a unit.

DEVELOPMENTAL TASKS OF THE CHILDBEARING FAMILY

With the coming of the first baby, the couple now becomes a family of three persons: mother, father, and baby. At the same time the inter-relationships within the family have jumped from one (husband-wife) to three (husband-wife, father-child, and mother-child). Husband and wife are typically in their mid-twenties as this stage begins, and thirty more or less as it ends two and one-half years after the baby's birth.

The developmental tasks of the family in the childbearing stage are basically concerned with establishing the young family as a stable unit, reconciling conflicting developmental tasks of the various members, and mutually supporting the developmental needs of mother, father and baby in ways that strengthen each one and the family as a whole.

With the coming of the first baby, there appears for the first time a new mother, in the sense that this woman has never been a mother before, a new father who must learn what it means to function as a father, and a new family that must find its own way of being a family. While the baby is learning what it means to become a human being by growing, developing, and achieving his developmental tasks, his mother is learning how to be a mother, his father is practicing what it means to be a father, and the new family is settling itself into family patterns for the first time in its history. This involves the simultaneous working out of the developmental tasks of the baby, the mother, the father, and the family-as-a-whole. The basic developmental tasks of the childbearing family are discussed briefly in the sections that follow.

ADAPTING HOUSING ARRANGEMENTS FOR THE LIFE OF THE LITTLE CHILD

In millions of families around the world, no special provisions are made for the infant and little child. He or she is carried about by the mother or an older sibling, either in arms, or in some kind of shawl, or sling or even wrapped tightly on a board. The baby sleeps with the parents until he is old enough to fend for himself with the other children of the household. There are many homes in the United States where a child never knows a bed of his own, where everything is "share and share alike" within the home from the baby's first appearance until he is grown and leaves for a home of his own.

As the standard of living improves among American families, giving the baby a special place of his own and readapting the family housing for the comfort and convenience of the little child has become the norm.

In traditionally oriented homes (Chapter Five), the goal in making these special arrangements is to keep the baby from annoying and disturbing adults, as well as to assure its comfort. In more developmental families, there is a conscious effort to provide the kind of facilities in which the child may grow at his best, be free to roam as he becomes ready, explore without hurt or restraint, and to learn from active manipulation how to master his environment and develop his own skills. This kind of family life involves adapting the home so that the normal destructiveness of the little child will not violate the parents' values of a pleasant comfortable home in which they as adults may continue to find satisfaction.

Developmental parents accept the fact that a little child is born with ten hungry fingers that must "get into things." They know that the rough and tumble of the baby's early exploration, soiling, and fumbling must be allowed for in the home they share with him. Rather than cooping him up indefinitely or forbid him access to their living quarters, they so arrange the household that he may enjoy it with them with a minimum of restraint. To avoid the continual "NO!" and to protect their belongings as well as their child, they child-proof the home.

CHILD-PROOFING THE HOME DURING THE CHILDBEARING STAGE
(Outlined suggestions for keeping little children from getting hurt
or destroying property)

Item	Danger	Child-Proofing Suggestions
Furniture	Tipping over on child	Select big-bottomed, heavy, plain pieces (esp. lamps and tables)
	Painful bumps	Rounded corners better than sharp
	Drawers dumped	Safety catch on all drawers (catch pegs at back hold them)
	Breaking treasured items	Pack away breakables or put in inaccessible places—use wall or hanging lamps instead of table and floor lamps wherever possible
	Soiling upholstery	Choose expendable items, or slip cover with washable fabrics, or upholster in durable, easily cleaned figured patterns that can take it (feet, sticky fingers, moist surfaces, etc.)
Floors and floor coverings	Chilling in drafts and cold surfaces	Weatherstrip under outside doors in cold weather, supplement heating at floor level, cover with rugs
	Slipping and falling	Avoid hazardous waxing, discard throw rugs, keep traffic lanes as clear as possible
	Soiling rugs	Choose colors that do not show dirt, in patterns rather than plain, select washable or reversible rugs, plan to discard after childbearing stage is over
	Marring floors	Cover with relatively indestructible surface, plan to refinish after heavy duty phases of family living pass
Walls	Marking and scratching	Choose washable papers or paints, or spray with washable plastic, convert a sizable section into blackboard (paint or large strips of paper) where child may mark, supply child with washable crayons, plan to redecorate when children are older.
Table tops	Scarring and staining	Cover with Formica, linoleum, terrazo, marble, or other surface not harmed by wetting, soiling, and pounding—use second hand items at first

The National Safety Council recommends putting gates at the top and bottom of stairs. Until the child has mastered the skills of going up and down safely, such a precaution allows the toddler to roam freely about the house without the danger of falling down stairs.

CHILD-PROOFING THE HOME DURING THE CHILDBEARING STAGE (*Continued*)
(Outlined suggestions for keeping little children from getting hurt
or destroying property)

Item	Danger	Child-Proofing Suggestions
Toys	Littered	Provide low shelves, and accessible storage places
	Harmful paints and surfaces	Select things child can suck and chew without harm
	Sharp edges and corners	Choose toys that will not hurt child in bangs and bumps
	Swallowing	Nothing smaller than a plum for baby
	Breaking	Give child sturdy things he cannot easily break (frustrating him, and you)
Bathroom fixtures	Falling baby	Provide convenient bathing, changing and toileting facilities for care of baby and little child
	Clinging child	Encourage child's independence as he becomes ready by low steps by wash bowl, low hooks for his towel, wash cloth and cup
	Training problems	Supply equipment he can manage himself when he is ready to care for his needs
	Running water	Allow for child's joy in water play by providing time and place for it with some supervision
Locked cupboards	Breaking treasures	Hang key high for door of good dish cabinet, etc.
	Swallowing poisons	Lock up paints, varnish, cleaning compounds, ammonia, lye, medicines, insecticides
	Inflicting wounds	Keep tools, guns, knives, and all other such objects locked away
Stairs and windows	Falling	Put gates at top and bottom of all stairways, give time to child as he learns to go up and down stairs, bar or tightly screen windows
Electric outlets	Shocking child	Cap low outlets, protect cords and keep to reasonable lengths, fence off with heavy furniture so child cannot introduce his finger, tongue or object into outlet
Entranceways	Cluttering	Provide shelves for rubbers, mittens, and other small objects; make room for baby buggy, sled, stroller, etc.

CHILD-PROOFING THE HOME DURING THE CHILDBEARING STAGE (*Continued*)
(Outlined suggestions for keeping little children from getting hurt
or destroying property)

Item	*Danger*	*Child-Proofing Suggestions*
	Soiling	Supply washable mats at outside doors to keep dirt from being tracked in, keep rubbers, boots, and wheeled objects near door
	Falling	Keep doorway gated or door closed, or screen locked when baby begins to get around
Kitchen	Burning	Provide play space near but not at the stove, keep handles of pans turned in rather than out
	Lighting gas	Make burner knobs one of the "No-Nos" that baby may not touch
	Lighting matches	Keep matches on high shelves, establish firm "No-No" policy on them
	Tripping workers	Fence off child's play area from main traffic lanes in kitchen, or provide high chair play during meal preparation
	Cutting	Hang knives high on wall
General	Hurting baby	Minor cuts, bruises, bangs, burns, etc., are taken in stride; major ones are turned over immediately to medical attention (keep doctor's number, and other resources on telephone pad)
	Damaging the house	Keep perspective of child being more important than things, use temporary, expendable things while children are small, plan to redo the place as youngsters near the teen years (they'll push for that anyway)

MEETING THE COSTS OF FAMILY LIVING AT THE CHILDBEARING STAGE

A baby born into a typical American family is fortunate. He will enjoy a higher standard of living than a child born in any other culture. His family will have a higher income year by year than would be average in any other country. The median family income in the United States was estimated at $6,900 in 1965 as we see in Table 15.

Even in a country of high income, and at a time of prosperity char-

TABLE 15. *Percentage of Families by Family Income,*
in the United States, 1965

Family Income before Taxes	Percentage of Families
Under $3,000	17%
$3,000 to $4,999	16
$5,000 to $6,999	19
$7,000 to $9,999	24
$10,000 to $14,999	17
$15,000 and over	8
Median: $6,900	100%

SOURCE: *Family Economics Review,* United States Department of Agriculture, September 1966, p. 20.

acteristic of this period in the American economy, millions of families have incomes below that considered adequate at current prices. And, many children grow up in low-income families with the deprivations of housing, nutrition, education, and other disadvantages of lower-class status discussed in Chapter Four.

The median money income of families in the United States has been steadily increasing. In 1964 it was about $6,600 before taxes, a full $1,000 more than the median family income in 1960.[1] Since prices also continue to rise, families' purchasing power increases slower than their income.

Even more pertinent for the college-educated middle-class couple is the fact that the first baby comes while they are still struggling to establish themselves financially. The young husband at the childbearing stage of the family life cycle is typically at the bottom of the vocational ladder with less income than he will have at any other time in his life as a worker. The typical pattern is for the man to start modestly and from then on to enjoy steady increases in income up to his forties in lower-paid jobs, and to his fifties in higher-paid positions, followed by gradual reductions as he nears, reaches and passes his retirement (Chart 13).

The costs of the family at the childbearing stage tend to balloon because it is then that the past, present, and future needs of the family are simultaneously part of the family budget. The first baby comes on the heels of the establishment stage of the family, when payments for furniture, equipment, house, car, and other high-cost items are still being made. The first child represents current costs in terms of doctor and hospital bills, baby furnishings, layette, special foods and medicines,

[1] *Current Population Reports: Consumer Income,* Series P-60, No. 36, June 9, 1961.

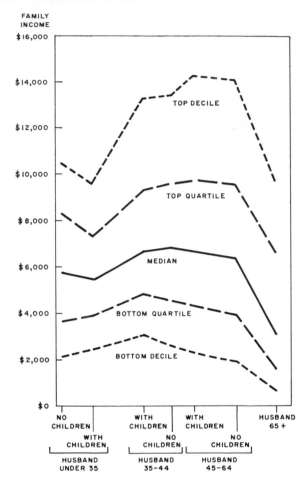

**CHART 13.   Dispersion of Family Income, for Husband-Wife Families
(United States, 1960)** [1]

baby-sitter fees, and at least some new clothing for the mother after
nine months of pregnancy. With the coming of the first child the future is sharply focused by realization of the importance of insurance.
Such protection means safeguarding the mother and children during the
childbearing and rearing stages, saving for the rainy days when sickness,
accident, or other crises drain the family purse, or put the breadwinner

[1] Reprinted by permission from Paul C. Glick and Robert Parke, Jr., "New
Approaches in Studying the Life Cycle of the Family," *Demography*, Vol. 2, 1965,
p. 201.

out of work, as well as financing dreams for education, cultural advantages, and a comfortable future for the family members.

As we have seen, this meeting of past, present, and future financial needs in the childbearing family stage spirals costs when family income is relatively low and when the wife is likely to be no longer gainfully employed. Therefore, the pinch is on, and making ends meet is a real challenge to the young family. Families each with its own problems and possibilities meet this developmental task in many ways.

The young father may get an additional part-time job in an effort to make ends meet. This will supply more income but at the cost of his time with his family, and possibly in fatigue, irritability, and strain. The young mother may go back to full-time employment soon after the baby is born. This will maintain the family income at the previous level, but it sacrifices the mother's full-time care of the child, their early hour by hour companionship with its satisfactions both for the baby and for the mother. Actually, if the mother has to replace herself in the home with a paid household helper, her work may not net the family much. If her mother, or his, is available for the early childcare and housework, the employment of the young mother may make financial sense, as it does in many lower-class homes.

Some young mothers have the kinds of salable skills that continue to supplement the family income even with a small child in the home. The young woman who can type, tutor, sew, or do specialized crafts (baking or cooking, or other money-making projects), can often continue to earn some money even during the active childbearing and rearing stages. Some young women can do such things easily and well. Others find extra activities beyond those of caring for the children and the household an added strain that cannot be comfortably handled.

The couple may borrow money for some high-cost purchases—mortgaging their future by that much but having the equipment when they need it most. Installment buying may be of this sort, with payments over a period of years for such things as the car, the refrigerator, the washing machine, and the other items that mean much when children are small. The danger is in loading up on installment purchases beyond the ability to pay comfortably over the months and years to come. Borrowing is feasible only if the family can see enough income in the foreseeable future to take care of the payment of the loan, with its accumulated interest charges, within a reasonable length of time. "Borrowing early in a period of financial strain is unwise, for it only serves to add interest charges to the already too heavy expenditures," is the counsel of one authority in family finance.[1]

Savings laid away earlier may be used for such items as the automobile, the first baby, or the furniture. Or, in some families, the grandparents pitch in with gifts that assure the young family of what they need as they need it. Some families can do these things well. Where there are tendencies to jealousy or rivalry between the two in-law families, or emotional immaturity and dependency on the part of one or both of the young parents, expensive gifts from grandparents may be hazardous.

"Making do" is one way of balancing the budget during this stage in the family life cycle. Many young families recognize that the household can be kept simple and inexpensive while the children are coming and growing, with furnishings that are expendable and with little importance put on appearance. Later, when the children are old enough to appreciate nice things and to share in their care, the old, inexpensive, beat-up things may be replaced.

Which course the young family follows in accomplishing this developmental task of meeting the costs of the family at the childbearing stage depends upon how they are approaching and meeting a number of their other developmental tasks of the period, especially those having to do with the allocation of responsibility, developing systems of communication, adapting relationships with relatives and friends, and working through a philosophy of life.

REWORKING PATTERNS OF MUTUAL RESPONSIBILITY AND ACCOUNTABILITY

The first child brings with him/her new responsibilities in terms of round the clock care, including the intricacies of feeding, bathing, soothing, and diagnosing distress signals. Daily laundry of baby clothing is a new responsibility. Making formula for the bottle-fed baby is a daily job. Cleaning up the household swollen by the new activities incident to child care is an everpresent responsibility. At the same time the former responsibilities of earning the family income, shopping, cooking,

---

[1] Howard F. Bigelow, *Family Finance* (Chicago: J. B. Lippincott Company, Revised Edition, 1953), p. 345.

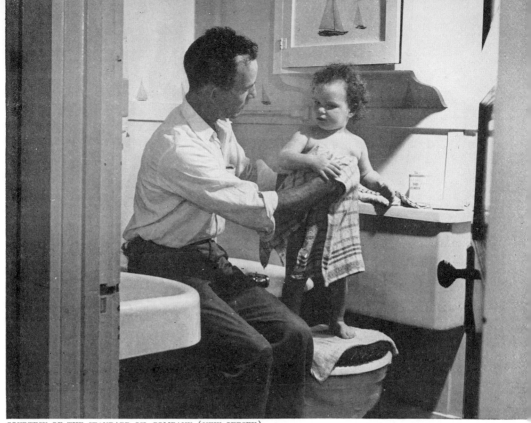

Baby's bath may be scheduled for the evening hours when the father is available for this and other intimate person-to-person responsibilities.

dishwashing, housecleaning, mopping, bedmaking, and all the rest continue as before.

There are some responsibilities that will be automatically allocated to one or the other of the parents: the father assumes the role of primary breadwinner, the mother of nursing the baby. Everything else that must be done in the young family may become the responsibility of either partner on either a short-term or a long-term basis. The usual pattern in the American family is for the wife to assume responsibility for child care, housework, laundry, and food preparation for both the baby and the adults, with the assistance of the husband in those chores in which he is particularly interested or capable. For instance, now that the young mother is confined with the care of the baby, the husband may assume more responsibility for marketing and other errands that he can take care of on his way home from work.

There is an increase in the number of families that define the father's role in terms of relating intimately to his children (Chapter Five, discussion of developmental fathers and families). In such homes the baby's bath may be scheduled for the evening hours when father as well as mother may actively participate. Similarly, changing the baby, airing the baby in leisurely Saturday afternoon walks, playing with the little child, putting the youngster to bed, feeding the baby, burping, cuddling, comforting, and all the other intimate person-to-person responsibilities of parent for child are being shared by the father as well as the mother in modern day families.

As both parents increasingly share the responsibilities for the family's welfare, certain chores may be relegated to the husband and others to the wife on a basis of individual strength. An example is found in the number of young husbands who take over some of the heavy cleaning and carrying jobs until the young mother has regained her strength and has the time and energy for all the housework again. It works the other way too. In some beginning families the shopping is done by both members of the pair in weekly marketing excursions. With the coming of the first baby, the wife now enjoys getting out of the house and taking the baby for a daily airing, and so now shops more often while she is out with the baby. Groceries are wheeled home in the carriage at the baby's feet and are no longer part of the weekend routines.

The wife, who is home most of the time with the baby, relates to the husband at his return home what has transpired through the day and how she and the child have fared. She brings up for his approval purchases made or contemplated and decisions that must be made one way or the other in the immediate and distant future. The husband in turn tells his wife of progress and problems on the job and goes over with her alternatives that may be theirs for improving their financial or vocational position.

As the baby grows he becomes accountable to his parents for the behavior that is expected. This has its beginnings long before the thirty-month age when the child is well launched into a set of expectancies of what to do when and how. What constitutes good behavior and what is "being bad" varies enormously by families, by cultural groups, and by developmental-traditional orientation. But in every home the child soon learns that he must assume certain responsibilties for himself and his conduct and that he is accountable to his parents for what he is and does. These responsibilities increase as the child grows; are least when he is a tiny infant; and grow as he develops more and more toward the "age of responsibility."

RE-ESTABLISHING MUTUALLY SATISFYING SEXUAL RELATIONSHIPS

It is usual for the sex life of the couple to decrease during the periods of pregnancy, childbirth, and postnatal days (Chapter Seven). By six weeks after the birth of the baby, the woman's pelvis is back to normal, the postnatal discharge has ceased, involution is complete, and normally she is physically able to enjoy an active sex life again. The re-establishment of their sex relationships is not a simple physiological problem; it has many intricate psychological aspects for both the wife and her mate.

Many a young mother experiencing for the first time the challenges of motherhood, becomes absorbed in its responsibilities and satisfactions so much that the husband is pushed into the background, unless he or she takes the initiative in keeping their mate-love central in the family. It may be the man of the house who re-establishes some of the wooing and courtship processes that will get them both occasionally out of the house with its constant reminders of the baby. The renewal of sweetheart roles will often rekindle the banked fires of desire in both of them. It may be the wife who takes the initiative in re-establishing full marital relationships as soon as she is ready. One of the first steps the wife takes in this direction is that of making herself attractive for her man again.

Throughout the pregnancy she may have felt the loss of her sexual attractiveness, as her body became swollen with child and the maternal functions gained ascendancy. Now that the baby has safely arrived and is well on the way to healthy infancy, the young mother is free to take an interest in becoming attractive to her husband again. She may get some stylish new clothes to fit this new slim silhouette of hers. She may get a new hairdo and pay new attention to her figure and skin care. Quite likely she will watch her diet to keep her weight in line during lactation at the same time that she assures her baby of sufficient milk.

Medically and emotionally there may be some specific problems. It is usual in most hospitals to perform an episiotomy, cutting the perineum enough to let the baby through without the danger of tearing maternal tissue. Normally the perineum heals in a few days, but the itching of the healing tissues continues a while. For some time afterwards, the memory of the pain in the sensitive area may make the re-establishment of sexual relations difficult. A young mother may complain that "the doctor sewed me up too tight," when the main trouble is the tightening of the tissues as she involuntarily tenses during stimulation of the area. Patient thoughtfulness on the husband's part, and active cooperation of the wife are usually all that is necessary for those who previously have known a good sex adjustment.

For couples whose early sex life has been frustratingly inadequate, the nursing period may be used as a protective device by the young mother. In some societies, and in some families here and now, the mother has been known to prolong the nursing of the infant as a way of protecting herself from the sexual advances of her husband. In still others, the young mother may complain of fatigue, ill-health, or pain as a way of avoiding the re-establishment of active sex life as long as possible.

Happy families soon find their way through the emotional and physical problems involved. The best of them find that the infant's call for attention may interrupt the most tender embrace from time to time. It is at such times that the couple's communication systems and philosophy of life stand them in good stead as they meet the baby's need and return to each other in good humor without the overtones of frustrated, disgruntled impulses spoiling their relationship one with another.

REFINING INTELLECTUAL AND EMOTIONAL COMMUNICATION SYSTEMS FOR CHILDBEARING AND REARING

Something new is added to family intercommunication when a baby comes into the household. The newborn makes his needs known through a series of signals and distress calls that have to be "received" by his parents with appropriate responses if he or they are to be comfortable. As he is able to communicate his wishes and feelings, and as his parents become increasingly skillful in understanding his communicative efforts, both baby and parents get a feeling of satisfaction in their interrelationship. When this developmental task is difficult, the baby and the parents find each other unsatisfying, even to the point of mutual frustration.

As the mother and father cuddle and fondle the baby, expressing their love for him in close person-to-person contacts, the baby learns to respond. He smiles when his mother or father comes near. He gurgles when they pick him up. He pats them when they care for him. He soon learns to hug, nestle, kiss, snuggle, and to express in the ways of

As a mother nurses her baby, she expresses her love by cuddling and holding him close—communication that even the littlest infant can "understand."

his particular family the love he feels in response to those who love him.

Long before the child is two years old, he has learned the basic response patterns appropriate for his little world. He has learned a degree of trust and confidence in his parents. He has learned how to express his annoyance and impatience with those around him. He has laid down the foundation of his emotional being in the loves and hates, fears and anxieties, joys and satisfactions that he has experienced and expressed during his early life with his family. His basic security as a personality rests upon the faith that he early develops in his world through his trust in his parents and his feeling that he is able to communicate, to be understood, and to have his needs met as they arise. By the time the family leaves the childbearing stage of the family cycle, the baby has learned the fundamentals of language and is talking in ways that may be understood not only by his parents, but also by others outside the family. He uses a growing number of concepts accurately and is fast becoming a fully communicating member of his family.

Husband and wife must re-establish effective communication as they become parents. They have new feelings to share in the prides, joys, anxieties, annoyances, and insecurities of early parenthood. The danger is that their marriage may be eclipsed by their new family roles. Feldman finds [1] that parents of infants talk less with each other, especially about personal things, than they did before their babies came. They tend to have fewer gay times, to laugh less, have fewer stimulating exchanges of ideas and to feel resentful more often. In general, the coming of the first baby has a sobering effect on the parents and a depressing effect on the marriage. Although satisfaction with marital companionship continues, the advent of children means that husband and wife tend to do less together and to grow apart from each other.[2]

Sharing one's mate with the newcomer involves still other communication systems in which there is mutual recognition of the multiple involvements of both the man and the woman as mates, as parents, and as persons. The young father now must recognize his wife as also "Mother" with the coming of their first baby. She must become accustomed to seeing her husband as also "Father" as soon as children come. Sometimes these terms are actually employed and continue throughout the

---

[1] Harold Feldman, "The Development of the Husband-Wife Relationship," a study supported in part by the National Institute of Mental Health, unpublished data received through personal correspondence, March 24, 1961, with permission.

[2] Robert O. Blood, Jr., and Donald M. Wolfe, *Husbands and Wives* (Glencoe, Illinois: The Free Press, 1960), pp. 156 and 174.

life of the family. In other families, these designations are used only occasionally in jest but they serve their purpose of assisting the partners to accept, express, and internalize the new roles as parents that both of the partners face.

The young family is successful in accomplishing the several-faceted developmental task of refining communication systems to accommodate the new constellation of emotional interactions when it emerges from the childbearing stage with a well-knit sense of being a family. When difficulties in achieving the task are unresolved, the family may emerge from the stage with problems of poor integration that carry over to complicate further stages in its development.

RE-ESTABLISHING WORKING RELATIONSHIPS WITH RELATIVES

With the coming of the first baby, grandmother comes into her own in many a home. She is welcomed as the one who holds things together during the baby's first days at home while the mother is fully absorbed in the baby's care and in regaining her strength. As the young mother is increasingly able to take over the full responsibility for her household with the assistance of the baby's father, the grandmother's role recedes in importance. About that time, other relatives begin to come by to see the new baby, call on the new mother, and bring gifts, advice, and warnings that have to be absorbed and dealt with one way or another.

In-law jealousies and juggling for power not infrequently emerge with the coming of the first baby. One parental family gives more, does more, demands more, or expects more of the little new family than does the other. If one or both of the parents is immature or on the defensive, the imbalance of grandparental interest may fan the flames of envy, jealousy, and insecurity to a white heat of passionate resistance.

In the mixed marriage, the interest of the grandparents in seeing that the new baby is baptized in the church of their faith rather than that of the other mate may become a battle royal, involving both grandparental families in armed camps in which "anything is fair in love and war." This may take the form of anything from covert hints and maneuvers to open aggression and abuse, as we saw in the many cases of in-law relationships both pro and con analyzed earlier.[1] Even if the home is of one faith there may be, with the coming of the first baby, inter-

[1] Evelyn Millis Duvall, *In-Laws: Pro and Con* (New York: Association Press, 1954), Chaps. 5 and 8.

ference in religious practices, financial plans, household routines, social activities, and so on until the young family finds its own autonomy as a family unit.

The childbearing family is now a unit in the larger family circle, with all the problems and promises appertaining thereto. As the young family establishes itself as a comfortably interdependent unit within the larger whole, giving and receiving in ways that are mutually satisfying, it is ready for the years of interlocking family interrelationships that lie ahead. No man can live to himself alone. Few families, even today in our age of individualism, are entirely independent. Most of us profit by serving and being served by our own flesh and blood, the brothers and sisters, parents, uncles, aunts, and cousins that make up our larger families.

FITTING INTO COMMUNITY LIFE AS A YOUNG FAMILY

Families tend to keep to themselves during the nesting time. Young families are apt to be highly mobile during the period when the young husband is transferred from place to place as he gets established vocationally. Community contacts in any one location tend to be temporary at best. Old friends and family are left behind. Old interests and group ties may be weakened. After a man and his wife have become parents they have little in common with their childless friends. They are not as available for gadding about as they were before the baby came. When the cost of a baby-sitter must be considered with every social affair the couple is invited to, they think twice before accepting the invitation.

Baby-sitters not only charge for their services, but they run up other costs as well. The inexperienced high school girl may give the young parents a feeling of severe insecurity that rises to fever pitch when some adolescent indiscretion is discovered. The older available woman may lack the physical stamina, the point of view, or the mental poise for dealing with the active little child. There has been such a shift in ideologies about the care of children since the older woman was herself a young mother, that it may be extremely difficult to trust to her the type of child-care procedures that seem important now (Chapters Three and Five). Even if the ideal baby-sitter is found and groomed for her tasks, there still remain the scheduling problems inherent in trying to fit together the needs of the young family with the available time of the sitter. In the "good old days," parents were freed for life as a couple in neighborhood and community affairs by the resident adults, who accepted as one of their roles in the larger family the staying with children that was expected from time to time. Nowadays it is much harder for the little new family, more removed from the extended family, to keep active in community life while their children are small.

Young parents today have developed some ingenious ways of working through this developmental task. In some neighborhoods, parents take turns minding each other's children, thus freeing each other for more social life. There are examples of parents' sitter-pools, by which parents sign up as available for the care of their neighbors' children in exchange for like service in return. One such sitter-pool is operated among twenty families with a rotating secretary who keeps track of the sitting-bank in which parents sit for others a certain number of hours and are repaid a like number of hours of sitting time when they go out. Holidays and hours after midnight count double, otherwise the exchange is an hour for an hour. One advantage is that the sitters are experienced young parents themselves. Other reported satisfactions are in serving in each other's families, enjoying the resources of each other's homes, and realizing through practical experience that one's own child is no worse than his agemates in similar homes. A disadvantage is that, while the one parent is doing duty in sitting for another family, the other parent is home alone with his or her own children. Since this is usually at the quiet hours of the family day, when the children are asleep and the adults free for their life as a couple, there may be something of a problem.

Even church-going presents problems for the couple with their first baby. Few churches have nurseries equipped to care adequately for a small child during the church service, although some are experimenting in that direction. Taking the baby along to church, so widely practiced in other cultures, is not feasible in most American churches today. The practice of one parent going to church while the other remains home with the baby is not satisfactory for the couple who want to participate as a unit. Much more frequent, although generally frowned upon as inadequate, is the tendency of young families with a child or children too small for church attendance to remain away from church. Sunday then is spent together as a family, at home, in short trips to the country, to visit relatives, or in various ways that satisfy their needs as persons and as families.

Among lower-class families there generally is more of the old-world custom of taking the baby along in shawl or bundle to any of the community or church affairs that continue to interest the mother of the family. But since such families rarely participate actively in the wide variety of community activities, family participation as such does not increase during the childbearing stage.

Upper-class families frequently have a nurse whose responsibility it is to care for the baby from the time it comes home from the hospital until he or she is old enough to be sent away to school. The nurse frees the mother and father from the day by day and night by night care of the little child, and so they are more apt to continue their previous activities in work and play, clubs and charities, benefits and concerts less disturbed by their parenting responsibilities (except in times of emergency such as the child's serious illness) than is the middle-class parent.

PLANNING FOR FURTHER CHILDREN IN THE FAMIILY

Most young parents today want two, three or more children.[1] If no planning for further children is done, one baby follows another at yearly intervals in the fertile family. This interval is shorter than many parents find desirable. Some couples marry late and want their babies just as fast as they can have them until the family reaches the desired size. Most couples today marry at a young age and want to space their children so that they can take the best care of them in ways that are most appropriate for them as a family.

It is possible to conceive again as soon as marital relations are resumed after the birth of the first child. Some women, believing that lactation postpones pregnancy, continue to nurse the first baby as long as possible in an effort to delay the coming of the second child. Others refuse to resume sexual contact with their husbands until they are ready to accept the responsibility of the possibility of another pregnancy. More effective today is the medical assistance given the couple that allows them marital access at the same time that they are relieved of further parenting responsibilities until they are ready for their next child. The belief is that a child should be wanted before it is born, and that this is more readily assured if the parents are helped to plan their families.

The procedure is a simple one. When the woman goes for her check-up six weeks following the birth of her child, her physician advises her on the practice that will best meet her situation, taking into consideration

[1] Ronald Freedman, David Goldberg, and Harry Sharp, "Ideals' about Family Size in the Detroit Metropolitan Area: 1954," *The Milbank Memorial Fund Quarterly,* Vol. XXXIII, No. 2, April 1955, pp. 187–197.

her anatomical requirements, religious affiliation, attitudes, preferences, and values as the representative of her family. This may be (with the advice of an obstetrician) some form of the rhythm method. It may be a diaphragm fitted to the mother's new requirements following the birth of her child. Or, it may be any other method the physician advises out of his knowledge of the particular family and their needs. The method is important. But even more important for the well-being of the family is the philosophy underlying whatever is done.

REWORKING A SUITABLE PHILOSOPHY OF LIFE AS A FAMILY

There is a five-fold crisis in family living at the childbearing stage that is essentially philosophical in nature:

1) Seeing through the drudgeries to the fundamental satisfactions of parenthood.
2) Valuing persons above things.
3) Resolving the conflicts inherent in the contradictory developmental tasks of parents and young children, and of fathers and mothers.
4) Establishing healthy independence as a married couple.
5) Accepting help in a spirit of appreciation and growth.

Faced with the daily round of diapers, dishes, and distractions, a young mother may feel weighed down with drudgeries to the point where she loses her sense of perspective. The young father burdened with his new responsibilities and pressures to make ends meet, may become chronically harassed and under strain. The young couple who sense through their daily duties the deep-down satisfactions involved in having their own child to care for, find ways to shrug off needless worries and to adopt a light-hearted approach to their family life and with each other. They find joy in little everyday happenings. They delight in their youngster's development, as well as in his emerging skills and cute doings and sayings. They discover the spiritual meanings of their own family living as they free themselves for the fulfillments of parenthood.

Things are in the saddle in many a family at the childbearing stage. The parents have invested a great deal of themselves and their resources into equipping a home they can be proud of. Along comes Junior with none of the adult values of neatness and cleanliness in his make-up, but rather bent on active exploration of as much of his world as he can get into his mouth, or pound to a pulp, or sit on, or wet and mess. The family soon has its back to the wall in the struggle of values as to which comes first—persons or things, parents or children. Ideally, each learns from the others in time. The baby learns that there are certain things that must not be touched, and certain values that are too precious to parents to ignore. While the parents are socializing their lusty little human, the infant in turn is changing a new mother and father into a set of experienced parents able to relax and take the daily issues.

If one's philosophy of family life centers in feeling that a good family is one where everyone always agrees with everyone else, one in which no voice is ever raised in protest, but all is sweetness and light, the childbearing stage is apt to be pretty difficult. For inherent in the period are contradictory developmental tasks and needs of parents and little children. Example: the parents need rest, sleep, and time for tender moments with each other; while a little child may clamor for attention, food, or special care at any hour of the day or night. Somehow, some way the fact of conflicting interests and values has to be seen, accepted, and lived with, if the family is to prosper.

It is at this stage that a family works through the dynamics of its primary and secondary orbits. The basic conflict is between the mother-child and the wife-husband relationship. If the young mother is so absorbed in her new mother role that her husband plays second fiddle, the family revolves around the mother-child orbit, with all the unfortunate aspects so widely recognized today. Struggling through conflicting pressures to the full realization of the importance of keeping the husband-wife relationship primary, often involves some tears, not a few tense moments, and a young mother torn by conflicting loyalties within herself. Resolving such a basic conflict rests first of all upon the philosophy of family life that sees the husband-wife relationship as central for the stability and well-being of the entire family.

Establishing healthy independence as a young family means cutting loose from the dependencies of childhood and standing on one's own feet. Fears of sponging, of imposing, of being "beholden," or of exploiting operate in this direction. Yet if the feeling that "our lives are our own, and what we do is nobody's business" prevails, it may be exceedingly difficult to get the help that is needed for a sick child, an ailing marriage, or a failing family.

Accepting help in the form of assistance and gifts from relatives, professional guidance of physicians, marriage counselors, child-guidance

The current practice of taking the baby to the physician for regular physical check-ups, preventive "shots," and vaccinations, protects the little child from many illnesses. Such a young family accepts the professional help of physicians, child-guidance experts, and others as needed, in a spirit of humility and with the recognition of the interdependence of all humans.

experts, or whatever is needed, is dependent in large measure upon the philosophy of the family.

If the young family is developing the philosophy of humility in open recognition of the interdependence of all humans, then they as family members can accept help with appreciation. Maturing families, as well as persons, grow from serving and being served by those in whom they have confidence. Especially now, the young father and mother can learn a great deal from parent-education experiences, as well as family counseling opportunities in which they talk over their problems, evaluate their progress, and plan for their future as a family.

If each new day in the life of the childbearing family started out without reference to those that had preceded, life might be hectic indeed. Each new situation would be faced without the benefit of precedents and established procedures. Each person would be confronted with a multitude of possibilities that could be frighteningly confusing. Each new developmental task of individual or family would be borne by the persons involved with its full weight. Fortunately the tasks of family life are not that heavy upon anyone, partly because of the early establishment of family rituals that help routinize into familiar patterns many of the aspects of living together around the clock and calendar. Rituals that are commonly part of the childbearing stage of the family life cycle are outlined below.

COMMON RITUALS OF THE CHILDBEARING STAGE

Rituals of awakening in the morning.
    Little child comes into parents' bed.
    Ritualized games and language play.
Breakfast rituals.
    Eating from special dishes.
    Names for foods and functions given by the baby used within the family.
Naps for baby and mother ritualized.
    Special blankets and toys.
    Ceremonies and routines.
Shopping on daily outings.
    Baby takes special possessions.
    Child allowed certain privileges.
Father's homecoming.
    Child watches for father from window.
    Father brings home gifts and surprises for baby.
    Mother and child welcome returning father in own special ways.

Bedtime bath for child.
 Special toys and procedures.
 Father may participate in particular functions.
Bedtime routines and ceremonies.
 Stories, songs, prayers at child's bedtime.
 "Drink a water" demands for further attention.
 Special light or customs to give child assurance.
Special holidays.
 Birthday celebrations ritualized.
 Visits to see relatives.
 Vacations and trips with baby.
 Photographing baby in special holiday settings.
 Sitter routines when parents celebrate as a couple.

Rituals add a great deal to the life of the childbearing family. They provide the workable routines that ease the parents' days and nights. They give the little child a sense of reliable, secure expectations of what comes next. And, they provide the simple, sweet sources of satisfaction that come to mean most in family living.

SUMMARY

The childbearing family goes through three phases in settling down to being a family, marked by changing moods, tempos, and feelings. There are predictable developmental tasks of the infant and young child that must be achieved in the childbearing family. The mother of the young child has developmental tasks she must accomplish as a mother, as a wife, as a person. The father at the childbearing stage has a series of complicated developmental tasks as a father, husband, and man that he must work through as a person. The developmental tasks of the childbearing family as-a-whole are several: adapting housing arrangements for the life of the little child (child-proofing the home during the childbearing stage), meeting the costs of family living at the childbearing stage, reworking patterns of responsibility and accountability, re-establishing mutually satisfying sexual relationships, refining intellectual and emotional communication systems for childbearing and rearing, re-establishing working relationships with relatives, fitting into community life as a young family, planning for further children in the family, and reworking a suitable philosophy of life as a family. Rituals of family living at the childbearing stage ease the parent's job, give security to the youngster, and bring satisfactions to the family.

SUGGESTED ACTIVITIES

1) Consulting authoritative child development sources for norms of development from birth through thirty months, make a master chart of the step by step progress the normal infant makes from the period of restless dependency to relatively poised independence as a little child able to communicate, get around, and master many aspects of himself and his world.

2) Review one or both of the films, *Helping the Child Accept the Do's* and *Helping the Child Accept the Don'ts* (Encyclopedia Britannica Films, Inc.; black and white, ten minutes each), with especial emphasis on the ways in which a child learns what is expected of him in a variety of situations.

3) Take pad and pencil to a nearby park, tot-lot, or other place where young mothers congregate with their babies. Record everything that is done and said by both a selected mother and her child for a five minute interval. Write a paper incorporating your verbatim record and interpreting the behaviors included in terms of the developmental tasks of both mother and baby that might be inferred at this stage, and in this situation.

4) Interview four mothers whose first babies are two years old or younger, on the question, "What part of the daily routine with your baby do you find hardest to work out comfortably?" Capture in your recording of the interviews not only the areas in which the mothers report difficulties but also their attitudes and feelings about themselves, their babies, and their adequacy as mothers in childbearing families. Comment critically on your findings in terms of the hazards young mothers find in achieving their developmental tasks during the childbearing stage.

5) Review the first 85 pages of *Fathers Are Parents, Too,* by O. Spurgeon English and Constance Foster (New York: G. P. Putnam's Sons, 1951) for implicit and explicit factors relating to the developmental tasks of the young father during the childbearing stage.

6) Write a letter to your sister who has told you of her concern over her first child's thumbsucking, telling her what is considered good practice in dealing with thumbsucking today, the developmental basis for the recommendations, and readings that may be still further helpful to her.

7) Outline a course of study to be used for a "Grandmothers' Refresher Course in Child Care" that would help a present-day grandmother bring up to date her concepts, ideas, and understandings of child development and guidance through the first three years of a baby's life. Contrast throughout present-day practices with those prevalent twenty to thirty years ago (when she brought up her children) using such references as were generally current then as manuals of baby care, in books, magazines, and government bulletins and pamphlets.

8) Prepare a double chart through a day in the life of 1) a traditionally oriented childbearing family, and 2) a developmentally oriented childbearing family making notations of all entries in which scheduling and procedures differ significantly between the two families.

9) Contrast expected family rituals at the childbearing stage for families at the lower-, middle-, and upper-class levels documenting your materials with quotations from James H. S. Bossard and Eleanor S. Boll, *Ritual in Family Living* (Philadelphia: University of Pennsylvania Press, 1950), Chap. 6, as well as excerpts from selected fiction and biography representative of the three class levels.

10) Chart the complementary and conflicting developmental tasks of the mother, the father, and the baby of the childbearing family, using the materials detailed in this chapter in the style developed in Chapters Six and Seven. Discuss the relative mutuality of this stage as compared with the previous two stages of the family life cycle.

READINGS

Aldrich, C. Anderson and Mary, *Babies Are Human Beings* (New York: Macmillan Company, 1954 Edition).

Auerbach, Aline B., *How to Give Your Child a Good Start* (New York: The Child Study Association of America, Revised 1961).

Baruch, Dorothy, *New Ways in Discipline* (New York: Whittlesey House, 1949).

Blood, Robert O., Jr., "Consequences of Permissiveness for Parents of Young Children," *Marriage and Family Living*, Vol. XV, No. 3, August 1953, pp. 209–212.

Blood, Robert O., Jr., and Wolfe, Donald M., *Husbands and Wives* (Glencoe, Illinois: The Free Press, 1960), Chapter 5.

Boek, Walter E.; Sussman, Marvin B.; and Yankauer, Alfred, "Social Class and Child Care Practices," *Marriage and Family Living*, Vol. XX, No. 4, November 1958, pp. 326–333.

Bossard, James H. S., and Boll, Eleanor S., *Ritual in Family Living* (Philadelphia: University of Pennsylvania Press, 1950).

Brody, Sylvia, *Patterns of Mothering* (New York: Basic Book, Inc., 1956).

Davis, M. Edward, *Natural Child Spacing* (Garden City, New York: Hanover House, 1953).

Duvall, Evelyn Millis, *Family Living* (New York: Macmillan Company, Revised 1961), Chaps. 15, 16, 17.

Duvall, Evelyn Millis, and Hill, Reuben, *Being Married* (Boston: D. C. Heath and Company, 1960), Chaps. 18, 19.

English, O. Spurgeon, and Foster, Constance J., *Fathers Are Parents, Too* (New York: G. P. Putnam's Sons, 1951).

Faegre, Marion L.; Anderson, John E.; and Harris, Dale B., *Child Care and Training* (Minneapolis: University of Minnesota Press, Revised 1958).

Greenhill, J. P., "The Birth of the Baby," Chapter 5 in Part Three in Fishbein, Morris, and Burgess, Ernest (eds.), *Successful Marriage* (Garden City, New York: Doubleday and Company, Revised 1955).

Hymes, James L., *Enjoy Your Child—Ages 1, 2, and 3* (New York: Public Affairs Committee, 1948).

LeMasters, Ersel, "Parenthood as Crisis," *Marriage and Family Living,* Vol. XIX, No. 4, November 1957, pp. 352–355.

Levy, David M., *Maternal Overprotection* (New York: Columbia University, 1948).

Louisiana Association for Mental Health, *Pierre the Pelican, Post-Natal Series* (New Orleans: Louisiana Association for Mental Health, 1528 Jackson Avenue, New Orleans 13, La.).

Martin, William E.; and Stendler, Celia B., *Child Behavior and Development* (New York: Harcourt, Brace, Revised 1959).

Ridenour, Nina, *Some Special Problems of Children* (Eight pamphlets published by the New York City Committee on Mental Hygiene, 105 East 22nd Street, New York, 10, New York, 1948).

Smart, Mollie Stevens, *Babe in a House* (New York: Scribner's, 1950).

Smart, Mollie Stevens and Russell, *Living and Learning with Children* (Boston: Houghton Mifflin, 1949).

Spock, Benjamin, *The Pocketbook of Baby and Child Care* (New York: Pocket Books, Inc., 1946).

Superintendent of Documents, Government Printing Office, Washington, D. C.:
    A Healthy Personality for Your Child (1952)
    Breast Feeding (1947)
    Foods Your Children Need (1953)
    Infant Care (1955)
    Your Well Baby (1949)
    Your Child from One to Six (1956)

Wiegand, Elizabeth; and Gross, Irma, *Fatigue of Homemakers with Young Children* (East Lansing, Michigan: Agricultural Experiment Station Technical Bulletin 265, March 1958).

The child is father of the man
WORDSWORTH

CHAPTER NINE

Families with preschool children

While the first child is between 2½ and 5 years of age, the preschool family typically has a second and possibly a third child, making a total of three to five persons, with the possibility of from three to ten interpersonal relationships. The possible positions in the family are husband-father, wife-mother, son-brother, and daughter-sister, each with its own developmental tasks. While the adults struggle with their child-rearing and personal tasks, the preschool child faces the crisis of initiative (expanding imagination) vs. guilt (developing conscience), while younger siblings retrace each in his/her own way the developmental stages the eldest has completed.

DEVELOPMENTAL TASKS OF PRESCHOOL CHILDREN

From the preoccupation of babyhood, the preschool child is emerging as a social being who can share with others, who participates as a member of his family, and who is ready for school. His pace of physical growth is slowing down, and many of his body activities are becoming routine. Progress in his emotional and intellectual development is increasingly apparent in his growing ability to express himself in speech and in his greatly increased acquaintance with his environment. The preschool child's chief developmental tasks are outlined below:

1) *Settling into healthful daily routines of rest and activity:*
   Going to bed and getting his needed rest without a struggle.
   Taking his nap or rest, and learning to relax when he is weary.
   Enjoying active play in a variety of situations and places.
   Becoming increasingly flexible and able to accept changes happily.

2) *Mastering good eating habits:*
   Becoming adequate in the use of the customary utensils for eating.
   Accepting new flavors and textures in foods with interest.
   Enjoying his food with lessening incidents of spilling, messing, and toying.
   Learning the social as well as the sensual pleasures of eating.

3) *Mastering the basics of toilet training:*
   Growing in his ability to indicate his needs for elimination.
   Cooperating comfortably in the toilet training program.
   Finding satisfaction in behaving appropriately as to time, place, and ways of toileting expected of boys/girls of his age in the culture.
   Becoming flexible in his ability to use the variety of resources, places, and personnel available to him.

4) *Developing the physical skills appropriate to his stage of motor development:*
   Learning to climb, balance, run, skip, push, pull, throw, and catch in whole body use of large muscle systems.
   Developing manual skills for buttoning, zipping, cutting, drawing, coloring, modeling, and manipulating small objects deftly.
   Becoming increasingly independent in his ability to handle himself effectively in a variety of physical situations and expectancies.

5) *Becoming a participating member of his family:*
   Assuming responsibilities within the family happily and effectively.
   Learning to give and receive affection and gifts freely within the family.
   Identifying with parent of the same sex.
   Developing ability to share his parents with another child and with others generally.

Recognizing his family's ways as compared with those of his friends and neighbors.

6) *Beginning to master his impulses and to conform to others' expectations:*

Outgrowing the impulsive, urgent outbursts of infancy.

Learning to share, take turns, hold his own, and enjoy the companionship of other children, and at times play happily alone.

Developing the sympathetic cooperative ways with others that insure his inclusion in groups.

Learning appropriate behavior for situations in which he is (times and places for noise, quiet, messing, nudity, etc.).

7) *Developing healthy emotional expressions for a wide variety of experiences:*

Learning to play out his feelings, frustrations, needs, and experiences.

Learning to postpone and to wait for satisfactions.

Expressing momentary hostility and making up readily afterwards.

Refining generalized joy or pain into discriminating expressions of pleasure, eagerness, tenderness, affection, sympathy, fear, anxiety, remorse, sorrow, etc.

8) *Learning to communicate effectively with an increasing number of others:*

Developing the vocabulary and ability to talk about a rapidly growing number of things, feelings, experiences, impressions, and curiosities.

Learning to listen, take in, follow directions, increase his attention span, and to respond intellectually to situations and to others.

Acquiring the social skills needed to get over feelings of shyness, self-consciousness, and awkwardness, and to participate with other people comfortably.

9) *Developing the ability to handle potentially dangerous situations:*

Learning to respect the dangers in fire, traffic, high places, bathing areas, poisons, animals, and the many other potential hazards.

Learning to handle himself effectively without undue fear in situations calling for caution and safety precautions (crossing streets, greeting strange dogs, responding to a stranger's offer of a ride, etc.).

Becoming willing to accept help in situations that are beyond him without undue dependence or too impulsive independence.

10) *Learning to be an autonomous person with initiative and a conscience of his own:*

Becoming increasingly responsible for making decisions in ways appropriate to his readiness.

Taking initiative for projecting himself into situations with innovations, experiments, trials, and original achievements.

Internalizing the expectancies and demands of his family and culture groups in his developing conscience.

Becoming reasonably self-sufficient in situations in accordance with his own make-up and stage of development.

11) *Laying foundations for understanding the meanings of life:*

Beginning to understand the origins of life, how the two sexes differ, and who he or she is as a member of his or her sex.

Trying to understand the nature of the physical world, what things are, how they work and why, and what they mean to him.

Accepting the religious faith of his parents, learning about the nature of God, and the spiritual nature of life.

The preschool boy or girl must achieve enough independence to be comfortable without his parents in a variety of situations. He or she must become reasonably self-sufficient both in the home and in outside settings, in keeping with his particular stage of development. The child who has preliminary practice in crossing streets, managing his outside garments, going to the toilet alone, washing his own hands, using his handkerchief, and in handling everyday routines, accidents and minor crises, will be ready to enter school feeling self-confident enough to be ready for its challenges. If his parents have introduced stories, songs, pictures, conversations, excursions, and creative play materials into his life, he will be able to enter school as a contributor as well as a recipient. When the preschool child has successfully accomplished the developmental tasks of this stage, he is ready to go to school. The check test on readiness for school attendance details some of the specific learnings derived from the preschooler's developmental tasks.

As a little girl "feeds her baby" she identifies with her mother by playing out what she sees as the feminine way to be. It is this identification with the parent of the same sex that is operating when a little girl trots around after her mother wanting "to help" in the things she sees her mother doing about the house. Similarly, the little boy frequently tags after his father, copying mannerisms, expressions, and ways of doing things down to the most meticulous detail.

CHECK TEST FOR THE CHILD'S READINESS FOR SCHOOL [1]

	Always	Usually	Sometimes	Rarely
1. The child knows his name, address, and father's name.				
2. He is free from those physical defects which can be corrected.				
3. He knows the way to school and can find his way home again.				
4. He has been taught how to cross streets.				
5. He recognizes policemen, is not afraid of them, and will follow their directions.				
6. He can go to the toilet, manage his clothing by himself, and conform to expected modesty patterns.				
7. He can hang up his coat, put on his outdoor clothing, and recognize his own belongings.				
8. He is content to stay with adults other than those he knows well.				
9. He has had opportunities to play with children his own age and gets along well with them.				
10. He is familiar with some of the places in the neighborhood which are of interest to children his age (post office, grocery store, fire house, a building under construction, etc.).				
11. He can entertain himself with constructive tasks for short periods of time.				
12. He is interested in books and will spend some time looking at them quietly.				
13. He attacks a new job willingly and welcomes new situations without fear.				

[1] Adapted freely from Fay Moeller, *Understanding Our Children*, Extension Service, University of Connecticut, Storrs, Connecticut, June 29, 1954 bulletin (mimeographed).

	Always	Usually	Sometimes	Rarely
14. He is in the habit of sharing certain household tasks with other members of the family.				
15. He is patient about waiting his turn and respecting property rights of others.				
16. He can keep his temper, his tears, and his other emotional outbursts under reasonably good control.				
17. He is curious about many things and, with a little help from an adult, can follow up his interests.				

DEVELOPMENTAL TASKS OF PARENTS OF PRESCHOOL CHILDREN [1]

Parents help the young child achieve his many developmental tasks by accepting his increasing range of skills and physical activity and by finding satisfactory roles in which physical help is gradually diminishing and other kinds of help gradually increasing. They must assume responsibility for supervising the child and yet avoid unnecessary worry and fear, whether in connection with a child's physical competence or growing social interests.

One of the perpetually surprising features of family life is the fact that it never stays put. No sooner has a fence been built to keep a 2-year-old out of the street than he is a 3-year-old, capable of understanding why he must keep to the sidewalk. The period of teaching the youngster to keep dry is succeeded by one of helping him to get used to sharing his parents with a new baby. Just as a child has reached a stage when his mental growth has made him an increasingly interesting companion, he is away at nursery school or kindergarten, and his parents begin to be outsiders, unaware of what is happening to him during a big share of his waking hours.

Parents who expect changes in themselves and in changing conditions will not find themselves washed up high and dry on the beach

[1] Freely adapted from Faegre, Marion L.; Hymes, James L., Jr.; Chandler, Caroline A., M.D.; and Work, Henry, M.D.; "Section III, Pre-School Family Stage," for the Committee on the Dynamics of Family Interaction, Preliminary Report, Evelyn Duvall and Reuben Hill, co-chairmen, National Conference on Family Life, February 1948 (mimeographed materials).

when their children are sailing merrily down the stream of life. They will have kept in the swim of things, will have found the necessary change and development exhilarating and enjoyable.

LOVING THE CHILD FOR WHAT HE REALLY IS

As their child enters a wider area of relationships and presses strongly for independence, parents need to maintain a sense of balance that recognizes helpfully that the child is still young, still dependent, and still in need of comfort and help in many areas.

He especially needs the comfort of being loved, appreciated, and enjoyed for himself. Both parents may need to check upon possible tendencies toward trying to make the child over, tweaking and pulling at him in little criticisms rather than giving encouraging and appreciative little pats. They must recognize that it is their job to help the child develop the capacities he has rather than to try to build up their self-esteem by pushing him beyond what he can do. Being aware of dangers in visiting "the curse of the norm" on any child and enjoying the unique individuality of each child are paired developmental tasks of prime importance.

CREATING TOGETHER AN ATMOSPHERE OF LOVE WITHIN THE HOME

Recent studies show [1] that wives and husbands at the preschool family stage have less emotionally-charged interaction with each other than they had earlier in their marriages. They have fewer arguments, feel resentful or misunderstood less often, and they tend less often to refuse to talk because they are angry with each other, now than they have since they married. At the same time, the marriage has fewer positive supports at the preschool stage than it formerly did. Husband and wife have fewer gay times away from home, 1) less often laugh together, 2) work together on a stimulating project, or 3) calmly discuss something with each other than formerly. By now the parents seem to have settled into the business of childrearing with fewer negative feelings and less fun as a married pair than they had earlier.

At this stage the parents may need to strengthen their creative partner-

[1] Harold Feldman, "The Development of the Husband-Wife Relationship," a study supported in part by the National Institute of Mental Health, unpublished data received through personal correspondence, March 24, 1961, with permission.

ship and express their affection in ways that will keep their relationship from falling to a humdrum level. Expression of affection for each other may seem like an odd "task" to set up, but lack of such expression ranks high among the grievances husbands and wives list when trying to analyze their sources of unhappiness.[1] Apparently it is easy to fall into the habit of assuming that the other partner will take for granted the love each really wants and needs.

WHOLESOMELY ACCEPTING THE WEAKNESSES IN THEMSELVES AND IN EACH OTHER

Somehow parents have to learn to take their unavoidable failures, mistakes, and blunders without piling up feelings of guilt, blame, and recrimination. One way of doing this is to try to be sympathetic toward, instead of full of blame for, each other's faults in connection with dealing with the children. In a day when so much emphasis is placed on parent-child relations, while so little is known about how to keep from foisting one's own frustrations and insecurities on one's children, parents need each other's help in striking a balance between worry and nonchalance, between self-recrimination and indifference. We all make mistakes, but if our basic attitudes are wholesome, loving and friendly, the mistakes are going to be more than offset by good feelings.

CONTINUING TO DEVELOP AS INDIVIDUALS AND AS A MARRIED COUPLE

This is a time when a man and woman must learn to nourish mutual tastes, interests, and friendships as an aid to making the satisfactions of marriage permanent and enduring; and to provide for each other the satisfactions that strengthen their belief in themselves and give them status. The many demands and pressures upon each parent may tend to leave little time for them to enjoy each other and the hobbies or pursuits that may have been initially responsible for drawing them together. The mother may be so concerned with the demands of child care and homemaking that she gives little thought to her need for continuing to develop as a person. The father may be so taken up with his work that he no longer takes time for just enjoying life with his wife.

[1] Lewis M. Terman et al., *Psychological Factors in Marital Happiness* (New York: McGraw-Hill Book Company, Inc., 1938), Chap. 5, "The Interpretation of Domestic Grievances."

FAMILY DEVELOPMENTAL TASKS AT THE PRESCHOOL STAGE

While the preschool child is achieving his developmental tasks, and the adults are attempting to accomplish theirs as parents and as husband and wife, the family as-a-whole is concurrently facing the family developmental tasks of the preschool stage:

1) Supplying adequate space, facilities, and equipment for the expanding family
2) Meeting predictable and unexpected costs of family life with small children
3) Sharing responsibilities within the expanded family and between members of the growing family
4) Maintaining mutually satisfying sexual relationships and planning for future children
5) Creating and maintaining effective communication systems within the family
6) Cultivating the full potentials of relationships with relatives within the extended family
7) Tapping resources, serving needs, and enjoying contacts outside the family
8) Facing dilemmas and reworking philosophies of life in ever-changing challenges

SUPPLYING ADEQUATE SPACE, FACILITIES, AND EQUIPMENT

Housing now should promote the growth of the preschooler, a good start for his younger sibling, and allow some privacy and comfort for the parents. Nothing can be a greater challenge to good family growth than inadequate room to work out the problems of group and individual maturation. When the entire neighborhood seems compressed and hemmed in through social barriers, the problem of full expression of the individual and the family is compounded. Play facilities, recreational areas, parks and their availability to all are important in providing an outlet for family tensions. Inefficient houses and inadequate household equipment complicate the mother's already onerous task of dividing her time between the needs of her children and the demands of the household. Many families achieve a high degree of family solidarity and goodwill by their ingenious collective use of too-tight quarters and too-limited facilities. But the fact that some families do well under severely limiting conditions does not thereby recommend the restrictions for general usage.

This is the stage when climbing, pulling, and hauling equipment gives the preschooler the large muscle exercise and skill development opportunities he needs, at the same time that it takes him out from under foot, assuring both his parents and his new sibling of some relief from his boisterous activity. Facilities adequate for the differential sleep and rest requirements of the several members of the family are a real asset. Parents now especially need privacy for their more intimate moments together without the everpresent interest of the inquiring preschooler, "Whatcha doing?" The child-proofing of the house mentioned earlier carries over into this stage with all its safeguards, especially now, when protecting the new baby without unduly restraining the preschool child, becomes an additional factor of importance.

MEETING PREDICTABLE AND UNEXPECTED COSTS OF FAMILY LIFE WITH SMALL CHILDREN

If the family income is fairly steady, it is possible to budget carefully for the normal expenditures of the growing family: so much for food, clothing, sitter fees, recreation, utilities, rent or house payments, and the rest. When the income fluctuates as it does with periods of unemployment or sickness or accident, major adjustments may need to be made.

The preschool stage is notorious for its unpredictabilities. The family may be getting along fine, with income matching outgo, when suddenly something happens that throws the whole financial picture out of focus. In early childhood there is a multiplicity of minor illnesses, any one of which can upset the family budget temporarily. Now when the older child ranges further afield in the neighborhood, to nursery school, kindergarten, play lot, park and beach, he comes in contact with many more children than he met as long as he was content in house and yard. These increased contacts multiply exposure to infections that make childhood diseases common for the preschooler and quite often for the baby sister or brother as well.

Accidents, falls, burns, and cuts are even more distressing because of the factor of suddenness that is added to the distress of actual incapacity. Children's accidents are frequently of great importance in the amount of guilt they arouse in the parents. When a long continued illness or an abrupt accident results in a deforming handicap or a crippling condition, it may necessitate critical shifts in the economic aspects as well as the emotional relationships of the family. Intelligent medical and social management are often necessary to keep the illness at the physical level from producing emotional maladjustment in its wake.

The high costs of medical care, continuing insurance drains, installment buying, debts, and mortgages complicate even well-planned family economics and are disastrous to those less carefully organized. Recent years have seen some advance in general recognition of such financial hazards facing young families with the development of such cushioning resources: group hospitalization and medical service plans, well-baby clinics, cooperative nurseries, child guidance clinics, mental hygiene services, family service facilities, parent education agencies, adult and child recreational programs, as well as special facilities for the care and education of all types of exceptional children. That such helpful resources are not yet generally available, or even known, to the rank and file of families who need them is all too true in most communities.

Nationally, grants-in-aid to the several states, funneled through the Children's Bureau, are available for maternal and child health, crippled children, child welfare services, etc., as is also the mental hygiene program under the United States Public Health Service.

The preschool family characteristically gets along on the single income of the husband. Only 15 per cent of all mothers of children under six are employed outside their homes.[1] This contrasts with 40 per cent of all wives working during the first year of marriage, and with 33 per cent of the wives in the labor force by the time all of the children have reached school age.[2] Now when little children must be cared for, it is the exceptional mother who leaves home to earn money, even at a time when family needs are great. This is the period when the family tightens its belt and tries to make ends meet on the husband's income alone.

SHARING RESPONSIBILITIES WITHIN THE EXPANDING FAMILY

Careful division of responsibility is needed at this time, when both mother and father may feel overworked. That the mother of young children is greatly overworked was publicly recognized in the widely discussed forum report, "The Plight of the Young Mother," in which the problem is introduced by these words:

[1] Paul C. Glick, "The Life Cycle of the Family," *Marriage and Family Living*, Vol. XVII, No. 1, February 1955, p. 8.

[2] *Ibid.*, p. 8.

Is our society asking too much of the young mother? Is it possible for her to give her children the best care when she must work as long as 100 hours a week—much more than is expected of people in business and industry—with no relief, even when her health is below par? Does this system produce the best results for the nation, for the community? [1]

Daily round-the-clock child care involving "chasing the children" who play in yard and neighborhood to properly supervise their play and protect them from danger, as well as attending to the needs of the infant, and doing the housework (marketing, cooking, baking, cleaning, dishwashing, sewing, washing, ironing), are generally assigned the young wife and mother in our society. In former days, these many responsibilities were divided among other grown and growing members of the family. In the old-fashioned farm family, there was always a pair of willing hands to mind the baby, or do an errand, or set the table. Margaret Mead reminds us that most primitive peoples recognize that it takes more than one adult to care for small helpless children and recommends that American families innovate ways of sharing small-child care more broadly today.

We have established a strange and lonely way of life, as grandmothers, aunts, grown daughters, and domestic help have progressively been banished from the home. We must devise new ways for real neighborhood sharing of the care of children, more cooperative nursery schools, more sharing of minor crises, so that the neighborhood takes over what the family used to do. And we need more generosity on the part of parents toward the grandparents, the childless aunts and uncles, all of whom could share a lot of the care of children if the parents were willing to really share their children. The present-day mother is alone in the house with her small children too much, and she has her hands too full.[2]

Until real help from the outside can be recruited, it may fall to the husband to share with his wife the tasks of childrearing and housekeeping through the preschool stage of the family life cycle. The young father returns home from work to find his wife busy with her end-of-the-day chores, the children irritably clinging to her while she tries to get the evening meal. He steps in and volunteers to take the children off her hands or to do some of the chores that she has not been able to finish through the hectic pace of the day. He may be tired but he comes in fresh from

<hr />

[1] The Fifth Journal Forum, "The Plight of the Young Mother," *Ladies' Home Journal*, February 1956, p. 61.
[2] *Ibid.*, p. 62.

the outside without the mutual annoyance and frustration that is so often a part of the young mother's hour by hour life with active young children. He can whisk them off for a frolic, or give them their baths, or take over their feeding with a light touch just because he has been out of the home all day. The more strenuous tasks of floor mopping, window cleaning, washing, or trash dumping may be saved for the man of the house by the woman whose strength is barely adequate for the many other demands upon it.

The high cost of labor, coupled with the great increase in home ownership, means that more men are taking over the repair and development projects around their homes. One estimate [1] indicates that men spend from 22 to 30 hours a week at such tasks as plumbing, carpentry, yard work, gardening and lawn-care, helping out in a family crisis, and working at special improvements. As one householder put it:

> I come home from the office, shuck off my coat, and the wife tells me whether I must become plumber, mason, gardener, electrician, cook, or baby-sitter. Around our place there's always a crisis.[2]

The apartment dweller is not so burdened with household service nor is the man in the higher income brackets, as Table 16 indicates.

TABLE 16. *Annual Income and Household Responsibilities of the Man of the House, 1956* [3]

Annual Income	Responsibilities Assumed by the Householder
Up to $4,500	Virtually all home repair work
$4,500–$7,500	Remodeling and restyling done personally
$7,500–$10,000	Easier jobs with professional hired for big painting and construction projects
Above $10,000	Some chores personally done, the rest planned and supervised

Some young families have established such heavy allocations of responsibilities to the young husband and father that he may be severely exploited by a wife who reserves more and more of the day's work for him to do when his day's work is presumably finished. The young husband

---

[1] Bruce Lee, "Who Works Longer—Husband or Wife?" April 29, 1956, pp. 7, 21, 22. Reprinted from *This Week* Magazine, copyright 1956 by the United Newspapers Magazine Corporation.

[2] *Ibid.*, p. 21.

[3] *Ibid.*, p. 22.

is apt to be sorely pressed for time and energy at this stage of his life. This is the time when the man of the house is trying to get ahead on his job. He possibly is taking an evening course or two with an eye to advancement. He may be doing what overtime he can get to help make ends meet. Even if he is willing to help out at home there is a limit to what any one person can do comfortably and well.

This is a time when it is necessary to have an equitable division of responsibility between mother and father on the basis of time, strength, interest, ability, and mutual concern for the well-being of the family. The man of the house may prefer taking the laundry to the laundromat if that is where he can meet and chat with the other fathers of the neighborhood. In another household, the young mother may choose to assume full responsibility for the laundry at home where she can keep the baby's things done up and some portion of the household linen taken care of on a daily basis. One family may decide to invest in an automatic washer the money that another family pays out for diaper services and laundrying. Whatever the decision, the important thing is that the members of the family agree to it as appropriate for their situation.

The preschool child is old enough to assume some real responsibilities. He gradually takes over more and more of his own care in toileting, washing his face and hands, dressing and undressing, and picking up his toys, with help or supervision as needed. As he enters the preschool period, he or she has begun to take a real interest in what is going on in the household and wants to participate. The little girl of two and a half or three begs to help make beds, to sweep the floor and to wash dishes when her mother is occupied with these tasks. The child identifies with the parent of the same sex and likes nothing better than acting out the sex role. Parents are wise not to discourage these efforts on the part of the small child "to help." They share with the child the jobs he or she can join in, not so much in the interest of the child's labor, but especially because helping makes the youngster a real participant in his family. The child learns thus to internalize his or her sex role.

The parent's burden varies greatly according to social class, with families of the upper classes hiring more domestic help in the form of housekeepers, cooks, maids, and infant nurses. Middle-class families spend little on domestic help; and lower-class mothers hire no help, themselves often available for day labor. The middle-class family invests more in labor-saving devices and equipment: electric washers and dry-

The preschooler is old enough to assume some real responsibility, and parents are wise to encourage this "help" as the child's way of participating in the family.

ers, dishwashing machines, vacuum cleaners, waxers, steam irons, mangles and other "wife-savers," that tend to be lacking in the lower-class home. Some struggling farm families, with more children than in the higher social levels on the average, carry and heat their water, cut and carry in their fuel, and raise, gather and process much of their food-stuffs in a daily round of "chores."

Many a young family sails smoothly through the preschool family stage in these days. Modern equipment in kitchen and laundry eases the load that the young mother must carry. Miracle fabrics are easy to keep clean and need practically no ironing. Prepared baby foods and frozen prod-

Modern automatic washers and dryers ease the load the young mother must carry and make some provision for the preschool child to assist in collecting and sorting the laundry.

ucts that can be readied for use in a few moments are a God-send. The modern young mother's ability to plan her work, putting the essential tasks on the agenda and letting the relatively unimportant things slide, removes much of the strain from daily routines. Spacing the arrival of the children so that each is assured the care it needs without unduly taxing the mother's strength does much to keep the young family on an even keel during the preschool stage when life can so easily become pretty hectic.

Success in achieving this developmental task is not just a matter of how much or how little there is to be done, but rather of how decisions are made, how roles are assigned, and how the several family members feel about their responsibilities. If each family member feels pride and pleasure in doing his tasks, if each is accountable to the others for common concerns, if each feels needed and appreciated, the family is finding happiness and integration as a working unit.

MAINTAINING MUTUALLY SATISFYING SEXUAL RELATIONSHIPS AND PLANNING FOR FUTURE CHILDREN

At this stage of the family life cycle, the parents have been through the full process of conception, pregnancy, childbirth, and establishment as a family. They are able to take further pregnancies more in their stride than was possible when the first baby came. But the very fact that there is already one child in the family adds its increment of responsibility to the second period of "infanticipating."

When mother goes to the hospital for the delivery of subsequent babies, father usually maintains the equilibrium at home. He gets his first youngster up in the morning and off to a good start in the day before he goes off to work. Not infrequently the young father takes his "vacation" from his job so that he can be at home to care for his firstborn while his wife is hospitalized for the second. The wealthy family keeps on the infant nurse for the care of the first and further children. In still other families a grandmother will take over the care of the household until the new baby and mother are firmly installed at home. Sometimes a toddler has to be "farmed out" to neighbors or friends while his mother spends her lying-in period away from home. In the larger cities homemaker services are increasing for just such assistance to families whose wife and mother is temporarily "out of service." One thing is sure, the American mother cannot take her family along with her when she goes to be delivered, as is possible in some other cultures.

When mother, father, and other family members are intimately involved in caring for the children, there tends to be more joint consultation about family size and more specific plans made for further children than in cultures where a man takes pride in sheer fertility and a woman's role is defined in terms of one pregnancy after another throughout her active reproductive life.

American couples want to have children. Men and women generally say they want to have two, three, or more children.[1] The figures from a study of eleven universities shown in Table 17 are fairly typical of college men and women.

---

[1] Ronald Freedman, David Goldberg, and Harry Sharp, " 'Ideals' about Family Size in the Detroit Metropolitan Area: 1954," *The Milbank Memorial Fund Quarterly*, Vol. 33, No. 3, April 1955, p. 195.

TABLE 17. *Number of Children College Students Expect to Have* [1]

Number of Children Expected	Men N — 2,008	Women N — 750
None	2%	1%
One	5	—
Two	25	13
Three	38	27
Four	23	31
Five or more	1	18
Don't know or no answer	5	9

Studies of the spacing of children agree that up to the third birth the interval between births tend to increase.[2] These longer intervals can be roughly seen as "breathing spaces" in which the young family re-establishes itself and mobilizes its resources after the birth of one child before attempting the next.

Finding the time, privacy, and energy for tender, close relationships as a married couple may be difficult when children are young. Sharing bed or room with a child old enough to be aware of what is going on robs a husband and wife of much-needed privacy. Days and nights of nursing a sick youngster rob even the most loving husband and wife of their ardor for each other. Just getting through the day's work may bring the couple to bed too tired for anything but sleep. Knowing from experience the power of their fertility tends to make the woman wary of her husband's approaches unless she has great confidence in the family planning procedures in operation. What once was entered into with joyous abandon, now may become a marital duty, unless they as a couple provide for their sex life together amid the welter of other demands.

CREATING AND MAINTAINING EFFECTIVE COMMUNICATION SYSTEMS WITHIN THE FAMILY

The tower of Babel had nothing on family life at the preschool stage. The baby babbles and gurgles and sputters and fusses and "practices" his

[1] Rose K. Goldsen, Morris Rosenberg, Robin M. Williams, Jr., and Edward A. Suchman, *What College Students Think* (Princeton, N. J.: D. Van Nostrand Company, 1960), p. 218.
[2] Gerald Leslie, Harold Christensen, and Glenn Pearman, "Studies in Child Spacing: IV. The Time-Interval Separating All Children in Completed Families of Purdue University Graduates," *Social Forces*, Vol. 34, No. I, October 1955, pp. 77–82.

vowels; the preschooler talks a blue streak, jumping from one topic to another and from the answer to one question to another miles removed; mother tries to get through to her preoccupied spouse and her energetic youngsters her suggestions, ideas, and feelings; and father grumbles out his frustrations oblivious to the goings-on around him.

With the coming of the new baby, the emotional constellations of the family shift as the firstborn accepts his displacement as well as he can and as the parents find a place in their home for the little newcomer at the same time that they safeguard the security of the older child. There may be a tendency for parents to be emotionally warmer with the second baby than they were with their first.[1] This probably is not so much that they love the second baby more, but rather that they have become more familiar with their roles, and so are able to relax and enjoy the new baby more fully than they could in their first experience as parents.

Understandable as the parents' feelings and emotional expressions are, it may be hard for the firstborn to accept their open display of affection for the little new rival. Therefore, the mother and father may need to create new modes of emotional communication with the older child that will give him the assurance that he is loved and needed and wanted for himself. Wise parents provide some special time with their firstborn when the new baby does not intrude. It sometimes helps to let the firstborn know that just because he is the older, he occupies a special place in their lives that no younger sibling can ever fill. Some increase in responsibility for the firstborn may be reassuring to him if it is not overdone. The older child sometimes has to let his parents know of his need for being babied too, in regressive acts: wetting himself when he has long since learned to be dry, wanting to take his milk from a bottle when he has already established more mature eating and drinking habits, wanting to be cuddled and fussed over as the baby is, even trying to put himself in the baby's place—literally in the buggy or the crib. These are signals a sensitive parent can read that indicate the older child's need for more close, demonstrable affection and attention than he has been getting. Ridiculing, belittling, ignoring, or denying a child's efforts to communicate his emotional needs cripple the communication systems and bottle up explosive feelings with unfortunate results to the youngster, the younger sibling, and the family-as-a-whole.

[1] J. K. Lasko, "Parent Behavior toward First and Second Children," *Genetic Psychology Monograph*, Vol. 49, No. 1, February 1954, pp. 99–137.

The child who is prepared for the coming of his new baby sister or brother, can take with less distress the jealousy and rivalry so usually generated by his displacement by the new rival. Before the baby comes, the older child needs from his parents an understanding of what is happening, an assurance that this is to be HIS baby as well as theirs and that they will love him after the baby comes, as they have before. In this a mother or father can get helpful books to read to the preschool youngster, as well as find sound guides on the early sex education of their children, of which the following are examples:

Ets, Marie Hall, *The Story of a Baby* (New York: Viking Press, 1948).

Faegre, Marion L., *Your Own Story* (Minneapolis: University of Minnesota Press, 1943).

Gruenberg, Sidonie M., *The Wonderful Story of How You Were Born* (Garden City, New York: Hanover House, 1952).

Hymes, James L., *How to Tell Your Child about Sex* (New York: Public Affairs Committee, 1949).

Levine, Milton, and Seligmann, J. H., *The Wonder of Life* (New York: Simon and Schuster, 1940).

Peller, Lili, and Mumford, Sophia, *Our New Baby* (New York: Vanguard Press, 1943).

Shane, Harold and Ruth, *The New Baby* (New York: Simon and Schuster, 1948).

Strain, Frances Bruce, *New Patterns in Sex Teaching* (New York: Appleton-Century-Crofts, 1951 edition).

Little children are so everpresent and so demanding of the time and attention of their parents, that husband and wife may need to inaugurate new times and ways for getting through to each other. The little children may be fed by one or both parents, and then put to rest while the parents have an occasional quiet meal together. Or, the preschooler can be given some special time of his own by either the father or the mother just before the family meal, so that he can relate the excitements of his day and get some of his more pressing questions out of the way before the family as a whole assembles for mealtime. One young family developed a "green light" system by which the "traffic" of conversation could flow in both directions across the table, each in its turn, thus assuring the parents of some access to each other between the gusts of chatter from their preschool youngsters.

This developmental task is being achieved in the family as each member of the family increasingly feels free to express his ideas, his feelings, and, his values with assurance of their acceptance by the others in the family. The expanding stage of the family life cycle is so explosive, and so full of new experiences, feelings, decisions, and needs to evaluate, that communication systems become extremely important at the very time that they are most difficult to keep open and in good working order. But few things are more important to happy family life.

CULTIVATING THE FULL POTENTIALS OF RELATIONSHIPS WITHIN THE EXTENDED FAMILY

At few stages in the family life cycle can relatives be as important as during the preschool period. Grandparents can do much to ease the pressures upon the parents while children are young. A loving relative who is on hand while the new baby is coming, and through the illnesses and accidents that occasionally hit the young family, cushions these crises in many a home. An aunt and uncle may get valuable experience at the same time that they relieve the young parents in child care. They may take over for a long evening or over a weekend or even for a week or two while father and mother slip off to regain their perspective as a couple on a brief vacation, on a business trip, or for a quick visit to old friends.

Problems come up, of course, when the substitute parents do not agree with the child guidance procedures or philosophy that the parents are trying to practice. A grandmother can "spoil" her young charges, in ways that take weeks to rehabilitate, if she is not aware of the parents' goals for their children. Or a too-rigid program of discipline suddenly imposed by some well-meaning aunt or uncle may boomerang in any number of ways. These things are being openly discussed in many families today in ways that allow the parents to brief explicitly any child-serving relative of what is the usual practice, and why; what the child is and is not customarily allowed to do, and why; and what routines are followed most conscientiously and which can be let slide when the situation warrants.

Children are remarkably resilient creatures and can take a great deal of inconsistency from the various adults that attend them, as long as they feel basically secure. Although there are some procedures and policies that are considered better than others according to sound child-development principles,[1] few children can be severely damaged by occasional

---

[1] James Walters, "Attitudes Concerning the Guidance of Children: A Study of the Differential Effects of an Introductory Course in Child Development on the Attitudes of College Women," Unpublished Ph.D. thesis (Tallahassee: Folrida State University, 1954).

lapses or changes of pace. Extremists who insist that grandparents are bad for children fail to see how much a child can learn from being differently handled by different persons or how much a youngster benefits from the sense of ongoing family relations he gets as he clamors for tales of when his mother or father was young. One nine-year-old puts both values neatly when he says solemnly, "I like to go to Grandma's house, because she scolds so soft, and she tells me all about the olden days when Daddy was a little boy just like me."

TAPPING RESOURCES, SERVING NEEDS, AND ENJOYING CONTACTS OUTSIDE THE FAMILY

One hazard of the family with little children is its preoccupation with itself. The young father is seen putting in a full day on his job, rushing to night school or union meeting to better his chances for advancement, and helping out at home in the many roles he feels are his in the family. The young mother is tied down with little children so much day after day that she may long for adult companionship, stimulation, and contact.

The little child will lead the family out into wider horizons if he is allowed to range further afield. He goes to nursery school and then to kindergarten, bringing home with him new problems and experiences and later taking his parents out to parents' meetings, neighborhood projects, and community affairs. The preschooler is big enough now to go to Sunday school, and often starts his family in church activities that carry through the years. Periodic trips to the pediatrician or family doctor for preventive shots and check-ups, as well as treatment for the various illnesses that befall him, bring both him and his parents into relationship with the health facilities of the community. His enjoyment of the park, the zoo, the playground, the fire department, and the bakery frequently gets his whole family out for jaunts into activities and facilities never before explored.

The young mother finds meanings in life as a person outside the family at intervals around her homemaking and childcare responsibilities. It may be in some parents' group, community service project, church circle, political campaign, course of study in the evening, or Saturday afternoon employment that she finds her identity as a woman and brings home, after a few hours of wider horizons, the perspective and point of view that enriches the family-as-a-whole. Here it is that the stereotyped reactions of the "Woman's place is in the home" or "Little children need a mother's care," if interpreted too rigidly, can be suffocating not only

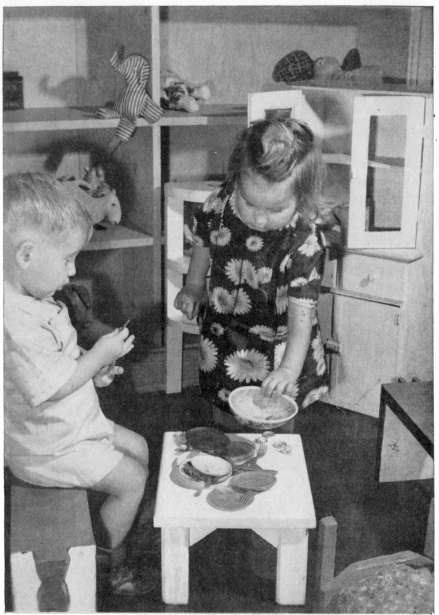

Nursery school offers a little child an opportunity to play with other children and to explore a variety of materials, settings, and situations—good ways of growing up, for the preschooler and for his family too.

to the young woman but to her family as well. A major complaint of college educated mothers of young children is that they long for intervals of adult association, mature stimulation, and challenging activities with persons their own age. This is one of the prime motivators back of the young mother's desire for a job. Openly recognized by the family, many opportunities besides gainful employment may appear as satisfying, unless the financial needs of the family require it.[1]

The young father driven through his twenties and thirties by efforts to get himself established vocationally and to keep his little family afloat financially, may push himself so hard that he has little time for continuing his interests as a person or for enjoying his family on their new horizons. This is especially true in some middle-class families, where mobility drives keep a man lashed by hopes for advancement and chained to his job and its demands. Upper-class fathers find it easier to keep up their club memberships (for business and professional reasons, it's true), and to maintain regular programs of recreation with other men as well as in the young married couple set. Lower-class families make the poorest articulations with the wider community in the health, recreational, educational, vocational, and social aspects of life, as studies previously quoted (Chapter Four) so emphatically indicate.

FACING DILEMMAS AND REWORKING PHILOSOPHIES OF LIFE

By the time the oldest child is four or five and the next baby already on the scene, the family is face to face with a number of dilemmas that challenge its ways of life. Kirkpatrick[2] mentions several that are particularly relevant at this stage of the family life cycle: (1) freedom versus order and efficiency, (2) free expression of personal potentialities versus stable goal expectations, (3) personal self-expression versus childrearing, (4) work achievement versus love-reproduction functions, (5) flexible training versus rigid childrearing, (6) high aspiration levels for children versus realistic expectations, (7) family loyalty versus community loyalty, and (8) extensive casual association versus restrictive intensive association. Each horn of each dilemma has its values and its price. Freedom

---

[1] Virginia Evans, "I Wanted to Go Back to Work," *McCall's*, March 1956, pp. 61–62, and Norman Cousin's Editorial, *The Saturday Review*, December 17, 1955, p. 22.

[2] Clifford Kirkpatrick, *The Family As Process and Institution* (New York: The Ronald Press, 1955), Chap. 4, "Family Types and Dilemmas."

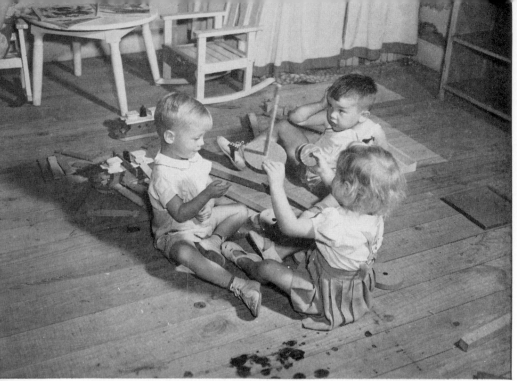

One of the dilemmas that challenge the preschool family is that of freedom (to clutter, to mess, to spill, and to play with a minimum of restraint) versus order and efficiency.

is greatly to be desired, but its price is conflict and confusion in the family. On the other hand, order and efficiency are values, but at the cost of personal frustration and submission to authority. And so it goes. Every family must work out in ways that make sense to its members and to itself as a unit, those answers to the eternal questions of life that make sense for them in their situations.

A simple "nonintellectual" family may deny its absorption in philosophical matters. Yet, every day is full of decisions and choices that depend upon how the family conceives of itself and what its operational definitions of life are. These conceptions of their common life are constantly undergoing change: (1) with the addition of each new member; (2) with the stimuli of other ways of life in the community and among their associates; (3) with the new ideas and insights any of the family members gets (in association with others, in reading, in educational, social, religious, and other contexts); (4) with the old and new tastes of joys and satisfactions that ought to be safeguarded; and (5) under the various stresses, strains, and challenges that back them to the wall and force them to take another look at life as they are living it.

SUMMARY

Families with preschool children are those whose first children are between 2½ and 5 years of age. There quite possibly is a second child, and sometimes a third, born into the family before the stage is completed, who will be preoccupied with the developmental tasks of infancy, while the preschool child is working on his developmental tasks, and the parents are attempting to accomplish those they face as parents, as married partners, and as persons. Family developmental tasks of this stage may be seen as (1) supplying adequate space, facilities, and equipment, (2) meeting predictable and unexpected costs of family life with small children, (3) sharing responsibilities within the expanding family, (4) maintaining mutually satisfying sexual relationships and planning for future children, (5) creating and maintaining effective communication systems within the family, (6) cultivating the full potentials of relationships within the extended family, (7) tapping resources, serving needs, and enjoying contacts outside the family, and (8) facing the dilemmas and reworking philosophies in everchanging challenges of family living.

SUGGESTED ACTIVITIES

1) Review Katharine Whiteside Taylor, *Parent Cooperative Nursery Schools* (New York: Bureau of Publications, Teachers College, Columbia University, 1954), looking especially for the ways in which cooperative nursery schools (1) help preschool children accomplish their developmental tasks, (2) assist parents of preschool children achieve their developmental tasks as parents and as persons, and (3) are of value to the family of the preschooler in its accomplishment of the developmental tasks of the preschool family. Document specifically task by task from explicit and implicit materials in the volume.

2) Outline a feasible program in preparation of the firstborn child for the coming of a new baby into the family, using references suggested in this chapter under the heading, "Preparing the Preschooler for the New Baby" and/or other sound materials. Discuss the relevance of each step in the program for the achievement of the goals for the child, and for the family.

3) Role-play several of the family situations presented in either Jackson's *Life Among the Savages* or McConnell's *Trampled Terraces* (full references in *Readings* for this chapter), portraying the child's as well as the parents' roles in each situation presented. Discuss the nature of the conflict between the developmental tasks of little children and the developmental tasks of parents of little children in each connection.

Indicate in what ways these are normal conflicts of developmental tasks between the generations or how they may be atypical of this stage. Document your opinions as far as you can from materials in your readings and in the chapter.

4) Copy on the blackboard one of Hank Ketcham's cartoons of *Dennis the Menace* showing a predicament in which the developmental tasks of the child are in opposition to those of his parents. Discuss.

5) Review the film *Preface to a Life* (29 minutes, sound, produced by Sun Dial Films, Inc., for National Institute of Mental Health, U. S. Public Health Service, 1950), looking especially into how a preschool child feels about the coming of the new baby into his family. What did the parents do that helped? What made the problem more difficult for the firstborn? What else might have been tried?

6) Invite a preschool teacher to tell you what she finds most usual in the behavior of her children. Discuss what the children seem to be after in these situations in terms of what you know about their developmental tasks.

7) Elaborate any one of Kirkpatrick's dilemmas of family life that particularly applies to the preschool stage, citing illustrations, and giving sources for both aspects of the dilemma you have chosen (see *Readings*).

8) Write a paper on the development of trust and of autonomy in early childhood, using as basic references, Erik Erikson, *Childhood and Society* (New York: W. W. Norton & Company, 1950), and Robert J. Havighurst, *Human Development and Education,* Part One (see *Readings*).

9) Discuss what is meant by the concept of a child's identifying with the parent of the same sex. Give illustrations, sources, and indicate the relationship between this tendency and the accomplishment of the developmental tasks of early childhood.

10) Write a paper on the role of the father in the preschool family, touching on the amount of responsibility he may assume in homemaking and childcare, and what effect he has upon the development of the child. (See English and Foster in your *Readings* as well as the discussion of division of responsibility in this chapter).

READINGS

Bacmeister, Rhoda W., *Growing Together* (New York: Appleton-Century-Crofts, 1947).

Baruch, Dorothy, *New Ways in Discipline* (New York: Appleton-Century-Crofts, 1949).

Bigelow, Howard F., *Family Finance* (Philadelphia: J. B. Lippincott Company, 1953), Chaps. 5, 6, and 7.

Burgess, Helen Steers, *How to Choose a Nursery School* (Public Affairs Pamphlet No. 310, 1961).

Breckenridge, Marian, and Vincent, E. Lee, *Child Development* (Philadelphia: W. B. Saunders and Company, Revised 1955).

Duvall, Evelyn Millis, *Family Living* (New York: Macmillan Company, Revised, 1961), Chaps. 15, 16, and 17.

English, O. Spurgeon, and Foster, Constance, *Fathers Are Parents, Too* (New York: G. P. Putnam's Sons, 1951).

Faegre, Marion L.; Anderson, John E.; and Harris, Dale B., *Child Care and Training* (Minneapolis: University of Minnesota Press, Revised 1958).

Faegre, Marion; Hymes, James; Chandler, Caroline; and Work, Henry, "Section III, Pre-School Family Stage," for the Committee on the Dynamics of Family Interaction, Preliminary Report, Evelyn Duvall and Reuben Hill, co-chairman, National Conference on Family Life, February 1948, unpublished materials.

Havighurst, Robert J., *Human Development and Education* (New York: Longmans, Green and Co., 1953), Chaps. 2 and 3.

Hendrickson, Norejane Johnston, *Teaching Preschool Children from Low Income Families* (Columbus, Ohio: 1787 Neil Avenue, 1965).

Hurlock, Elizabeth B., *Developmental Psychology* (New York: McGraw-Hill Book Company, Revised 1959), Chaps. 5, 10, and 11.

Jackson, Shirley, *Life Among the Savages* (New York: Farrar, Strauss and Young, 1953).

Jones, Eve, *Natural Child Rearing* (Glencoe, Illinois: The Free Press, 1959).

Ketcham, Hank, *Dennis the Menace* and *More Dennis the Menace* (New York: Henry Holt and Company, 1953).

Kirkpatrick, Clifford, *The Family as Process and Institution* (New York: The Ronald Press Company, Second Edition, 1963), Chap. 4, "Family Types and Dilemmas."

Langdon, Grace, and Stout, Irving, *These Well-Adjusted Children* (New York: John Day Company, 1951).

Martin, William E., and Stendler, Celia B., *Child Behavior and Development* (New York: Harcourt, Brace, Revised 1959).

McConnell, Raymond, *Trampled Terraces* (Lincoln, Nebraska: University of Nebraska Press, 1950).

Parsons, Talcott, and Bales, Robert, *Family, Socialization and Interaction Process* (Glencoe, Illinois: The Free Press, 1955), Chapter 2, "Family Structure and the Socialization of the Child."

Read, Katherine H., *The Nursery School: A Human Relationships Laboratory* (Philadelphia: W. B. Saunders and Company, 1966).

Smart, Mollie and Russell, *An Introduction to Family Relationships* (Philadelphia: W. B. Saunders and Company, 1953).

Spock, Benjamin, *The Pocketbook of Baby and Child Care* (New York: Pocket Books, Inc., 1946).

Stone, L. Joseph, and Church, Joseph, *Childhood and Adolescence* (New York: Random House, 1957), Chaps. 6 and 7.

Children begin by loving their parents; as they grow older they judge them; sometimes they forgive them.

OSCAR WILDE
The Picture of Dorian Gray

CHAPTER TEN

Families with school children

The stage of the family life cycle characterized by schoolage children starts when the first child goes to school, at five to six years of age, and continues until he or she becomes a teenager at thirteen. Before the end of this period, it is likely that the family has seen the birth of younger siblings and that the family has reached its maximum size in number of members and of interrelationships. Typically the American family at this stage consists of four to six persons who maintain from six to fifteen interpersonal relationships. The possible range in age is from infancy (youngest child) through forty plus or minus (father) while the eldest is a schoolager. The parents' crisis continues to be that of self-absorption versus finding fulfillment in rearing the next generation. The schoolage child's developmental crisis is risking a sense of inferiority as he develops the capacity of work enjoyment (industry). The family developmental tasks revolve around the major goal of reorganization to make way for the expanding world of schoolagers.

These are busy, full years of family living, with children running in and out of the house, with many projects underway, the adults busy keeping the household in good running order and following their youngsters out into wider contacts in the larger community. Concurrently, the schoolager, his younger siblings, his parents, and his entire family work at their developmental tasks, sometimes in harmony, sometimes in discord, but always with the urgency that accompanies growth.

COURTESY OF THE LIBRARY OF CONGRESS

When the eldest child reaches school age, his next younger sibling is probably a preschool child and still a third may be on the way.

DEVELOPMENTAL TASKS OF SCHOOLAGE CHILDREN

The first-born now is learning all that is involved in becoming an acceptable schoolage boy or girl. Longitudinal studies [1] indicate that earlier problems such as destructiveness, temper tantrums, and overactivity decline rapidly through the school years. But first-born children, more than their younger siblings evidence problems of excessive demands for attention, restlessness in sleep, and physical timidity between 6 and 12. First-born girls especially have problems indicating tension and withdrawal at 6 and again at 11. First-born boys now have more withdrawing and internalizing patterns than do second-born boys, who tend to be more overt and aggressive. The developmental tasks of schoolage boys and girls are both in terms of continuing previous learnings and opening up whole new areas of life.

[1] Jean W. Macfarlane, Lucile Allen, and Marjorie P. Honzik, *A Developmental Study of the Behavior Problems of Normal Children between Twenty-One Months and Fourteen Years* (Berkeley: University of California Press, 1954), pp. 146–186.

1) *Learning the basic skills required of school children:*
   Mastering the fundamentals of reading, writing, calculating, and the scientific rational approach to solving problems.
   Extending understandings of cause and effect relationships.
   Developing concepts essential for everyday living.
   Continued development in ability to reason and to do reflective thinking.

2) *Mastering the physical skills appropriate to his development:*
   Learning the games, the sports, and the various roles in activities pursued by children of his age and sex in his community (ride a bike, swim, skate, play ball, row a boat, climb a tree, etc.).
   Developing abilities needed in personal and family living (bathe and dress himself, care for his clothing, make his bed, cook and serve food, clean up after activities, maintain and repair simple household equipment, etc.).

3) *Developing meaningful understandings of the use of money:*
   Finding socially acceptable ways of getting money for what he wants to buy.
   Learning how to buy wisely the things he most wants with what he has, and to stay within his available resources.
   Finding the meanings of saving for postponed satisfactions.
   Reconciling differences between his wants and his resources, and those of others both poorer and richer than he.
   Getting basic orientation into the nature of money in everyday life in the family and in the larger community.

4) *Becoming an active, cooperative member of his family:*
   Gaining skills in participating in family discussions and decision-making.
   Assuming responsibilities within the household with satisfactions in accomplishment and belonging.
   Becoming more mature in giving and receiving affection and gifts between himself and his parents, his siblings, and his relatives within the extended family.
   Learning to enjoy the full resources and facilities available within the family, and to take initiative in enriching them as he becomes able.

5) *Extending his abilities to relate effectively to others, both peers and adults:*

> Making progress in his ability to adjust to others.
>
> Learning to stand up for his rights.
>
> Improving his abilities both to lead and to follow others.
>
> Mastering expectancies in simple conventions, rules, customs, courtesies, and standards of his family and groups.
>
> Learning genuinely cooperative roles with others in many situations.
>
> Making and keeping close friends.

6) *Continuing the learnings involved in handling his feelings and impulses:*

> Growing in his ability to work through simple frustrations.
>
> Exploring socially acceptable ways of releasing negative emotions effectively.
>
> Becoming more mature in channeling feelings into the ways and time and places appropriate within his culture.
>
> Gaining skill in sharing his feelings with those who can help (parents, teachers, close friends, scout leaders, etc.).

7) *Coming to terms with his or her own sex role both now and as it will become:*

> Learning what is expected as appropriate behavior for boys, for girls, for men, for women, for married people, for parents, and grandparents.
>
> Clarifying knowledges about the nature of sex and reproduction.
>
> Adjusting to a changing body in the pubertal growth spurt as teen years approach; (accepting the new size and form, function and potentials of pubertal growth).
>
> Thinking wholesomely ahead to what it will be like to be grown up as a man or woman.

8) *Continuing to find himself as a worthy person:*

> Identifying with his own age and sex in appropriate ways.
>
> Discovering many ways of becoming acceptable as a person; gaining status.
>
> Growing in self-confidence, self-respect, self-control, and self-realization.
>
> Extending the process of establishing his own individuality.

9) *Relating himself to loyalties beyond the moment and outside himself:*
> Finding new meanings in religion, in the universe, in the nature of things.
>
> Discovering satisfactions in music, art, drama, nature, and the literature of his culture, appropriate to his age.
>
> Devoting himself to group goals (scouts, boys' and girls' clubs, etc.).
>
> Laying foundations for patriotism, for pride in men's achievements through history, and for a sense of belongingness to the human race.
>
> Gaining experience in essential morality in action at home and with others.
>
> Learning and accepting the eternal realities of birth, death, and infinity.

How well a given boy or girl accomplishes any of these many complex developmental tasks before he or she enters the teens depends on many things. It depends first of all on how good a start that particular child had in development through the early years of childhood. The little child who succeeded in achieving most of the developmental tasks of infancy, early childhood, and the preschool years continues on in these achievements as his or her horizons expand through the school years. Success depends upon how many opportunities there are for development in the home, in the school, and in community life. It depends in large measure on how skilled parents and teachers are in anticipating, recognizing, and providing growth opportunities for the child's developmental tasks as they come along. But children differ widely, as do parents. And, while children are struggling through their growth stages, the parents too are hard at work on their developmental tasks.

DEVELOPMENTAL TASKS OF PARENTS OF SCHOOL-AGE CHILDREN

Parents are expected to make most of the adjustments during the early years of childhood, but they are just as human, with their own needs and strivings, as they were before they married, or as they will be during the empty-nest stage as parents who no longer have to reckon with the imperious demands of offspring. The parents know full well that they are needed through the bustling years of the school-age period. But by this time, the household routines have become established and the children are growing at a less rapid rate than they did as infants or preschoolers. Parents now can get their children in focus and understand them better because they are not changing so fast, and because parent-child intercommunication is better. Schoolage children generally are satisfied with their relationships with their parents, and are involved to a considerable degree in family activities, according to one study of 730 fifth-graders.[1] No other stage appears to offer so much in family solidarity.

BEING SENSITIVE TO AND PROVIDING FOR CHILDREN'S GROWTH NEEDS

A recurring challenge to modern parents is to provide opportunities for the child to do things for himself which are within his abilities. It is helpful to the accomplishment of the child's developmental tasks if he can share in family decisions, responsibilities, and opportunities. Family discussion and joint planning offer openings for schoolagers to join with their parents and their brothers and sisters in establishing family policies and getting firsthand experience in democratic interaction and orderly ways of doing things.

Overly cautious parents may curtail their school child's activities because they fear he will be hurt. Actually, the accidental death rate for schoolage children is lower than at any other time in the life cycle. The National Safety Council[2] estimates accidental deaths per 100,000 population of each age group as: 18.4 for 5–14-year-olds, 44.0 for under 5-year-olds, 56.1 for 15–24-year-olds, 42.1 for 25–44-year-olds, 52.2 for 45–64-year-olds, and 157.4 for those over 65 years of age. Thus in the chance of meeting accidental death, the schoolager statistically is more than twice as safe as his parents, nearly three times as safe as his grandparents, and more than eight times as safe as his retired great-grandparents. School children who tend to have accidents more than others are found to have emotional problems, and to have parents who are anxious, insecure and nonassertive.[3]

---

[1] Glenn R. Hawkes, Lee G. Burchinal, and Bruce Gardner, "Preadolescents' Views of Some of Their Relations with Their Parents," *Child Development*, Vol. 28, No. 4, December 1957, pp. 393–399.

[2] National Safety Council, *Accident Facts, 1960 Edition*, p. 14.

[3] Irwin Marcus, Wilma Wilson, Irvin Kraft, Delmar Swander, Fred Southerland, and Edith Schulhofer, *An Interdisciplinary Approach to Accident Patterns in Children*, Society for Research in Child Development, Monograph No. 76, Vol. 25, No. 2, 1960, pp. 53–54.

Parents are under pressure from neighbors and other members of their social class to have their children measure up to the demands and expectancies of the culture. This tends to shape even the most developmental family into more traditional lines as soon as the children reach school age, as we saw in Chapter Five. "What will the neighbors think?" or "What will the teacher say?" are powerful pressures to conform in the · school-age family. When traditional striving for good manners collides with developmental conceptions of parent-child rapport, the traditional patterns win out in most homes studied. Two examples:

Billy, age 10, hurries home to snatch his lunch and get back for an important school football game. As he gobbles, he tells his mother excitedly all about the team. As he pauses for breath, his mother breaks in severely, "Billy, take your elbows off the table. How many times must I tell you? And, stop eating so fast!"

Immediately Billy wilts. He obediently removes his elbows and hurries through the remainder of the meal in silence . . .

Mother has a point. Billy will have to learn good manners. But what is more important at the moment—good manners or good feelings shared between mother and son? How ready will Billy be next time to share his excitements with his mother?

. . . . .

Mary dashes home from school. She breaks in on her mother's club meeting with all the ladies sitting around. Mary is 12, happy, friendly, and outgoing. She is unself-conscious. She says cheerily, "Hello, Mrs. Brown," as she stumbles over Mrs. Smith's feet.

Mother rises to the situation. She must teach Mary some manners right now. She must save her own face by scolding Mary. So she speaks, sweetly but pointedly, "Mary, my dear! Do look where you are going!" Then she turns to her guests, saying, "Mary is just at the awkward age, so you'll have to excuse her."

Is Mary's face red? Does she approach the next roomful of guests with more or with less ease as a result of this experience? Has her feeling of friendliness increased or decreased? Is she closer to or farther from her mother now?

ENJOYING LIFE THROUGH CHILDREN'S EYES

Parents who can relax and enjoy their children, find life unfolding all around them as they see it through children's eyes. Long-forgotten joys and pleasures are renewed as they are shared with children who delight in them. New vistas and fresh perspectives from different vantage points open up with a child companion. What might have been an ordinary

Parents who can relax and enjoy their children find life unfolding all around them.

business trip turns out to be an adventure when a ten-year-old goes along:

> I was at the meetings in Omaha for three days; took Janice along, and we had a great time. As you would guess, I did many things I would not have done had I gone alone: climbing on foot to the top floor of the hotel and looking out over the city from the fire escape; climbing to the very top seat in Omaha's immense auditorium; walking all the way across the Missouri river bridge to Council Bluffs and standing midway on the bridge with one foot on the Iowa side of the line and the other foot on the Nebraska side; going to the top of the Woodman of the World Building . . .
>
> There was much other fun too: being proud of how sweet she looked; enjoying her ways of packing and unpacking; watching her select items at Bishops Cafeteria and her enjoyment of her favorites; appreciating the fact that she surprised me the second afternoon and did the wash for us in the bathroom sink . . . observing the things she enjoyed most . . . People without children miss half the fun in the world! [1]

[1] David Fulcomer, personal communication; see also Benjamin Spock, "The Wonderful World of Little Children," *Ladies' Home Journal*, June 1960, pp. 47–58.

What Is a Boy? [1]

BY ALAN BECK

Between the innocence of babyhood and the dignity of manhood we find a delightful creature called a boy. Boys come in assorted sizes, weights, and colors, but all boys have the same creed: To enjoy every second of every minute of every hour of every day and to protest with noise (their only weapon) when their last minute is finished and the adult males pack them off to bed at night.

Boys are found everywhere—on top of, underneath, inside of, climbing on, swinging from, running around, or jumping to. Mothers love them, little girls hate them, older sisters and brothers tolerate them, adults ignore them, and Heaven protects them. A boy is Truth with dirt on its face, Beauty with a cut on its finger, Wisdom with bubble gum in its hair, and the Hope of the future with a frog in its pocket.

When you are busy, a boy is an inconsiderate, bothersome, intruding jangle of noise. When you want him to make a good impression, his brain turns to jelly or else he becomes a savage, sadistic, jungle creature bent on destroying the world and himself with it.

A boy is a composite—he has the appetite of a horse, the digestion of a sword swallower, the energy of a pocket-size atomic bomb, the curiosity of a cat, the lungs of a dictator, the imagination of a Paul Bunyan, the shyness of a violet, the audacity of a steel trap, the enthusiasm of a firecracker, and when he makes something he has five thumbs on each hand.

He likes ice cream, knives, saws, Christmas, comic books, the boy across the street, woods, water (in its natural habitat), large animals, Dad, trains, Saturday mornings, and fire engines. He is not much for Sunday School, company, schools, books without pictures, music lessons, neckties, barbers, girls, overcoats, adults, or bedtime.

Nobody else is so early to rise, or so late to supper. Nobody else gets so much fun out of trees, dogs, and breezes. Nobody else can cram into one pocket a rusty knife, a half-eaten apple, 3 feet of string, an empty Bull Durham sack, 2 gum drops, 6 cents, a sling shot, a chunk of unknown substance, and a genuine supersonic code ring with a secret compartment.

A boy is a magical creature—you can lock him out of your work shop, but you can't lock him out of your heart. You can get him out of your study, but you can't get him out of your mind. Might as well give up—he is your captor, your jailer, your boss, and your master—a freckled-face, pint-sized, cat-chasing, bundle of noise. But when you come home at night with only the shattered pieces of your hopes and dreams, he can mend them like new with the two magic words—"Hi Dad!"

What Is a Girl? [1]
BY ALAN BECK

Little girls are the nicest things that happen to people. They are born with a little bit of angelshine about them and though it wears thin sometimes, there is always enough left to lasso your heart—even when they are sitting in the mud, or crying temperamental tears, or parading up the street in mother's best clothes.

A little girl can be sweeter (and badder) oftener than anyone else in the world. She can jitter around, and stomp, and make funny noises that frazzle your nerves, yet just when you open your mouth, she stands there demure with that special look in her eyes. A girl is Innocence playing in the mud, Beauty standing on its head, and Motherhood dragging a doll by the foot.

Girls are available in five colors—black, white, red, yellow, or brown, yet Mother Nature always manages to select your favorite color when you place your order. They disprove the law of supply and demand—there are millions of little girls, but each is as precious as rubies.

God borrows from many creatures to make a little girl. He uses the song of a bird, the squeal of a pig, the stubbornness of a mule, the antics of a monkey, the spryness of a grasshopper, the curiosity of a cat, the speed of a gazelle, the slyness of a fox, the softness of a kitten, and to top it all off He adds the mysterious mind of a woman.

A little girl likes new shoes, party dresses, small animals, first grade, noise makers, the girl next door, dolls, make-believe, dancing lessons, ice cream, kitchens, coloring books, make-up, cans of water, going visiting, tea parties, and one boy. She doesn't care so much for visitors, boys in general, large dogs, hand-me-downs, straight chairs, vegetables, snow suits, or staying in the front yard. She is loudest when you are thinking, the prettiest when she has provoked you, the busiest at bedtime, the quietest when you want to show her off, and the most flirtatious when she absolutely must not get the best of you again.

Who also can cause you more grief, joy, irritation, satisfaction, embarrassment, and genuine delight than this combination of Eve, Salome, and Florence Nightingale? She can muss up your home, your hair, and your dignity—spend your money, your time, and your temper—then just when your patience is ready to crack, her sunshine peeks through and you've lost again.

Yes, she is a nerve-racking nuisance, just a noisy bundle of mischief. But when your dreams tumble down and the world is a mess—when it seems you are pretty much of a fool after all—she can make you a king when she climbs on your knee and whispers, "I love you best of all!"

A recurring challenge to modern parents is providing opportunities for children to do things within their abilities. A school-age child is able to do a great many things about the house and to carry real responsibilities with the joy of knowing that she or he is a participating member of the family.

LETTING THE CHILD GO AND GROW

Encouraging a child's growth involves letting him go. As the school years progress, there are longer and longer absences from home. He is away from home through the school hours, which often include the lunch period as well as morning and afternoon sessions. If he or she is getting normally involved in sports, and clubs, and friendship groups, the after-school hours increasingly are given to these interests, with the youngster coming home tired and bedraggled just in time for the evening meal. There are frequent requests to spend the evening at someone else's home and occasions when spending the night with a close buddy is terribly important. Soon there are weekend trips with scouts or other youth groups, and then come the longer periods during summer vacation when children of school age are off to camp or visiting relatives for weeks at a time. All this is good for the child's development of independence, widening social experience, and general personality growth.

As children become increasingly involved with friends their own age, their orientation increasingly is toward their peers. Parents can encourage these associations, for research [1] shows that children who are well-adjusted family members tend to retain family identifications, norms, and values even as they associate with others. Mothers with emotionally satisfying friendships may find it easier to let their children go. Unfortunately, however, those old enough to have schoolage children tend to have fewer close friends than do both younger and older housewives.[2]

Schoolagers often quote other adults as authority figures. A secure parent can take a child's "But the teacher says so," as an indication that the youngster is stretching away from home in intellectual as well as physical respects, with new models, new attitudes, and new viewpoints to explore beyond the immediate family. Parents who can empathize with their children's interests and loosen the apron strings at this point have less difficulty untying them in another few years, when the youngsters become teenagers.

Parents who cultivate interests beyond their children probably have

[1] Charles E. Bowerman, and John W. Kinch, "Changes in Family and Peer Orientation of Children between the Fourth and Tenth Grades," *Social Forces*, Vol. 37, No. 3, March 1959, pp. 206–211.

[2] James H. Williams, "Close Friendship Relations of Housewives Residing in an Urban Community," *Social Forces*, Vol. 36, No. 4, May 1958, pp. 358–362.

Among school-age children, the afternoon hours are increasingly devoted to friends and interests that friends enjoy together. This is good for children's development of independence and general personality growth.

less difficulty letting them go than do those who devote their lives to their children. Ongoing research at Cornell [1] finds husbands and wives with schoolage children working together on projects more often than do those at either the preschool or the teenage stage of the family life cycle. This is the time when building a boat, equipping a summer camp, and fixing up the house preoccupy father and mother. Now too, entertaining others in the home and going as a family to company picnics and social affairs with the husband's work associates are at an all-time high.[2] Such activities shared with the children suggest an over-all parental stance of involvement in whole-family pursuits that may or may not develop into continuing interests for the married pair as a couple.

FAMILY DEVELOPMENTAL TASKS AT THE SCHOOLAGE STAGE

Married seven years or more, by the time their eldest is in school, the husband and wife have been parents for at least six years and have settled into familiar ways with each other and with their children. The developmental routes traversed by the oldest child are gone over again by the younger children each in his turn, each in his own way. Family developmental tasks at this stage include:

1) Providing for children's activity and parents' privacy
2) Keeping financially solvent
3) Cooperating to get things done
4) Continuing to satisfy each other as married partners
5) Effectively utilizing family communication systems
6) Feeling close to relatives in the larger family
7) Tying in with life outside the family
8) Testing and retesting family philosophies of life

PROVIDING FOR CHILDREN'S ACTIVITY AND PARENTS' PRIVACY

Now that families live mostly in cities, towns, and suburbs, homes are smaller and space is more limited, both indoors and out, than it once was

[1] Harold Feldman, "The Development of the Husband-Wife Relationship," a study supported in part by the National Institute of Mental Health, unpublished data received through personal correspondence, March 24, 1961, with permission.

[2] Robert O. Blood, Jr., and Donald M. Wolfe, *Husbands and Wives* (Glencoe, Illinois: The Free Press, 1960), pp. 158–159.

(see Chapter Three). Thanks to better nutrition and preventive medical care, today's children are bigger, stronger, and more vigorous—age for age—than was true a generation or two ago. No comparable change has occurred in the desire of parents for privacy and a little peace and quiet in their lives. Todays' developmental family's house during the preschool and school-age periods is cluttered, toy-strewn, and noisy.

Providing outlets for the needed exploration and activity of vigorous growing children within the limits of cramped housing, small yards, remote playgrounds, traffic-filled streets, and cranky neighbors is not an easy task. Lower-class neighbors in some places settle the problem by letting the children roam the streets, play in the alleys, and run the risks of life and limb. Social clubs and settlements set up programs that help in some of these congested areas, but the needs are still unfulfilled. Upper-class families usually have more space and, except for those urban cliff-dwellers who live in crowded metropolitan apartment houses, have areas the children can call their own to play in, either on the home grounds or at their private schools. Many middle-class families feel the pinch in living so closely with their children in common living quarters; space requirements must be worked out in elaborate rituals and routines.

This is the time when many families move out of congested areas and into the suburbs, where children can have space for play, enjoy congenial companions, and attend good schools and community activities. The price that these families pay for such a move is real, both in monetary and psychic terms.[1] The family reorganizes itself around a mother-head. Father comes home too tired and is there too infrequently to play the role he could if he lived nearer his work.

The irony is that just when a man is most needed around the house for all the repairs and refurbishing that are part of home-ownership, the man is not as readily available as he was when they lived in the city, where services around the place were provided without tapping the man of the house. The pressure is eased somewhat by the five-day week, which gives father to his family Saturdays and Sundays—unless the golf bug bites him first, that is!

[1] See Richard and Katherine Gordon, and Max Gunther, *The Split-Level Trap* (New York: Bernard Geis, 1960); and John Keats, *The Crack in the Picture Window* (Boston: Houghton Mifflin, 1957).

KEEPING FINANCIALLY AFLOAT

The triple threat of keeping up payments, keeping up with the Joneses, and keeping out of debt is a real strain now. Costs will zoom even higher before there is any relief. But now, when the firstborn is in school and younger children are coming along, comes the bulging budget characteristic of expanding families. In low- and moderate-income families where food, clothing, and medical costs are always a big part of the household expenses, these items take a big bite out of what money there is. Fixed costs such as car expenses, rent or house payments and maintenance, utilities, insurance, bus and lunch money, as well as all the expected items like dues, school collections, allowances, recreation add to the financial burden. No wonder many a family man may look a little frayed at times.

Moonlighting, in which the man of the house takes a second job to make ends meet is not uncommon now. Before the end of the school-age period, Junior may have a paper route and be earning some of his own money; and Mother may have found a full- or a part-time job that fits the demands of her growing brood. Of those living with their husbands, 35 per cent of all mothers of children aged 6 to 17 are in the labor force.[1] If the mother of schoolage children is widowed or no longer living with her husband the chances are three out of five that she is working.[2] Financial factors are not the only reasons why mothers with children work outside the home, but statistically the lower the husband's income, the more likely is the wife to be gainfully employed.[3] Except for the first couple of years of marriage, the schoolage stage is the time when the wife is most likely to be working.[4] Grandparents help out by giving the grandchildren clothing, taking the family on vacation trips, purchasing big items of equip-

[1] National Manpower Council, *Womanpower* (New York: Columbia University Press, 1957), pp. 68–69.
[2] *Ibid.*, p. 65.
[3] Blood and Wolfe, *op. cit.*, p. 98.
[4] "After all the children have reached schoolage, nearly one-third of the wives are in the labor force. Aside from the first couple of years of marriage, this is the period when the wife is most likely to be supplementing the husband's earnings by working outside of the home." Paul C. Glick, "The Life Cycle of the Family," *Marriage and Family Living*, Vol. XVII, No. 1, February 1955, p. 8, and National Manpower Council, *Womanpower, op. cit.*, pp. 68–69.

ment,[1] sitter services, and nursing care through childhood sicknesses and childbirth of the little newcomer.[2] Income tax exemptions for the children and unemployed wife are a help, but are by no means adequate to cover the costs of childrearing at this stage of family living.[3] Many a middle-class father gets what overtime he can, or pieces out his earnings with a part-time job during his "leisure" hours.

The lower-class family frequently solves the problem by the mother's employment, leaving the children under the casual supervision of whomever happens to be home. The upper-class family's financial problems are less, for by definition the upper-class home is more affluent. But even so the strain of keeping up appearances, sending the youngsters to the proper private schools, maintaining memberships in exclusive clubs, and participating in the right charities adds up faster than the money rolls in, in many a supposedly well-to-do family. Here the problems are compounded by pride. What lower-status families can do without losing face become last resorts to the families "on the hill."

COOPERATING TO GET THINGS DONE

Each family has its own ways of getting things done. Mother does everything. Father pitches in as he can. Older children care for the younger ones. Grandmother may be close enough to help out. A maid works by the day or month. Some way or another food has to be purchased, prepared, and served. Clothes have to be washed, ironed, mended, and put away. Dishes have to be washed, the house cleaned, beds made, and belongings put where they belong. The too-young, the too-sick, and dependent members of the family must be cared for, and extended family relationships must be kept in good repair. Someone must answer the doorbell, the phone, the questions of the youngsters, and the demands of salesmen. Someone has to plan the meals, supervise the spending, and attend to the special and the everyday routines, in even the sketchiest family situation.

---

[1] Marvin B. Sussman, "The Help Pattern in the Middle Class Family," *American Sociological Review*, Vol. 18, No. 1., February 1953, pp. 22–28.

[2] Evelyn Millis Duvall, *In-Laws: Pro and Con* (New York: Association Press, 1954), pp. 89–99.

[3] Reuben Hill estimates that income tax exemptions meet about 1/20th of the cost of rearing his children in any given year; each child's exemption is worth from $50 to $75 cut in tax per child per year, while it costs on the average $1,000 a year per child to rear him or her to age 18 (Louis Dublin, and Alfred Lotka, *The Money Value of a Man* [New York: Ronald Press, 1946], Chapter 4, pp. 44–58).

Casual impressions of homemaking in this push-button age are that now the housekeeping day has been so shortened, thanks to these marvels of science, that there is really very little to do around the house. Actually quite the opposite is the case. A recent study of 52 Midwestern home-makers with two to four school-age children indicated that these women spent more time in laundering now than was spent by a similar group of homemakers twenty-five years ago, automatic washers to the contrary notwithstanding! [1] Interpretations are two: (1) our miracle fibers take special care and no longer can the family wash all go through together and (2) our standards are higher; we have more clothing, and we expect to be cleaner now than we did a generation ago.

Increased standards of living put a heavier load of responsibility on the home than used to be expected. It is no longer enough to put food on the table. It must be a carefully balanced meal, supplying just the right number of calories for the individual family members; attractive in color; tasty as to the right combination of textures, flavors, and personal preferences; full of vitamins, body-building proteins, minerals, and even trace minerals. It isn't enough to keep a child neat, clean, and obedient; today we must be concerned for his growth as a personality (Chapter Five). It isn't enough to keep a man's shirt buttons on; now a wife must be concerned and interested with all that goes into mending a wounded ego, and keeping her husband a growing, happy person. It isn't enough to keep house for the family; now a woman is expected to do her share of community housekeeping in working for a school bond issue, getting out to parent-teacher meetings, and helping run the block meeting, or whatever is the pressing issue of the day. It is the plethora of new tasks and expectations that take the time and energy of families at this stage in the life cycle.

Cooperation is the answer, not only for getting things done, but for helping everyone grow in the process. What becomes "a chore" if one person gets stuck with it all the time, becomes "a project" when the whole family pitches in and works together to get a job done. Cooperative efforts in meal preparation-serving-cleaning up make for pleasant companionship as well as shared responsibilities. Daily routines, weekly cleaning, and seasonal gardening, housecleaning, leaf-raking, and holiday preparations are planned by the family; tasks are allocated on the basis of inter-

[1] Dorothy G. Van Bortel, "Conception of Woman's Role in the Home in Two Social Classes," reported at the Seventh Annual Symposium, the University of Chicago, Committee on Human Development, February 25, 1956.

est, ability, and preference and are accomplished with family members working side by side.

In a nation-wide study[1] of boys in 4th through the 8th grades in public, private, and parochial schools, the Survey Research Center asked the boys, "What things that you do at home or in school or with your friends, make you feel important and useful?" The largest percentage of the 11- to 13-year-olds (40 per cent) mentioned some adult role around the house. The next most frequent mention was that of achievement and use of skills (28 per cent). Other high ranking items were "recognition by parents and adults" (12 per cent), and "giving help" (18 per cent). These findings are in line with the general tendency of children to find satisfaction in working constructively with adults as members of a team.

CONTINUING TO SATISFY EACH OTHER AS MARRIED PARTNERS

If the woman has received good postnatal care and has established a satisfactory sex response in the marriage, she now is at the peak of her sexual powers. Her main problem now is in getting over enough of her busyness to relax and give herself wholeheartedly to her husband. The man old enough to have schoolage children is beyond the peak of his sexual capacities, but still a virile man with needs not only for sexual intercourse, but also for the renewal of faith in himself as a man that a truly loving wife can give him so well.

The couple successful in accomplishing this developmental task is usually one who keep their love for each other central in their family life. Yet the evidence is that wives are decreasingly satisfied with their husbands' love through the family life cycle.[2] Mothers of preschool children are more satisfied with their husbands' affection than any other group of wives. But, by the time the schoolage stage of the family life cycle arrives, fewer wives are satisfied with the affection they receive from their mates—a decline that continues through the rest of the marriage.

EFFECTIVELY UTILIZING COMMUNICATION SYSTEMS

It may be that decline in mates' satisfaction with each other results from the eclipse of the husband-wife relationship by the responsibilities

[1] Survey Research Center, *A Study of Boys Becoming Adolescents* (Ann Arbor: University of Michigan, 1960, p. 215.
[2] Blood and Wolfe, *op. cit.*, p. 232.

of parenthood. The schoolage family is a network of communication ties, with possible interpersonal relationships numbering fifteen in the four-child family. The children now are full of experiences to relate, questions to ask, and sheer exuberance to express. Each is uniquely at work on his developmental tasks within his position in the family. Boy or girl, first-born or younger child, each struggles to establish his identity as a person in the family, who is and must be different from his siblings.[1] Unless they are twins, their ages differ so widely that their interests as children of school age, preschool stage, and infancy are worlds apart. Yet they compete for the resources of the family (the use of the television set is a good example[2]), for status and affection, and for the special recognition that all children need in intimate association.

The schoolage youngster comes home from his rigorous day in class-room and playground full of the pent-up emotions that could not be fully expressed in front of teachers and classmates. He brings his frustrations, disappointments, and unexpressed hostilities home, where he very likely takes them out on the first available family member. This is not to be condemned. One of the chief functions of family life is to serve as an emotional reconditioning center for its members. But this does not make for peace and quiet. On the contrary, feelings explode all over the place, the children get into squabbles seemingly without provocation. Junior topples over the baby's blocks, baby scrawls in Mary's book, she teases Junior, and they are at it again.

One group of mothers exploring children's squabbles in their own homes discovered that most of the quarreling took place in the late afternoon between the time the school children returned home and the evening meal was served. Hypothesizing that a juice break might build up blood sugar levels and reduce tension, these mothers found that after-school snacks alone did not decrease the number and length of the episodes of tension. However, the squabbles decreased significantly in the homes where the mother awaited her school children's return home with an interest in their feelings and reports of the day.[3]

These results of a very simple experiment parallel those of the famous

---

[1] Helen L. Koch, *The Relation of Certain Formal Attributes of Siblings to Attitudes Held Toward Each Other and Toward Their Parents,* Society for Research in Child Development, Monograph Serial No. 78, Vol. 25, No. 4, 1960.

[2] Robert O. Blood, Jr., "Social Class and Family Control of Television Viewing," *Merrill-Palmer Quarterly,* Vol. 7, No. 3, July 1961, pp. 205–222.

[3] Unpublished study by the author.

studies [1] of factory workers in which it was the *attention* paid the people that increased their work output and job satisfaction. They give a challenge to family members who must weather the emotional storms that generate outside to blow their full fury within the home. Not only the children, but father and mother too, bring home their tensions and unresolved conflicts from office, factory, or PTA meetings. The family that is satisfactorily providing effective means by which tensions can be drained off before they become either chronic or critical, is one that keeps communication free and full.

One mother who is aware of the importance of these functions, when her husband is in a particularly exacting and trying spot, has the makings of a picnic supper in her pantry for the occasional afternoon when her husband comes home looking as though he has had "one of those days." As soon as she takes a good look at her husband's face, she suggests a picnic for the whole family, or a quiet tete-a-tete for just the two of them, with the children having their picnic supper on the back porch or yard. This is a way of not only helping her husband work through a difficult job, but is also effective in maintaining the kind of sensitive communication needed in the hurly-burly of family life.

It works the other way too. An emphatic husband returning home to find his wife at the end of her rope, with the youngsters irritable and the house a mess, may take her out for dinner, with a quickly imported sitter for the children more than paying for her charge in the release the husband and wife get when they need it most.

A husband and his wife appear to be less likely to discuss something calmly together at the schoolage stage than at any time since their marriage. Now they are more likely to argue, and to overtly work through their disagreements with a stimulating exchange of ideas than they did at the preschool stage, or will again when they reach the teenage stage of family life. Such open communication may account for the further findings of the Feldman studies that husbands and wives with schoolage children less often feel misunderstood and resentful, and they now are less prone to refuse to talk because they are angry with each other.[2] Ventilated feelings generally do not accumulate in repressed resentments.

[1] F. U. Roethlisberger and W. J. Dickson, *Management and the Worker* (Cambridge, Massachusetts: Harvard University Press, 1940).
[2] Feldman, *op. cit.*

When children's horizons are expandng and life is so full of so many wonderful things, the whole family can glow and grow with its younger members.

The most valuable aspect of marriage from the wife's point of view is companionship in doing things with her husband. This outranks all other aspects including love, understanding, standard of living, and the chance to have children, in the eyes of most wives.[1] The Detroit Area Study further finds that the more education a wife has the more likely she is to be satisfied with her husband's companionship. College-educated wives, usually married to college-educated husbands, are more satisfied with their marital companionship than are wives on any other educational or income level.[2]

When communication systems are open within a family, love can flow through, removing the waste products of everyday living and renewing the spirit of every member. For love is a two-way flow, going and returning between each person and the next, taking away one's hates and angers and bringing back the warmth of belonging and the joy of living in a family. Like a river that purifies itself as long as it keeps running freely, so the stream of human emotions within a family

[1] Blood and Wolfe, *op. cit.*, p. 150.
[2] *Ibid.*, pp. 170–171.

renews and refreshes the human spirit so long as communication systems run free.

FEELING CLOSE TO RELATIVES IN THE LARGER FAMILY

Relatives come into their own during the school-age stage of family living. When a boy is old enough to handle himself with some independence, his uncles and cousins may take him along on a fishing trip, to ball games, and all the rest of the activities that delight the young man of the family. A school-age boy or girl is old enough to visit relatives for a week or more, even a whole summer vacation without becoming homesick or being too dependent upon a hospitable household. Going to grandparents' home for special holidays is a thrill now, when the children are old enough to appreciate such treats, and to take care of their own needs and interests in new settings with only casual supervision.

With family routines fairly well established and the children knowing the ropes of everyday family living, it is possible for them to take over for a few days at a time with a visiting relative keeping a general eye on things, while the parents leave for a brief holiday or business trip. "Sitting" now becomes a mutual process in which the youngsters share their interests and achievements with the aunt, uncle, or grandparent in charge, at the same time that they tap this rich source of family-lore and gain a sense of the continuity of family living from those who knew their parents when they were small.

Even more important than what the relatives *do* for the school-age boy or girl, is what they *are*. In even the most homogeneous family, there are so many differences in personality strengths and weaknesses, behavior patterns, and value systems represented in the members of the extended family group, that these variations are of great interest to all. The family is worried about one of its black sheep who has stepped out of line again, and hashes over his past history, the details of the current escapade, and their opinions as to why he has turned out so badly. The family is proud of some honor bestowed upon one of its relatives and proudly exhibits mementos of the glorious moment, the picture of the person with prestige, and regales even the most casual visitor with the wonderful qualities that have helped this special one turn out so well. One relative is ill, another is mentally unstable, a third is out of work, still another is leaving for an extended voyage, and so on and on through the multitude of permutations and combinations of experiences and predispositions represented in the members of any family.

All this is grist for the children's mill. As they get close to these differing relatives and hear them discussed in the family, they see value systems in action. They find themselves lining up on one side or the other in accordance with their own personality needs and tasks of the moment. The twelve-year-old girl may ardently defend some impulsive cousin who has run away to be married in defiance of her family, not because the girl actually believes that such actions are wise, but because this represents for her the emancipation she is mobilizing for and has not yet accomplished personally. The ten-year-old boy may idolize a young uncle who flexes his muscles and talks big about the manly art of self-defense, not because he is going to turn out to be a prize fighter, but because growing up to be a strong man is the boy's goal for himself.

Feeling close to the relatives of the family is accomplished through the years in the letter-writing, visiting, holiday observances, vacation sharing, gift giving, services rendered and received, and all the other ways in which the members of the family maintain contact with each other. The process is futhered by the family loyalties that bind the family together, regardless of what any member may or may not do. The task is delayed or incomplete in the little family in which such high standards of perfection are maintained that it ostracizes any relative who steps out of line. Sniping at in-laws is one way of venting hostilities against the mate. Or mutual dislike of any relative on either side of the family may be a common bond between a couple. Complete harmony in the larger family is rarely realized, but, to the extent to which it is achieved, it contributes much to the ongoing life of the family.

TYING IN WITH LIFE OUTSIDE THE FAMILY

The schoolager takes the family with him out into the larger community. Pressure is on the parents to become active in the parent-teacher association, to visit the school for special parents' functions, to participate in parents' study groups, and to become an active part of community life as soon as their children are enrolled in school.

Father now gets tied into father-son affairs with his boy through church and youth programs, as well as in the informal going and coming within the neighborhood. As soon as the youngster becomes a Little Leaguer, he becomes a part of the male set in town, with other men and boys recognizing him and his father and the rest of the family in ways that are new and exciting.

Mother is asked to bake a cake for a scout bake-sale or to help serve at a Campfire Girls' mothers' tea. She may take on the job of den-mother, or teach a Sunday School class, or help her youngsters canvass for Red Cross funds, as soon as her own children are drawn into community projects and group life.

Life in the larger community becomes of more personal interest when children are intimately involved. Raising interest in a new school building or getting pledges for the Community Fund, or a special neighborhood project now makes sense in a personal way, when the family's own children are directly benefited. Candidates for political office may have been only remote pictures in the newspaper before; now they are seen for the issues for which they stand, for the kind of family life they represent, and for what they promise to do for the welfare of the community. Corruption may once have seemed like something that is always with us; but when children get out into the streets, ridding the city of its harmful elements becomes urgent family business. The teacher shortage, once a general social problem, now becomes an imminent family concern. And so it goes. As the child grows up and goes forth into the world, he takes his family with him into larger and larger circles of interest and influence. Widening participation in community life helps mature the family as well as the individual, and this is one of the developmental tasks that must be tackled and worked through together.

TESTING AND RETESTING FAMILY PHILOSOPHIES OF LIFE

As soon as the yard child gets out into the street and begins to go to school, he comes face-to-face with ways of life that are different from those of his family. Some of these variations on the theme of life, look good to him and he brings them home in questions about and demands for a new order of things. The family then must test its way of life in terms of child-introduced, community pressures. Something has got to give. Either the family gives way to the child's pleas that "all the other kids are doing it," or the youngster faces up to the finality of "this is the way we do it in *our* family." Either outcome is the result of some testing and review of the merits and penalties of a certain stand or value.

By the time the boy or girl reaches the third or fourth grade in school, these culture conflicts may be in the form of episodes of open rebellion. The preadolescent finds adults generally trying. Both boys and girls are skeptical of the other sex and band together in tight little groups of children of the same age and sex. Boys now reject such adult-imposed "sissy stuff" as cleanliness, obedience, and politeness, and often become antagonistic, rebellious, uncooperative, restless, and very noisy. Dr. Luton D. Ackerson studying 5,000 nondelinquent boys and girls at the Illinois Institute for Juvenile Research, found that behavior problems are more frequent among the nine- to thirteen-year-olds than among any other age group—more fighting, rudeness, and disobedience among preadolescent children than among either the younger or the older age groups.[1] These problems are so characteristic of the third- to sixth-grader, that Fritz Redl defines preadolescence as, "That phase when the nicest children begin to behave in the most awful way." [2]

Another study of third- to sixth-grade boys finds that those children whose parents were both coercive and autonomy-granting were successfully assertive academically as well as in social influence and friendship.[3] Such data suggest strongly that schoolagers need firm controls from their parents, as well as a chance to prove themselves autonomously. Other significant adults—teachers, scout leaders, relatives and friends of the family further reinforce family values for a child.[4]

When mother and father have successfully undertaken their developmental tasks of developing a workable philosophy of life in the earlier stages of their marriage and in their individual personality development, they can accept the querying and the challenging of the schoolage boy or girl without being personally threatened or feeling personally attacked or repudiated.[5] It is when one or the other of the parents feels basically insecure about the area under question that confusion reigns and the family fails to make progress in refining and developing its way of life to meet the test of real life situations. Actively interpreting why some

[1] Quoted in *Junior Guidance Newsletter* (Chicago: Science Research Associates, December 1952).

[2] *Ibid.*, p. 1.

[3] Lois Wladis Hoffman, Sidney Rosen, and Ronald Lippitt, "Parental Coerciveness Child Autonomy, and Child's Role at School," *Sociometry*, Vol. 23, No. 1, March 1960, pp. 15–22.

[4] Carle C. Zimmerman and Lucius F. Cervantes, *Successful American Families* (New York: Pageant Press, 1960).

[5] O. Spurgeon English and Constance Foster, *Fathers Are Parents, Too* (New York: G. P. Putnam's Sons, 1951), Chap. 6.

Religious practices on a whole-family basis may help a youngster feel secure.

things are wrong and others right, why some actions are good and others bad, are aspects of this developmental task that families face all through the schoolage stage. Such teaching is not easy, especially in this day and age when family values are changing.[1] But nothing is more important to a family's basic integrity, or to a youngster's sense of what he and his family stand for, in a world where individuals have to stand for something, lest they fall for anything.

CHALLENGES AND RESOURCES OF FAMILIES WITH SCHOOL CHILDREN

Families with schoolage children present at least seven challenges today: (1) economic pressures (four out of five families at this stage are in debt[2]), (2) limited space in home and neighborhood, (3) ethnic and racial tensions in changing communities, (4) inadequate school facilities for a rapidly growing population, (5) poor articulation of home and school, (6) unsolved and undetected child behavior problems, and (7) neglected and rejected children growing up in inadequate homes.

[1] Daniel R. Miller and Guy E. Swanson, *The Changing American Family* (New York: John Wiley & Sons, 1958), and other sources quoted in Chapter Five.

[2] John B. Lansing and Leslie Kish, "Family Life Cycle as an Independent Variable," *American Sociological Review,* Vol. 22, No. 5, October 1957, p. 514.

Resources paralleling the sevenfold challenge in brief suggestive summary are:

1) Financial plans to spread the costs of rearing children
2) Increase and improvement of housing suitable for families with children, and of neighborhood facilities for active play
3) Widespread intergroup education, and interpretation of the meanings and methods of living in a democratic melting-pot culture
4) Rapid expansion of school facilities, teacher recruitment and education with enlightened public support
5) Parent-teacher cooperation in improving conditions for children and encouraging home-school teamwork through effective PTA programs, etc.
6) Widely accessible child-guidance services, effective mental health education, and adequate programs in parent education and family counseling
7) Community welfare programs to strengthen families and to provide supplemental services for children whose homes have failed them.

SUMMARY

The schoolage stage of family life represents the crowded years that begin with the firstborn going off to school and flow into the teen years as he becomes a teenager. Younger children have already arrived, and are hard at work on their developmental tasks, while the schoolager works out his at the growing edges of the family where all is new both to it and to him. He faces a multitude of growth responsibilities as he makes a place for himself at school, with his peer group and with other adults, and becomes a participating member of his family and of the larger community. His parents meanwhile are occupied with their tasks as parents, as a married couple, and as individuals. Family developmental tasks of this stage may be summarized briefly: (1) providing for parents' needs for privacy, quiet, and order during the children's vigorous years; (2) keeping financially afloat while the family nears the flood stage of its needs; (3) cooperating to get things done; (4) continuing to satisfy each other as married partners; (5) elaborating communication systems within the expanding family; (6) feeling close to relatives in the larger family; (7) tying in with life outside the family; and (8) testing and retesting family philosophies of life.

The schoolage family has its challenges in dovetailing the many developmental tasks of all members of the family in harmonious satisfying ways. It has its rewards in the sense of accomplishment that comes from both individual and group achievements, as well as in the family solidarity that is peculiarly meaningful at this stage.

SUGGESTED ACTIVITIES

1) Carefully review the research on the effects of working mothers on their children, their marriages, and their personality development (see reference in Chaps. 3 and 10), and debate the proposition, "Resolved that mothers with school children should be full-time homemakers."

2) Visit a session of a parents' study group, record what happened, especially the questions asked during and after the meeting. Interpret the parents' questions in terms of what is known about their developmental tasks at this stage of family life.

3) Plan a budget for a schoolage family with three children for a) a low-income family, b) a medium-income family, and c) a high-income family. Base your figures on current prices and standards of living in your community. Discuss the ways in which the three budgets differ, and why.

4) Review the School-Age Study Course in the *PTA Magazine* for the current year, relating the materials covered to the developmental tasks of the school-age family.

5) Write a paper on the pros and cons of moving to the suburbs as children reach school age. Interview at least one middle-class family which has chosen to remain in the city, and a family from a similar social status which has recently moved to a suburb for anecdotal material on the rewards and regrets of suburban vs. urban living.

6) Develop a critique of the philosophies of child development at Yale University under Dr. Arnold Gesell and under Dr. Milton Senn, by comparing the references under the two names in your *Readings*.

7) Prepare a list of recommendations for parents of schoolage children who want to keep their marriage relationship from being overshadowed by their responsibilities as parents. Document with statistical and clinical evidence, and gear to both preventive and remedial proposals.

8) Role play three ways of handling children's quarrels within the family where there are two or more children of school age or younger. Discuss your feelings and behaviors and relate to relevant materials in this chapter and its references.

9) Review Carleton Washburne's *The World's Good* (New York: John Day Company, 1954), for ways in which parents and teachers can help push out a child's horizons toward world-mindedness and interest in other peoples around the globe.

READINGS

Barclay, Dorothy, *Understanding the City Child* (New York: Franklin Watts, 1959).

Brim, Orville G., Jr., *Education for Child Rearing* (New York: Russell Sage Foundation, 1959).

Duvall, Evelyn, and Hill, Reuben, *Being Married* (Boston: D. C. Heath and Company, 1960), Chapter 20, "Bringing Up Your Children."

English, O. Spurgeon, and Foster, Constance, *Fathers Are Parents, Too* (New York: G. P. Putnam's Sons, 1951), Chapter 6, "The Latency Period."

Frank, Mary and Lawrence K., *How to Help Your Child in School* (New York: The Viking Press, 1950).

Gesell, Arnold, and Ilg, Frances, *The Child from Five to Ten* (New York: Harper & Brothers, 1946).

Ginzberg, Eli, ed., *The Nation's Children* (New York: Columbia University Press, 1960, 3 volumes prepared for the Golden Anniversary White House Conference on Children and Youth, 1960).

Havighurst, Robert J., *Human Development and Education* (New York: Longmans, Green and Company, 1953), Part Two: "Middle Childhood."

Hawkes, Glenn R., and Pease, Damaris, *Behavior and Development from 5 to 12.* (New York: Harper & Brothers, 1962).

Hoffman, Lois Wladis, "Effects of Maternal Employment on the Child," *Child Development*, Vol. 32, No. 1, March 1961, pp. 187–197.

Lane, Howard A., and Beauchamp, Mary, *Understanding Human Development* (New York: Prentice-Hall, 1959).

Lewis, Gertrude M., *Educating Children in Grades Four, Five and Six* (Washington, D. C.: United States Department of Health, Education and Welfare, Office of Education, 1958).

Macfarlane, Jean W.; Allen, Lucile; and Honzik, Marjoria P., *A Developmental Study of the Behavior Problems of Normal Children between Twenty-One Months and Fourteen Years* (Berkeley: University of California Press, 1954).

Martin, William E., and Stendler, Celia B., *Child Development: The Process of Growing Up in Society* (New York: Harcourt, Brace, 1953).

Miller, Daniel R., and Swanson, Guy E., *The Changing American Parent* (New York: John Wiley & Sons, 1958).

National Manpower Council, *Work in the Lives of Married Women* (New York: Columbia University Press, 1958).

Prescott, Daniel A., *The Child in the Educative Process* (New York: McGraw-Hill Book Company, 1957).

Senn, Milton J. E., "The Epoch Approach to Child Development," *Woman's Home Companion*, November 1955, pp. 40–42, 60–62.

Stolz, Lois Meek, "Effects of Maternal Employment on Children: Evidence from Research," *Child Development*, Vol. 31, 1960, pp. 749–782.

Stone, L. Joseph, and Church, Joseph, *Childhood and Adolescence* (New York: Random House, 1957), Chapters 8 and 9.

Strang, Ruth, *Helping Your Gifted Child* (New York: E. P. Dutton & Co., 1960).

Weil, Mildred W., "An Analysis of the Factors Influencing Married Women's Actual or Planned Work Participation," *American Sociological Review*, Vol. 26, No. 1, February 1961, pp. 91–96.

Old and young, even of the same breed, find themselves at different phases in the vital cycle, and cannot agree in mood, opinion, impulse or affection. Contact means restraint on both sides, and a hearty unison can seldom be established except amongst comrades of the same age.
GEORGE SANTAYANA

CHAPTER ELEVEN

Families with teenagers

A family enters the teenage stage of the family life cycle when the oldest child becomes thirteen, and leaves it when the first child departs for marriage, for work, or for military service, as a young adult. Typically six or seven years in the teenage stage, the family may spend but three or four years as is the case of the very early marriage, or the school-dropout who goes to work at sixteen. The stage lasts much longer when the first child to be launched delays his leaving home until he or she is in the twenties or thirties or later.

The father at the teenage stage is usually close to or in his forties, with his wife on the average of two years younger, entering the stage in her mid-thirties and leaving it typically in her mid-forties. By this time she is in her menopause, and possibly has a "change of life baby" as the late-arriving infant is sometimes called. The other children by this time are most likely schoolagers.

A family with four sons and daughters is made up of six persons, holding a maximum of four positions. (1) husband-father, (2) wife-mother, (3) son-brother, and (4) daughter-sister. Each has its relevant developmental tasks as parents, as teenager, as schoolager, and as younger child. Father and mother cope with the adult crisis of guiding the next generation with the possible risk of interpersonal impoverishment. The adolescent struggles toward a sense of identity against the danger of identity diffusion, inability to "take hold" or fixation on a negative identity. Concurrently, the schoolager is busy learning to make things and to prove his ability to produce, the preschool child adventures in curiosity and initiative against the tendency to feel guilty and vindictive; the possible late-born infant is laying down a sense of trust in his world so critical at his stage of development. The over-all family goal at the teenage stage is that of loosening family ties to allow greater responsibility and freedom in readiness for releasing the young adult-in-the-making.

AMERICAN TEENAGERS TODAY

Adolescents in America are so frequently used as scapegoats that popular opinion makes them out to be a generation of troublemakers who will become juvenile delinquents unless somebody gets tough with them. This negative attitude toward children in the second decade of life is seen to be [1] rooted in our larger insecurities as parents and as a people. Its bitter fruits are exaggerated fears of the teen years, and of teenagers themselves. Many families which have survived the busy, full years of childhood tense up and prepare for the worst at the first sign of adolescence.

Actually only a small percentage of teenagers ever become delinquent. Estimates of incidences of adolescent norm-violation vary by community and between investigators. On a national scale, between 2 and 5 per cent of all teenagers are brought to the attention of police for violations ranging from trespassing or breaking curfew, to murder and manslaughter. Granted that teenage gang rumbles and vicious vandalism are not to be discounted, the plain fact is that the vast majority (95 to 98 per cent) of America's teenagers are law-abiding citizens.

Some adolescents are more vulnerable to delinquent behavior than others. Delinquency research projects concur that most teenage violators are lower-class youngsters. Delinquents from other social classes are more apt to be emotionally disturbed, as is clear from Dr. Miller's estimations of delinquency distribution, Table 18.

Further light on the problems of teenagers is seen in the pathways they follow into adulthood. It is estimated that in America today, 30 per cent of the boys and 20 per cent of the girls find the path to adulthood blocked, and have great difficulty reaching responsible adulthood.[2] These are the youngsters who drop out of school at fifteen or sixteen with a history of failure, frustration, and maladjustment in school, home, and work.

[1] William C. Kvaraceus, Walter B. Miller and others, *Delinquent Behavior* (Washington, D. C.: National Education Association, 1959), Volume 1, pp. 24–31.
[2] Robert J. Havighurst, "Adolescence and the Postponement of Adulthood," *The School Review*, Spring 1960, pp. 52–62.

TABLE 18. *Distribution of "Delinquent" Individuals*

Social Class Status	Demonstrable Emotional Disturbance	Little or No Serious Emotional Disturbance	Percentage of All Delinquents
Lower Class	15%	70%	85%
Non-Lower Class	10%	5%	15%
	25%	75%	100%
		Degree of Emotional Disturbance	

SOURCE: Walter B. Miller, *op. cit.*, p. 54.

Until 1900, 80 per cent of the boys and 90 per cent of the girls typically left school by age fifteen. The median age for leaving school at the turn of the century for the boys was 14, when he went to work on a farm, or as an apprentice in a trade or business. Most girls finished grade school and then went to work in their own or other people's families until they married and established their own homes. This classic pattern, typical of the centuries that preceded our own, no longer fits in today's world and so more often brings frustration and maladjustment to the teenager who follows it.

In today's complex society, two other pathways to adulthood are more promising. One, followed by 10 to 15 per cent of youth in 1900, now attracts from 50 to 70 per cent of American teenagers who finish high school and go to work at steady jobs where their wage levels are protected, and their tenure is relatively secure. This is the modal group today, involving little role discontinuity in steps that lead smoothly for most young people from high school graduation to learning a skilled or semiskilled operation, getting a steady job with promotions and fringe benefits assured, finding a mate, and establishing a comfortable home.

The third pathway to adulthood is not quite so simple, but offers many rewards for advanced education, technical competence, and initiative. It is followed by those who work toward a high level of education and training before they become self-supporting. These young people finish college and tend to go on for graduate or professional education. Since 1900 this group has increased from 4 to 22 per cent of all young men, and from 1 to 12 per cent of all young women in the United States.[1]

A farm youngster in an agricultural economy suffers few of the handicaps that would be his in a highly industrialized technical society. A

[1] Walter B. Miller, *op. cit.*, pp. 53–54.

1960 study[1] of Iowa farm boys found that although their high school grades and social participation were as high as their urban classmates, they got less encouragement from their parents for education beyond high school than did the city boys; they less often had plans for any education beyond high school; they less frequently planned on going to college; and they more often planned to enter occupations with lower income and prestige than did their city counterparts.

Achievement drive in a teenager appears to be closely related to his family relationships. Those with low drives for achievement tend to come from families when there is (1) a close mother-son relationship marked by dependence, (2) low standards of the "not caring" sort, and/or (3) too high and too early expectations beyond the child's readiness and ability.[2] Another study of adolescents' vocational aspirations found that high aspirers more frequently report (a) feelings of parental rejection, (b) demonstration of favoritism to a child in the family, (c) less attachment to parents, (d) less childhood happiness, and (e) other indications of unsatisfactory interpersonal relationships in the family[3] from which escape may be seen as lying up the occupational ladder.

Distinguishing between two types of intellectual ability as high in IQ tests, and high in creativity, a University of Chicago team found that the high IQ adolescent appears to prefer safety, while the adolescent with high creativity chooses the anxieties and delights of growth. Parents of high IQ students tend to recall more financial difficulties in their childhood, and so may have felt more insecurity than did the parents of parents of students with high creativity, who tend to take risks, permit divergence, and to emphasize their children's openness to experience, values, interests, and enthusiasms.[4]

The dominant values of the period of history in which a youth grows up greatly effects his vocational dreams. Contemporary studies found 3,892 high school boys reporting what they want to be in the following

[1] Lee G. Burchinal, "What's Your Son Going to Do?" *Iowa Farm Science*, Vol. 14, No. 9, March 1960, pp. 16, 17, 18.

[2] David C. McClelland, "Cultural Variation and Achievement Motivation," paper delivered at the Twelfth Annual Symposium of the Committee on Human Development, University of Chicago, April 15, 1961.

[3] Russell R. Dynes, Alfred C. Clarke, and Simon Dinitz, "Levels of Occupational Aspiration: Some Aspects of Family Experience as a Variable." *American Sociological Review*, Vol. 21, No. 2, April 1956, pp. 212–215, see Chap. 12 for further detail.

[4] Jacob W. Getzels and Philip W. Jackson, "Family Environment and Cognitive Style," *American Sociological Review*, Vol. 26, No. 3, June 1961, pp. 351–359.

rank order: nationally famous athlete (37.3 per cent), jet pilot (31.6 per cent), atomic scientist (25.6 per cent), and missionary (5.7 per cent). The same investigation finds girls looking to the more visible occupations open to the modern woman in this rank order: model (32 per cent), nurse (29.2 per cent), schoolteacher (20.6 per cent), and actress or artist (18.4 per cent).[1]

Teenagers' interests and concerns with problems vary too with the times. Replicating a 1935 study of 1,641 junior and senior high school students with a 1957 comparable investigation of 1,165 teenagers, Harris finds significant increases within the 22-year-period in interests of both sexes in love and marriage, home and family relationships, and getting along with others. In 1957, both boys and girls significantly ranked those problems of interpersonal relationships with parents, love, and marriage as higher than children in the 'thirties.[2] The dominant concern of modern teenagers with home and family problems was evident too in the poll in which 6,181 youth participated following the Midcentury White House Conference on Children and Youth, wherein the top fifteen problems ranked as "very important" by one-third to one-half of the youth were as follows: [3]

Percentage of Youth Reporting	As "Very Important" Problem
56%	Unhappy relationship between mother and father
56%	Draft and threat of war
49%	Developing healthy attitude toward sex
48%	Being misunderstood by parents
47%	Finding the right job
46%	Use of narcotics
45%	Finding the right girl or boy
42%	Responsible driving of automobile
37%	Use of alcohol
35%	Religious uncertainties
34%	Lack of respect for property rights of others
34%	Racial discrimination
33%	Religious discrimination
32%	Lack of close friends of my own age
32%	Lack of good home suitable for friends

[1] James S. Coleman, *Social Climates in High Schools* (Washington, D. C.: U. S. Office of Education, 1961), p. 11.

[2] Dale B. Harris, "Sex Differences in the Life Problems and Interests of Adolescents, 1935 and 1957," *Child Development,* Vol. 30, No. 4, December 1959, pp. 453–459.

[3] "Unhappy Homes and Draft Lead Youth Problems," *Progress Bulletin,* National Midcentury Committee for Children and Youth, January 1953, pp. 1 and 7.

ADOLESCENTS AND THEIR PARENTS

Adolescence is a period of strain in most families as teenagers attempt to establish their identity and emancipate themselves from their parents. This is a time when parents feel that their children undervalue them, and when adolescents believe that adults generally depreciate teenagers. Widely separate studies find, however, that adolescents have a higher opinion of adults than do their parents, that both generations have favorable opinions of teenagers, and that adolescents rate parent-adolescent relationships more favorably than do their mothers or fathers.[1]

Conforming teenagers who less often break rules and regulations tend more than others to have favorable images of their families, to rate their parents' discipline as fair, and their family relationships as democratic and affectionate.[2] There is also evidence that lower-class families value conformity and respectability more than do middle-class parents whose children tend more to be encouraged to develop as persons in their own right.[3]

Gradually through adolescence, the teenager shifts his orientation from his family to his friends as Table 19 indicates.

TABLE 19. *Percentage of Students by Grade and by Orientation*

Orientation Toward	Grade in School						
	4th	*5th*	*6th*	*7th*	*8th*	*9th*	*10th*
Family	87.1	80.5	80.2	66.7	41.7	44.7	31.6
Neutral	6.9	12.2	11.2	9.3	18.3	22.4	20.2
Peers	5.9	7.3	8.6	24.1	40.0	32.9	48.1
N	101	82	116	108	115	85	79

SOURCE: Charles E. Bowerman and John W. Kinch, "Changes in Family and Peer Orientation of Children Between the Fourth and Tenth Grades," *Social Forces*, Vol. 37, No. 3, March 1959, pp. 206–211.

[1] Robert D. Hess, and Irene Goldblatt, "The Status of Adolescents in American Society: A Problem in Social Identity," *Child Development*, Vol. 28, No. 4, December 1957, pp. 459–468; and Patricia Henderson Maxwell, Ruth Connor and James Walters, "Family Member Perceptions of Parent Role Performance," *Merrill-Palmer Quarterly*, Vol. 7, No. 1, 1961, pp. 31–37.

[2] W. L. Slocum and Carol L. Stone, "A Method for Measuring Family Images Held by Teen-Agers," *Marriage and Family Living*, Vol. XXI, No. 3, August 1959, pp. 245–250.

[3] Elias Tuma and Norman Livson, "Family Socioeconomic Status and Adolescent Attitudes toward Authority," *Child Development*, Vol. 31, No. 2, June 1961, pp. 387–399; Evelyn Millis Duvall, "Conceptions of Parenthood," *American Journal of Sociology*, Vol. 52, No. 3, November 1946, pp. 193–203; and Melvin Kohn, "Social Class and Parental Authority," *American Sociological Review*, Vol. 24, No. 3, June 1959, pp. 352–366, and other references in Chapter Four.

Each adolescent must come to terms with his own family situation as he matures. Whatever the family strengths and weaknesses, they eventually must be faced and accepted as his "givens" by any teenager. Other resources in the community may be tapped as the adolescent realizes that he need no longer look solely to his family for all he requires to mature into effective adulthood. What he must accomplish as the developmental tasks of adolescence are outlined briefly below.

DEVELOPMENTAL TASKS OF TEENAGERS [1]

1) *Accepting one's changing body and learning to use it effectively:*
    Coming to terms with new size, shape, function, and potential of one's maturing body.
    Reconciling differences between one's own physique and that of agemates of the same and other sex, as normal and to be expected variations.
    Understanding what puberal changes mean and wholesomely anticipating maturity as a man or as a woman.
    Caring for one's body in healthful ways that assure its optimum development.
    Learning to handle oneself skillfully in the variety of recreational, social, and family situations that require learned physical skills.
2) *Achieving a satisfying and socially accepted masculine or feminine role:*
    Learning what it means to be a boy or girl in one's culture.
    Anticipating realistically what will be involved in becoming a man or a woman.
    Finding oneself within the leeway of sex-role expectations and practice allowed by one's family and community.
3) *Finding oneself as a member of one's own generation in more mature relations with one's agemates:*
    Becoming acceptable as a member of one or more groups of peers.
    Making and keeping friends of both sexes.
    Getting dates and becoming comfortable in dating situations.
    Getting experience in loving and being loved by one or more members of the opposite sex.

[1] Freely adapted from the schema used by Robert J. Havighurst, *Human Development and Education* (New York: Longmans, Green and Co., 1953), Chaps. 9, 10, 11.

Finding oneself as a member of one's own generation involves making and keeping friends of both sexes.

> Learning how to get along with a wide variety of agemates in school, neighborhood, and community settings.
>
> Developing skills in inviting and refusing, solving problems and resolving conflicts, making decisions, and evaluating experiences with one's peers.

4) *Achieving emotional independence of parents and other adults:*

> Becoming free of childish dependencies upon one's parents.
>
> Developing more mature affection for parents as persons.
>
> Learning how to be an autonomous person who is capable of making decisions and running one's own life.
>
> Growing through the dependence of childhood and the impulsive independence of adolescence to mature interdependence with

others (parents, teachers, and all authority figures, especially).
Learning to be an adult among adults.

5) *Selecting and preparing for an occupation and economic independence:*

Seeking counsel and getting specific knowledges about possible fields of work within the limits of real possibilities.

Choosing an occupation in line with interests, abilities, and opportunities.

Preparing oneself through schooling, specialized training, and personal responsibility to get and hold a position.

Getting try-out or apprenticeship experiences wherever possible in the lines of future vocational interests.

6) *Preparing for marriage and family life:*

Enjoying the responsibilities as well as the privileges of family membership.

Developing a responsible attitude toward getting married and having a family.

Acquiring knowledge about mate selection, marriage, homemaking, and childrearing.

Learning to distinguish between infatuation and more lasting forms of love.

Developing a mutually satisfying personal relationship with a potential mate through processes of dating, going steady, effective courtship, and becoming involved with a loved one.

Making decisions about the timing of engagement, marriage, completion of one's education, fulfillment of military service requirements, and the multiple demands upon young people of marriageable age.

Becoming ready to settle down into a home of one's own.

7) *Developing intellectual skills and social sensitivities necessary for civic competence:*

Developing concepts of law, government, economics, politics, geography, human nature, and social organization which fit the modern world.

Gaining awareness of human needs and becoming motivated to help others attain their goals.

Acquiring problem-solving methods for dealing effectively with modern problems.

Gaining abilities to communicate competently as a citizen in a democracy.

Becoming involved in causes and projects outside oneself and becoming a socially responsible person.

8) *Developing a workable philosophy of life that makes sense in today's
world:*

Achieving a mature set of values and the ethical controls that characterize a good individual in one's culture.

Desiring and achieving socially responsible behavior.

Selecting worthy ideals and standards to live by and identify with.

Practicing and working through the meanings of religious experience that motivate and inspire.

Finding oneself in the universe and among one's fellowmen in
meaningful ways.

> *Each youth sustains within his breast*
> *A vague and infinite unrest.*
> *He goes about in still alarm,*
> *With shrouded future at his arm,*
> *With longings that can find no tongue.*
> *I see him thus, for I am young.*
> BY AN OKLAHOMA HIGH SCHOOL BOY

Adolescents' developmental tasks were originally derived from intensive longitudinal studies, as described in the *Preface.* More recently,
young teenagers have been able to identify their developmental tasks, as
Dales' use of scalogram analysis illustrates.[1] Planning youth programs in
terms of the developmental tasks of various age-groupings in ways that
make possible the measurement of progress now seems possible.[2] Criteria
for success or failure and for early, expected, and late accomplishment
of each of the developmental tasks of adolescence would give even a
finer cutting edge to this useful tool.

Traditional tendencies in thinking, feeling, and behaving often hinder
and delay a young person's development. Attitudes of shame, guilt and embarrassment hurt, while wholesomeness helps a youth's full acceptance of
himself and of other persons. Finding one's self vocationally is delayed by

[1] Ruth J. Dales, "A Method for Measuring Developmental Tasks: Scales for
Selected Tasks at the Beginning of Adolescence," *Child Development,* Vol. 26, No. 2,
June 1955, pp. 111–122.

[2] Al J. Hummel and Clifford A. Smith, *The Task Method of Program Planning*
(Omaha, Nebraska: Omaha Young Men's Christian Association Publications, 1959).

tendencies to live in a world of dreams and fantasy; it is helped by the willingness to cope with reality and the courage to explore real possibilities. Preparing for marriage and family life is blocked by outmoded restrictions and limitations in education and greatly helped by forward-looking programs for equipping young men and women to become competent husbands and wives, fathers and mothers. Becoming a competent citizen is often side-tracked by outmoded biases and stereotyped ideas ("you can't buck the system"); it moves straight toward its goal with worthy adults to emulate in determining a sound, acceptable set of values. Finding oneself as a person means coming to terms with one's self, as one was, as one is, and as one might become. Acceptance, encouragement, and guidance are pivotal requisites for many a teenager in accomplishing these manifold tasks of growing up.

DEVELOPMENTAL TASKS OF THE ADULTS AS PARENTS, AS SPOUSES, AS WORKERS, AS HOMEMAKERS, AND AS PERSONS IN THE FAMILY WITH TEENAGERS

Traditional tendencies in thinking, feeling, and behaving often are hazards for both parents as we see in the charts that follow.[1]

THE MAN OF THE FAMILY
AS FATHER

Developmental Tasks, Goals, and Responsibilities	Traditional Tendencies in Thinking, Feeling, and Behaving
Providing "good" patterns for the roles of the growing adult man, loving husband, and accepting father.	Inability to regard adolescent "cockiness" and impudence as growth manifestations but interpret them as attacks upon parental dignity.
Learning to understand each child as an individual, believe in and trust him, respect his personality and delight in seeing him grow into adoles-	Tendency to more or less unconsciously look upon adolescent child as his rival for the attention of others and in importance and prestige.

[1] Freely adapted from Leland H. Stott, chairman, Robert G. Foster, Robert J. Havighurst, and Fritz Redl, "Section V, The Family with Teenagers," for the Committee on the Dynamics of Family Interaction Preliminary Report, Evelyn Duvall and Reuben Hill, co-chairmen, National Conference on Family Life, Washington, D. C., February 1948, mimeographed materials.

Developmental Tasks, Goals, and Responsibilities	*Traditional Tendencies in Thinking, Feeling, and Behaving*

cence and adulthood, and thus maintaining the confidential, affectionate and companionable relationship earlier established. Providing time to spend with adolescent on a companionable basis, and to get the youth's point of view.

Understanding that growth is not identical with "improvement," that what the adolescent *needs* is often *not* what he seems to "deserve." Also that what the youngster *needs* has no relationship to the kind of treatment the father received when young.

Fear of loss of control, hence the tendency to be more autocratic toward the adolescent. Tendency to deal with child in terms of his own adolescent experiences—either try to repeat or to avoid what happened to himself. (Repeat the strict handling he received from his own parents, or avoid all firmness, not in terms of the child's needs but because of what happened to him.)

Getting insight into, and a realistic evaluation of his own emotional reactions, not to stifle or hide them, but to avoid consciously or unconsciously over-reacting to them in dealing with the child.

Tendency to fear his own emotions (fear of "spoiling" child through the expression of affection and so become unduly cold and over-strict).

Arriving at a common understanding and cooperating with mother on matters of guidance and control of children.

Assumption of an authoritarian attitude, following perhaps the pattern of his own parental home, and attempting arbitrarily to order the lives and activities of his older children, without consultation with mother, or the young people.

Taking no particular interest, and assuming no part of the responsibility for the guidance and control of children.

THE WOMAN OF THE FAMILY
AS MOTHER

Developmental Tasks, Goals, and Responsibilities	*Traditional Tendencies in Thinking, Feeling, and Behaving*
Providing "good" patterns for the roles of the *growing* adult woman, wife, and mother. Being alert to matters of her personal and social behavior, dress, and appearance that the adolescent may or may not be proud of.	Tendency not to think of her own attitudes, behavior and appearance as being important for adolescent children.
Trying to understand each child as an individual, believing in and trusting him, respecting his personality and delighting in seeing him grow into adolescence and adulthood, and thus maintaining a confidental, affectionate and companionable relationship with the adolescent as well as with the younger children. Understanding also that what the child needs in the way of guidance has no relationship to the kind of treatment she herself received when young.	Tendency to be anxious upon seeing the child grow up. Tendency to deal with the adolescent in terms of her own adolescent experiences—either repeat, or try to avoid what happened to herself (repeat strict handling of own parents, or avoid firmness, not in terms of child's needs but because of what happened to her). Tendency more or less unconsciously to feel that the adolescent daughter is her rival—is replacing her in the attention of the father—is outdoing her in attractiveness.
Understanding that growth is not identical with "improvement," that what the adolescent *needs* is often not what he seems to "deserve."	Tendency to be over-concerned with "improvement" in the child's behavior in relation to certain stereotypes of socially acceptable conduct.
Getting insight into, and a realistic evaluation of her own emotional reactions, not to stifle or hide them, but to avoid consciously or unconsciously over-reacting to them in dealing with the adolescent.	Tendency to fear her own emotions (fear that her strong affection for child is "spoiling" and to try to compensate by becoming unduly cold and overstrict, or fear of her rejecting and aggressive wishes may result in a compensatory suppression of all control and firmness with an "overdose of overprotection.")

THE MAN OF THE FAMILY
AS HOMEMAKER AND PROVIDER

Developmental Tasks, Goals, and Responsibilities	*Traditional Tendencies in Thinking, Feeling, and Behaving*
Taking a renewed interest in the activities of the home and cooperating with and supporting wife in adapting the household routines to the changing and varied demands of the family members at this stage.	Tendency to resist changes and to be irritated at variations from routines he has become accustomed to.
Relieving his wife of some of the actual work and assuming a share of the responsibility of the family and household management—encouraging and facilitating participation of children in the daily work.	Tendency to hold to the point of view that housework is woman's work and beneath the dignity of men. Tendency to follow the pattern of home participation set in his own parental home and to take for granted that that pattern is normal and desirable.
Taking on more responsibility in the management of interpersonal relationships and problems, particularly in relation to adolescent children.	Feeling that the handling of the children is their mother's job and responsibility.
Regarding his responsibility for providing for the material requirements and the general economic security of his family as taking precedence over his own desires to speculate or to quit.	Irresponsibility in the matter of providing financially for the family— tendency to take chances and go into financial ventures that jeopardize the economic security of family, or to run away in one escape or another.
Acquainting the rest of the family with the realities of the family's financial situation and thus enlisting their intelligent sharing of responsibility.	Feeling that the money he makes is his own—that after all money matters are a man's business.
Enlisting the participation of the family in making decisions regarding important expenditures or financial ventures, and regarding the equitable sharing and apportioning of the family funds.	Feeling that he, as head of the family, should continue to maintain complete control of the family finances.

THE MAN OF THE FAMILY
AS HOMEMAKER AND PROVIDER (*Continued*)

Developmental Tasks, Goals, and Responsibilities	*Traditional Tendencies in Thinking, Feeling, and Behaving*
Accepting and encouraging the wife's sharing of the economic burden of earning the family living if she is so talented and so minded.	Feeling that to provide the income to support the family is the task of man alone.

THE WOMAN OF THE FAMILY
AS HOMEMAKER AND FAMILY MANAGER

Developmental Tasks, Goals, and Responsibilities	*Traditional Tendencies in Thinking, Feeling, and Behaving*
Checking on her health needs and habits and taking steps to insure strength and energy for the job of making a home for a family with adolescents.	Tendency to neglect her own health at a time of life when it is especially important.
Reviewing her work habits and routines with the purpose of adapting them to the real needs and demands of all members of the family, including herself.	Tendency to overstress the housekeeping aspects—orderliness, cleanliness, things always in their places. Tendency either to follow slavishly or to repudiate the homemaking patterns of her parental home.
Reviewing homemaking schedules and routines with the view of obtaining optimum family participation and satisfaction.	Tendency to perfectionism—husband or children not able to participate in homemaking activities because they cannot do them to suit her.
Managing the family budget efficiently—buying economically, and with an understanding of the nutritional requirements and other material needs of the family. Devising means of keeping family, including the father, informed as to costs, available goods and relative values and enlisting their intelligent cooperation in the use of the family's resources.	Tendency to be extravagant, or unwise in buying. Failing to cooperate fully with the "provider" or to enlist his sympathy and his understanding of the problems of managing efficiently the household budget. *Struggling* with the children rather than helping them to understand the problems of "making ends meet."

Developmental Tasks, Goals, and Responsibilities	*Traditional Tendencies in Thinking, Feeling, and Behaving*
Acquiring the attitudes, knowledge and skills necessary to create a "home atmosphere" which is comfortable, wholesome, easy, friendly, happy, and *to take joy and professional pride in that accomplishment.*	Tendency to feel that the status of the homemaker is low in comparison with business or professional work. Assuming an attitude of one betrayed —an attitude of self-pity. Failing to see the challenge or the possibilities for satisfaction and development in homemaking.

THE MAN OF THE FAMILY
AS HUSBAND

Developmental Tasks, Goals, and Responsibilities	*Traditional Tendencies in Thinking, Feeling, and Behaving*
Maintaining or reinforcing habits of personal care and grooming.	Tendency to "let down" with the approach of middle age, to be careless in care of clothes and in personal care and grooming.
Strengthening his attitudes of acceptance with respect to his wife—to be able more than ever to recognize the necessity for, and her right to be different—to be as she is, and to be able really to accept her thus.	Tendency to hold to a preconceived notion as to personality, talents and behavior of a wife. Tendency to follow or to repudiate compulsively the husband-wife relationships of own parents.
Maintaining or re-establishing habits of outward courtesy and attentiveness toward wife and a genuine concern for her comfort and welfare.	Tendency to take wife for granted, to forget to be courteous or to show appreciation of her, or concern for her welfare and comfort.
Understanding the needs and tendencies of his wife at this particular stage and be increasingly alert to ways of facilitating her personal growth and satisfactions.	Tendency to assume a self-centered individualistic attitude in his relationships with wife, to be concerned with his own satisfactions,—to be self-centered and exploitive in marital relations.

THE MAN OF THE FAMILY
AS HUSBAND (*Continued*)

Developmental Tasks, Goals, and Responsibilities	*Traditional Tendencies in Thinking, Feeling, and Behaving*
Cultivating a closer confidential and sharing relationship with his wife; to share with her his experiences—his triumphs and worries, etc. Being really interested in her activities, domestic and social. Regarding her as a partner and sharer in all aspects of their life together.	Tendency to regard men's and women's spheres of action as separate, to feel that he must maintain his authority, that a "woman's place is in the home," "has no business working outside the home," "has no sense about money," "it's her job to take care of the kids."
Cooperating in the development of new joint interests, activities, hobbies, etc.	Tendency to want to "take it easy" —to follow old established habits in the use of leisure resisting something new.

THE WOMAN OF THE FAMILY
AS WIFE

Developmental Tasks, Goals, and Responsibilities	*Traditional Tendencies in Thinking, Feeling, and Behaving*
Maintaining and enhancing her personal attractiveness and charm.	Tendency to "let down" with the passage of years—to forget the importance of being personally attractive, particularly to her husband.
Showing tender concern about husband's health and welfare. Being sympathetic with his need for quiet, for understanding and occasional "ego inflation."	Tendency to take husband for granted; to be nagging and critical when he needs sympathy and understanding; to be thoughtless and inconsiderate toward him.
Being understanding of her husband's needs for affection and response and to be able to respond to them adequately.	Inability to respond maritally with warmth and affection, or to be self-centered, responding or not responding according to her present whim.

Developmental Tasks, Goals, and Responsibilities	Traditional Tendencies in Thinking, Feeling, and Behaving
Being able to accept her husband's differences and peculiarities with sympathy and with interest.	Tendency to continue to try to make her husband over after her own preconceived notions, which may represent a compulsive adherence to, or a repudiation of the husband-wife relationships of her own parents.
Maintaining or acquiring a genuine interest in husband's business or profession and thus being able to function as an understanding and sympathetic listener, confidant and sharer in his triumphs and worries.	Boredom in relation to husband's work; tendency to be disparaging of his job, lack of appreciation of its importance, nagging with respect to the prestige value or income from the job.
Encouraging the development of additional joint activities and interests with husband.	Lack of inclination to participate in the type of activities in which husband is interested.

THE MAN OF THE FAMILY
AS A PERSON

Developmental Tasks, Goals, and Responsibilities	Traditional Tendencies in Thinking, Feeling, and Behaving
Adjusting to the realities of constantly growing older—accepting realistically his present age and stage of development with its limitations as well as its potentialities for satisfactory functioning and enjoyment.	Tendency to continue to base feelings of personal prestige on the exploits and accomplishments of youth, maintaining image of self, established in youth. Tendency to feel that life is "passing him by." Feeling that the supreme pleasures and satisfactions of life are limited to youth and young manhood.
Keeping "up-to-date" on current thinking, social attitudes and changing folkways and mores.	Tendency to continue to think in terms of the norms and social standards of his youth, failing to move along with the times.

THE MAN OF THE FAMILY
AS A PERSON (*Continued*)

Developmental Tasks, Goals, and Responsibilities	*Traditional Tendencies in Thinking, Feeling, and Behaving*
Broadening interests and knowledge and thus growing in terms of civic and social responsibility.	Tendency to become so engrossed in making a living or achieving business or professional success as to have no time or energy for growth in other areas. Tendency to attitude that "politics is rotten business" and that government is the business of incompetent, irresponsible, and corrupt individuals.
Bolstering feelings of adequacy and self-confidence and personal worth by constantly developing new personal skills, hobbies, etc.	Tendency to foster basic feelings of inadequacy through lack of growth in skills and personal proficiency (sometimes compensated for in rigid, unyielding, domineering behavior toward wife, children and associates).
Continuing to work toward his personal ideals and goals of achievement, always in terms of the realities of his own resources and limitations.	Tendency to seek to become, and to attain *through his child* the ideals and goals of achievement which he failed to achieve in his own life.

THE WOMAN OF THE FAMILY
AS A PERSON

Developmental Tasks, Goals, and Responsibilities	*Traditional Tendencies in Thinking, Feeling, and Behaving*
Adjusting to the realities of constantly growing older—to approaching middle age. To accept realistically and with equanimity her present age and stage of development with its limitations and its potentialities for satisfactory functioning and enjoyment.	Tendency to feel that she is "missing out," that life is passing her by. Becoming anxious, irritable, complaining or discouraged. Trying to "have her fling" while she can, or to recapture the appearance and the pleasures of youth.

Developmental Tasks, Goals, and Responsibilities	*Traditional Tendencies in Thinking, Feeling, and Behaving*
Keeping up-to-date on current thinking, social attitudes, and changing folkways and mores.	Tendency to fall "behind the times" because of her preoccupation with home duties, tendency to neglect, or sacrifice and submerge self for family.
Developing new interests and broadening scope of activities outside the home and thus maintaining or re-establishing herself as an independently growing, yet interacting member of the family group.	Tendency to limit activities and interests more and more exclusively to home and family and thus to have no time or energy for growth in other areas. Tendency to feel that civic and political problems are not the concern of women.
Bolstering feelings of personal adequacy and worth by developing new skills, hobbies, interests, and commitments.	Tendency to compensate for inadequacy feelings by controlling or domineering over others by means of various devices or to "outdo" others in appearance, clothes, or show of wealth, etc.
Continuing to get satisfaction from her own efforts toward the achievement of personal ideals and goals.	Tendency to live and to experience the realization of her own dreams and ideals through, and in the life and the triumphs of her daughter.

If each of the adult members has been able realistically to accept himself as he is—his physique, with its weaknesses and strengths, its defects and superiorities, his sex and the sex role he must play, his age and stage of maturity, all without inner conflict and undue sensitivity—he thus has set the pattern for a similar sort of self-acceptance on the part of the children. The adolescent girl then has the pattern for accepting with satisfaction her role as a girl and woman; and the boy, even though he may be small in stature or a bit behind schedule in his physical development, has before him a healthy pattern to follow and an understanding attitude in his parents to help him to live happily with himself and his family. Inseparable from the attitude of self-acceptance in the family is the tendency for each family member to accept the others as a matter of course with a basic respect that is founded in mutual understanding.

FAMILY DEVELOPMENTAL TASKS AT THE TEENAGE STAGE

While mother and father, teenager and younger siblings are working out their developmental tasks within the traditional tendencies and social pressures that oftentimes thwart and hinder them, the family as a whole is busy at the essential family developmental tasks of the teenage stage:

1) Providing facilities for widely different needs
2) Working out money matters in the family with teenagers
3) Sharing the tasks and responsibilities of family living
4) Putting the marriage relationship into focus
5) Keeping communication systems open
6) Maintaining contact with the extended family
7) Growing into the world as a family and as persons
8) Reworking and maintaining a philosophy of life

PROVIDING FACILITIES FOR WIDELY DIFFERENT NEEDS

At no time in the family life cycle do family members feel as intensely about the house and its facilities as they do during the teenage family stage. Now the teenager's need for acceptance in larger social circles makes him (even oftener when she is a girl) push for nicer, better, bigger, more modern furnishings and equipment. The house that some years ago was child-proofed and stripped of all breakable elegance, now must bloom in the styles of the period as teenagers see the house as a reflection of themselves and their family. One of the first signs of adolescence noted by mothers is a critical attitude of the youngster about the physical features of the home. The Harvard studies of the health and development of normal children find that with the onset of adolescence youngsters tend to compare their homes unfavorably with others in the community; they find it hard to accept the fact that they cannot use the telephone for hours on end, and they feel they should have top priority for the use of the bathroom.[1]

The dating adolescent girl wants an attractive setting in which she can entertain her boy and girl friends. She needs some privacy in these facilities at least part of the time away from the everwatchful eyes and

[1] Ruth M. Butler, "Mothers' Attitudes Toward the Social Development of Their Adolescents," *Social Casework*, May–June 1956, reprint page 3.

ears of younger siblings, parents, and other family members. The rest of the family needs to be somewhat protected from the noisy activities of teenagers, with their radios turned up full-blast, the record player grinding out the same popular tune over and over again, the giggles, the chatter, the shrieks, and the endless telephone conversations that mean so much to teenagers and yet so often fray the nerves of adults. Now, when so much emphasis is put upon popularity and social life, most families want to encourage their teenagers in their social growth and so do what they can to provide the facilities for it.

The teenage boy starts dating a little later, and he dates less frequently than the girl of the same age.[1] He does less of his dating and entertaining at home than does the girl, and so tends to demand less in refurbishing and "style." The pressures he puts on the home as a teenager are more apt to be in space for his hobbies and for his gang of buddies. As the fellows gather in the basement to fix a model plane, or in the yard to "soup up" the jalopy, or over the short wave set in his room, there is bound to be some invasion of the house and its supplies for food and drink and rags and string and all the other necessities that go into the completion of a project—and a man!

Teenagers tend to crowd their parents in the use of household equipment as they begin to adopt adult ways. One study finds[2] that in the shared equipment and space for leisure activities of teenagers and other members of the family, there are too many activities of diversified nature carried on in the same room. Listing them as (1) quiet or private—reading, study, etc., (2) social—entertaining guests, music, records, television, etc., and (3) active—dancing, painting, carpentry, etc., the investigators recommend creating three distinct activity areas: private, social and active, and using them interchangeably depending upon the demands of the various family members.

The extent of teenagers' use of the home for leisure activities is seen in a survey made by the Social Welfare Council of the Oranges and Maplewood, N. J., the results of which are shown in Table 20.

The top-ranking activity, "doing homework," suggests still another need

[1] Samuel Lowrie, "Factors Involved in the Frequency of Dating," *Marriage and Family Living*, Vol. XVIII, No. 1, February 1956, pp. 46–51.

[2] Jerre L. Withrow and Virginia Y. Trotter, "Space for Leisure Activities of Teen-Agers," *Journal of Home Economics*, Vol. 53, No. 5, May 1961, pp. 359–362.

TABLE 20. *How Teenagers Spend Their Leisure Time* [1]

Percentage of Teenagers	Leisure-time Activity	Number of Hours a Week Reported
83.8	Doing homework	9.2 hours
81.0	Watching television	11.3 hours
77.6	Listening to radio	9.7 hours
61.0	Talking on the telephone	4.4 hours
47.5	Having dates	8.2 hours
46.3	Doing nothing at all	8.0 hours

for the teenage family's facilities—a place suitable for study. Where an atmosphere conducive to study is provided and teenagers are expected to finish their assignments before relaxing with their parents in front of the television set or around a snack on the kitchen table, the early evening pressures are off whole-family equipment. A portable radio in the youngster's room gives him or her "company" for study but does not intrude on concentration as does television. Examples of adult interest in intellectual and cultural things, as well as patterns of work habits and family expectations, facilitate the teenager's effective use of study times and places. It isn't as easy for the lower-class youngster whose home offers few if any of these models and resources.

While the teenager is crowding the house with his or her dating, recreational, and work interests, younger siblings are growing up with their interests and needs to be taken into account. Younger brothers and sisters often resent teenage interests and activities and the break in customary patterns of former years of play together. At the same time, father and mother continue to be persons with rights and needs for a little peace and quiet in their lives. The home that fulfills this multidimensional demand for adequate facilities during the teenage stage has some tall stepping to do, with adaptations and elaborations that more than likely cost money—plenty of it, as we see in the next section.

WORKING OUT MONEY MATTERS IN THE FAMILY WITH TEENAGERS

The teenage family feels pressures for physical expansion and renewal of its facilities. Junior campaigns for a new car. Sally needs a party dress.

[1] Reported in *Time*, September 29, 1952.

The refrigerator is no longer large enough to meet the demand for snacks and meals of the many appetites represented in the family. It would be nice to have another bathroom, or a second TV set, or a deep freeze, or a rumpus room, or a den where mother and father could find some place to call their own when the teenagers are entertaining, or some new furnishings to replace "this old stuff" that is suddenly so hideous in adolescent eyes. All the while, father sees costs of college, social life, and weddings ballooning up ahead of him.

Adolescents are very much concerned with the problems of money. Many of our junior and senior high school young people have difficulty keeping up with school expenses and feel embarrassed because of lack of funds.[1] Dates cost money—clothes and grooming for the girl, and, for the boy, actual financial layout for entertainment and food on the date. There is a wide range of the costs of a date, all the way from less than a dollar for something simple to a great deal of money for elaborate special affairs. One study of freshmen and sophomore college students reports that they spend $2 to $3 for routine dates, $5 to $6 for special dates, and $20 to $35 for big affairs like homecoming, in a range of dating costs running from less than $1 to $300 (reported by a former member of the armed services).[2]

This is the time when a teenager gets a part-time job that will not interfere too greatly with his school work and yet will bring him some regular money of his own. When employment is good, a teenage boy can find work in his neighborhood shop or store, golf links, or garage. The adolescent girl is in demand as baby-sitter, household helper, and in many places as saleswoman or clerk in local store or office. These may be valuable experiences if they do not cut short the young person's educational program and if the income from self-employment may be jointly recognized in the family as of special interest to the adolescent.

Families differ greatly in money practices. Some appropriate the children's earnings as part of the family income as once was traditional. Others consider the child's earnings as his to do with as he or she pleases. Still others keep a supervisory eye on teenagers' earnings, and while they

[1] Martin Bloom, "The Money Problems of Adolescents in the Secondary Schools of Springfield, Massachusetts," *Doctor of Education thesis,* New York University, 1955.

[2] Ruth Connor and Edith Flinn Hall, "The Dating Behavior of College Freshmen and Sophomores," *Journal of Home Economics,* Vol. 44, No. 4, April 1952, pp. 278–281.

The teenage girl is in demand as a baby-sitter—a valuable experience as well as one way of earning money of her own.

respect the young person's wishes, try to counsel for wisdom in planning for future needs. There are still some traditional homes in which either the father or the mother holds the purse strings and the young people have no voice in the family finances. In growing numbers are the more democratically oriented families in which family income and expenditures are discussed and money planning is done jointly with all members of the family participating. In these homes, young people gain experience in handling money and in dealing with financial problems, at the same time feeling that their wishes and rights are being considered in the family as they grow up.

There was a time when women had little say about the family monies. Linnie Day had to wheedle her way into her husband's closely held moneybags, according to Clarence Day's vivid descriptions of his family at the turn of the century.[1] Since World War II, there has been a rapid increase in women workers, especially among the over-35 wives.[2] As a wife gets and holds a job, she brings her earnings home to swell the family coffers and she becomes more of an economic partner in the getting and spending of the family income. This makes sense, especially in the family where the children are old enough so that they do not require the full-time attention of the mother. In fact, some evidence indicates that the adjustment between adolescents and their parents is better when the mother is employed part-time than when she is a full-time homemaker.[3] One interpretation is that as children become adolescent and need to untie the apron strings, the task is less difficult if the mother is not entirely dependent upon her children for her sense of being needed. If she has a part-time job, she not only helps out financially, but very likely she widens her horizons and enriches her role in her family as she becomes a self-sufficient person as well as wife and mother. Individual women and families differ widely, and many wives find it impossible or impractical to work outside the home. With the removal of traditional taboos about women working, a family has a choice about the matter today. That so many families in the teenage stage find that economic and emotional pressures are eased when the mother has some gainful employment is a trend worthy of note.

SHARING THE TASKS AND RESPONSIBILITIES OF FAMILY LIVING

As children grow up into the teens, they are able to assume more and more responsibility for themselves and for the household. Authority that once rested entirely in the parents now can be shared with the adoles-

---

[1] Clarence Day, *Life with Father* (New York: Alfred A. Knopf, 1935).

[2] United States Bureau of the Census, "Women Past Thirty-Five in the Labor Force: 1947 to 1956," *Current Population Reports,* Series P-50, No. 75, July 1957.

[3] Ivan Nye, "Adolescent-Parent Adjustment: Age, Sex, Sibling Number, Broken Homes, and Employed Mothers as Variables," *Marriage and Family Living,* Vol. XIV, No. 4, November 1952, p. 331; also research in progress under Margaret S. Jessen of the Woodland Public Schools, Woodland, California on "Factors in Parents' Understanding of Adolescent Attitudes," reports that working mothers tend to show more understanding than mothers at home.

cents in the family as they become ready. The traditional family, with its father-head, is on the wane in twentieth-century America, with democratic patterns more frequent in families with teenagers.[1] Teenagers are still accountable to their parents, but progressively assume more and more responsibility for their behavior and for the well-being of the family as a whole.

Middle-class family rituals are evidenced in cooperative activities of adults and teenagers working together at jointly assumed responsibilities. Father and son wash and wax the family car on Saturday afternoon. Mother and daughter together do the weekend cleaning and straightening up in the house. The children are usually expected to assume some responsibility for the care of their rooms and personal belongings, with help as needed from their mothers more than their fathers. The wife and mother generally prepares the food, assisted by children upon occasion. With the move to more informal out-of-doors eating, father often presides over the hot dog pit with the assistance of others in the family.

Studies show that most household tasks are jointly undertaken by the various members of the family, with no one member assuming complete responsibility for any one activity. Too frequently, however, teenagers are found doing the simpler, less interesting jobs such as setting and clearing the table (by the girls), and removing the trash by the teenage boy —the major chore that he claims as his own in most families. The parents take on the more important activities—the mother preparing the meals and the father fixing broken things—which might give teenagers and their younger brothers and sisters pride in achievement.[2]

Mother and father clearly hold the balance of power in deciding who will participate in the various activities involving family members. Although most decisions are jointly made by two or more family members, significantly more parents than teenagers have a voice in the social activities that effect them. For example, four out of five fathers (83.8 per cent) decide who uses the family car, a decision that about half of the mothers (51.9 per cent), less than one out of four teenage sons (23.8 per cent), and 13.4 per cent of the teenage daughters have a voice in making. Twice as many parents as teenagers decide who will go on outings or

[1] Vivian Briggs and Lois R. Schulz, "Parental Response to Concepts of Parent-Adolescent Relationships," *Child Development*, Vol. 26, No. 4, December, 1955, pp. 279–284.

[2] Theodore B. Johannis, Jr., "Participation by Fathers, Mothers, and Teenage Sons and Daughters in Selected Household Tasks," *The Coordinator*, Vol. 6, No. 4, June 1958, pp. 61–62.

summer vacations, and half again as many mothers as teenage daughters decide who will use the living room.[1]

It is the father who earns the money (97.9 per cent), pays the bills (97.9 per cent) and shops for the family car (91.3 per cent). Mother has the major voice in selecting the household equipment, furniture, and clothing for the family. Less than half of all teenagers polled participate in any of the family economic activities.[2]

PUTTING THE MARRIAGE RELATIONSHIP IN FOCUS

By the time father and mother have been married fifteen or more years, they may have become so preoccupied with their parenthood responsibilities that their marriage no longer holds a central place in their lives. The man of the house tends to be absorbed in his work roles and associations. His wife carrying through the years major responsibility for the home and children may feel "bogged down," work-worn, and devoid of the glamor that her teenagers' magazines portray so fetchingly. Putting the marriage back in focus may be a major family developmental task at this stage.

Studies of husband-wife relationships [3] through the family life cycle, find a steady decline in the wife's satisfaction with her husband's love as the children grow older. At the teenage stage of the family life cycle, the middleaged husband shows little of the ardor that his teenagers demonstrate in their lovemaking. The wife feels taken for granted, always on tap to serve family needs, with few of the fulfillments that are supposed to go with marriage.

Wives about the same age as their mates are more satisfied with marital love than wives older or younger by four or more years.[4] The middleaged woman, old enough to have teenage children may be especially vulnerable. The college educated find greater fulfillment in their marriages than do those with less education,[5] possibly because their schooling meant deferred gratification in adolescence and the development of a richer repertoire of emotional and sexual expression.

[1] Theodore B. Johannis, Jr., and James M. Rollins, "Teenager Perception of Family Decision Making about Social Activity," *The Family Life Coordinator*, Vol. VIII, No. 3, March 1960, pp. 59, 60.

[2] Theodore B. Johannis, Jr., "Participation by Fathers, Mothers and Teenage Sons and Daughters in Selected Family Economic Activity," *The Coordinator*, Vol. VI, No. 1, September 1957, pp. 15, 16.

[3] Blood and Wolfe, *op. cit.*, p. 232.

[4] *Ibid.*, p. 227.

[5] *Ibid.*, p. 229.

As the family reaches the teenage stage, its children are more active socially than they were at younger ages. Boyfriends call for the adolescent daughter whose excitement in getting ready for her dates has a certain contagion that carries over to her parents, who relive in her some of their courtship experiences. Now husband and wife drive their teenagers to parties and various social events, where they with other adults are expected to stay as chaperones. This may explain in part why married couples with teenagers more often have a gay time away from home than they did when their oldest child was still a schoolager.[1]

Now that the oldest child is old enough to leave in charge of the home for short intervals, husband and wife are freer to get away for an occasional evening, or to have a weekend trip together from time to time as the husband's schedule allows. Letting the adolescents perk things up in the family as they want to is often fun for the parents as well as the youngsters. As mother gets a smart new hat, she gets the feelings that go with it and once more attracts her husband's interest in her as a woman. When father gets into the tweed jacket his son insists is right for him, he assumes the gay blade air that seems appropriate, he throws back his shoulders, pulls in his tummy, and woos his own wife as only he can charm her. Keeping a marriage vigorously alive consists of much more than so-called marriage hygiene: it rests upon the eagerness of the husband and wife to attract and be attractive to the other— with the life and the lilt that is to be found in a radiantly alive marriage.

KEEPING COMMUNICATION SYSTEMS OPEN

The major problem in communication at this stage of the family life cycle is being available to each other both as husbands and wives and as parents and children. Parents with teenagers and parents with children at the preschool stage, experience a collapse in the exchange of ideas more than at any other period in the life of the marriage.[2] The man and wife appear to be so involved in keeping the family intact and in order that their own contact with each other intellectually and emotionally is damaged. The adolescents are so absorbed with their problems and so noisy in their interaction with each other and with the younger

[1] Feldman, *op. cit.*
[2] *Ibid.*

children in the family that the parents may have little opportunity for interchange of their own thoughts and feelings.

They now keep their ideas to themselves, they now have fewer arguments than they had earlier in their marriage, even though both husband and wife feel misunderstood quite as often as they did when their eldest was of schoolage.[1]

It is generally agreed that one function of communication in marriage is that of sharing with one's partner the good and the unpleasant events which have happened during the day while each has been at work at his or her own tasks. Yet, few of the wives in the Detroit Area Study spontaneously mentioned interaction with their husbands after a bad day. During the honeymoon stage of the marriage 70 per cent of the brides appear to have kept their problems to themselves. This percentage of wives increases as the marriage continues until at the teen-age stage, 98 per cent of the wives report neither positive nor negative interaction with their husbands at the end of a bad day.[2] It is safe to assume that the reason is not that mothers of adolescents have no bad days, but rather that their communication with their husbands has declined to the place where they no longer burden their mates with their problems.

Although a few teenagers are found to report all their difficulties to their mothers and fathers, most of them have trouble confiding in their parents.[3] Sex and petting are the two subjects ranked by both boys and girls as most difficult to discuss with their parents. Four out of five boys had trouble talking about sex with their fathers, and 84 per cent with their mothers. Nine out of ten girls had trouble discussing sex with their fathers, and 64 per cent with their mothers; 12 per cent of the girls were totally blocked from talking about sex with their mothers, 24 per cent with their fathers, and 10 per cent had no communication whatever with their parents in these areas. In the light of the developmental tasks of adolescence, it may well be that parents' silence in such matters of critical concern accounts for some of the mutual alienation and suspicion that exists between teenagers and their parents.

---

[1] *Ibid.*

[2] Blood and Wolfe, *op. cit.* p. 188.

[3] Marvin C. Dubbé, *What Do Your Adolescents Tell You?* (Portland, Oregon: E. C. Brown Trust, undated mimeographed report; and Marvin C. Dubbé, "What Young People Can't Talk Over with Their Parents," *National Parent-Teacher*, Vol. 52, No. 2, October 1957, pp. 18–20.

Family projects and whole-family interests help keep communication systems open within the teenage family.

Little children can be openly dependent. Teenagers frequently find irritating, evidences of their continuing need for their parents. Watch a central school letting out in the afternoon. As the children come to find parents waiting to take them to a picnic or music lesson, the younger child not unusually welcomes his mother with enthusiastic warmth. Not so the junior or senior high school student, who more typically resents his parents' presence near the school building and has been known to greet his mother with the critical query, "What are you doing here?"

Parents, who have been considered perfect by little children, come in for criticism [1] and fault-finding as these same children reach adolescence. The schoolboy brags about his father's prowess and boasts of his mother's beauty. The same young fellow as a teenager groans over his father's old-fashioned behavior and begs his mother not to appear at a parent-teacher meeting in "that old hat." Adolescent criticism of parents is evidence of the young person's struggle to free himself from his close

[1] Ruth M. Butler, *op. cit.* p. 8.

emotional attachment to his parents and to mature in his relationship to them.

The teenager who achieves emancipation from his parents emerges as a young adult capable of mature affection for his mother and father as persons. He becomes an autonomous person, capable of reciprocal interdependence with his father and mother, and of mature feelings of genuine affection and appreciation for them. But in the meantime, through adolescence, relationships between the generations are frequently strained.

There is some normal slackening off of telling parents everything as children get into their teens. Then it is normal for intimate confidences to be shared first with close friends within the peer group, and only secondarily with the parents and other significant adults. Adults who recognize how normal it is for young people to identify now with their own generation, as they must if they are to emerge as full-fledged adults, restrain from the prying pressures that only serve to alienate them further from their teenagers.

Wise parents guide their adolescents with a loose rein, letting them have their heads, knowing that they will not stray too far from the fold if they are not driven from it. Being available for companionable chats now and then is better than letting loose a barrage of questions as soon as the teenager sets foot inside the door. Adolescents need parents and go to them willingly in families where communication systems are kept in good working order.

Some families experience more alienation between generations than do others. Ethnic groups in which the parents hold to the old ways, while the young people reach out to the new, find it hard to bridge the growing chasms between the generations. In general, middle-class and upper-class families maintain more democratic patterns of interaction and have fewer problems with their adolescent youth than do lower-class families.[1]

Youth is ever more explorative, daring, and "up to the minute" than are parents. Young people enjoy that contrast. They want to be out ahead. But it is also exceedingly important to the adolescent for Dad and Mom

---

[1] Leonard G. Benson, "Family Social Status and Parental Authority Evaluations among Adolescents," *Southwest Social Science Quarterly*, Vol. 36, No. 1, June 1955, pp. 46–54; also Ivan Nye, "Adolescent-Parent Adjustment—Socio-Economic Level as a Variable," *American Sociological Review*, Vol. 16, No. 3, June 1951, pp. 341–349; and Henry S. Maas, "Some Social Class Differences in the Family Systems and Group Relations of Pre- and Early Adolescents," *Child Development*, Vol. 22, No. 2, June 1951, pp. 145–152.

not to get *too* far behind. They take pride in their parents' progressive point of view and in their social and civic activities and interests. They are concerned about the way their parents look and behave in public. For parents to possess some social grace and an interest in cultural activities and events apparently gives the young person the needed sense of pride in them that makes communication free and full.

MAINTAINING CONTACT WITH MEMBERS OF THE EXTENDED FAMILY

The teenage stage of the family life cycle is the testing time for the immediate relatives. If they pass youth's rigorous standards of acceptability they can contribute much to and gain much from association with the young relatives. If they remain rigidly rooted in "old-fashioned" ways and ideas, young people eschew them heartily and will avoid them except under duress. An understanding grandparent can bridge the gap not only between the first and third generations but also between grandchild and parent. A sympathetic uncle, aunt, or cousin has a real role to play as a home away from home—a parent once removed, a guide without the heavy hand of authority, or the wise counselor who is not too close to the teenage boy or girl. The narrow-minded "old maid," male or female, married or unmarried, is rarely a welcome guest in the teenage family, for he or she brings too much implied criticism and personifies too clearly the frustrations that burden youth.

Broad-gauged or narrow, generous or stingy, wise or foolish, relatives have to be taken in their stride in most families.

You dare not offend Aunt Amy no matter what you think of her. You can not go live with your sophisticated cousin however much you would love it. You need not imitate drifting Uncle Mike regardless of how much you envy his freedom. You go to family gatherings and size them all up, maintaining the courtesies that are expected, and learning a great deal about your roots and your forebears as you see these kinfolk in action.

When graduation day arrives, and your relatives sit there beaming up at you, you can afford to be proud of your family, and glad to be a part of them. You want to be worthy of them, and to measure up to their expectations of you. You recognize yourself as a member of the larger family group, and feel sorry for the boy and girl in your class who have no family to call their own.

Younger cousins and other relatives may idolize the teenager and play significant parts in his or her development. Relatives have a real place in the family, less perhaps in the teenage family than before or after, but

COURTESY OF THE LIBRARY OF CONGRESS

Telephoning becomes especially important as teenagers begin to reach out for associations with persons of their own generation.

a place, nevertheless, that is real and a part of family living that is important.

GROWING INTO THE WORLD AS A FAMILY AND AS PERSONS

The teenage family ranges farther afield than it ever has before. The children are now old enough to enjoy a whole family vacation to more distant points of interest than before was feasible. Trips to historic shrines and cultural areas now take on real meaning for the family. Individually, horizons expand too. The teenager goes off with his friends for a weekend or a summer. Father is away on business trips from time to time. Mother is sent as a delegate to the state or national convention of her favorite organization. The family is beginning to scatter in a preview of the individualization characteristic of the empty nest stage just ahead.

Teenagers normally reach out for associations with people outside the family. The adolescent boy or girl must identify with the younger generation. Social growth is dependent upon friendships with members of both sexes and on the activities that go with dating, courtship, and becoming involved emotionally with one or more members of the other sex. During the entire second decade of life, members of the peer group are especially important to the young person. It is in the face-to-face contacts with friends of one's own age that decisions are made, skills are developed, and values are weighed in everyday interaction. Guidance, confidences, and counsel from beloved older friends (teacher, minister, youth leaders, etc.) may be more important to the teenager than one suspects. Such close ties outside the family may threaten the parent who is not prepared to release the teenage child. Accepting the teenager's intimate friends and the confidences that young people normally share, parents can take adolescence in their stride. Otherwise this task of growing out to others may be frightening for the parents who stand by and resist or retreat.

A frequent example is found in the teenager's early love experiences. For him or her the crushes and infatuations of early adolescence are important and especially precious. If one or both of the parents ridicule these early involvements as "puppy love" or ignore them as "kid stuff," they alienate their own youngster and only rarely weaken the outside ties. When the family can make this special friend welcome at home, treat him or her and the relationship with respect, and take it for what it is and nothing more, both the family and the adolescent are free to grow through the experience to new levels of maturity.

Group life is a magnet for the adolescent. Many a teenager wants to belong to more organizations and get into more activities than can comfortably be carried. He or she wants to belong to the band or the glee club, to the drama group or the ball team, to social clubs and hobby groups. Life is opening up and everything must be tried and tested. Political organizations and social action groups quite distant from the family's orientation may be explored, as much to see what they are like as to stretch away from the family's affiliations into those peculiarly one's own.

Parents who can take these adventures of their youngsters as a normal part of growing up, without feeling unnecessarily afraid or personally threatened, can argue the merits of this cause or that with their budding citizen without going off the deep end in repression or repudiation. Families who can go along with their young people in the various explorations into new ways of looking at things can grow up with the flexibility that the modern age requires.

REWORKING AND MAINTAINING A PHILOSOPHY OF LIFE THAT FITS THE NEW LEVELS OF DEVELOPMENT AS A FAMILY AND AS MEMBERS OF A CHANGING WORLD

A family cannot be buffeted about by every social wind that blows and feel steady and strong within itself. Conversely, a family that does not bend with the pressures of the times will break under their stress. With no convictions and values, the family is a tumbleweed, without roots or stability. With a philosophy of life that is too rigid and narrow, a family risks alienation of its teenagers and grown children and its own integrity as a unit.

The stresses of adolescence that so often shake families to their roots often grow out of conflicting value systems of the old and the new generation. Parents were brought up in one way of life, where definite standards of right and wrong prevailed. Circumstances have changed; teenage young people see life situations differently. The developmental tasks for the family involve holding fast to those verities that have continuing meaning, while venturing forth into wider, broader orientations that new levels of development and experience require. Successful in this concurrent maintenance and testing of values and truths by which life is lived, families weather the storms that beset them without losing their integrity as units or as individual members.

POSITIVE VALUES IN TEENAGE FAMILY LIFE

Family life, with its potentials for promoting human growth, becomes complicated and often threatened by the struggle and clash of diverse strivings, emotional difficulties, misconceptions, and rationalized behavior of individual family members. It is, nevertheless, the area of life from which come some of the deepest satisfactions in human experience. Fulfillment comes from adequate functioning. Those forms of functioning involved in human interaction can be the most satisfying of all.

Adults and youth in the family group are constantly striving toward their goals as persons and as family members. Many of the growth tasks and needs in terms of which the teenager strives to function are consistent and harmonious with the desires and felt responsibilities of the parents. But usually some yielding and a lot of "accepting" may be necessary on the part of youth as well as by the parents. It is in the very process thus of arriving at an integration of purposes (dynamic interaction) that both grow and experience deep satisfaction.

The adolescent, for example, needs to function more and more as a free agent in his own right. He is striving toward an independent adult status. The parent normally delights in the young person's attainments in the direction of adult-like functioning, and from them derives the satisfaction of the fulfillment of his own purposes and responsibilities. In adolescent strivings toward independence, however, there are likely to be some fumblings, errors in judgment, and behavior that looks like arrogance, impudence, and lack of respect for his elders. Parents are inclined to feel these concomitants of growth as threats to their status—assaults upon their dignity as parents. But parents can, through experience and some effort, come to take them for what they are, and become yielding and understanding.

The young person, on the other hand, senses any resistance the parent may feel to his strivings and awkward attempts at independence. He is inclined to resent that resistance. But if he also senses in his parent's behavior a genuine interest in his problems and some evidence of an understanding acceptance of him, he is able to yield a bit, eventually to accept the advice and counsel of his parent. Each grows through understanding the other. They both grow in their ability to accept others as they are. The relationship between them then grows closer, more affectionate and companionable.

In our culture the smallness of the family group limits the personal sources from which the child can draw for security and a sense of belonging. The kind of persons his parents happen to be, therefore, is for him an exceedingly important matter. If they are secure and growing individuals, happy in their relationships with each other, they are the greatest source of inner security a youngster can have. They not only provide a home atmosphere in which he can feel secure, but they also set the pattern of attitudes and interpersonal relationships which is conducive to human adjustment and growth.

When mutual respect for each other's point of view and a real concern for each other's well-being and peace of mind is the prevailing pattern of interaction, the child is inclined to follow that pattern. As he increasingly does so the adult's confidence in him grows. He is allowed to assume more and more responsibility for his own activities and conduct. In such matters, for example, as being in at night he will not need to be *told* when he must be home. He clears his plans with his parents and gradually takes on the full responsibility himself. Because of his regard for his parents and his desire not to cause them worry or inconvenience, and especially because he knows they trust him, he meets family standards on his own responsibility. He thus achieves self-control and personal integration.

Parents need the love, confidence, and the respect of their teenage children. They need it for the sense of success and accomplishment it gives them, for they have invested a great deal of themselves in the rearing of those sons and daughters. But they gain and maintain that love and respect only as they meet dependably, day by day, the developmental needs of their children. During adolescence those needs are just as vital as at any other period of the child's development, and the understanding parent is just as necessary in the adequate meeting of those needs. Adolescents do want parents. Not only this, they really need parents.[1]

HAZARDS OF THE TEENAGE STAGE

Families with adolescents struggle with pressures on their resources, facilities and space to accommodate the wide variety of conflicting needs, interests, and activities typical of this stage in the family life cycle. Breakdown in communication between parents and youth and between the married partners is a real possibility at this time, and maintaining a vigorous marriage relationship strong enough to survive the release of the children is an ongoing challenge.

Teenagers today face hazards resulting from their down-grading in the public mind, as well as in the actual problems of delinquency, truancy, unwholesome recreation, confusions about love, sex, and marriage, too-early involvement, and blocked pathways to adulthood. Unrealistic pressures in many communities for precocious commitment sexually and emotionally compound youth's problems in social maturation.

Anxious, threatened, insecure parents and those with the handicaps of outmoded traditional attitudes and ways fail to give their adolescents effective, acceptable guidance, and too often alienate their children. As

[1] Katharine W. Taylor, *Do Adolescents Need Parents?* (New York: D. Appleton Century Company, 1938), p. 15.

teenagers attempt to establish their identity and to emancipate themselves from their dependence upon their parents, they present urgent challenges to their families and to themselves. Both over-dependency and over-rebelliousness increase the difficulties in both generations in loosening the apron strings and allowing the maturing young person to find himself.

IMPLICATIONS FOR NEEDED SERVICES

If the hazards to constructive family interaction are to be removed, and individual and family functioning in the various tasks is to be mutually more satisfying, the vicious circles of faulty thinking, negative attitudes, and hostile feelings about roles and relationships in family life which are perpetuated and passed on from parents to children must somehow be broken. The adolescent period, when young people question the authority of their elders, is an opportune time to make this break. It is then that relationships between the generations and between the sexes are of vital concern.

Educational programs in the principles of human development and interaction as they apply to boy-girl relationships and to marriage and family life are indicated for both youth and parents.[1] Teachers and leaders capable of forthright instruction, effective group guidance and competent counseling should increasingly be selected, trained, and employed for both formal and informal programs in family life education.

Expansion of present parent education programs to include principles of adolescent development, and methods of working with youth would greatly help. As parents learn what to expect of their adolescents, and which teenage experiences can be encouraged and which curtailed, they can prevent some unfortunate escapades and contribute to the security of the teen years. Parents' help in improving community facilities for teenagers often improves relationships in the family as well as abroad. Mutual interpretation of each generation to the other through joint sessions to consider common concerns, to plan social activities and to develop effective social codes have proven their worth.[2] Competent professional leadership is invaluable at this point in helping each generation

---

[1] 1960 White House Conference on Children and Youth, *Recommendations* (Washington, D. C.: U. S. Government Printing Office, 1960), pp. 12–15.
[2] Evelyn Millis Duvall, *Family Living* (New York: Macmillan Company, 1961), pp. 108–112.

Many a teenager wants to belong to young people's organizations and to get into youth activities, now when life opens up beyond his family.

accept the values of the other and reach mutually comfortable solutions to their problems.

SUMMARY

Teenagers today face special problems which confuse both them and the adults who live and work with them. While they struggle with their developmental tasks, and their parents work at theirs amidst the handicaps of traditional approaches, the family must accomplish its tasks which at the teenage stage are: (1) providing facilities for widely different needs, (2) working out money matters, (3) sharing tasks and responsibilities, (4) putting the marriage relationships in focus, (5) keeping communication systems open, (6) maintaining contact with extended family members, (7) growing into the world as a family and as persons, and (8) reworking a philosophy of life at the teenage stage. There are many hazards to be overcome and challenges to be met, which call for the development and extension of programs for parents, youth, and families.

Young people need wholesome recreation that they can plan and carry out themselves, with adult support and supervision.

SUGGESTED ACTIVITIES

1) Write up a case study of some teenager whom you know well, listing the developmental tasks that he or she is working on, with anecdotal material illustrating the relative success or failure with which each task is being achieved. Document.

2) Pull together into focus the developmental tasks of the man of the teenage household, as father, husband, provider, homemaker, and individual, with especial reference to the ways in which these various roles may possibly conflict with one another. Write a paper on contradictory roles of the father of teenagers as you hypothesize them from this analysis.

3) Popular opinion once had it that a married woman with children should not work outside the home. Using data from this chapter and from related readings and research, refute the traditional stereotype in a paper on "When an Outside Job for Mother May Benefit a Teenage Family."

4) Interview a personnel manager of a local business or industry employing married women with teenage children. Ask him about his experience with mothers as workers considering such factors as: reliability, permanence, loyalty, days off in sickness, accident rate, manual skills, abilities to work with people, and other relevant points. Find out what opportunities this business concern provides for older workers to learn while they work through special courses, incentives for continuing education, etc.

5) Conduct an informal discussion among teenagers whose mothers work outside the house on a part-time or a full-time basis. Focus the discussion on how the adolescents feel about having their mothers work. Encourage full freedom of expression of both positive and negative attitudes as well as of the detailed anecdotal material that breathes life into the responses. Keep notes sufficient to write up the group interview as an exploratory report of how adolescents feel about having their mothers work.

6) Explore what some communities are doing in the development of parent-youth codes in which both parents and teenagers discuss together their various conflicts over social standards and come to mutually acceptable agreements on a number of specific issues. Representative codes are published in the following sources:

Evelyn Millis Duvall, *Family Living* (New York: Macmillan Company, 1950 and 1955 and 1961 editions), pp. 134–136, 134–137 and 108–112 respectively.

Evelyn Millis Duvall, "Community Codes by Common Consent," *The National Parent-Teacher,* December 1954, pp. 8–10.

Evelyn Millis Duvall, "Toward a Parent-Youth Code for a Midwestern City," *Journal of Home Economics,* Vol. 46, No. 1, January 1954, pp. 36–37.

See if you can find others being developed in neighborhoods near you. Visit one or more sessions, talk with some of the parents and teenagers, and write up your findings, impressions, and evaluations of such endeavors as helping teenage families meet one or more of their developmental tasks.

7) Arrange a simple production of *High Pressure Area,* a short skit available from the National Association for Mental Health, 1790 Broadway, New York 19, N. Y., depicting a provocative situation between an adolescent girl and her family. Discuss your reactions to the skit by identifying one by one with each of the principal characters: analyzing how the person felt and why, what he or she did and why, how he or she might have responded differently, and how these different responses might have altered the others reactions and the course of the story.

8) Write a letter to your Superintendent of Schools, to your State Department of Education at your state capital, to the National Association of Secondary School Principals, 1201 Sixteenth Street, N.W., Washington 6, D. C., and to the United States Department of Health, Education and Welfare, Social Security Administration, Washington 25, D. C. In each case, inquire about what is being done in educating teenagers for friendship, love, marriage, and family living in the schools known to them. Collect and analyze your findings in the light of what you believe the need to be for education of a young person for mature living with the significant others of his life now and in the foreseeable future.

9) Discuss the following situations from case excerpts developed by Dr. Hazel Ingersoll, Department of Home Life, Oklahoma A&M College, Stillwater, Oklahoma:

a) Judy's mother loves to see Judy have a good time. She would, by her own admission, "work her fingers to the bone" for Judy. She wants Judy to have the most clothes and the most dates! She is overcome with joy when she is selected May Queen. She even suggests that she has a stage career all lined up for Judy. "And I'll go with her to see that she gets along all right. She will need me, then, more than now. And maybe she will meet and marry some rich nice young man." Meantime Judy's mother neglects her own appearance and has no life of her own apart from her child. She was widowed young after an early marriage and a frugal upbringing. What do you think are the mother's developmental tasks? How do they affect Judy? What suggestions do you have for Judy's mother? for Judy?

b) Father grumbles constantly at Junior (a teenager) about his using the car, his carelessness of dress and his language. Junior appears to be gone with the gang most of the time these days and often doesn't get his chores done. Father, when he can catch him, deluges his ears with tales of "when I was young, young man, I had to take my girl friends by bus to the movies. No sense in this *always* having to use the car!" or "My father always insisted that I clean up my room and mow the lawn before I went to play baseball. You are just spoiled! Now is the time you learned to do a little work. Why at your age I was earning my own spending money. I don't see what has got into this younger generation." What are the developmental tasks of father and son? In what ways might they be accomplished? What may happen if the present situation persists? Why?

10) Review Richard E. Hamlin, *Hi-Y Today: A Report of the National Study of the Hi-Y and Tri-Hi-Y Movement* (New York: Association Press, 1955); Al J. Hummel and Clifford A. Smith, *The Task Method of Program Planning* (Omaha, Nebraska: YMCA of Omaha, 1959); and the Survey Research Center, University of Michigan's studies: *Adolescent Girls* (1956), *Adolescent Boys* (1955), and *A Study of Boys Becoming Adolescents* (1960), for guidance in building a program designed to help a specific age group of teenagers to accomplish their

developmental tasks of 1) achieving a satisfying and socially acceptable masculine or feminine role, and 2) finding oneself as a member of one's own generation.

READINGS

Bernard, Jessie; Buchanan Helen E.; and Smith, William M., Jr., *Dating, Mating & Marriage* (Cleveland, Ohio: Howard Allen, Inc., 1958).

Coleman, James S., *Social Climates in High Schools* (Washington, D. C.: U. S. Government Printing Office, 1961).

Coleman, James S., *The Adolescent Society* (Glencoe, Illinois: Free Press, 1961).

David, Opal D., ed., *The Education of Women* (Washington, D. C.: American Council on Education, 1959).

Duvall, Evelyn Millis, *Love and the Facts of Life* (New York: Association Press, 1963).

Duvall, Evelyn Millis, *Today's Teen-Agers* (New York: Association Press, 1966).

Faegre, Marion L., *The Adolescent in Your Family* (Washington, D. C.: Children's Bureau Publication 347, Revised Edition 1955).

Frank, Mary and Lawrence K., *Your Adolescent at Home and in School* (New York: The Viking Press, Inc., 1956).

Friedenberg, Edgar Z., *The Vanishing Adolescent* (Boston: Beacon Press, 1960).

Havighurst, Robert J.; Bowman, Paul; Liddle, Gordon; Matthews, Charles; and Pierce, James, *Growing Up in River City* (New York: John Wiley & Sons, Inc., 1962).

Hummel, Al J.; and Smith, Clifford A., *The Task Method of Program Planning* (Omaha, Nebraska: Young Men's Christian Association of Omaha, 1959).

Hurlock, Elizabeth B., *Developmental Psychology* (New York: McGraw-Hill Book Company, Second Edition, 1959), Chapters 7, 8, and 9.

Mohr, George J.; and Despres, Marian, *The Stormy Decade: Adolescence* (New York: Random House, 1958).

Nye, F. Ivan, *Family Relationships and Delinquent Behavior* (New York: John Wiley & Sons, 1958).

Peck, Robert F.; and Havighurst, Robert J., *et al. Psychology of Character Development* (New York: John Wiley & Sons, 1960).

Seidman, Jerome M., ed. *The Adolescent—A Book of Readings* (New York: Holt, Rinehart and Winston, Inc., Revised Edition, 1960).

Strang, Ruth, *The Adolescent Views Himself* (New York: McGraw-Hill Book Company, Inc., 1957).

Stone, L. Joseph, and Church, Joseph, *Childhood and Adolescence* (New York: Random House, 1957), Chapters 10, 11, 12, and 13.

Wittenberg, Rudolph, *Adolescence and Discipline* (New York: Association Press, 1959).

PART **3**

Contracting families

There is a time for holding close and a time for letting go. What happens as families launch their young adults into lives of their own? With what do middleaged parents fill their years in the empty nest? Why are problems of aging families of special interest now? And, what makes the dynamics of family interaction so potentially explosive at every stage of the life cycle?

This time, like all times, is a very good one if we but know what to do with it.

EMERSON

CHAPTER TWELVE

Families as launching centers

There comes a time when the young of the family are ready to be launched from the home base and to sail off into a life for themselves. In twentieth-century American families this stage usually begins late in the teen years. It is sharply marked by the young person's departure from home to marry, to take a full-time job, or to begin military service or college—each of which removes the person from the parental home, never again to return as a child.

This stage begins with the first child leaving home as a young adult; it ends with the emptying nest as the last child leaves home for a life of his or her own. This stage may be an extremely short one, as is the case in the family with one child, a daughter who marries the year she graduates from high school. The stage may extend over a considerable period of time, even for the duration of the family, as happens in an occasional family in which an unmarried son or daughter stays dependent in the home through the years. In mid-century United States the stage typically lasts six to seven years (Chapter One).

The processes of launching start during the earlier life cycle stages of the family, as the child and young person prepares for the decisions that will shape his future. His or her vocational future is planned or is left to chance long before the young person is out of school. Educational plans are formed or they go by default early in the high school years. Timing for his military service depends in part upon his educational decisions. His or her marriage readiness is determined by previous successes or failures in making heterosexual adjustments. The process of cutting apron strings characterizes the teen years and sets the stage for the son's or daughter's emergence as an emancipated young adult. No matter how abrupt this may seem to be, the departure of the young person from his home is a process that goes on through the years.

From maximum size at the beginning of the stage, the nuclear family shrinks during the launching period to the original married pair. From the multiplicity of interpersonal relationships with all the children home characteristic of the beginning of the stage, the family leaves this stage in its development with but one: the husband-wife relationship. Before the stage is completed, the husband-father may also be a grandfather, and the wife-mother a grandmother, as the first-married son or daughter bears children. Thus later-launched siblings now hold positions of son-brother-uncle, and daughter-sister-aunt. Similarly, with the marriage of the first child, the mother becomes a mother-in-law, the father a father-in-law, and their children brothers- and sisters-in-law of the newly recruited members of the family by marriage.

The launching stage is marked by the simultaneous release of the family's children and the recruitment of all new members (and their families) by marriage. Personal positional developmental tasks continue for the parents: as mother, homemaker, wife, person, and probably mother-in-law and grandmother; as father, provider, husband, person, and possibly father-in-law and grandfather. Each of the children have their developmental tasks as young adults and younger children in the family of orientation, and as they marry as husbands and wives in the establishment phase of their family of procreation. Family developmental tasks are critical as the family shifts from a household with children to a husband-wife pair. The major family goal is the reorganization of the family into a continuing unity while releasing matured and maturing young people into lives of their own.

FACTORS AFFECTING THE YOUNG ADULT'S LIFE PLANS

Some young people plan farther ahead than do others. In general, as social class rises, the interest in life planning, and the ability to predictably plan one's life increases. A study of 2,700 public, private, and trade high school students, and 349 Yale undergraduates, explored the question, "How far ahead have you planned your life?" The percentage of high school students planning five or more years ahead doubled from the lowest to the highest social class (from approximately 20 to 40 per cent).

The researchers conclude that "length of life planning had a reliable posi-tive correlation with both the occupational and educational status of the young respondents' fathers." [1]

A further factor related to the young adult's plans for his life is the mobility of his family. Upward mobile parents tend either to carry their children along with them or to encourage their young people to climb; young people from nonmobile families tend to remain static in the great majority of cases (85 per cent in one recent study).[2]

Significantly more boys than girls tend to make extended life plans,[3] probably because a girl knows her future will be greatly influenced by her marriage and the plans of her husband. In both sexes there is more upward mobility drive among those whose family and interpersonal relations have been difficult than among those whose early interpersonal relations have been satisfying.[4] One relevant study shows that high levels of aspiration of 350 university students are related to (1) feelings of not being wanted by parents, (2) favoritism shown by parents, and (3) little attachment to parents (Table 21).

These findings support current psychoanalytic assumptions and gen-

TABLE 21. *Interpersonal Relationships in the Family and Aspirational Level of 350 University Students* [5]

Feelings of Not Being Wanted by Parents	Levels of Aspiration		Favoritism Shown by Parents	Levels of Aspiration		Degree of Attachment to Parents	Levels of Aspiration	
	HIGH	LOW		HIGH	LOW		HIGH	LOW
Father	(N = 117)	(N = 223)	Father	(N = 95)	(N = 188)	Father	(N = 110)	(N = 222)
Some	41.9	24.7	Yes	45.3	30.9	Much	33.6	50.9
None	58.1	75.3	No	54.7	69.1	Little	66.4	49.1
Mother	(N = 122)	(N = 223)	Mother	(N = 95)	(N = 188)	Mother	(N = 123)	(N = 223)
Some	34.4	20.2	Yes	41.1	25.0	Much	52.8	66.8
None	65.6	79.8	No	58.9	75.0	Little	47.2	33.2

[1] Orville G. Brim, and Raymond Forer, "A Note on the Relation of Values and Social Structure to Life Planning," *Sociometry*, Vol. 19, No. I, March 1956, pp. 54–60.

[2] Carson McGuire, "Conforming, Mobile and Divergent Families," *Marriage and Family Living*, Vol. XIV, No. 2, May 1952, p. 113.

[3] Orville G. Brim and Raymond Forer, *op. cit.*, p. 58.

[4] Evelyn Ellis, "Social Psychological Correlates of Upward Social Mobility among Unmarried Career Women," *American Sociological Review*, Vol. 17, No. 5, October 1952, pp. 558–563; and Karen Horney, *The Neurotic Personality of Our Time* (New York: Norton and Company, 1938) pp. 162–187.

[5] Data from Russell R. Dynes, Alfred C. Clarke, and Simon Dinitz, "Levels of Occupational Aspiration: Some Aspects of Family Experience as a Variable," *American Sociological Review*, Vol. 21, No. 2, April 1956, Tables 1, 2, and 3, pp. 212–215.

eral social theory that unsatisfactory interpersonal relationships in the family of orientation are significantly related to high aspirational levels and that satisfactory relationships are related to low aspirational levels. Thus we see that some young people, whose family life has been unhappy, struggle to better themselves as soon as they can cut loose from family ties. In some cases the high levels of aspiration are fantasies not related too closely to what is realizable. In others actual social mobility results from realistic efforts to improve.

The final factor influencing the young person's vision of who he may become, is the factor of identification with some older person who serves as a model for the emerging young adult. The girl identifies with her teacher and wants to be just like her when she grows up. The boy greatly admires his coach or his leader at the YMCA and goes off like his hero for specialized training, possibly at the same college and professional school. In such cases, the young adult patterns himself after the much admired adult and so makes the decisions and follows the course that bring him closer to his ideal.

To summarize, factors influencing the young adult's life planning and specific decisions upon leaving his family of orientation, tend to operate in the following directions:

1) The higher the social class of the parents, the farther ahead the young person plans his life
2) Young people from upward mobile families tend to continue climbing
3) Young men tend to plan further ahead than do young women
4) Young people from unhappy homes tend to have higher levels of aspiration than do young adults from satisfactory family backgrounds
5) Young people who identify closely with an admired adult tend to pattern themselves after that older person in their own life plans.

DEVELOPMENTAL TASKS OF YOUNG ADULTS

The developmental tasks of young adults in the United States are intertwined with the decisions that must be made concurrently along several related lines. Throughout his life as a child and teenager, the individual has lived within the expectancies of his age and grade. Now, upon his emergence from the norms of the age-grade system, he steps out into a life of his own, with his success or failure largely dependent upon the choices he makes as an individual. This very freedom is confusing, as Robert Havighurst so vividly points out:

Early adulthood seems . . . to be a period of storm and stress in America, and especially in the middle-class part of American society. The basic reason for this, when expressed in sociological terms, is that this is a relatively unorganized period in life which marks a transition from an age-graded to a social status-graded society. During childhood and adolescence one climbs the age ladder, getting new privileges and taking on new responsibilities with each step up the ladder. The ten-year-old has such and such privileges and such and such responsibilities, which enable him to look down on the eight-year-old, but also cause him to look up to the twelve-year-old. He climbs the age ladder, rung by rung, year by year, knowing that each step up gives him more prestige, along with new tasks and pleasures.

This simple age-grading stops in our culture somewhere around sixteen to twenty. It is like reaching the end of the ladder and stepping off onto a new, strange cloud-land with giants and witches to be circumvented and the goose that lays the golden eggs to be captured if only one can discover the know-how.

In the adult society prestige and power depend not so much on age as on skill and strength and wisdom, and family connections. Achieving the goals of life is not nearly so much a matter of waiting until one grows up to them as it was in the earlier years. There must be a strategy, based on an understanding of the new terrain, which can only be got by scouting around and getting the lay of the land for a few years. This is what young people do, and it often takes several years to learn how to get about efficiently and to go where one wants to go in the adult society in America.[1]

CHOOSING A VOCATION

In some cultures a young man is expected to follow in his father's footsteps and carry on the family business. In the United States this pattern tends to hold largely in the upper-class families, where wealth and holdings necessitate grooming the sons of the family to carry on the family traditions. Young people today face many more vocational possibilities than were formerly available. In 1870 there were but 338 vocations, in contrast to many thousands by the middle of the twentieth century (20,000 by 1940,[2] and 50,000 estimated more recently with rapid development since World War II in electronics, atomic fission, radar, television, plastics, medical and chemical advances etc.).[3]

Historically, a young woman groomed herself for marriage; all other interests were secondary. Today, a girl may be marriage-minded but

---

[1] Robert J. Havighurst, *Human Development and Education* (New York: Longmans, Green and Company, 1953), pp. 258–259.

[2] *Occupational Dictionary* (Washington, D. C.: U. S. Department of Labor, 1940).

[3] *Job Guide for Young Workers*, 1956–57 Edition (Washington, D. C.: Superintendent of Documents, 1956).

COURTESY OF THE LIBRARY OF CONGRESS

As more fields open up for women, girls face vocational choices that will serve them through the years both before marriage and after.

she believes in women seeking public offices,[1] and she may look forward to carrying some vocational interests both as an unmarried woman, and as a wife and mother. During the first year of marriage some 40 per cent of American wives work outside the home. In 1952, one-third of all families had two earners—the husband and the wife.[2] Marriage still holds first place in the future plans of the great majority of American girls, but many of them think realistically also in terms of developing vocational skills that will serve them well through the years both before marriage and after. As more and more fields open up for women workers, girls as well as boys face inevitable vocational choices.

[1] Harold Christensen and Marilyn M. Swihart, "Postgraduation Role Preferences of Senior Women in College," *Marriage and Family Living*, Vol. XVIII, No. 1, February 1956, pp. 54–55.
[2] Paul C. Glick, "The Life Cycle of the Family," *Marriage and Family Living*, Vol. XVII, No. 1, February 1955, p. 8.

Occupational decisions do not have to be made from among the many thousands of potential vocations. For any one young adult, the factors influencing his life plan tend to limit his fields of interest, and to influence the direction his life work will take. Yet within a given direction, there still is much that must be learned about specific vocations, and about one's individual aptitudes, interests, and preferences. Try-out experiences in part-time jobs, summer employment, and apprentice-like opportunities are helpful to many young people. Vocational guidance is available in many schools. Testing and counseling programs are designed to help young people find themselves in an occupational field suited to their personal abilities and social availability.

Parents who encourage their sons and daughters to explore various possibilities and to get the training needed for the chosen field greatly assist their young people to accomplish this developmental task. Attempting to force a young person into a field in which he or she is not personally interested often results in parental disappointment and failure of the young adult in an area in which he has little or no interest or ability.[1]

GETTING AN EDUCATION

The choice of a vocation determines in large measure the amount and the kind of education the young person must pursue. Conversely, the education the young person has obtained greatly influences his vocational opportunities. Tony, who drops out of high school to get "quick money" that will allow him to buy a car and entertain his girl, thereby limits his future possibilities for vocational choice and advancement. The economic advantage of an education is strikingly apparent in the relationship between the amount of education and the lifetime earnings of an American, as of 1956 (Table 20).

In dropping out of school, Tony, in the case above, is depriving himself and his family of the more than $100,000 that he might have earned if he had gone on through college. Of course, as we saw in Chapter Four, lower-class young people have less chance of finishing school and still less likelihood of graduating from college than do young people from

[1] Dr. Dean J. Plazak of Bethesda, Maryland reported to the 1956 meeting of the American Psychiatric Association in Chicago, that "A study of midshipmen discharged from the U. S. Naval Academy shows few wanted to go there in the first place, but came as a means of raising family prestige or because their father desired it." Reported in *Chicago Daily News*, May 1, 1956, p. 15.

TABLE 22. *Estimated "Life-Time" Income for Men by Amount of Education* [1]

Education	Life-Time Earnings
4th grade or less	$ 72,000
8th grade	116,000
12th grade	165,000
1–3 years of college	190,000
College graduate	268,000

SOURCE: Derived from 1950 Census of Population, Vol. IV, Special Reports, PE, No. 5B, Education, Table 12.

the higher-class levels. So, economic and vocational advantages and disadvantages tend to be "socially inherited," in the sense that they tend to pass from generation to generation. The mobile young person from a lower-class home may push on through school even though no one in his family ever graduated from high school before. In doing so, he greatly increases his vocational and economic future. Using the census figures of Table 22, we find his life earnings as a high school graduate come to $49,000 more than might have been expected had he dropped out of school at the eighth grade. This means that each year of high school is equivalent to $12,250 in cash earnings in the years ahead.

Getting an education is especially important today when there are relatively few nonskilled jobs, in comparison with the large number of highly skilled occupations requiring specialized training. A good general educational background is important not only for earning a living, but especially for living a life. The educated person who knows his way around in the physical and biological sciences, the humanities, and the social sciences, is at home in much more of the world than the relatively illiterate. Every citizen today should have enough orientation to know how to tackle a problem and how to think through a point.

The question of how much education a girl should have has been often discussed. The general consensus today is that education is important for a woman, as a worker, as a wife and mother, as a citizen, and as a person. The girl with an education has something to offer that assures her of a better job at more money than is generally available to the less well-educated woman. The statement "when you educate a

[1] From Paul C. Glick and Herman P. Miller, "Educational Level and Potential Income," *American Sociological Review*, Vol. 21, No. 3, June 1956, page 310.

woman, you educate a family" recognizes that the woman's cultural background becomes the foundation of her family. Whatever she has learned
of music, the arts, literature, medicine, history, philosophy, and religion
can become part of the children's day-to-day education in the home.
As a citizen and as a person, education is quite as important for a
woman as it is for a man. This is recognized by members of both generations today. A study of 1,100 college girls and 752 of their mothers
found between 80 and 95 per cent of both groups feeling that a woman
should have an education equal to her husband's.[1] Now, when so many
men of college age leave school for military service, it is not unusual to
find the woman the better educated of the two, both among courting
couples and young married people.

Both schools and families face real challenges for helping boys
and girls get an adequate education. Schools that gear their educational
offerings to the needs and readiness of their students, that provide
effective counseling services and social opportunities, that use testing
programs that are not flagrantly class-biased, help the young person
who might otherwise become discouraged and drop out to remain in
school for as long as is feasible. Lyle M. Spencer lists four things that
schools can do to help children from the lower classes continue their
education, when he says,

Research studies and the experiences of school staffs who have tackled this
problem suggest some of the most promising approaches:
1) *Help teachers understand class differences.*
   While 6 out of 10 pupils are from lower socio-economic groups, 90 per
   cent of their teachers have a middle-class orientation and tend to stress
   middle-class views about manners, ambition, and aggressiveness. . . .
2) *Recognize that IQ tests may be biased in favor of pupils from upper
   socio-economic groups.*
   No valid evidence has been produced to show that native intelligence
   varies according to social status, yet the average IQ of adolescents in the
   lowest socio-economic group is from 20 to 23 points below that of higher
   groups. . . .
3) *Eliminate stumbling blocks for lower-class pupils that exist in the school.*
   . . . Eliminate 'hidden tuition costs' and expensive school customs . . .
   broaden participation (of the students), and . . . modify factors in the
   cliques that are cruel to other pupils.

[1] Arlene Sheeley, Paul H. Landis, and Vernon Davies, *Marital and Family Adjustment in Rural and Urban Families of Two Generations* (Pullman, Washington: The
State College of Washington, May 1949), Bulletin No. 506, pp. 6–7.

4) *Help pupils to understand our social status system.*
. . . Help all pupils by giving them a realistic idea of their opportunities in life, the statuses that go with them, and the "rules of the game" through which young people can preserve their socio-economic position or move to a higher status." [1]

Families encourage their sons and daughters to get an education when they express real interest in the student's school progress. Other family helps include (1) providing opportunities for the pupil's participation in both academic and extracurricular activities, (2) maintaining intellectual interests within the family, and (3) refraining from pressing the young person to premature work to support the family before his or her educational program has been completed. These things are easier for some families than for others (Chapter Four), but as education becomes generally more highly valued, more families want to make the effort.

SATISFYING MILITARY SERVICE REQUIREMENTS

Before a young fellow is out of his teens, he faces the possibility of military service. He may volunteer for service in order to "get it over with." He may wait until he is drafted, deferring it as long as the law allows. Official estimates in 1956 are that about 80 per cent of young men in the United States see military service before they are 26 years old.[2] It is possible that the percentage may decrease in the future.

A young man over 18 years of age may be deferred as 4-F (unqualified by some physical or mental defect). He may be deferred if he is in some essential industry. If he becomes a father before the draft gets to him, he has greatly increased his chances of avoiding service. As long as he remains in school, he is not as likely to be drafted. But if he is qualified, available, and not deferred as a student, father, or essential worker, the chances are that he will serve his hitch in service sometime early in his twenties.

Military service is a responsibility that thrusts itself upon a young

[1] Lyle M. Spencer, *Guidance Newsletter* (Chicago, Illinois: Science Research Associates, April 1953), pp. 1–2.

[2] "Our experience indicates that about four out of five of our young men who are not fathers, and who are otherwise physically and mentally qualified and available, can expect to enter military service before they reach age 26." (Admiral Arthur W. Radford, Chairman of the Joint Chiefs of Staff, in a recent speech, quoted in *U. S. News & World Report*, April 20, 1956, p. 55.)

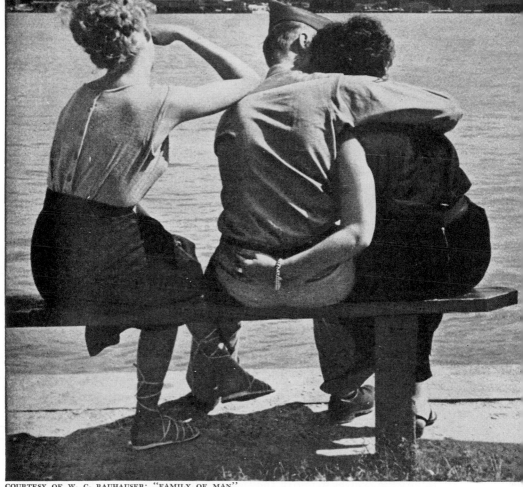

COURTESY OF W. C. RAUHAUSER: "FAMILY OF MAN"

Military service comes at a time when a young man is fitting himself for a vocation, completing his education, choosing a wife, and getting married.

man at the time when he is leaving home to establish a life of his own.[1] It comes at the time when he is working on the universal developmental tasks of fitting himself for his vocation, completing his education, becoming socially acceptable, choosing a wife, getting married, and settling down in a home of his own. Questions of the timing of military service, education, work, and marriage are difficult. Should the young man volunteer for service directly from high school and count on his veterans' benefits to help him complete his education when he has finished his

[1] Disruption of plans "ranks as concern number one affecting attitudes toward military service held by university students in the study": Edward Suchman, Robin Williams, Jr., and Rose Goldsen, "Student Reaction to Impending Military Service," *American Sociological Review*, Vol. 18, No. 3, June 1953, p. 302.

military service? Or should he get just as much education as he can before Uncle Sam catches up with him? Should he attempt to get a job and at least start his vocation before he goes into service, with the hope of establishing seniority on the job? Or, is it better to get his service behind him before becoming vocationally established? Will he be wise to get things settled with his girl and get married before he is pulled off into service? Or will it be more advisable to postpone marriage until he can really settle down in a home of his own? If he does marry before military service, will his wife try to follow him as far as she can? Or should she try to maintain a home base for them both until he is out and can join her in homemaking?

These are but a few of the many questions that come tumbling in upon both the young man and the girl who loves him as he reaches draft age. There is no single answer to any of these questions. One way that may be wise for one fellow, or couple, may not work out well for another. Each young man, each young woman, each young couple today must work out the solution that makes the most sense in their particular situation. That so many young adults accomplish this task so well is a credit to the generation of young adults today. At the same time, it is understandable that many fellows and girls are anxious, baffled, and bewildered by the multitude of major decisions that must be made during this period. The impulsive, the impetuous, the hysterical fringe of the young adult population who rush into some premature "solution" (only to find themselves in one of the traps for the unwary) are the problematic minority.

There are many community, church, school, and family aids to young men and women facing the likelihood of military service. Today, more than ever before, young people need opportunities to think through, under qualified leadership, the many paths that stretch ahead for them, of which military service is but one. Boys need some preparation for what to expect in service, what the alternatives are, and how to choose the time that will be best for each of the demands and responsibilities they face as young adult males. Girls in their teens and early twenties are ready for discussion of what it means to be a woman, whom to marry, and when and what their role is in the many months and miles of separation from lover or husband that military service imposes. Together the sexes face the developmental tasks of dating, courtship, marriage and family establishment, in the midst of a military economy, as they enter the launching years. The decisions about military service are made with vocational, educational, social, marital, familial and personal values all crowding in for multifocused attention.

BECOMING MARRIAGEABLE

Today's young people have full responsibility for finding a place for themselves among their peers, making friends, getting dates, and becoming the kind of marriageable young men or women who can win and hold a mate. This is not an easy task. Many young women who are of good marriage potential miss out because of shyness, social ineptness, and inability to get along comfortably with eligible young men. Some of our most able young men lose themselves so completely in their vocational interests that they miss out on normal social contacts with members of the other sex. A man may be a good engineer or an outstanding physician, but if he has not learned to get along pleasantly with women and to find deep satisfaction in warm friendships with one or more especially compatible women, he may be easy prey for some unscrupulous female when the time comes for him to marry. There are many instances of a young man of outstanding ability hurriedly plunging into marriage with some relatively inferior woman largely because he has not developed the social, emotional, domestic sides of his personality.

Leonard S. is a case in point. He is a brilliant scientist. But in social affairs he feels lost. He is embarrassed at meeting new people. He is shy and uncomfortable with women generally. His conversational abilities are limited to the field of his specialty and superficial comments about the weather. He is now nearly twenty-seven, has never gone seriously with a girl, doesn't know how to dance, and has no contacts with mixed groups of young adults his own age. Several weeks ago, a girl behind the salad counter at the corner cafeteria began to flirt with him. At first he blushed and stammered some nonsensical reply. She told him she thought he was "real sweet," and on her day off brought her dinner out to eat with him. Things moved fast from then on, and they are to be married next Saturday. Leonard's family is shocked at his marrying a lower-class girl who never went beyond sixth grade. Leonard has questions himself about what he is getting into. The girl's family is happy about the financial security she will acquire by the marriage, but openly ridicules Leonard as a "brain." But, at the moment, Leonard is powerless to stop the affair.

Surely there are many factors contributing to such a situation as Leonard faces. The obvious ones are social inexperience and lack of competency with others in personal and social relationships. Failures in accomplishing these developmental tasks become problems for many teenagers and young adults. Such continuing failures seriously block or distort the processes that lead to marriage.

Getting the feeling of belonging to one's own generation is a major developmental task of the second decade of life. The young person who feels that he or she is personally attractive and socially acceptable is able to make the decisions about occupation, education, military service and the other elements of life-planning without insistent dreams of friendship and popularity distorting his vision. The young man or woman who has attained some measure of success in social situations is able to move among members of both sexes, to make and keep friends, to date and go steady, to choose a mate wisely and become engaged through the process of association that leads to marriage.

What it takes to get into the leading crowd reflects the values of the youth culture which may vary greatly by size and type of community. In most schools, the path to popularity is through athletics for boys and activities for girls. In smaller schools where more young men are headed for the professions, intelligence and good scholarship may be (to a lesser extent than athletics) a road to social acceptance.[1]

Among college students there is general agreement on the traits preferred in members of the other sex both as dating and as marriage partners. Both men and women students rate as "crucially important" in a date such qualities as (1) well-groomed and well-mannered, (2) sense of humor, (3) considerate, (4) emotional maturity, (5) ambitious and industrious, (6) health and vitality, and (7) sensible about money. Preferred traits for marriage partners include these seven qualities, plus the trait of affection (by more than 80 per cent of both men and women). Much more than in dating partners, students value in marriage partners such characteristics as similar background, normal heredity, good earner or cook, intellectual, and religious nature.[2] An eleven university survey shows roughly similar percentages of men and women students listing such qualities of their ideal mate as highly important.[3]

[1] James S. Coleman, *The Adolescent Society* (Glencoe, Illinois: Free Press, 1961).
[2] Lester E. Hewitt, "Student Perceptions of Traits Desired in Themselves as Dating and Marriage Partners," *Marriage and Family Living*, Vol. XX, No. 4, November 1958, pp. 344–349.
[3] Rose K. Goldsen, Morris Rosenberg, Robin M. Williams, Jr., Edward A. Such-

No area is more confusing than that of sex expression before marriage. Both sexes have increasingly greater freedom. But premarital chastity continues to be the desirable alternative for many college students, with about a third feeling that premarital sex relations could never be justified, a fifth saying that virginity is a highly important factor in mate selection, and nearly two-fifths "not sure" they would break their engagement if this rule were broken.[2] More men than women are permissive in their sex attitudes and behavior. But, as love enters the relationship, men are only half as likely to engage in premarital intercourse, (and women more than twice as apt to go all the way) with their loved ones as with friends and acquaintances.[3]

Reviewing changing sex standards, Reiss finds the majority of college men today adhering fairly closely to the double standard, modified by a feeling that abstinence is really the best policy. Most college women tolerate the double standard but feel that abstinence for both sexes before marriage is preferable, and that petting with affection is sometimes acceptable.[4]

Kirkendall's research into six levels of attachment (from prostitute and pick-up to fiancée) between premarital sex partners, suggests that such criteria as increasing trust, integrity and self-respect within the interpersonal relationship be used as a basis for making moral judgments.[5]

Sex is not a simple biological response, but reflects the personalities of the partners and expresses the type of persons they are more dramatically than any other type of behavior. Sex is not and cannot be a strictly private affair of concern only to the partners, for it is at the core of family life and is of central social concern. One of the most difficult tasks for a young man or woman is determining what is best in the expression of love and sex at a time when society no longer draws a clear line between right and wrong. A valid sex code that protects social, family, and personal values must be built.[6]

---

man, *What College Students Think* (Princeton, N. J.: D. Van Nostrand Company, 1960), page 90.

   [2] *Ibid.*, p. 94.

   [3] Winston Ehrmann, *Premarital Dating Behavior* (New York: Henry Holt & Company, 1959), p. 179.

   [4] Ira L. Reiss, Premarital Sexual Standards in America (Glencoe, Illinois: Free Press, 1960), pp. 250–252.

   [5] Lester A. Kirkendall, *Premarital Intercourse and Interpersonal Relationships* (New York: Julian Press, 1961).

   [6] Sylvanus M. Duvall, *Men, Women and Morals* (New York: Association Press, 1952); and "Sex Fictions and Facts," *LOOK*, Vol. 24, No. 8, April 12, 1960, pp. 47 ff.

TABLE 23. *Significant Differences Between Percentage of Students Preferring Specified Characteristics in Casual and Serious Dating Partners for All Students, for Men Students and for Women Students* [1]

Items	Per cent of Respondents Choosing Item Personal Preferences	
	CASUAL DATES	SERIOUS DATES
A. *Discriminations Made by Both Sexes*		
1. Is emotionally mature	84.2	100.0
2. Is dependable	87.8	99.3
3. Is a well-rounded person	84.6	98.5
4. Is affectionate	69.6	97.6
5. Is a good listener	88.3	97.4
6. Gets along with friends of own sex	80.6	96.4
7. Is ambitious and energetic	65.3	84.7
8. Person has my family's approval	24.5	72.1
9. Knows how to dance well	52.6	31.9
B. *Discriminations Made by Men Students*		
10. Has good sense, is intelligent	88.4	100.0
11. Is an intelligent conversationalist	85.3	100.0
12. Is honest, straightforward	80.0	96.8
13. Is willing to join a group	82.1	93.7
14. Has polished manners	66.3	81.1
15. Doesn't have a reputation for petting	38.9	74.7
16. Doesn't have a reputation for necking	34.7	67.4
17. Dates popular students only	9.5	3.2
C. *Discriminations Made by Women Students*		
18. Is willing to neck on occasion	34.3	67.7
19. Is willing to pet on occasion	8.2	32.1
20. Is good looking, attractive	61.2	45.5
21. Goes to popular places	38.8	22.6

The researcher observes from these data,

The over-all impression given . . . is one of increasing rapprochement between the sexes as they begin to get serious with one another. Moreover, this rapprochement centers about themes of emotional maturity, intelligence, and affectionateness which appear conducive to marital adjustment.[2]

[1] Robert O. Blood, Jr., "Uniformities and Diversities in Campus Dating Preferences," *Marriage and Family Living*, Vol. XVIII, No. 1, February 1956, p. 43.
[2] *Ibid.*, p. 44.

Success in dating and in becoming marriageable seem to be dependent upon a number of factors. There is evidence that such success is closely related to personal and family background. One study finds that:

The seniors not dating presented a more negative, less wholesome picture in family relationships, feeling of self-regard, and social relations than did the other seniors. . . .
. . . A relatively large number of young people had worried during childhood about their physical characteristics, development and appearance. These students had had and were still having difficulty in their relations with others because of shyness and sensitivity . . .
The most significant finding with respect to their *social relationships* was the relatively large number of young people who, by their senior year in high school, were having few social contacts, especially with the other sex.[1]

Opportunities for gaining social experience as well as for dating, appear to be related to the social class of the young person's family (Chapter Four). In general, a larger percentage of young people in the higher social classes date and they date more frequently and with more persons than do boys and girls from the lower socio-economic groups.[2]

Success in dating and in gaining social experience tends to be cumulative. The more dating is done, the smoother it becomes. Studies of the frequency of dating, among both high school and college students, indicate that from the ages of sixteen to twenty-one years, the frequency of dating increases with age; furthermore, the earlier university students had begun to date in their teens, the more frequently they dated in college.[3]

Frequency of dating is significantly related to one's dating status. Those who are playing the field have fewer dates than do those who are going steady or are engaged. Among college students the findings of one study are:

Among the men those going steady in each age classification date around twice as frequently as those playing the field. Among the women . . . those going steady or engaged date much more frequently than those playing the

[1] Opal Powell Wolford, "How Early Background Affects Dating Behavior," *Journal of Home Economics*, Vol. 40, No. 9, November 1948, pp. 505, 506.
[2] A. B. Hollingshead, *Elmtown's Youth* (New York: John Wiley and Sons, Inc., 1949), pp. 229–230.
[3] Samuel H. Lowrie, "Factors Involved in the Frequency of Dating," *Marriage and Family Living*, Vol. XVIII, No. 1, February 1956, pp. 49–51.

field. These differences are statistically highly significant for each sex and for all age levels, except eighteen among the women.[1]

Table 24 shows data on dating frequency for both sexes, ages 18 through 21, by dating status among university students.

TABLE 24. *Mean Number of Dates Per Week by Sex, Age, and Dating Status of University Students Dating the Previous Month* [2]

Age	MEN					WOMEN				
	Playing Field		*Going Steady*			*Playing Field*		*Going Steady*		
	Mean	No. of Stu-dents	Mean	No. of Stu-dents	Critical Ratio *	Mean	No. of Stu-dents	Mean	No. of Stu-dents	Critical Ratio *
18	1.2	110	2.5	39	4.6	2.0	119	2.5	68	1.9
19	1.5	165	2.8	90	8.3	2.2	129	2.9	100	3.5
20	1.7	112	3.5	77	8.3	2.2	105	3.6	69	6.0
21	1.8	91	3.2	55	5.5	1.9	62	3.6	66	6.8
Total	1.5	478	3.0	261	—	2.1	415	3.1	303	—

* A critical ratio of 3.5 or over is considered statistically significant, that is, the relationship between the two variables is such that it can not be attributed to chance.

Going steady is usually defined as dating exclusively one person with whom there are generally recognized expectations, loyalties, and some mutual identification.[3] It has arisen in recent years, with the coming of large, heterogeneous high school populations and complex urban communities, for what seem to be several interrelated reasons, in the words of young people themselves:

1) "If you go steady, you are more sure of a date when you want one." (*Date insurance.*) [4] Table 23 shows clearly that those university students who go steady have significantly more dates than those who play the field. Among high school students a frequent observation is, "If you go at all, you have to go steady."

2) "You aren't anybody in our school if you don't go steady." (*Group acceptance.*) High school students report that going steady is important for status reasons, and that "going steady was the thing to do in my high school." [5]

[1] *Ibid.* pp. 48–49.
[2] *Ibid.*, p. 49.
[3] Robert D. Herman, "The 'Going Steady' Complex: A Re-Examination," *Marriage and Family Living*, Vol. XVII, No. 1, February 1955, pp. 36–37.
[4] Ruth Connor and Edith Flinn Hall, "The Dating Behavior of College Freshmen and Sophomores," *Journal of Home Economics*, Vol. 44, No. 4, April 1952, p. 280.
[5] Robert D. Herman, *op. cit.*, p. 39.

3) "Be seen twice with the same person, and you are going steady—the crowd sees to that." (*Social pressure.*) If John dates Mary a couple of times over the weekend, by Monday they are going steady whether they have decided to or not, for by then their friends line up behind them as a pair and expect them to go steady from then on.[1] Such social pressure is found in many high school, community and campus situations.

4) "Going steady is a lot easier and safer than dating unknowns." (*Personal security.*) A girl knows what her steady boy friend will expect of her on a date, she is secure with him as she can not be with a strange boy whom she may or may not be able to manage. A boy is secure knowing his steady girl expects him, and finds it easier and cheaper to go steady than to play the field. There is probably less exploitation in going steady than in random dating, as Herman observes.[2]

5) "We would rather go steady than to date anyone else available." (*Mutual preference.*) The two persons prefer each other to any other possibilities on the scene. They may be fond of each other, and so prefer associating with one another than with other more casual dating partners.

6) "When you go steady, you learn to adjust to one person, and to become more mature in your understanding of each other." (*Mature association.*) In this sense, going steady is good preparation for marriage based upon companionship and mutual understanding.

Adults and many young people themselves see some of the problems related to going steady. In general, these tend to be: (1) going steady limits social contacts, (2) going steady interferes with work responsibilities and takes up too much time, (3) going steady often brings more emotional and sexual involvement than the two people are ready for, and (4) it is hard to get out of going steady after both names have been coupled together for a long time. Young people tend to agree that it is not wise to go steady too soon before the two people have had some general experience with members of the other sex. They recognize generally that going steady is not wise if the two people are to be separated for a considerable period of time. Then their social life will be severely curtailed if they try "to be true to each other" and yet they are not close enough to participate socially as a couple. College men and women are particularly aware of the importance of breaking off going steady when the two people have outgrown each other. The solu-

[1] Evelyn Millis Duvall, *Facts of Life and Love for Teenagers* (New York: Association Press, revised 1956), p. 347.
[2] Robert D. Herman, *op. cit.*, p. 40.

tion of the dilemna of becoming seriously involved with a steady who will not be a suitable mate is difficult to work through comfortably, posing a serious problem in present-day patterns in going steady.

The most favorable situations for those who want to become more marriageable are found in the families, in the schools and colleges, in the community programs that foster wholesome contact between the sexes in a wide variety of interests and activities. The responsibility is upon the young man or woman, to develop the social skills, and to introduce oneself into the situations where mingling with congenial persons is increasingly comfortable and competent. For those young adults who have reached marriage age without accomplishing this developmental task, there are at least two types of supportive services that might be helpful. The first is the introduction service that offers help, for a small charge, to those desiring friendship or marriage.[1] The second is the group counseling or educational programs designed to help socially inept young men and women develop the specific skills, social graces, and personal adequacies needed to become more marriageable. Many churches, YMCA's, YWCA's, and other community agencies sponsor "Charm Schools," classes in "Personality Development," and other programs designed particularly to assist the slow-developing young adult to become more socially adequate. The American Institute of Family Relations in Los Angeles has a well established service called a *Human Relations Program* that is widely publicized as a "How to Be Marriageable" course.[2] The program is two-fold: individual testing and counseling on the personality potentials and problems; and group discussion under the leadership of a staff member. Health, grooming, speech, posture, leisure-time pursuits, job-satisfaction, living conditions, and marriage ideals and dreams all come into the program. The time may come when such programs of remedial socialization are widespread, just as programs in remedial reading, remedial speech, and the like are now generally available.

In summarizing this section, we recognize the relevancy of the concept of the "teachable moment" (Chapter Two) in the process of becoming marriageable. If the person as a young teenager learns to dance and to

[1] Ernest W. Burgess and Harvey J. Locke, *The Family: From Institution to Companionship* (New York: American Book Company, 1953), pp. 354–362.

[2] Norma Lee Browning, "Want to Find a Husband?" *Chicago Tribune Magazine,* October 9, 1955, p. 51; and the series of articles on "How to Be Marriageable" that appeared in the *Ladies Home Journal,* through the Spring of 1954.

date and to associate with his peer group acceptably, while the others are working on these same tasks, he gets group support in his efforts. When he is awkward the others are too, so the learning process is tolerable. But if, for some reason, he or she has been delayed in this particular task, it will be more difficult later on when it must be done in relative solitude, carrying the added burden of feelings of personal inadequacy and social isolation (Chapter Eleven). Social success in the past facilitates success in present efforts. The process of becoming marriageable is one that typically goes on through the entire second decade, and some of the third decade of life for many, many persons.

LEARNING TO APPRAISE AND TO EXPRESS LOVE FEELINGS APPROPRIATELY

Learning to love is a lifetime achievement. It begins in infancy, it flowers in the teens and twenties, bears fruit in the rich full years of childbearing and rearing, and colors and warms life throughout the rest of life. At no stage of life is it more difficult to assay and to express responsibly than in the teen and young adult years when it is confused and intertwined with maturing sex drives.

In a culture that allows freedom of access between the sexes from an early age, and establishes marriage on the basis of being in love, it is not surprising to find young people repeatedly asking three questions about love and its expression: (1) What is love? (2) How can you tell when you are really in love (enough to build a marriage on)? and (3) How far is it wise to go in physical expression of love and sex interests before marriage? Each of these questions is complex. There are no completely satisfying or well-substantiated answers to any of these questions. Yet, when so many young men and women want to base their behavior upon some understanding of what is involved, it behooves us to rally resources that are available for their use.

What is love? Love is the most powerful force known to man. It is indeed "the greatest thing in the world." It is also the most mysterious, and the hardest to describe. In the outline below we see some outstanding attempts at definition or description made by men and women of various orientations through the years:

The Apostle Paul	Love is patient and kind; love is not jealous or boastful; it is not arrogant or rude. Love does not insist on its own way; it is not irritable or resentful; it does not rejoice at

wrong, but rejoices in the right. Love bears all things, believes all things, hopes all things, endures all things.

I CORINTHIANS, 13:4–7

The poetess Elizabeth Barrett Browning

How do I love thee? Let me count the ways.
I love thee to the depth and breadth and height
My soul can reach, when feeling out of sight
For the ends of Being and ideal Grace.
I love thee to the level of every day's
Most quiet need, by sun and candlelight.
I love thee freely, as men strive for Right;
I love thee purely, as they turn from praise.
I love thee with the passion put to use
In my old griefs, and with my childhood's faith.
I love thee with a love I seemed to lose
With my lost saints,—I love thee with the breath,
Smiles, tears, of all my life!—and, if God choose,
I shall but love thee better after death.[1]

The anthropologist Ashley Montagu

To love and to be loved is as necessary to the organism as the breathing of air. Insofar as the organism fails in loving, it fails in living, for to live and love is, for a human being, the equivalent of healthy living. To live as if to live and love were one is not simply an ideal to be achieved, but a potentiality to be realized, a destiny to be fulfilled.[2]

The human relations professor F. Alexander Magoun

Love is the passionate and abiding desire on the part of two or more people to produce together the conditions under which each can be and spontaneously express his real self; to produce together the intellectual soil and an emotional climate in which each can flourish, far superior to what either could achieve alone. . . .

Love is concerned with the realities of life; not with ideas about romantic idealism which cannot be embodied in life. Love sees faults as well as virtues. Love knows and unhesitatingly accepts the fact that no one is perfect. . . .

Love is self-discovery and self-fulfillment through healthy growth with and for the other person.[3]

The biologist and philosopher Julian Huxley

As a biologist, but also as a human being, I want to affirm the unique importance of love in life—an affirmation badly needed in a tormented age like ours, where vio-

[1] "How Do I Love Thee?" from the Standard Book of British and American Verse (Garden City, New York: The Garden City Publishing Co., 1932), pp. 431–432.

[2] Ashley Montagu, ed., *The Meaning of Love* (New York: The Julian Press, Inc., 1953), p. 19.

[3] F. Alexander Magoun, *Love and Marriage* (New York: Harper & Brothers, 1948), pp. 4, 16, 17.

lence and disillusion have joined forces with undigested technological advance to produce an atmosphere of cynicism and crude materialism. . . .

Personal love is indispensable both for the continuation of the species, and for the full development of the individual. Love is part of personal education; through love, the self learns to grow. . . . Love is a positive emotion, an enlargement of life; it leads on toward greater fulfillment and counteracts human hate and destructive impulses.[1]

The human development educator Daniel A. Prescott

Love involves more or less empathy with the loved one. . . . One who loves is deeply concerned for the welfare, happiness, and development of the loved one. . . . One who loves finds pleasure in making his resources available to the loved one . . . the loving person seeks a maximum of participation in the activities that contribute to the welfare, happiness, and development of the loved one. . . . Love is most readily and usually achieved within the family circle but can be extended to include many other individuals. . . . The good effects of love are not limited to the loved one but promote the happiness and further development of the loving one as well. . . . Love is not rooted primarily in sexual dynamics or hormonal drives, although it may well have large erotic components.[2]

The psychologist and philosopher Harry A. Overstreet

The love of a person implies, not the possession of that person, but the affirmation of that person. It means granting him, gladly, the full right to his unique humanhood. One does not truly love a person and yet seek to enslave him—by law or by bonds of dependence and possessiveness.

Whenever we experience a genuine love, we are moved by this transforming experience toward a capacity for good will.[3]

The psychiatrist Smiley Blanton, M.D.

. . . It is in the joyful union of a man with a woman that the jangled forces of life fall at last into harmony. Here, in the eternal longing of one to join with the other, we may discern an infinite wisdom distilled from billions of years of patient evolution. Here lies the primordial pattern of all our striving and all our bliss. It is the secret spring that

[1] Julian Huxley, "All about Love," *Look,* Vol. 19, No. 14, July 12, 1955, p. 29.
[2] Daniel A. Prescott, "Role of Love in Human Development," *Journal of Home Economics,* Vol. 44, No. 3, March 1952, pp. 174–175.
[3] Harry A. Overstreet, *The Mature Mind* (New York, W. W. Norton and Co., 1949), p. 103.

animates our deepest desires and shapes our loftiest dreams. It generates the restless tension, the driving energy, that ever moves us to aspire and to achieve. From its profound yearning comes all creation, whether of the body or spirit. Man and woman, united in loving endeavor, truly encompass the sum and substance of human life.[1]

The sociologist Clifford Kirkpatrick

Every human is born into a culture which provides certain viewpoints and expectations in regard to love. There may be emphasis upon free sex expression, property values, kinship ties, love security, love adventure, aggression and tenderness. The present-day American culture is sex-repressive but does place a high value upon romance and defines "falling in love" as the basis for marriage. The romantic complex nurtured in the medieval courts of love has been powerfully strengthened by movies, romance magazines, popular music and the example of others. Young persons of dating age fully expect that sooner or later they will be caught in the magic spell of love and experience the pangs and delights which seem inevitable. . . .[2]

By the time a young person reaches the late teens and twenties he or she is experienced in loving. One of the most important things he or she has learned within the family through the years of childhood and adolescence is to learn to love.

Love does not simply spring forth some moonlight night without warning. We do not *fall* in love. We *learn* to love through a lifetime of experience in loving. By the time boy meets girl, a great deal has happened to both of them to make them ready for their interest in each other. In fact, by that time they both are old hands at loving, in many ways. Each has grown up through the phases of emotional maturity to the place where he and she are capable of loving and being loved. In a real sense we *grow* into love, both individually and as couples.[3]

If, through the years of growing up within the family, the young adult has learned how to love and be loved, he or she is ready for the urgent developmental tasks of appraising love feelings in terms of readiness for marriage. If there has been deprivation or distortion of love

[1] Smiley Blanton, M.D., "Love or Perish," *Woman's Home Companion,* Jan. 1956, p. 70, copyright, 1956, The Crowell-Collier Publishing Co.

[2] Clifford Kirpatrick, *The Family as Process and Institution* (New York: The Ronald Press Co., 1955), pp. 272–273.

[3] Evelyn Millis Duvall, *Facts of Life and Love for Teenagers* (New York: Association Press, Revised Edition, 1956), p. 257.

through the years of growing up, it may be exceedingly difficult to achieve and gauge the level of mature love that is needed as a foundation for a successful marriage.

The young person often needs a functional answer to the urgent question, "Is this *it?*" If the marriage is to be based upon love, it becomes imperative to know whether the feeling one has toward a particular person is "the real thing," especially when love comes and goes, as apparently is quite usual. One study of 896 love affairs of college men and women, found that 644 of them (71.8 per cent) had been broken off.[1]

Another study of 500 college girls found half the students reporting that they had had five to seven or more infatuations between the ages of 12 and 18.[2] Such multiple experiences are confusing and give rise to the question of the differences between infatuation and "real love." One convenient device used by college women themselves is to call past loves "infatuations," and to reserve the designation "love" for any present involvement.[3] More helpful may be the distinctions between infatuation and love that may be made from the findings of contemporary studies, a few of which are summarized in Table 24.

Opportunities for discussion, individual and group counseling, education for marriage, premarital conferences, and confidential relationships with trusted adults in the family, the community, the church, and in schools and colleges, prove helpful to many young adults who are at the point of making personal decisions on the basis of the mutuality and potential permanence of their love feelings. High school and college teachers report that it is not unusual for some young people to break off unpromising affairs during and after completion of a course in Preparation for Marriage.[4] This may be a measure of the effectiveness of the educational program in being of real and practical help. The students otherwise might have found themselves trapped in too impulsive, immature, or unsuitable marriages. Parents who have maintained effective two-

---

[1] Clifford Kirkpatrick and Theodore Caplow, "Emotional Trends in the Courtship Experience of College Students as Expressed by Graphs with Some Observations on Methodological Implications," *American Sociological Review*, Vol. X, No. 5, October 1945, pp. 619–629.

[2] Albert Ellis, " A Study of Human Love Relationships," *The Journal of Genetic Psychology*, Vol. 75, 1949, p. 64.

[3] *Ibid.*, p. 69.

[4] Personal communications.

TABLE 25. *Differences between Infatuation and Love* [1]

Infatuation	Love
1. Is the term applied to past attachments, oftentimes	1. Is the term used to refer to a current attachment, usually
2. Focuses frequently on quite unsuitable persons	2. Object of affection is likely to be a suitable person
3. Parents often disapprove	3. Parents tend to approve
4. Feelings of guilt, insecurity and frustration are frequent	4. Is associated with feelings of self-confidence, trust and security
5. Tends to be self-centered and restricted	5. Kindlier feelings toward other people generally are associated
6. Narrowly focusses on but a few highly visible or fantasied traits	6. Broadly involves the whole personality
7. Most frequent among young adolescents and immature persons	7. Grows through the years with emotional maturity
8. Simultaneous attachments to two or more at the same time are possible	8. Loyalty centers in mutual commitment and involvement
9. Can reoccur soon after a previous affair is over	9. May slowly develop again after a previous lover has gone
10. Boredom is frequent when sexual excitement dies down	10. An ongoing sense of being alive when together precludes boredom
11. Partners depend upon external amusement for fun	11. Joy is in many common interests and in each other
12. Little change in the relationship over time	12. Relationship changes and grows with ongoing association
13. Shallow sensations come and go	13. Deepening feelings provide steady warmth as more of life is shared
14. Problems and barriers are usually disregarded	14. Problems are tackled and worked out as they arise
15. Romantic illusions have little regard for reality	15. Faces reality with faith in growth and improvement
16. Tends to last but a short time	16. Tends to last over a long period of time
17. Little mutual exploration of personality values and aspirations	17. Shares hopes and dreams, feelings and meanings
18. May be stereotyped "romance for romance's sake"	18. Tends to be highly individual, unique and person-centered
19. Can exploit the other as a person	19. Has a protective, nurturing, caring concern
20. A poor basis for marriage	20. Enough to build a marriage on, perhaps—if other things are right

way, open, non-judgmental communication with their growing children may be of special help as the young people work through their entangling alliances as best they can.

[1] Evelyn Millis Duvall and Reuben Hill, *When You Marry* (Boston: D. C. Heath Company, Revised Edition, 1967), pp. 40–41, quoted with permission.

Whether a love affair goes on into marriage or breaks off after a few dates, there still remains the question of the degree of expression of affection between the two lovers. How much intimacy is appropriate to various situations and relationships? How far is it wise to go before marriage? These are two questions especially pertinent today. It is generally agreed that two lovers need to express their affection for each other, not only for their emotional well-being and development, but as good preparation for marriage. There is general recognition too that there is a progression of intimacy through the process of dating, going steady, being engaged, and getting married. Holding hands, kissing goodnight, and the lighter forms of contact are typical early in the relationship. As the involvement increases there is commensurate development of intimacy patterns through what young people themselves generally recognize as "necking," "light petting," "heavy petting," and "going all the way." At what point an unmarried couple stops depends upon a number of factors.

According to one research study of two university populations, "there is a striking tendency for females to be less tolerant than males with respect to petting to climax, premarital sex intercourse, intercourse with prostitutes, and extramarital sex intercourse." [1] The influence of social class is seen in a study within another state university student group:

The marked tendency of males to descend the social ladder for dating companions seems to be motivated primarily by a desire to find willing sexual partners. [2]

Similar findings are reported from other studies, indicating that girls from the lower classes are more willing and available sexual partners than those from higher educational and social levels. [3] Boys, too, show striking differences in premarital sex experience by social class as indicated by level of education achieved. Studying the percentage of total sex outlet in intercourse with companions among 16–20 year old boys,

[1] Clifford Kirkpatrick, Sheldon Stryker, and Philip Buell, "Attitudes towards Male Sex Behavior," *American Sociological Review*, Vol. 17, No. 5, October 1952, p. 586.
[2] Winston H. Ehrmann, "Influence of Comparative Social Class of Companion upon Premarital Heterosexual Behavior," *Marriage and Family Living*, Vol. XVII, No. 1, February, 1955, p. 52.
[3] August B. Hollingshead, *Elmtown's Youth* (New York: John Wiley and Sons, 1949), pp. 232, 240; and Alfred C. Kinsey *et al.*, *Sexual Behavior in the Human Female* (Philadelphia: W. B. Saunders Company, 1953), p. 78.

Kinsey found the highest percentage of sex intercourse among the least well-educated: 50.62 per cent among males with less than eighth grade education, 39.49 per cent among males with high school education, and 9.13 per cent among males with some education beyond high school.[1]

Other factors related to premarital sex experience are gleaned from a study of premarital pregnancies in which higher frequencies were found, (1) during the depression years when marriage was more difficult, (2) among people who married young, (3) among couples who were married in a civil or secular ceremony, and (4) for those who were classified occupationally as laborers.[2]

The moral, as well as the emotional and psychological aspects of premarital sex behavior have been widely discussed.[3] A sociological exploration of the factors that distinguished happily married from divorced couples found, "A significantly larger per cent of divorced than happily married men reported premarital intercourse."[4] Another student of the question suggests that the romantic ideal and permissiveness in sexual practice before marriage may be incompatible, when he says,

When a couple chooses to "go all the way," it should be prepared for the possibility that the romantic bubble may collapse in the process.[5]

He cites loss of the sense of mystery, and of the image of perfection, as well as the waning of interest in the other when the two have "gone the limit," as factors that may start one or both members of the pair to wondering if they were really meant for each other after all, with the possible outcome of a broken love affair and a search for a new partner.

The individual young man or woman faces the question of premarital sexual behavior not so much in terms of the findings of studies as in terms of conceptions of self. The young person who sees himself or

[1] Alfred C. Kinsey et al., Sexual Behavior in the Human Male (Philadelphia: W. B. Saunders Company, 1948), p. 378.
[2] Harold T. Christensen, "Studies in Child Spacing: I—Premarital Pregnancy as Measured by the Spacing of the First Birth from Marriage," American Sociological Review, Vol. 18, No. 1, February 1953, p. 52.
[3] Sylvanus M. Duvall, Men, Women, and Morals (New York: Association Press, 1952), Chapter 9, "The Morality of Fornication;" and Bibliography, pp. 319–330.
[4] Harvey J. Locke, Predicting Adjustment in Marriage (New York: Henry Holt and Company, 1951), p. 133.
[5] Robert O. Blood, "Romance and Premarital Intercourse—Incompatibles?" Marriage and Family Living, Vol. XIV, No. 2, May 1952, p. 108.

herself as a person with a future, who has long-term professional and personal goals has a basis for conforming to traditional codes of premarital chastity; while the individual whose past has been bleak, whose future seems to offer little, and who tends to see himself as a creature of impulse feels there is nothing much worth waiting for. Success in the developmental tasks of building an adequate self-concept and meaningful philosophy of life through the years of childhood and adolescence in the family contributes to success in this task of learning to express responsibly the love and sex feelings of young adulthood.

CHOOSING A MARRIAGE PARTNER

Three factors are found to play a part in choosing a life partner: propinquity, homogamy, and complementarity. Persons of both sexes tend to marry those who live and work near them. Residential propinquity is significantly related to mate selection in both urban and rural populations, in various regions and among the several racial groups. Studies of marriages in Philadelphia, Pennsylvania, and in New Haven, Connecticut, in the thirties, both found more than half of the couples living within twenty blocks of each other at the time of their marriage.[1] In a later study in New Haven, one of the original researchers discovered an even higher percentage (an increase of 18.4 per cent) of marriages among persons residing within an area of twenty blocks.[2] Studies in rural counties in Michigan and Minnesota turned up 58 per cent and from 58 to 70 per cent of the couples living in the same county respectively.[3]

A recent study of both Negro and white marriages in Nashville, Tennessee, finds that residential propinquity operates significantly more frequently among the colored than among the white populations (79.6 per cent of the Negroes, as compared with 46.6 per cent of the white

[1] James H. S. Bossard, "Residential Propinquity as a Factor in Marriage Selection," *American Journal of Sociology*, Vol. 38, 1932–33, pp. 219–224; and Maurice R. Davie and Ruby Jo Reeves, "Propinquity of Residence Before Marriage," *American Journal of Sociology*, Vol. 44, 1938–1939, pp. 510–517.

[2] Ruby Jo Reeves Kennedy, "Premarital Residential Propinquity and Ethnic Endogamy," *American Journal of Sociology*, Vol. 48, 1942–1943, pp. 580–584.

[3] Howard Y. McClusky and Alvin Zander, "Residential Propinquity and Marriage in Branch County Michigan," *Social Forces*, Vol. 19, 1940, pp. 79–81; and Donald Mitchell, "Residential Propinquity and Marriage in Carver and Scott Counties, Minnesota," *Social Forces*, Vol. 20, 1941, pp. 256–259.

couples living within a twenty block radius).[1] Several factors possibly related to the high propinquity tendencies are suggested: (1) segregation, (2) neighborhood organization, and (3) neighborhood self-sufficiency (schools, churches, shopping centers, etc.).[2]

Homogamy, the tendency of marriage partners to have similar characteristics, has been shown in scores of studies of many characteristics, in thousands of couples, by hundreds of social scientists through recent decades.[3] Homogamy is especially evident in tendencies to marry within the same group, as Hollingshead has pointed out in his study of all marriages in New Haven during 1948:

> The data presented demonstrate that American culture, as it is reflected in the behavior of newly married couples in New Haven, places very definite restrictions on whom an individual may or may not marry. The racial mores were found to be the most explicit on this point. They divided the community into two pools of marriage mates and an individual fished for a mate only in his own racial pool. Religion divided the white race into three smaller pools. Persons in the Jewish pool in 97.1 per cent of the cases married within their own group; the percentage was 93.8 for Catholics and 74.4 for Protestants . . . The ethnic origin of a person's family placed further restrictions on his marital choice. In addition, class position and education stratified the three religious pools into areas where an individual was most likely to find a mate. . . . In a highly significant number of cases the person who marries is very similar culturally to one's self.[4]

Neither propinquity nor homogamy tell us how mates are chosen within a pool of eligibles. To explore the theory of complementary needs as a factor in the dynamics of individual choice, Winch and others have conducted a series of studies that indicate that individuals tend to marry those persons who are purposefully *unlike* in significant personality characteristics.[5] The senior author concludes,

[1] Alan C. Kerckhoff, "Notes and Comments on the Meaning of Residential Propinquity as a Factor in Mate Selection," *Social Forces*, Vol. 34, No. 3, March 1956, pp. 207–213.

[2] *Ibid.*, p. 212.

[3] A carefully selected bibliography of studies on homogamy is found in the footnotes of August B. Hollingshead, "Cultural Factors in the Selection of Marriage Mates," *American Sociological Review*, Vol. 15, No. 5, October 1950, pp. 619–627.

[4] *Ibid.*, p. 627.

[5] Robert F. Winch, Thomas and Virginia Ktsanes, "The Theory of Complementary Needs in Mate Selection: An Analytic and Descriptive Study," *American Sociological Review*, Vol. 19, No. 3, June 1954; and Robert F. Winch, "The Theory of Complementary Needs in Mate-Selection: A Test of One Kind of Complementariness," *American Sociological Review*, Vol. 20, No. 1, February 1955, pp. 52–56.

The bulk of the evidence, therefore, supports the hypothesis that mates tend to select each other on the basis of complementary needs.[1]

The element of personal choice is strongly influenced by powerful unconscious needs that apparently strive to be met through a mate whose personality complements rather than replicates one's own. In such interplay of mutually complementary need patterns may be the answer to the question of "What can he see in HER?" That marriage partners may tend to choose those whose life style, and personality patterns mutually strengthen and encourage their development as persons, is a theory that may yield still further insight in further research.

Granted that persons generally tend to marry those individuals who live and work nearby, and to choose mates from within their own social, religious, and racial groups, an increasingly large number of mixed marriages are taking place today. How successful marriage is that crosses religious, racial, nationality, or socio-economic group lines depends upon a number of interrelated factors: (1) the motivation for the selection of the marriage partner, (2) responsibility of the sweethearts and mates for bridging the gulfs between them, and their families, (3) ability of the two people to live with their differences. Since there are usually more problems in building a marriage that spans two different cultures, the two people face a greater task, and more is expected of them both in maturity and in responsibility than might be necessary in a homogamous union.

Choosing a suitable partner for marriage can be and often is a confusing task. Families help by standing by with assurance, encouragement, and opportunities for free exploration and development of available possibilities. Premarital counseling and education has proven of invaluable aid to many young men and women who want to be sure before they plunge into anything as serious as marriage.

GETTING ENGAGED

Getting engaged may seem like a pleasant "task" to set up for young adults, but it is a many-faceted responsibility that is not easy for many a couple. Some of the more frequent questions young people ask about the engagement period are:

[1] Robert F. Winch, "The Theory of Complementary Needs in Mate Selection: Final Results on the Test of the General Hypothesis," *American Sociological Review*, Vol. 20, No. 5, October 1955, p. 555.

How soon should a couple get engaged?
How long should an engagement be?
Is it necessary for the man to ask the girl's father for her hand in marriage?
Why does an engagement ring mean so much to a girl?
How much freedom should be allowed the engaged couple?
Does engagement mean "no stepping out?"
Is it necessary to reveal your past to your fiance (é)?
Is it natural to have doubts about your engagement? about yourself?
What are justifiable reasons for breaking an engagement?
How can an unsatisfactory engagement be terminated without being painful?
What is the engagement period for?
What should be discussed during the engagement period?
Is it wise for two people to visit each other's families before they marry?
How can you know when you are really ready for marriage? [1]

No two persons will ever answer such questions in the same way. The answers to most engagement questions depend upon the two people, the nature of their relationship, the motivating forces within them both, their dreams, disappointments and readiness. The way they conduct their engagement is predictive of their marriage success, as we see from how closely the engagement success scores parallel the marriage success scores of both men and women in the longitudinal study of 666 couples through engagement into marriage by Burgess and Wallin, reported in Table 26.

TABLE 26. *Relation between Engagement Success and Marital Success for Men and Women* [2] (Percentage Distribution for 666 Couples)

Engagement Success Scores	MEN Marriage Success Score			WOMEN Marriage Success Score		
	Low	Inter-mediate	High	Low	Inter-mediate	High
High (180 and over)	0.0	16.0	84.0	0.0	9.1	90.9
Median (150–159)	6.7	38.7	54.7	6.7	32.2	61.1
Low (100–109)	40.0	40.0	20.0	28.6	57.1	14.3

[1] Taken from questions discussed in Evelyn Millis Duvall and Reuben Hill, *When You Marry* (Boston: D. C. Heath and Company, Revised Edition, 1953), Chapter 5, "The Meaning of an Engagement," pp. 87–106; and in Evelyn Millis Duvall, *Facts of Life and Love for Teenagers* (New York: Association Press, Revised Edition, 1956), Chapter 16, "Getting Engaged," pp. 361–383.

[2] Ernest W. Burgess and Paul Wallin, *Engagement and Marriage* (Chicago: J. B. Lippincott Company, 1953), excerpts from Table 81, page 547.

Engagement rituals contribute to the success of the engagement period. Many an engaged pair share the rituals of their respective families as a way of giving a sense of belonging to both families, and also as a way of selecting those common rituals that both may enjoy and want to continue in their own family-to-be. Having Sunday dinner with his or her family, participating in family celebrations, going on family picnics, and attending church and community functions with one or the other family are illustrations of the way rituals in the engagement weave the couple into the larger family life.

Some engagement rituals are oriented toward the future in anticipating and preparing for their marriage and family life. Ritualized house-hunting, Saturday afternoon window shopping, contributing to the piggy bank for special funds, calling on recently married friends, having a series of premarital conferences, and attending courses for engaged couples, all are practices that tend to emerge in engagement as future-oriented rituals.

By the time the couple is ready for marriage, it will have accomplished several important purposes of the engagement period: (1) to place themselves as a pair in their own eyes, and in the eyes of both families and their mutual friends, (2) to work through intimate systems of communication that allow for exchange of confidences, and an increasing degree of empathy and the ability to predict each other's responses, (3) to plan specifically for the marriage that lies ahead, in terms of both the practical decisions of where and on what, as well as the value consensus of how the common life will be lived.

BEING MARRIED

Being married is a multiple developmental task for both partners. If the marriage is to get off to a good start in its establishment phase (Chapter Six), several important jobs must be satisfactorily accomplished when the two people marry. The two people face several urgent questions as they become one in marriage: (1) Are our parents with us or against us in our marriage? (2) Where will we live, and on what? (3) Are we both really ready to settle down in marriage? (4) How well prepared for marriage are we? (5) What kind of ceremony will we have?

A marriage that starts off with the blessing of both sets of parents has much smoother going than if one or both families oppose the match. Modern young people growing up in an era of extreme individualism may operate under the illusion that they are not marrying into each other's families, and that what anyone else, including their parents, thinks about their marriage is none of their business. Actually the opinions of both families are very important, and influence the marriage either positively or negatively in many crucial ways through the years. The task of coming to terms with real attitudes about the proposed marriage within both sets of families is urgently relevant.

ONE IN THREE COUPLES WED ON "SHOESTRING" headlines a release in early 1956.[1] The report goes on to say that 35 per cent of all newlyweds are married on an income of less than $60 a week (about $3,000 a year). How young couples manage on so little is a story in itself. About 10 per cent of young married couples live with their families. Others are receiving regular assistance from their families in the form of money, food or gifts. Many of the young marriages take place when they do because of the willingness and the ability of the girl to work.

The too-young couple may be getting themselves caught in the tender trap of love and marriage, as a woman professor of education warns:

Funny . . . how ideas about love and marriage change with something so unromantic as the national economy. In the depression years of the 1930's the average young woman was willing or at least reconciled to waiting before mating. Now she knows that her parents can and probably will help. And she knows she can get a job that will enable her husband to manage. It may well be an uninteresting (if fairly well-paid) job with no chance for advancement, but she can thereby Help Her Husband with His Education—or make it possible for *him* to take, if necessary, a thirty-six-dollar-a-week-job with a whale of a future. Perhaps she has always wanted to work her way up in a New York publishing house—or with the Department of State in Washington. She drops her plans like a hot cake to follow her husband to the spot on the globe where he can do what he wants to do—and she can't. It doesn't occur to her until later that she has walked wide-eyed into a trap.

She does not stop to think that, while the early sacrifices of the ardent young bride can be made with happy generosity, they will lead to later resentment when she discovers that she is an uninteresting person, unqualified for either self-respect or respect of others in a world that has moved ahead without her, where her own growth has been slowed and stunted. The husband will forget, in time, that it was she who helped him win success and grow beyond her very reach, that it was she who took upon herself the limiting routines and denied her own personal goals.

An early marriage . . . can trap the husband as well as the wife. He is

---

[1] "One in Three Couples Wed on 'Shoestring,'" *The Family Economist* (New York: Institute of Life Insurance, December, 1955), release January 6, 1956, page 1.

COURTESY OF THE LIBRARY OF CONGRESS

Many young marriages take place when they do today because of the willingness and ability of the girl to work.

not allowed the time and leisure for intellectual growth. His perceptions and judgments are sharpened only in his own professional directions. Weighed down by his desperate pressures in earning power, he has too many responsibilities too early—financing his wife, the two, three or four babies, the mortgage. He does not have the leisure to write, experiment, explore, create. He too is cramped and harassed.[1]

Readiness for marriage is measured most easily by chronological age. Data on age at marriage by success in marriage indicate that teenage marriages are the riskiest of all. However, the number of birthdays an individual has had is not as good an indication of his or her readiness for marriage as is emotional age, or maturity as a person. Discriminating questions like these are pertinent: Am I really ready to stop playing around and settle down with one person in marriage? Am I grown up

[1] Kate Hevner Mueller, "The Marriage Trap," *Mademoiselle,* Spring 1955, taken from release from *Mademoiselle,* pp. 1 and 2.

enough to be responsible for my own behavior without blaming someone else, or "running home to mother" when I get in a jam? Am I emotionally weaned from my parents? Are my motives for marriage to this person at this time sound and mature? Are we both prepared for what lies ahead for us?

Such questions as these, and many others, are usually freely discussed in functional courses in marriage and family living. Studies have shown that college students are generally appreciative of such course work, their attitudes ranging from "favorable," to "strongly favorable." [1] Of the married graduates who had taken the course in "Marriage and the Family" at Florida State University between 1930 and 1946, 34.8 per cent responded to a poll by saying they believed the college course had helped them "a great deal," 52.8 per cent, "helped somewhat," and 12.4 per cent "made no difference." [2] An evaluation of the effectiveness of the course at Syracuse University summarizes findings in part as follows:

. . . Students enrolled in a functional course in Family Relationships do make significant gains in their understanding; they do gain insights which they, themselves, consider to be of personal value; they do apply these understandings and insights in their efforts to solve personal problems they are currently experiencing on campus . . . individuals who formerly have had the course and who are now married are applying learnings and insights derived from the course. These people feel the application of learnings derived from the course has contributed much to the quality of their marriages.[3]

Courses in preparation for marriage are offered by many public and private schools, YMCAs, YWCAs, and other youth-serving agencies in many communities. Churches of all three faiths increasingly assume responsibility for preparing their teenage and young adult constituents for marriage and family life. The Pre-Cana and Cana Conferences under Roman Catholic auspices, the excellent materials (course outlines, books, pamphlets, film-strips, recordings, leader's guides, etc.) published by many Protestant denominations for their work in Christian Family Life

[1] Lawrence S. Bee, "Student Attitudes toward a Course in Courtship and Marriage: Educational Implications," *Marriage and Family Living*, Volume XIII, No. 4, Fall, 1951, pp. 157–160.

[2] George H. Finck, "A Comparative Analysis of the Marriages and Families of Participants and Non-Participants in Marriage Education," *Marriage and Family Living*, Vol. XVIII, No. 1, February 1956, p. 63.

[3] Virginia Musick Moses, "A Study of Learnings Derived from a Functional College Course in Marriage and Family Relationships by Students as Undergraduates and as Married Alumni," unpublished dissertation, Syracuse University Library, 1955.

Formal and informal education for marriage clears up many of the confusions young adults have about when and how and whom to marry.

programs, as well as the outstanding work being done in many Jewish groups are all resources that may be tapped.

Specific plans for the wedding may be for anything from a simple home ceremony, with just members of the family present, to elaborate society affairs running into thousands of dollars and months of preparation. The average wedding today costs $1,000, including $250 for the bride's gown and accessories,[1] an outlay few families can comfortably afford.[2]

Whatever the type of ceremony, the most important factors are the *persons*, rather than the things. A wedding that is planned to meet the needs of the situation, in accordance with the wishes of the families, and the values of the couple is a many-faceted responsibility involving a number of specific decisions.[3] These tasks are usually jointly assumed by the couple and their parents, with the bride and her parents taking the major responsibility for the social aspects of the affair.

[1] Alexandra S. Potts, "Brides: The Nation's Billion Dollar Babies," *Public Relation Board Newsletter*, Vol. 7, No. 9, June 1961, pp. 3 and 4.
[2] Robert Wacker, Jr., "Our Wild Extravagance . . . The Great Big Wedding," *McCall's*, January 1960, pp. 50, 51, 117, 118.
[3] Evelyn Millis Duvall and Reuben Hill, *Being Married* (Boston: D. C. Heath and Company, 1960), Chapter 9, "Your Wedding Plans," pp. 171–191.

DEVELOPMENTAL TASKS OF FAMILIES AS LAUNCHING CENTERS

The popular stereotype has the family playing a passive role as its young adults leave home for lives of their own. Like Horatio Alger, the youth is seen striding from the door darkened by the figure of his weeping mother, to go into the world and make his fortune. In reality, most families today, as they always have, play active roles over a considerable period of time in getting their young people successfully launched into the world.[1]

While the first child is at work getting established as an autonomous young adult there probably are one or more younger children still in the family, each with his or her own developmental tasks to accomplish. So, the family's tasks are not only in assisting the young adult to become successfully autonomous, but also in maintaining a home base in which the other members of the family can thrive.

Family developmental tasks at the launching center stage are:

1) Rearranging physical facilities and resources
2) Meeting the costs as launching center families
3) Reallocating responsibilities among grown and growing children
4) Coming to terms with themselves as husband and wife
5) Maintaining open systems of communication within the family and between the family and others
6) Widening the family circle through release of young adult children and recruitment of new members by marriage
7) Reconciling conflicting loyalties and philosophies of life

REARRANGING PHYSICAL FACILITIES AND RESOURCES

These are the accordion years of family life. The young adult's room lies empty through the college year, or while he is away for service, only to suddenly become swollen over a holiday or through a leave, with the young person and his or her friends swooping in for a few days and nights. The family goes along on an even keel for some weeks, and then must mobilize itself and all of its resources for a wedding, or a graduation, or both, that keeps the household humming and house bulging at the seams.

The physical plant is sorely taxed at this stage. The family car that Dad uses to get to work and that is needed for the weekly shopping, is

[1] Marvin B. Sussman and Lee Burchinal, "Parental Aid: Prospects and Implications for Family Theory," mimeographed materials, September 1961.

in constant demand by the young man or woman of the family with engagements far and wide looming large in importance during the launching stage. Teenage siblings clamor for their share of the use of the car, the telephone, the TV set, and the living room, until, as one harassed father described it, "This is the stage of life when a man is dispossessed in his own home." A mother comments somewhat ruefully that she doesn't mind the noise and the expense of young people in the home, but she will be glad to regain the use of her own living room when the courting couples have finally found homes of their own. Few families complain when facilities are sorely taxed at this stage of family living, but the fact remains that for many, the flexible rearrangement of available resources to meet the variety of functions within families at the launching center stage, is a task indeed.

MEETING THE COSTS AS LAUNCHING CENTER FAMILIES

With some exceptions, families at this stage are at the peak load of family expenses. These are the years when the young adult needs financial help to carry him or her through college or other educational plans, to get specialized training and experience, to get established in the "starvation period" of any of the professions, to pay union initiation fees and dues as workers, to finance the wedding, and the new home-in-the-making. Such costs are over and above the already established expenditures budgeted for the family. Many young people today help earn what they can as young adults always have, but few are in a position to contribute heavily to the family budget at the very time that they are establishing themselves independently.

Chart 14 clearly indicates that family expenditures are highest when the oldest child is about nineteen, in families of one, two or three children. Costs mount until this period and rapidly decline as the children are launched. Only the family with no children escapes this peak load that comes typically twenty to twenty-five years after the parents' marriage.

These are the years when a man is glad he is near the peak of his earnings (Chapter Eight, Chart 13); but even so, some supplementation may be necessary to carry the additional expenditures that go with launching center functions. The husband may do overtime as a laboring man, or get a summer job as a teacher, or a part-time job around the edges of his regular position whatever he does. His wife now is possibly

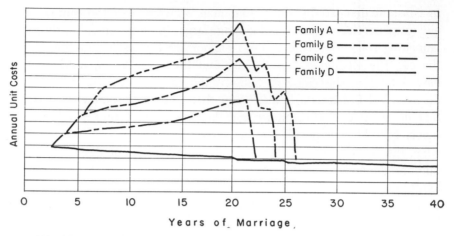

CHART 14. Relative Annual Cost of Supporting Four Families for Forty Years [1]

"Family A consists of a husband and wife who bring up three children, a boy born at the end of the second year, a girl born at the end of the fourth year, and a boy born at the end of the sixth year of their married life.

"Family B consists of a husband and wife who bring up two children, a boy born at the end of the second year, and a girl born at the end of the fourth year of their married life.

"Family C consists of a husband and wife who bring up one child, a boy born at the end of the second year of their married life.

"Family D has no children."

"It is assumed in each case that the husband and wife were married when he was 25 and she was 23, and that each family supports each of its children for 19 years, providing them with a high school education. On the 19th birthday, each child leaves home and becomes self-supporting."

in the labor force, as 30 per cent of wives 45–65 years of age were in 1955.[2] The young adult and other children in the family possibly have jobs of some kind, on a part-time basis while in school, and full-time after education is completed. These sources of income may not be suf-

---

[1] Howard F. Bigelow, *Family Finance* (Chicago: J. B. Lippincott Company, 1953), p. 333.

[2] United States Bureau of the Census (see details in Chapter Eleven).

Tasks and responsibilities are allocated among the members of the family on the basis of interest, ability, and availability.

ficient to meet such special costs as are involved in an expensive wedding, or college tuition and fees. The family may float a loan or borrow on life insurance or increase the mortgage on the house or tighten its belt wherever it can to meet the current emergencies. Providing for a family at the launching center stage is a task, as few will deny.

REALLOCATING RESPONSIBILITIES AMONG GROWN AND GROW-ING CHILDREN IN THE FAMILY

Young adults and older teenagers thrive with real responsibilities of their own. Now is the time when father and mother can sit back and let the children run their own affairs in many a situation. These are the years when the "smothering Mom" is a liability, and a Dad who is too prone to "snoopervise" is a threat to the autonomy of the young adult. The happy family at the launching center stage is one in which tasks and responsibilities are allocated among the members of the family on the basis of interest, ability and availability.

The successful accomplishment of this task depends upon the flexibility of roles of the two parents as well as the growing abilities of the young adult(s) and younger siblings to assume and carry through effectively the tasks of the household. As young adults begin to take on more real responsibility for their own and for the family's welfare, the parents play the complementary roles of letting go, and standing by with encouragement, reassurance and appreciation.

COMING TO TERMS WITH THEMSELVES AS HUSBAND AND WIFE

Being a parent is not easy at any stage in the child's growth. In many ways being a parent of older youth today is the hardest of all. For parents often vicariously live through all the terrors and threats of emancipation that beset their youth, at the same time that they as people are living through the "crisis of the middle years."

Being middleaged today is a far more powerful business than it used to be in the day of Whistler's mother. Then, a woman in her forties was physically and psychologically ready to retire to her knitting. Today's middleaged woman, thanks to better nutrition, medical services, lightened burdens at home, and shifting feminine roles, still has a "head of steam up" both physiologically and emotionally. She is apt to be vigorous, often feeling better than she has in her whole life. Even menopause, the dread of women in earlier eras, now can be taken in stride (Chapter Thirteen). The woman with nearly grown children has found her strengths and her weaknesses. She has tasted the sweetness of affection and learned to enjoy creative companionship with her husband and children. Husband and wife now more often than they have in years work together on projects and have stimulating exchanges of ideas.[1]

Now, suddenly, before she has quite prepared herself for it, her children are no longer children; they are taking their confidences and their loves outside. Her husband is engrossed in the peak of his business or career. Her house is in order. And she—where does she go from here? What loves can take the place of those so suddenly torn away? What tasks will absorb the energies and the skills that cry for channeling? If she clings to her children she is a "Mom." If her interests in her husband's career become too absorbing she is a "meddler." If she spends her time in a dizzy round of matinees, bridge parties, and beauty parlors, she is a "parasite." If she devotes herself to a quest for her soul through

[1] Harold Feldman, "The Development of the Husband-Wife Relationship," a study supported in part by the National Institute of Mental Health, unpublished data received through personal correspondence, March 24, 1961, used with permission.

devious cults and sundry religions, she is suspect. Her salable skills are at least two decades old where she left them when she married to make her place in her home. These are but a few of the questions the wife must face in her middle years (Chapter Thirteen).

And the man, the middleaged father—what of him? Are the middle years any easier on him than on his wife? Can he more comfortably help his children launch themselves into the shadowy adulthood in which he is to be but a small part? Does he too face tasks as a person that shake him to his very roots, and cry urgently for attention just when his youngsters scare him with their first efforts at "trying their wings?"

There is evidence to indicate that men too face a crisis in the middle years, for the basic problem is the same for men and women alike. Briefly it is this. Throughout their lusty twenties and pushy thirties most American men, driving to "get ahead," fasten their eyes on distant goals and dream hopefully of success. But few reach the top. Even those who do, struggle to maintain and improve their position in the competitive scheme of things where others are always jockeying for more favorable positions. The glamour dies in the struggle, and "success" for too many American men in their forties and fifties is but ashes in the mouth.

The multitude of hard-working fathers who never reach the top must face the realities of their limitations, and accept their lot for what it is, mediocre and bitter though it may be. "I am just a minor guy in a minor rut, living life in a minor key," says one man.

Men are further troubled by signs of diminished masculinity, so ever dear to American males. The slowing up characteristic of the middle-aged father, seen in contrast with the youthful vigor of his growing sons and daughters, is personally threatening to many men. Lessened potency and sexual excitation is too frequently attributed to monogamous monotony. The "dangerous period" for men comes when a man must prove his virility to himself, even with more youthful partners if need be. With the burden of guilt that this carries, is it any wonder that he is too easily upset by his son's girl-troubles or his daughter's involvements? The timing of launching, both for parents and for young adults, today is unfortunate. Two types of crises piled one on top of the other means trouble in many homes.

The question of "how well have we done by our children?" is pertinent. In the dark hours of the night, parents toss with the haunting fear that some how, some way, they might have done a better job with those children who are now beyond their parental ministrations. Parents recognize that the family at the launching stage is being evaluated on its success through its products, the children. Yet the problems of their achieving full adulthood maritally, vocationally, and intellectually are so many and the solutions so few!

Someday we will know more about these things. We will be prepared for the head-on collisions of children and their parents bent on urgent, not-to-be-denied tasks. Today we stumble along doing amazingly well considering all the threats with which we live in these launching center stages.

MAINTAINING OPEN SYSTEMS OF COMMUNICATION WITHIN THE FAMILY AND BETWEEN THE FAMILY AND OTHERS

Being able to get through to each other in the family is especially important during the launching stage. This is the time when the young adult is emerging from his family, and is working through some of the most important and the most complex tasks of his life. The young person who can freely bring his questions and his alternative solutions to his parents as sounding boards can get invaluable help through their perspective, at the same time that the family avoids the hazards of feeling "left behind" or "discarded."

Only an understanding non-judgmental family can hope to keep the confidence of its young adults, busy with the gaining of true autonomy. Families who "make a scene" or create an issue over some youthful blunder lose, at least for the moment, contact with the young person at the very time when the generations may need each other most. This is especially true in the relationships the young adult is establishing outside the family. If the parents are unduly critical of visiting boy friends, a girl often has to make a choice between complying with her parents' wishes or being true to her "heart" and loyal to her friend(s). This is a lot to ask of a young person. Yet, the evidence is that parental disapproval of boys dated has increased appreciably in the last three generations.

Table 27 summarizes data from a study made of young college-trained, married women, their mothers, and their maternal grandmothers, in which a pattern emerges of increasing frequency of disapproval of boys dated, with the youngest generation reporting more disapproval than either the mothers or the grandmothers had known in their time.

TABLE 27. *Parental Approval of Boys Dated in the Early Courtships of Respondents from Three Married Female Generations* [1]

Parental Approval	First (Grandmothers)	Generations Second (Mothers)	Third (Young Wives)
Did not approve	62	91	109
Did approve	104	89	69
Uncertain	25	20	22
Unknown	9	0	0
Total	200	200	200

The reasons for such a significant increase of parental disapproval of the boys a girl dates are a matter of conjecture. One may result from rapid social change in which each generation departs farther from its predecessor than the former had from its parents. A second may be that the increase in social contacts in the larger community brings girls into contact with more boys and young men of whom parents disapprove than was possible in more limited situations characteristic of an earlier day. Still a third possible explanation is that parents had more control over courting couples and dating choices in former times and were therefore more likely to approve the dating partners than today when friends are selected by the young person with little assistance from the family.

Families at the launching center stage walk the tightrope between the pressures from outside the family and the forces of cohesion that integrate the family as a unit. This developmental task is one of the most difficult to achieve satisfactorily. It is competently accomplished if a solid foundation of good parent-child relationships has been established, and if now at the "proving time" the young adults feel that whatever happens, their family is back of them, with faith in their ability to work things through, and willingness to look at any situation, with loving concern.

WIDENING THE FAMILY CIRCLE

With the first marriage of one of the children of the family comes the first experience of sudden expansion of the extended family to include both the new family unit being established, and also with more or less

[1] Marvin R. Koller, "Some Changes in Courtship Behavior in Three Generations of Ohio Women," *American Sociological Review*, Vol. 16, No. 3, June 1951, p. 367.

interaction, the family of the son- or daughter-in-law. The family in its earlier expanding stages took upon itself one child at a time (except in multiple births), and that as a tiny infant. The widening of the family circle at the launching center stage is dramatically different in two major respects: (1) the addition is multiple, consisting of the entire family of in-laws and (2) the additional persons are at varying levels of maturity with a preponderance of adults.

The situation is complicated by the fact that while the young adult of the one family is intimately known within his or her own family, he or she, for awhile, remains an outsider to the young mate's family of orientation. If there is too close a bond between one young adult and his or her parents, it is difficult to establish the new unit with equilibrium, as we see in the following analysis:

Every married couple belongs to three families. They belong first of all to themselves. They are the WE of the new family they are founding together. But, at the same time they belong also to *his* family, and to *hers*. If they are to establish a strong family unit of their own, they must inevitably realign their loyalties to the place where *our* family comes before either *yours* or *mine*.

"This is the elemental triangle of married living. Unless the cohesive force in the new family unit is stronger than that which ties either of the couple to the parental home, the founding family is threatened, as we see in the figures.

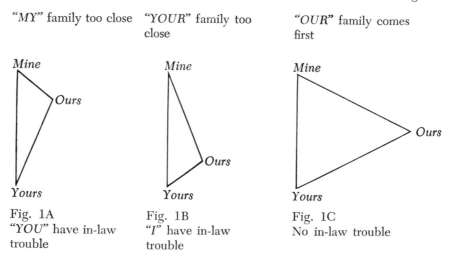

"MY" family too close	"YOUR" family too close	"OUR" family comes first
Fig. 1A	Fig. 1B	Fig. 1C
"YOU" have in-law trouble	"I" have in-law trouble	No in-law trouble

In Figure 1A, "YOU" have in-law trouble because "MY" family is too close. It may be because I am still immature and not ready to emancipate myself from my parental home. It may be that one or more members of my family is possessive and finds it difficult to let me go. It may be that circumstances within my family require from me more loyalty and attention than I can comfortably give at the time that I am involved in building my own home and marriage. Whatever the reason, if the forces pulling me/us toward loyalties to "MY" home are too strong, the development of "OUR" common sense of identity is delayed or weakened.

In Figure 1B, "YOUR" family is too close, and so "I" have in-law trouble. Because "YOU" are bound so tightly to "YOUR" family, I am pulled away from mine, and "WE" make little progress in establishing "OURS."

In Figure 1C, "OUR" family unit comes first in our joint loyalties. We are threatened neither by the ties that bind us to "YOUR" family, nor by the bonds that unite us to "MINE." We are able to make progress as a new family because the force of our common identification pulls us out and away together into a home of our own. Now we can share in the common heritage of both your family and mine because we are not threatened by the pull from either. Only thus are WE free to enjoy being members of the entire extended family, without the stress of in-law strains.[1]

RECONCILING CONFLICTING LOYALTIES AND PHILOSOPHIES OF LIFE

In establishing his autonomy as a young adult, the son or daughter of the family has to question at least some of the premises by which life in his family has been lived. These are the days when many a young person tries out conflicting ways of life in an effort to test his background and catch a glimpse of his potential future. When a young adult is being launched from his home base into a life of his own, it is the one time within his life span when he will be free to pull loose from old allegiances without basic threats and instabilities.

The young man or woman critically reviews his life within his family of orientation and makes comments from time to time that may severely challenge his parents and their ways with him. Ruth Ann startled her parents one night with her observation that she would never make last year's hat do, and look as shabby as her mother in order to let any child of hers go to college. The fact that the family's sacrifice had been for *her* college education was not irrelevant! Junior soberly reflects one night when his father is working late at the office that life is too short to spend couped up on any job; he promises himself that when he gets out into life of his own, he will never knuckle under to any position the way he

[1] Evelyn Millis Duvall, *In-Laws: Pro and Con* (New York: Association Press, 1954), pp. 278 and 279.

has seen his father do through the years. Young Sam, son of a prominent Republican leader, is active in a leftist organization in college. Mary, brought up in a pious home, refuses to continue in church as soon as she gets a job in the mill. Illustrations are nearly as numerous as young people themselves. In one or more ways many young people repudiate their parents and strike out for ways of their own. This is especially true for the mobile youngster whose drive thrusts him upward in social climbing, or whose resistance pushes him downward in the social scale.

Many young adults from conforming homes rather unquestioningly follow through the life style established by their parents. But even the most stable are in some ways different from their parents, if only that they are emerging as young adults into a different world than that in which their parents established themselves. In times of social change there are inevitable shifts in ways of life from one generation to the next, so that the task of reconciling differences between the generations becomes almost universal.

Some young people get into trouble as they push out into strange new ways. Queenie in Noel Coward's *This Happy Breed,* runs off with a married man, is deserted, tries to make a go of running a teashop in Southern France, and finally is brought back home to a reconciliation by a loyal lover who grew up next door. Not all youthful mistakes are as critical. Not all turn out so well in the end. But in some way or other most young people blunder as they try their wings and attempt to fly off into life on their own. Parents who are patient while these efforts are being made are of far more help than those who stand by clucking their fears as the fledgling leaves the nest. Families who stand by with assurance and encouragement, giving help as needed, especially in any of life's firsts (first formal party, first job, first trip away from home, and the rest), give their young people the stable home base that is needed for a successful launching.

While the young adults are gaining strength to live independently, and showing by their words and actions that their lives are not going to be complete carbon copies of their parents, the younger children in the family may be torn by the obvious conflicts between their parents and their older siblings. It is normal for younger children in the family to value highly the attitudes and judgments of their older brothers and sisters. During World War II when large numbers of young men left for military service, there was a sudden upsurge of juvenile delinquency among the next younger teenage boys. Two explanations were given, one that they felt unneeded in the sense that their older brothers were needed, and secondly, that their models of behavior in showing what a young man is and does were no longer at home to keep them in line. Very possibly there were other factors operating too. But the influence of older young people on the lives of their younger brothers and sisters is not to be denied.

Families that keep a secure home base for the younger members of the family during the launching center stage are those that attempt to accept comfortably the way of life the young adult has chosen. They do not feel too threatened by it. They help the younger siblings see that there are many good ways to live a life, and that when his time comes, he too will find his way for himself.

In a democratic society, in a democratic home, such a course is not hard to follow. Difficulties come in the autocratic, rigid ways in which little latitude is allowed, and where all must follow the one path already established by the dictator of the family.

SUMMARY

Families enter the launching center stage as the first child leaves home as a young adult. The stage ends as the last child departs leaving the parents in their empty nest. The stage may be short or long; typically it lasts from six to seven years. Developmental tasks of young adults in the United States include the following: choosing a vocation, getting an education, satisfying military service requirements, becoming marriageable, learning to appraise and to express love feelings appropriately, choosing a marriage partner, getting engaged, and being married. The developmental tasks of families as launching centers include: meeting costs as launching center families, reallocating responsibilities among grown and growing children in the family, coming to terms with themselves and with each other as husband and wife amid the threats of the launching period, maintaining open systems of communication within the family and between the family and others, widening the family circle to include the new relatives by marriage within the extended family, and reconciling conflicting loyalties and philosophies of life.

This is a period full of teachable moments for the young adult and for all those who live with and love him. New possibilities, new problems, and new ways bring new tasks for the young person to accomplish. He is helped to achieve his developmental tasks as a young adult by family members who have confidence in him and who encourage him to become an autonomous person in his own right. He may find especially meaningful the courses, counseling, and guidance offered in many communities to assist the young adult in one or more of his growth responsibilities.

Parents at this stage are breaking the patterns and habits of two decades, as they let their children go. Never again will the relationship between themselves and their offspring be quite the same. Fathers and mothers who successfully launch their children into the world are usually those whose emotional lives do not depend upon the continuing dependence of their children. This is the time when their ways of life are being challenged by their own flesh and blood. This is either a threat or a challenge depending upon their basic security in a democratic acceptance of difference.

SUGGESTED ACTIVITIES

1) Review Jan de Hartog, *The Fourposter* (New York: Random House, 1952), Act Three, Scene 1, pp. 89–104. Then, chart the indicated developmental tasks of both Agnes and Michael, as they meet the crisis of the marriage of their daughter, by listing the revealing phrases (quotes) in the left hand column, and the developmental task implied on the right hand column of your paper. Interpret and summarize.

2) Compare the launching of a conforming son as revealed in the character of young Apley in John P. Marquand's *The Late George Apley* (Boston: Little, Brown and Company, 1937), with the mobile climber depicted in the character of Sammy in Budd Schulberg's *What Makes Sammy Run?* (New York: Bantam Books, 1945). Indicate in what significant ways the two patterns differ, and how the various developmental tasks of young adulthood are accomplished by the young men.

3) Review Edward Strecker, *Their Mother's Sons* (Philadelphia: Lippincott, 1946) and Phillip Wylie, *Generation of Vipers* (New York: Rinehart, 1942) with special reference to the theory of "momism." Write a paper on possible explanations for the phenomenon of "momism" in contemporary American culture.

4) Review Edward Streeter, *Father of the Bride* (New York: Simon and Schuster, Inc., 1948), looking especially for the hazards a father faces in letting his daughter go in marriage. Write a paper outlining ways of minimizing these hazards in making wedding plans.

5) Poll the class on the question, "Is it wise to get as much education as is possible before going into service or getting married?" Tabulate replies and document with verbatim statements of the various positions taken. Discuss in terms of what you know about the multiple developmental tasks young adults face today.

6) Write an autobiography outlining specifically the factors in your life history that played some direct or indirect part in your choice of a vocation. Consider such factors as the social class placement of your family, your mobility drives, your sex, your identification with some significant adult, vocational guidance and tests you have had, as well as other factors that are relevant.

7) Visit a class in personality development in your local YMCA, YWCA, church or other community group, and observe what is being done to help young adults become more marriageable in your area. Write a report of your findings.

8) Write a paper on how much parents should try to influence the choice of a life mate. Give illustrations of parents who have tried to exert too much influence and those who have seemed not to care enough about the choice of their child's life partner. Show possible consequences of each extreme.

9) Chart the pros and cons of parental subsidy in the marriage of their young adult children. Summarize with a documented paper showing why you have placed the items mentioned where you did.

10) Debate the proposition that there are more intrafamily conflicts at the launching center stage of the family life cycle than at any other period.

11) Discuss one or more of the following situations adapted from case excerpts developed as class discussion stimuli by Dr. Hazel Ingersoll, Department of Home Life, Oklahoma A&M College, Stillwater, Oklahoma:

a) Jack and Martha came from different home backgrounds and from different parts of the country. Martha's parents had hoped she would marry a western boy. Jack wants Martha's parents to accept him and his New England ways; Martha wants to please his parents as well. During the engagement period they plan to spend their vacations in each others' homes. How will they go about really getting to know and understand the early childhood experiences of each other? How can they use this interest in each other's background to further their relationships with their prospective in-laws? How can they come to understand and appreciate the differences in their upbringing? In what ways will these explorations facilitate their marriage adjustment?

b) Judy and her widowed mother have always been very close. Now Judy's mother thinks John is taking Judy away from her. Her whole life has been wrapped up in Judy. She is encouraging Judy to delay marriage and to go on with her career. She says, "We've worked and sacrificed so much for your education. Now you are giving up everything to marry this stranger!" John feels he is unwanted, so he has avoided Judy's mother as much as possible. Judy's mother cries and becomes ill when Judy talks about marriage, and because Judy can't bear to hurt her mother, she is considering asking her to live with John and her. John objects. What is the real problem here? What might Judy do? John? Judy's mother? Judy and John as a couple? What developmental tasks does each individual face in this situation?

c) Al's parents had his life all planned. He was to devote his life to medicine as his grandfather had done. After completing medical training they envisaged him married to one of his own set and settled nearby. But Al, aware that he must soon enter military service, married Louise, a classmate, a girl his parents had never met. Louise had planned to finish school (one year more) and then work. But she became pregnant. Al, wanting her to have good care, asked his parents to take her in until his return. Louise objects because she feels the parents-in-law will treat her like a child and try to run her life. What developmental tasks are inherent in this situation for Louise, for Al, and for his parents? What difficulties may arise in the young couple's efforts to launch themselves as a separate family unit? What possible outcomes are there to the problem situation? Which course will best assure the various members and the two family units of achieving their developmental tasks?

d) Mary Ann's father "dotes" on her and thinks no man could ever be good enough for his daughter. Mary Ann, an only child, is very devoted to her father, so much so that she has chosen a man who is very much like him. Bill, her fiancé, resents the affection and attention Mary Ann gives her father; and the father wastes no words in his criticism of Bill. The father is accustomed to taking Mary Ann with him to games, etc. Now Mary Ann wants to go with Bill, or wants her Dad to include Bill. But the tension between the men makes her uncomfortable. What is the source of Mary Ann's difficulty? What developmental task(s) is she struggling with? What can be done to better the relationship, by each of the three persons?

e) Beverly is a city girl who is engaged to Tom, a student in the College of Agriculture, who is going back to the ranch in partnership with his father. Beverly does not know anything about being the wife of a rancher. How best can she learn her new roles on the ranch? What may be involved in her relationship with her prospective mother-in-law who is an experienced rancher's wife? What hazards and challenges, what resources and advantages do both of the young people face in the accomplishment of their developmental tasks in the months ahead?

READINGS

Blood, Robert O., Jr., *Anticipating Your Marriage* (Glencoe, Illinois: The Free Press, 1955).

Burgess, Ernest W., and Wallin, Paul, *Engagement and Marriage* (Philadelphia: J. B. Lippincott Company, 1953).

Cavan, Ruth Shonle, *American Marriage: A Way of Life* (New York: Thomas Y. Crowell Company, 1959).

Christensen, Harold T., *Marriage Analysis* (New York: The Ronald Press Company, 1958).

Christensen, Harold T., and Swihart, Marilynn M., "Postgraduation Role Preferences of Senior Women in College," *Marriage and Family Living*, Vol. XVIII, No. 1, February 1956, pp. 52–57.

David, Opal D., ed., *The Education of Women—Signs for the Future* (Washington, D. C.: American Council on Education, 1959).

Duvall, Evelyn Millis, and Hill, Reuben, *Being Married* (Boston: D. C. Heath and Company, 1960).

Duvall, Evelyn Millis, *In-Laws: Pro and Con* (New York: Association Press, 1954).

Duvall, Evelyn M., and Sylvanus M., eds., *Sex Ways—In Fact and Faith* (New York: Association Press, 1961).

Duvall, Sylvanus M., *Before You Marry* (New York: Association Press, Revised Edition, 1960).

Duvall, Sylvanus M., *Men, Women and Morals* (New York: Association Press, 1952).

Ehrmann, Winston, *Premarital Dating Behavior* (New York: Henry Holt & Company, 1959).

Goldsen, Rose K., Rosenberg, Morris, Williams, Robin M., Jr., and Suchman, Edward A., *What College Students Think* (Princeton, N. J.: D. Van Nostrand Company, 1960).

Havighurst, Robert J.; Bowman, Paul; Liddle, Gordon; Matthews, Charles; and Pierce, James, *Growing Up in River City* (New York: John Wiley & Sons, 1961), Chaps. 8, 9, 10.

Hurlock, Elizabeth B., *Developmental Psychology* (New York: McGraw-Hill Book Company, Second Edition, 1959), Chaps. 10, 11.

Johannis, Theodore B., Jr., "Married College Students and Their Honeymoon," *The Coordinator*, Vol. VII, No. 3, March 1959, pp. 39–40.

Kirkendall, Lester A., *Premarital Intercourse and Interpersonal Relationships* (New York: The Julian Press, 1961).

Kirkpatrick, Clifford, *The Family as Process and Institution* (New York: The Ronald Press, 1955), Chaps. 13–18.

Landis, Judson T., and Mary G., *Building a Successful Marriage* (New York: Prentice-Hall, Inc., Third Edition, 1958).

Lantz, Herman R., and Snyder, Eloise C., *Marriage, an Examination of the Man-Woman Relationship* (New York: John Wiley & Sons, 1962), Chapters 5 and 6, "Love in the Man-Woman Relationship;" and Chapter 8, "Necking, Petting, and Premarital Sexual Intercourse."

LeMasters, E. E., *Modern Courtship and Marriage* (New York: The Macmillan Company, 1957).

Locke, Harvey J., *Predicting Adjustment in Marriage: A Comparison of a Divorced and a Happily Married Group* (New York: Holt and Company, 1951).

Martinson, Floyd M., *Marriage and the American Ideal* (New York: Dodd, Mead & Company, 1960), Part 2.

McKee, John P., and Sherriffs, Alex C., "Men's and Women's Beliefs, Ideals, and Self-Concepts," *American Journal of Sociology*, Vol. LXIV, No. 4, January 1959, pp. 356–363.

Mudd, Emily Hartshorne, *Man and Wife* (New York: W. W. Norton & Company, 1957).

Reiss, Ira L., *Premarital Sexual Standards in America* (Glencoe, Illinois: The Free Press, 1960).

Sussman, Marvin B., "The Help Pattern in the Middle Class Family," *American Sociological Review*, Vol. 18, No. 1, February 1953, pp. 22–28.

Teacher-Leader Packet for Users of the E. C. Brown Trust Film, *Early Marriage* (Portland, Oregon: E. C. Brown Trust, 1960).

Thomas, John L., *The American Catholic Family* (Englewood Cliffs, N. J.: Prentice-Hall, Inc., 1956).

Woods, Sister Frances Jerome, *The American Family System* (New York: Harper & Brothers, 1959), Chapter 10, "The Contracting Family."

Sing a song of seasons!
  Something bright in all!
Flowers in the summer,
  Fires in the fall.
      ROBERT LOUIS STEVENSON

CHAPTER THIRTEEN

Families in the middle years

The family life cycle stage of the middle years starts with the departure of the last child from the home and continues to the retirement of the husband or the death of one of the spouses. This may be a period of only a few months or years as in the case of a late launching of a son or daughter, or an early retirement of the man of the house. The stage may abruptly stop with the premature death of either husband or wife. It may be delayed indefinitely by a dependent child who stays on at home.

Typically in the latter half of the Twentieth Century, the period of the middle years lasts longer than any stage in the family life cycle that a couple has had since their marriage. Up to the turn of the century, the likelihood was that a woman was widowed before her last child left home; or the mother may have died before seeing the first of her children married. Now the married couple have an average of fourteen years together between the departure of their last child and the death of the first spouse (Chart 1, page 13, and Chart 15, page 390).

The period of the middle years is new to this century for several reasons. Fewer children, spaced early in the marriage give the parents an early release from child bearing and rearing. Medical advances postpone the time when death of the husband or the wife breaks the marital bond. More adults live out their life span in good health now than previously could be expected. So, nowadays, most married pairs can expect a "breathing spell" between the busy years of childrearing and the aging years when retirement, decreased physical vitality, reduced social

Median Age of Wife

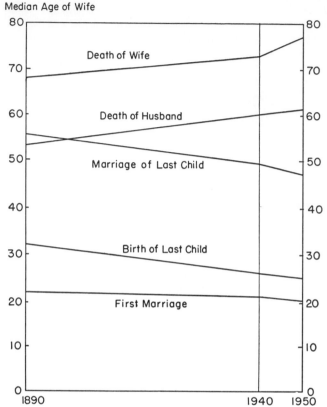

CHART 15.   Stages of the Life Cycle of the Family in the United States: 1890, 1940, and 1950.[1]

life, and finally the death of first one and then the other of the pair must be anticipated.

The husband and wife are usually in their early fifties when they enter the postparental phase of the middle years, and somewhere near their mid-sixties when the man's retirement takes them into the final stage of the family life cycle. Throughout the middle years the married couple alone constitute the nuclear family, maintaining their husband-wife interaction as the central interpersonal relationship. Now each member occupies several positions with multiple roles in the family: husband, father, father-in-law, and grandfather; and wife, mother, mother-in-law, and grandmother, each of which has its complex developmental tasks.

[1] Paul C. Glick, "The Life Cycle of the Family," *Marriage and Family Living,* Vol. 17, No. 1, February, 1955, p. 4, Figure 1.

The crisis of this period is essentially that of accepting responsibility for life as mature adults, without which there is dispair, disappointment and disgust in the later years of life.

The departure of the grown children from the home to establish their independence is a turning point for the family. In American life, mothers and fathers are expected to observe a hands-off policy toward their married children. The daily stream of thought, activities, tenderness and love that once flowed from parents to children now must be diverted into other channels in order to allow the young married couple the opportunity to establish their own new family life.

Ever since MacIver dubbed this "the stage of the empty nest,"[1] it often has been discussed in terms of abandonment, when the middle-aged parents after devoting their lives to their children now are deserted, and thereafter find life bleak and barren. Recent evidence from the Kansas City Studies of Adult Life, find that there is a dip in over-all adjustment among 50–55-year-old adults that resembles what is popularly known as "middleage depression." Not systematically associated with the sexual climacteric, or otherwise simply explained, there is a temporary period of poor adjustment in the lives of many otherwise normal men and women in their fifties.[2]

Rather than society withdrawing from the middleaged and aging person, it has been suggested that the individual goes through a process of disengagement between himself and society. Data from a panel of healthy adults between the ages of 50 and 70 within the Kansas City longitudinal studies point toward a perception of constriction even before life space actually decreases, following retirement. A person is seen as going through a process of mutual withdrawal in which disengagement begins in the sixth decade with a shift in self-perception, accompanied by a constriction in the variety of interactions, to be followed by a reduction in the amount of time spent in the company of others, eventually resulting in a self-centered and idiosyncratic style of behavior among the aged.[3]

[1] R. M. MacIver, *Society, A Textbook of Sociology* (New York: Rinehart, 1937), pp. 199 ff.

[2] Robert F. Peck, *What Is Normal?* (Austin, Texas: The Hogg Foundation for Mental Health, 1961), p. 4; and "Measuring the Mental Health of Normal Adults," *Genetic Psychology Monographs*, Vol. 60, 1959, pp. 197–255.

[3] Elaine Cumming, Lois R. Dean, David Newell, and Isabel McCaffrey, "Disengagement—A Tentative Theory of Aging," *Sociometry*, Vol. 23, No. 1, March 1960, pp. 23–35.

These are the years when a couple can tour the countryside, take a trip to faraway places, and enjoy their freedom for a weekend or a season.

Reactions to the middle years of life after the children have been launched vary. A Washington State University study [1] appears to corroborate the disengagement theory when it finds that mothers whose last child has left home participate less in community activities and are significantly more lonely at the empty nest stage than they were before. At the same time Axelson finds no significant difference in the degree of satisfaction in seven basic areas of life as mothers and fathers move into the postparental period. Their financial worries and concern for the children now decrease significantly, while satisfaction with their marital adjustment and the activities they share with each other increase as their children marry and leave home.

Some middleaged husbands and wives go in for a variety of self-enriching pursuits that range all the way from refurbishing the home,

[1] Leland J. Axelson, "Personal Adjustment in the Postparental Period," *Marriage and Family Living*, Vol. XXII, No. 1, February 1960, pp. 66–68.

renewing their formal and informal educational pursuits, to taking extended trips together to faraway places.

The empty nest is not as empty for some as it is for others. It can fill up with grandchildren, as one grandfather in his early fifties observes, "What's all this about the empty nest? The old nest here is bursting at the seams with five wonderful grandchildren and two sons-in-law extra —all besides the two daughters who used to roost with us!" It can be a time of fulfillment in which for the first time in a woman's life she is free to live on her own terms. For the first twenty years she did what her parents wanted her to do. For the next twenty-five years she did what her children wanted her to do. Now she and her husband are free to do what they want to do—if they can achieve the developmental tasks of this stage.

DEVELOPMENTAL TASKS OF MIDDLEAGED ADULTS

Failure to accomplish the developmental tasks of any stage in life leads to unhappiness and difficulty with later tasks, while success leads to satisfaction at the time and greater ease with future tasks. The middleaged adults who are lonely and depressed may well be having more difficulty achieving their developmental tasks than are those whose satisfaction with life continues after the children have departed. One aspect of the Kansas City Studies of Adult Life finds social class differences in the ways men and women take the middle years of life. The upper lower-class man or woman views the years between 40 and 60 as decline in which he or she is "slowing down," "a has-been." The upper middle-class man sees the middle years as the period of his greatest productivity and major rewards, the "prime of life." The upper status woman feels the loss of her children from the home, but also a sense of mellowness and serenity when "You enjoy life—you're comfortable with yourself and the world—you're no longer *adjusting* as you were before." [1]

Intensive research over the past decade has been fruitful in describing the patterns followed by men and women in various walks of life as they enter, pass through and leave the period of the middle years. The relative success or failure of men and women in the middle years of life is best appraised, as at younger stages in the life cycle, by their achievement of the developmental tasks as middleaged adults, outlined as:

[1] Bernice L. Neugarten and Warren A. Peterson, "A Study of the American Age-Grade System," *Proceedings of the Fourth Congress of the International Association of Gerontology*, Merano, Italy, July 14–19, 1957, Vol. 3, Sociological Division, pp. 497–502.

1. Setting adolescent children free and helping them to become happy and responsible adults.
*1a. As aunt or uncle, serving as model and, on occasion, as parent-substitute for nephews and nieces.
2. Discovering new satisfactions in relations with one's spouse.
*2a. Working out an intimate relationship with brothers and sisters.
3. Working out an affectionate but independent relationship with aging parents.
4. Creating a beautiful and comfortable home.
5. Reaching a peak in one's work career.
6. Achieving mature social and civic responsibility.
7. Accepting and adjusting to physiological changes of middleage.
8. Making an art of friendship.
9. Making a satisfying and creative use of leisure time.
10. Becoming or maintaining oneself as an active club or organization member.
11. Becoming or maintaining oneself as an active church member.

> * Roles which unmarried people may perform more fully than the average person, as a partial substitute for the roles of parent and spouse.[1]

The developmental tasks of middle adulthood have a biological basis in the gradual aging of the physical body; a cultural basis in social pressures and expectations; and a personal origin in the individual life style and self-concept that the mature adult has developed. Personal aspirations are by nature idiosyncratic and highly individual, and therefore difficult to gauge. Social expectations, on the other hand, tend to be general within a given culture and so can be listed and scored. It is possible to appraise an individual's success in his social roles as one measure of his achievement of his developmental tasks as a mature adult.

Basically, the developmental tasks of the middle years may be seen as a complex of social roles. A social role is defined as a pattern of learned behavior, appropriate to a given social status. A social role is developed by an individual as his response to what is expected of him by others, modified by his own perceptions, values, and aspirations.

A man or woman in modern society is expected to fill such social roles as (1) parent, (2) spouse, (3) child of aging parent, (4) homemaker (male or female), (5) worker, (6) user of leisure time, (7) church member, (8) club or association member, (9) citizen, and (10) friend. The

---

[1] Robert J. Havighurst and Betty Orr, *Adult Education and Adult Needs, A Report, Center for the Study of Liberal Education for Adults,* 940 East 58th Street, Chicago 37, Illinois, 1956, p. 9.

quality of a person's life is judged generally by the way he or she fills these roles. When performance approaches the ideal expectations of American society generally, it is rated "high"; when performance is average (4 to 5 on a 0–9 scale) it is rated "medium"; while failure is rated "low." Actual scores on performance in each of ten social roles for men and women in four social classes in the Kansas City study, gives the multi-celled picture seen in Table 28.

TABLE 28. *Performance Scores of Kansas City Adults on the Developmental Tasks of Middleage* [1]

Area	Men (Age 40–70) Social Class *				Women (Age 40–70) Social Class *			
	I	II	III	IV	I	II	III	IV
Parent	6.00	5.50	5.21	3.90	6.44	5.48	5.88	4.84
Spouse	6.00	5.57	4.87	4.13	6.17	5.94	5.46	3.62
Child of Aging Parent	5.89	6.06	5.89	5.00	5.75	5.90	5.94	5.75
Homemaker	5.64	5.70	5.55	4.38	5.93	4.86	5.40	3.68
Worker	7.31	5.67	5.36	3.54	6.25	5.97	4.50	3.61
Leisure	5.97	5.64	4.21	3.50	6.32	5.05	4.33	2.66
Church Member	4.19	3.39	3.19	3.06	4.70	3.57	4.23	4.18
Club and Ass'n	5.55	3.03	2.47	1.89	5.13	2.34	1.91	0.84
Citizen	5.21	4.11	3.64	3.44	4.57	4.01	3.06	3.91
Friend	5.27	4.38	4.02	3.75	6.32	4.59	3.85	2.52

° I—Upper-middle; II—Lower-middle; III Upper lower; IV—Lower-lower (as defined by Warner and other writers on social class in America).

Several observations are of interest in comparing the performance scores on the developmental tasks of middleage (Table 27) by social class, sex, and social role. In general we note that:

a) The higher the social class, the higher the performance score on developmental tasks for both men and women in all social roles.

b) Women tend to get higher scores than do men in such roles as parent and church member; but men do better than women as club and association members and as citizens, generally for all social class levels.

c) Scores range from .84 (lower-class women as club and association members) to 7.31 (upper middle-class men as workers) with more than half (47 out of 80) getting "medium" scores between 4 and 6; 24 out of 80 scoring less than 4 ("low"); and 9 of the 80 scoring over 6 or "high medium."

[1] *Ibid.* p. 32.

COMPLEMENTARY ROLES OF HUSBAND AND WIFE
IN THE MIDDLE YEARS

One student of the roles played by middleaged husbands and wives finds a direct relationship between the complementarity of their roles during the postparental years and their satisfaction with the period. Three-fourths of the husbands and wives interviewed evaluated the postparental phase of the family life cycle as better than or as good as the preceding stages, and only three individuals reported the postparental stage as worse than earlier periods of the marriage.[1]

Complementary roles have been defined as, "interlocking systems in which each unit shapes and directs the other units in the system. This effect is reciprocal; changes in one role cannot be made without corresponding changes in other roles which are involved in it. For example, changes in the role of wife will be accompanied by changes in the role of husband; changes in the role of employer will involve changes in the role of employee. Changes in the role of mother will involve changes in the role of the father and in the role of the child." [2] Following this definition, Deutscher describes six different patterns of complementarity in the Kansas City middle-class panel of middleaged adults that he interviewed: [3]

1) *Reciprocal bolstering*, through appreciation, consideration and standing by with encouragement through crisis.

2) *Mutual activities*, in increased recreational pursuits that both enjoy together.

3) *Relaxing together*, as "joint idlers in a restful paradise of peace and quiet."

4) *Joint participation in husband's occupation*, in which the wife becomes absorbed in helping her husband in his work.

5) *Constructive projects*, in which both members of the couple join forces to fix things up, in one project after another.

6) *Separate interests*, as husband remains absorbed in his work and the wife goes on with what interests she has or can find.

[1] Irwin Deutscher, *Married Life in the Middle Years* (Kansas City, Missouri: Community Studies, Inc., May 1959), Publication 126, page 44.
[2] Eugene L. Hartley and Ruth E. Hartley, *Fundamentals of Social Psychology* (New York: Knopf, 1952), pp. 495–496.
[3] Irwin Deutscher, "Husband-Wife Relations in Middle-Age: An Analysis of Sequential Roles Among the Urban Middle Classes," Unpublished manuscript, Department of Sociology, University of Missouri, July 1954, pp. 122–130.

The self and other role images of both men and women appear to change as they grow older, in two distinctly different patterns. Men, oriented primarily outside the family in their young adulthood, show a gradual decline in affective expressiveness, and a withdrawal from emotional investments as they age. In contrast, as women move through the middle years, they become more self-confident, emotionally more expressive, more expansive and in some ways even dominant over their husbands.

The young woman is a bland figure, lacking in autonomy and symbolizing tenderness, intimacy and sexuality. The more mature woman is the key figure in the family, struggling with problems of retaining and controlling the young, channelling her own needs for self-assertion, with great depths of feeling symbolized by impulsive, egocentric qualities. Women stress the aggressive qualities of the older woman, while men see her either as benignly maternal or as domineering.[1]

DEVELOPMENTAL TASKS OF THE WIFE AND MOTHER IN THE MIDDLE YEARS

1) *Helping grown and growing children to become happy and responsible adults:*

> Setting young adult children free as autonomous persons.
>
> Freeing herself from her emotional dependence upon her children.
>
> Relinquishing her central position in the affection of her grown and growing children, and sharing them freely with their husbands, wives and friends.
>
> Standing by with assistance as needed, without hovering and smothering.
>
> Withdrawing from active motherhood roles and diffusing nurturance drives into wider areas of mothering (through community service, interest in children and young people generally).
>
> Accepting her young adult sons and daughters and their husbands, wives, and children as dear friends whose independence is respected and promoted.
>
> Enjoying her grandchildren without intruding and meddling.

2) *Discovering and developing new satisfactions as a wife with her husband:*

[1] Bernice L. Neugarten and David L. Gutmann, "Age-Sex Roles and Personality in Middle Age: A Thematic Apperception Study," *Psychological Monographs* Vol. 72, No. 17, 1958, No. 470, pp. 32–33.

Giving her husband the encouragement, reassurance, support and appreciation he needs as a middleaged man.

Enjoying her part in joint activities as a couple again.

Exploring new hobbies, vacation possibilities, friendship groups and community projects they both may enjoy as a pair.

Becoming a desirable and desiring companion.

Plumbing the possibilities of deep and abiding intimacy, in mutual understanding, empathy, and the sense of unity as a couple.

3) *Working out an affectionate and independent relationship with aging parents:*

Helping her own and her husband's parents find wholesome happy ways of living out their sunset years.

Assisting both sets of aging parents find satisfactory supports for their failing powers as needed.

Giving the expressions of interest, affection, and care that aging parents need from their grown children.

Serving as a buffer as need be between the demands of aging parents and the needs of the young adults, emerging in the family.

Weathering the inevitable illnesses, accidents, and eventual death of aging parents in wholesome, supportive ways.

4) *Creating a pleasant, comfortable home for her husband and herself:*

Refurbishing the home for couple-living after the children have grown.

Reworking household facilities and routines for ease and comfort of upkeep.

Investing time, energy and resources in making home a place of enjoyment and comfort according to the interests and values of husband and wife.

Getting satisfactions from achieving proficiency in one or more of her chosen roles.

Sharing the family home at intervals with grown children, grandchildren and friends with satisfaction in hospitality.

Giving, receiving and exchanging hospitality with grown children with mutual interdependence and freedom.

5) *Finding satisfactions in her work if she is an employed woman:*

Becoming more relaxed about the quantity of her work.

Making progress in line with her powers, wisdom, and proficiencies as a woman on the job.

Getting real satisfactions from being of service, being creative, being recognized as competent, and being a pleasant colleague and a growing person.

Balancing the values of her work with those of her homemaking and other roles to avoid strain and grossly unequal devotion to any one.

6) *Achieving mature social and civic responsibility:*

Becoming alert and intelligently informed about civic affairs and her role in them.

Taking an active part in one or more organizations at work on civic and political problems in the neighborhood, community, nation, or world.

Giving time, energy, and resources to causes beyond herself and her home.

Working cooperatively with others in the mutual responsibilities of citizenship.

Committing herself to the democratic ideal in any of its many manifestations.

7) *Accepting and adjusting to the physical changes of middle age in healthful ways:*

Taking menopause in her stride with whatever medical and psychological supports may be needed.

Accepting changes in skin, hair color, body tone, energy output, and physical rhythms without distress.

Eating a well-balanced diet high in proteins, fresh fruits and vegetables.

Keeping her weight within normal limits.

Getting a healthful balance of sleep and exercise.

Going periodically for medical and dental check-ups and following prescribed routines.

Dressing comfortably and attractively to please both herself and others.

Relishing the bloom and pace of maturity as a woman.

8) *Making an art of friendship:*

Cherishing old friends for themselves and the mutual experiences and values that have been built together through the years.

Choosing new friends from among the many interesting new contacts with "our kind of people" as well as novel, refreshing personalities.

Enjoying active social life with friends of both sexes and a variety of ages.

Giving and receiving freely in social interaction with her friends.

Accepting at least a few friends into close sharing of real feelings with intimacy and mutual security.

Becoming an increasingly friendly person who values her friends and her friendships highly.

9) *Using her leisure time creatively and with satisfaction:*

Choosing the interests and activities that she finds most personally rewarding without yielding too much to social pressures and "styles."

Learning to do some things well enough to become known for them among her family, friends and associates.

Losing herself sufficiently in one or more areas of interest so that she gets creative satisfactions from her leisure hours.

Balancing her program of leisure activities with active and passive, collective and solitary, service-motivated and self-indulgent pursuits.

Keeping alive and interested in the world around her and her part in it.

10) *Becoming or maintaining herself as an active club or association member:*

Choosing her affiliations with discrimination.

Assuming real responsibilities in those she considers important.

Refusing conflicting, contradictory or too burdensome invitations with poise.

Getting a sense of pleasure and satisfaction from her affiliations.

Enjoying a sense of belonging with kindred minds and spirits.

Working through her own ways of dealing with intraclub tensions, power systems and personality problems within the membership, comfortably and effectively.

11) *Becoming or maintaining herself as an active church member, as may be socially expected and personally meaningful:*

Finding a soul-satisfying place for herself in a religious affiliation in which she has an abiding faith.

Holding one or more responsible positions within the church.

Gaining personal satisfaction from worship and the rituals, ceremonies, and celebrations of her church.

Contributing her services and her resources to the upkeep of her church.

Serving in ways that help her contribute her best talents to the causes and purposes in which she believes.

Discovering new depths and meanings in the brotherhood of man and the Fatherhood of God that go beyond the fellowship of her particular church.

Any woman who accomplishes all this is quite a woman! No one is expected to score high on every task, now or at any other time of life. Certain social roles that are expected in some communities are not important in others; *i.e.*, church membership. Some tasks will proceed smoothly and well. Others will labor or go by default. In those areas where she builds upon past successes, the middleaged woman will be likely to find happiness and relative success in the tasks of the middle years. In the tasks in which she has had past difficulties, failures or little experience, her accomplishments in the middle years may reflect her inexperience or incompetence.

Some of the developmental tasks of the middle years are particularly difficult for the middleaged woman, partly because she does not relish them. It is an unusual woman who really enjoys relinquishing her active role as mother, to see her children, whom she has loved and cared for for twenty years, pack their suitcases and leave home. A woman's children represent for her, more than they do for her husband, not only an emotional investment of her adulthood until now, but also the main reason for her existence. Throughout her life as wife and mother, her children have been her job. Now, when they leave, she feels that they take with them her very reason for being. Unless she has prepared herself through the years for a life beyond her children, helping them become independent adults is apt to be a highly unpleasant and difficult job for her.

Difficult too, may be the re-establishment of a close companionship with her husband now that the children have grown. If she has been a "devoted mother" she may have put the children first, and her husband in second place in her thoughts and actions through the years. Now it may come as a shock to realize that she hardly knows this man of hers in terms of his deepest hurts and disillusionments, his dreams and aspirations, or even how he really feels about her. She may feel that they have grown apart through the years of childrearing while he had to keep his

Re-establishment of a close relationship with her husband is especially important now that the children have grown and gone.

nose to the grindstone to make ends meet, and she was so everlastingly busy with the thousand and one details of homemaking. She may find life dull and drab in the same old routines with him day after day, and long for a fling that will help her get a taste of LIFE before it is too late, as Fran Dodsworth attempted (Sinclair Lewis, *Dodsworth*, New York: Harcourt Brace and Company, 1929). She may find initial efforts to get close to her husband now peculiarly embarrassing, self-conscious, and hardly worth the effort. But, if she has maintained a real fellowship with her mate as their children were growing up, she does not have as far to go now in re-establishing a meaningful companionship. Husband and wife have learned what to expect of each other. They have already established some personally delightful little whimsicalities as well as a deeply meaningful unity so that further fellowship is a constant discovery and delight.

A third developmental task that tends to be shunned by the middle-aged woman in American culture is that of coming to terms with her age and the processes of aging. There is such a high valuation on youth in society at large, that she fears for her status, her acceptance, her desirability, her very security in the gradual loss of her youth. Now, more than ever, she wants to feel that she is attractive. The appearance of gray hair, wrinkles in her skin, flabbiness in upper arm and abdomen may be frightening reminders that she is no longer the appealing young thing she once was. She may lie about her age and prop up her sagging tissues, with society approving. She may paint on an artificial complexion, with the disapproval of some of her friends and associates. Or she may cultivate the charm of maturity that will see her through for several decades. Marlene Dietrich, Claudette Colbert, Helen Hayes, and countless other women have proven that the years need not rob a woman of the charm of true femininity.

Some developmental tasks of the middleaged wife and mother are highly motivated and relatively pleasantly undertaken. Now, as at other times in the life cycle, there are certain teachable moments that are full of eagerness to learn and grow and achieve. The woman may get a special pleasure in helping her husband rearrange their lives, to "live it up" a little now, when their responsibilities are not as great as they have been and their income is still near its peak. It may be fun to expand their recreational budget to take a trip or build a summer place, or join a club they haven't been able to afford before. Redoing their home as a place they are proud to call their own may become a joyful task, highly motivated, and richly rewarding in ways for all to see.

Becoming a satisfied and satisfying grandmother may be another easy, happy developmental task. In wanting to become worthy of these exciting new roles with these wonderful little people who are indeed her "own flesh and blood," she may take a refresher course in child care, and learn more now than she ever knew about children and child development, her nature as a person, and of life itself.

Difficult or easy, late or soon, every wife and mother faces her new developmental tasks in her own way with the coming of her middle years. She is successful if she finds happiness and satisfaction in this stage of living. As she meets life's challenges now she prepares herself for the aging years that lie ahead. She is all of a piece, building on what has gone before, and laying the foundation now for what still lies ahead.

DEVELOPMENTAL TASKS OF THE HUSBAND AND FATHER IN THE MIDDLE YEARS

1) *Setting young adult children free and helping them become happy, responsible adults:*

Getting along with grown children as friendly equals in most areas of life.

Encouraging grown children to make their own choices of clothes, college, military service, friends, marriage partner, job, etc.

Supporting grown children where necessary, unobtrusively and without any strings attached.

Being an advisor as requested, and an impartial "listener" for young people who are trying to work out their problems.

Expecting grown children to want and need autonomy, privacy and freedom.

Giving and receiving affection and attention from grown children and their families.

Becoming a pleasant, beloved grandfather who finds joy in his grandchildren.

2) *Discovering and developing new satisfactions with his wife:*

Giving his wife the reassurance, the recognition (both in private and in public), the appreciation and the affection she needs as a middleaged woman.

Enjoying being with his wife and participating with her in a variety of shared activities.

Feeling close to his wife with mutual understanding and empathy.

Sharing his work, his thoughts, his feelings and his hopes and disappointments with his wife, and encouraging her to tell him of hers.

Developing mutually satisfying ways of attracting and holding her interest in him as a man, a male, and as a husband.

3) *Working out an affectionate and independent relationship with aging parents:*

Being friendly without too much dominance or dependence in relations with his own and his wife's parents.

Taking responsibility for failing parents as needed in ways that help them maintain their self-respect.

Keeping in touch with the needs, interests, and plans of his parents.

Working through, with the others involved, the best possible living arrangements when parents no longer are able to live by themselves.

Interpreting aging parents and young adult family members to each other as needed.

Giving personal support as illnesses, accidents, and eventual death of one or both parents bring their crises to the bereaved one(s).

4) *Creating a pleasant, comfortable home:*

Taking a real interest in the physical upkeep of the home.

Assuming responsibility for the care of the heavier chores around the house, basement, and yard.

Helping plan for and taking a real interest in decorating the home and keeping it nice.

Enjoying full partnership in planning for the home, its remodeling, redecorating, and ongoing routines.

Taking pride in his and in his wife's accomplishments in making the home a good place to live in as a couple.

Finding pleasure in having grown children home at intervals for celebrations, vacations, and in times of need.

Assuming his share of responsibility for entertaining friends, associates, and members of the extended family.

5) *Working productively and efficiently in his job:*

Liking his work and doing well in it.

Being able to lead and to follow, to give and to take orders comfortably on the job.

Coming to terms with the degree of success that is his without regret or recriminations.

Getting satisfactions on his job from: friendships with associates, feeling of being needed and of service, self-respect and prestige, and feeling of creative productivity.

Taking his work at a more leisurely pace as time goes on, letting established routines and wisdom on the job take the place of earlier over-zealous drive.

Letting younger men take over without threat of lost status, and planning for his eventual retirement constructively.

6) *Achieving mature social and civic responsibility:*

Keeping informed and enjoying discussing civic affairs and national and international problems.

Understanding where he fits into the pressure groups and politics of the society.

Taking active part in some one or more movements for community improvement, civic reform, or national and world conditions.

Encouraging his wife and family to be good citizens.

Standing for democratic practices and the good of the whole in issues where vested interests may be at stake.

7) *Accepting and adjusting to the physical changes of middleage in healthful ways:*

Getting regular medical and dental check-ups and keeping physically fit.

Using the glasses, hearing aid, or other helps prescribed for him as needed.

Eating what is good for him, in healthful quantities, avoiding excesses in rich, caloric foods, and keeping tobacco use and alcohol consumption within reasonable limits.

Getting some physical exercise appropriate to his age, strength, and endurance.

Dressing comfortably and attractively with attention to good grooming and the self-respect of cleanliness, neatness and appropriateness.

Wearing his mature years with poise, without undue concern over such inevitables as balding, graying hair, and lessening vitality.

8) *Making an art of friendship:*

Choosing friends of various ages with mutual interests and ongoing satisfactions.

Enjoying old and new friends of both sexes in a variety of settings, rituals, and functions.

Reciprocating hospitality and finding satisfactions in both roles of host and guest.

Being gracious to his wife's friends and associates, for themselves as well as for his wife's sake.

Sharing feelings intimately with close friends in whose fellowship he feels basically secure.

Considering himself a warm friendly person with others generally.

9) *Making satisfying and creative use of leisure time:*

Welcoming the increased leisure of the middle years as a chance to do all the things he has never had time for before.

Choosing some activities that have personal meaning for him as well as doing some things for fellowship primarily.

Mastering some arts and skills sufficiently to gain recognition and a heightened sense of self-respect and pride from his workmanship.

Losing himself in some of his pursuits so that he is never at a loss for things to do.

Sharing an increasing number of his leisure time activities with his wife.

Keeping alert and alive to the world around him.

10) *Becoming or maintaining himself as an active club or association member:*

Dropping the unrewarding affiliations that may have interested him early in his career but that may be burdensome or boring now.

Attending meetings and assuming responsibility in the associations he considers important.

Finding satisfactions in using his talents and abilities in group activities.

Enjoying fellowship with like-minded people.

Becoming a mature "elder statesman" in diplomatic roles within the relationships of his clubs.

11) *Becoming or maintaining himself as an active church member, as may be socially expected or personally rewarding:*

Coming to terms with what religion and his church mean to him.

Holding responsible positions in his church.

Finding personal satisfactions through the various rituals, activities and programs of the church.

Enjoying the opportunities for service available through the church and its related activities.

Being increasingly willing to lose himself in causes that are bigger than he is, and in movements that go beyond the present.

The husband and father in the middle years finds some of his developmental tasks easier than the parallel tasks his wife is facing. It probably is easier for him, than it is for her, to encourage the autonomy of their children, largely because the children have been her main responsibility, her Number One job through the years of their growing up. It usually is easier for a middleaged man to find ongoing satisfactions in his work than it is for his wife whose employment has probably been secondary to her homemaking responsibilities through the years.

In some areas of life the man in the middle years of the family life cycle may find difficulties greater than those his wife is facing. He may

Grandfatherhood can be a challenging task for a man who does not know what to do with little children.

refuse to recognize his decline in vitality, and brag that he can work and play as vigorously as he did twenty years ago. He may have been so preoccupied with his work through the years of getting established that he has built little foundation for more relaxed living with his wife and family. He may be dismayed in the face of so much leisure now available, and postpone much-needed vacations, or hurry back from those he takes, largely because he has never learned to play. Some men even feel guilty if they "play" since recreation used to be considered wasteful of time rather than re-creative.

After years of tight financing, and trying to make ends meet within the pressures of his growing family, he may find that he has built habits of scrimping and "making do" that now are inappropriate. It may be a struggle for him to cooperate with his wife in making their home pleasant and comfortable. He may seem to be "tight" with their money now when they might be enjoying it in ways that are rightfully theirs. He is likely to be uncertain about how much should be saved for the future and how much could be spent for today's pleasure.

Even grandfatherhood can be a challenging task. During the years when his own children were growing up he may have been so involved outside the home that he never seemed to have the time for close companionship with them that now is possible with his grandchildren. He may not know what to do with little children, and so miss out on some of the joys and satisfactions that otherwise would be his. He can find peculiar pleasure in his grandchildren, and contribute richly to them and to the entire family from the wisdom and richness of his years.

A man is sometimes a better father to his grandchildren than he was able to be to his own children. He is getting older now and the years have passed so swiftly that he is suddenly aware of all that he has missed. He wants to make up for lost time and one way to do it is to enjoy his grandchildren and savor their youth, though he had little inclination for this sort of thing when his own children were small . . .

. . . . .

. . . Grandfather, who has read many men and women in his lifetime. often catches the tremble in the lip or the hangdog look of shame that a busy parent misses beneath the overt defiance. Being a wise man he has relinquished the intense competition of his earlier days, the ceaseless striving to keep up with the Joneses, get ahead of a business rival, or acquire a new-model car every year. He has learned to be content with his lot whatever it may be. He is relaxed enough to have fun with his grandchildren and that is the master recipe for being good friends with children.

A thoughtful, well-seasoned, leisured man in a home where there are young children can be of great service in their well-rounded development. Grandfather has time to mend a broken toy or coax a stubborn one to work. He can read or tell stories. He is not too busy to admire the shape of a pebble a young one discovers on the beach and wonder with him about it—why it is different from all the others, from what far shores the ocean waves washed it, where it got its opalescent gleam.

. . . . .

Children need grandparents who have come to terms with life and accept it philosophically as parents seldom have yet learned or had time to do. When those who are at the beginning of the journey hold hands with those who have travelled a long way and know all the turns in the road, each gains the strength needed by both. They are like the pair who were seen wandering together in the summer over the winding paths of a Maine island in Casco Bay.

"My grandfather takes me everywhere," the small boy told a summer visitor happily.

"He doesn't know it," the white-haired man smiled, "but he's the one who takes *me*. I'm blind, you see." [1]

A man may flee from the new expectations and possibilities of middle-age. He may bury himself blindly in his accustomed work and refuse to anticipate his impending retirement. He may neglect his wife, his grown children, his grandchildren, and his friends. He can deny his own failing strength, and refuse to accept his feelings of regret, frustration, disappointment and panic. He may fail in any or all the developmental tasks of this stage of life, and be miserable in the process, nursing his neurotic symptoms and his grudges until he chucks it all in an early grave soon after retirement. Such failures to meet the challenge of the middle years do happen, but they are not necessary.

A husband and father who is willing to keep on growing can, during his middle years, reap the harvest of good living, that he has sown in earlier years. He can relax and enjoy the fruits of his labors, in the sense of "You Can't Take It with You," or in the spirit of this being "the last of life for which the first was made." He can rediscover the richness of marriage, the satisfactions of fellowship with grown children, the warmth of friendship, the excitement of adventure and novel experience, the rewards of creative productivity. But not one of these automatically "comes due" at this time, without effort on his part. They all are satisfactions that accrue from success in achieving the developmental tasks of this stage of life. When he does a good job in them, he finds the happiness that goes with their successful accomplishment. As long as there is life, there can be growth, and the middle years are no exception.

PROGRESSIVE DISENCHANTMENT AND DISILLUSIONMENT

What has been called "the crisis of the middle years," seems in the light of recent research to be more like a continuation of the process of disenchantment that continues throughout life. Studying men's and women's attitude changes from courtship through engagement into marriage, Hobart found men more quickly disillusioned than women after marriage especially in the more romanticized areas of life. Postmarital disillusionment is especially characteristic in such areas as personal freedom,

---

[1] O. Spurgeon English and Constance J. Foster, *Fathers Are Parents, Too* (New York: G. P. Putnam's Sons, 1951), pp. 260–261, 268–269 and 271.

marital roles, having children, in-law relationships, values on neatness, savings and money, and attitudes toward divorce.[1]

Study of Burgess and Wallin's 1,000 couples investigated from engagement into marriage now continues after they have been married up to 20 years. Between the early and the middle years of marriage two evidences of disenchantment are noted: (1) a general drop in marital satisfaction and adjustment; and (2) a loss of intimacy—less frequent kissing, reciprocal settlement of disagreements, and more loneliness. The marital adjustment score declines more than any other from the early to the middle years of marriage.[2]

There is further evidence that many men and women fail to find happiness in the middle years. A study of the marital happiness and unhappiness of married persons (as rated by their brothers and sisters) reveals the forties and fifties as a difficult period for married women, and the fifties as particularly hard for men.[3] The women's problems revolve around their joblessness as mothers when their children no longer need their services, the decreasing adequacy of their middleaged husbands as sexual partners, and the problems of the menopause. For men, the unhappiness of the middle years tends to center in their occupational problems.

. . . Two groups of men are identified by our informants. One consists of men who have attained some degree of prominence and success in their chosen field, only to find that their wives have not kept pace with them in their upward climb. Such men often make a determined effort to remain loyal to their mates. Some of them are reported as succeeding; others fail and are aware of it; and still others appear to their siblings as failing in spite of outward evidences of success.

A second group of men, identified by their siblings, are in their fifties and have failed, absolutely or relatively, in their occupational efforts. Such failures lead them to rationalizations: they never had a chance to succeed, they say. Their wives were no help to them. If it were not for the handicaps which their wives imposed, they would have succeeded, as did other men. Such wives become scapegoats for the failure of their husbands. The husbands find com-

---

[1] Charles W. Hobart, "Disillusionment in Marriage and Romanticism," *Marriage and Family Living*, Vol. XX, No. 2, May 1958, pp. 156–162.

[2] Peter C. Pineo, "Disenchantment in the Later Years of Marriage," *Marriage and Family Living*, Vol. XXIII, No. 1, February 1961, pp. 3–11.

[3] James H. S. Bossard and Eleanor S. Boll, "Marital Unhappiness in the Life Cycle," *Marriage and Family Living*, Vol. XVII, No. 1, February 1955, pp. 10–14.

fort in the development of feelings of self-pity and animosity toward their wives.[1]

The findings of a study of 8,300 American business leaders and their wives, seem to show that business success depends not so much on whom a man marries, or on what his wife does, as on his talents, energies, and his singleness of purpose.[2] If these findings apply to vocational success generally, then it must be that a great many men unfairly blame their wives for their failures, to the impairment of the marriage relationship. If, at the same time, middleaged women complain about the inadequacies of their husbands as sexual mates, as Bossard and Boll find many of them do, then the probabilities are that the marriage itself is threatened in the middle years.

Happiness in the middle years is an indication of success in one's developmental tasks, and of good adjustment to the process of growing older. For example, a study of parents of university students finds that social participation is associated with life satisfaction among both men and women.[3] Life Satisfaction Rating Scales[4] designed to measure relative success in the middle and later years use five criteria: (1) Zest vs. apathy (enthusiasm of response and degree of ego-involvement), (2) Resolution and fortitude (personal responsibility for one's life), (3) Congruence between desired and achieved goals (feeling of success in accomplishments one feels are important), (4) Self-concept (physical, psychological and social attributes), and (5) Mood tone (spontaneous positively toned affective terms for people and things). Each of these criteria rated on a five-point scale from high to low yield an index of life satisfaction that distinguishes between individuals and between groups. The nonmarried (single, separated, divorced, and widowed men and women) have significantly lower life satisfaction scores than do married, suggesting that disenchantment is less within than outside of marriage.

[1] Bossard and Boll, *op. cit.*, p. 14.

[2] W. Lloyd Warner and James C. Abegglen, "Successful Wives of Successful Executives," *Harvard Business Review*, March–April issue, 1956; also by the same authors, *Business Leaders in America* (New York: Harper & Brothers, 1956).

[3] Arnold M. Rose, "Factors Associated with the Life Satisfaction of Middle-Class, Middle-Aged Persons," *Marriage and Family Living*, Vol. XVII, No. 1, February 1955, pp. 15–19.

[4] Bernice L. Neugarten, Robert J. Havighurst, and Sheldon S. Tobin, "The Measurement of Life Satisfaction," *Journal of Gerontology*, Vol. 16, No. 2, April 1961, pp. 134–143.

FAMILY DEVELOPMENTAL TASKS IN THE MIDDLE YEARS

The middle years in the family are a challenge to more than the individual husband and wife as middleaged adults. This stage has its full complement of family developmental tasks that are necessary for family survival, continuity, and growth. These family developmental tasks can be briefly outlined as follows:

1) Maintaining a pleasant and comfortable home.
2) Assuring security for the later years.
3) Carrying household responsibilities.
4) Drawing closer together as a couple.
5) Maintaining contact with grown children's families.
6) Keeping in touch with brothers' and sisters' families and with aging parents.
7) Participating in community life beyond the family.
8) Reaffirming the values of life that have real meaning.

MAINTAINING A PLEASANT AND COMFORTABLE HOME

Most couples own their own homes by the time the last child is launched. Indeed, home ownership is more likely now than at any other stage in the family life cycle: 37.3 per cent of the young married, 52.5 per cent of young couples with youngest child under six, 66.7 per cent of young marrieds with youngest child six or older, 69.9 per cent of older married with children, and 71.4 per cent of those whose children have been launched.[1] The chances are nine out of ten that the middleaged couple stay on in the family home after their children have grown and gone.[2]

Reasons for remaining in the family home are several. The most powerful is probably the sense that this *is* home to husband and wife. Here their habits are built into the place. Here are their friends, neighbors, and the familiar ways of life that perhaps mean much to both of the couple. The husband still is on the job and he is accustomed to going and coming from this place. The children come home for special celebra-

---

[1] John B. Lansing and Leslie Kish, "Family Life Cycle as an Independent Variable," *American Sociological Review*, Vol. 22, No. 5, October 1957, pp. 512–519.

[2] Paul C. Glick, "The Life Cycle of the Family," *Marriage and Family Living*, Vol. XVII, No. 1, February 1955, Table 2, page 7. (The 10.3 per cent of husbands moving in the middle years compares with 55.8 per cent of husbands under 25 years of age, 32.9 per cent of husbands 25–34 years of age, and 18.2 per cent of husbands 35–44 years old who change their place of residence.)

A man may wish he had saved enough during the peak years of childrearing to feel secure in the middle and later years of life.

tention: (1) learning to spend money for personal gratification after years of self-sacrifice and thinking first of the children and their needs, and (2) planning for a secure old age.

Planning financially for the later years is highly motivated during middleage. Few parents want to be beholden to their grown children for support during their own old age. They realize that neither Social Security nor Old Age Assistance will keep them on anything more than a subsistence level. They may not have accumulated enough during the peak years of childrearing to make them feel as adequately prepared for the uncertainties of their later years as they would like. And so they continue the pattern of putting their money away for a rainy day that has been established through their earlier years in the family. National analyses of saving by age groups indicate that middleage families tend to be the biggest savers, and to place more emphasis on building up a reserve than any other age group.[1]

Planning for old age should include recognition of the fact that the average age at which men die is lower than the average age at which women die. In the older age groups, there are many more widows than widowers. In fact, after age 70 there are more widows than women living with husbands. Men need to provide not only for their own support in old age, but for the support of their widows. This is more than a matter of stocks and bonds and life insurance. It means helping prepare the wife to fend for herself if and when she is left alone.

Few happily married women want to think of widowhood as a personal possibility. Yet, when one or more of their husband's friends or associates drop off in the prime of life, they begin to realize the importance of preparing for what may become inevitable for them too one day. Several steps in preparing for widowhood are indicated: (1) Find one or more close confidants besides the husband. A good woman friend will do. An understanding lawyer-friend, a sensitive pastor, or an old-friend-of-the-family may be tapped to serve as counsel and confidential ear when widowhood comes. (2) Make sure that both husband and wife know the full state of their financial affairs. The older pattern of the husband carrying the full responsibility for the money matters in the marriage meant that many mature women were as babes in the woods when their husbands died. They were easy prey for charlatans and sundry "widows' rackets." Today's couples more often share responsibility for financial planning through the years and so leave the widow better prepared to carry on when she is left in charge. (3) Encourage one or more absorbing interests in life that keep pulling toward the future. A crocheted afghan is a start, but it is not enough for most women. Active work in the community gives her something to grow on and into. A job outside the home may do it. Whatever it is, a woman in the middle years must have something to live *for* as well as to live *on*. If it can be both, she is doubly protected.

If the middleaged wife works, as do nearly a third of the married women 45–54 years of age,[2] the increased family income may be welcome

---

[1] Dorothy A. Brady and Marsha Froeder, "Influence of Age on Saving and Spending Patterns," *Monthly Labor Review*, Vol. 78, No. 11, November 1955, pp. 1240–1244.

[2] Paul C. Glick, *op. cit.*, p. 7.

A woman for whom widowhood is a personal possibility must have something to live *for* as well as on. Hobbies and interests such as gardening can continue to bring a sense of being creatively worthwhile.

for future security planning as well as for luxuries and pleasures. A combined income now may make it possible for the couple to buy a nice home, or fix up the old one, or take a long-dreamed-of trip abroad, spend a winter holiday in a southern clime, or budget more lavishly for their clothes and personal grooming than was possible before now. Some husbands are secure enough as males not to be threatened by their wives' earning power, enjoying the economic partnership involved in team earning, shared planning, and joint spending.

Learning to "live it up" may be more difficult a task in the middle years than is planning for the future. When two people have been future-oriented throughout their whole life together as a pair, it is not easy to suddenly shift into spending for present pleasures. Getting away for an occasional holiday while the children were growing up has prepared some couples for their freedom in the middle years. Spending something for immediate fun and pleasure through the years, even when the going has been rough, gives some basis for relaxing and just enjoying life now. Even finding pleasure in freedom and in enjoying life has to be learned, as many a lonely middleaged or older person discovers. This is the nature of developmental tasks, built on the past, pointed toward the future at every stage of the life cycle.

CARRYING HOUSEHOLD RESPONSIBILITIES LIGHTLY AND TOGETHER

Typically, the middleaged couple has no one but themselves to worry about in the daily routines of living. The grown children are in homes of their own; aging parents are being cared for independently; and the husband and wife are alone in the home, free to plan their daily routines as they will, without others' schedules to burden them.

Occasionally a married son or daughter will return home for a few weeks or months through a stint in military service, or for special training, or during an illness. Then the old place is crowded as two families try to live as one, getting into each other's way, and having to work out new ways of doing old chores.

There may be times when the only way to care adequately for aging parents is to bring the dependent one into the home. Then husband and wife divide the care of the aging or invalid one as best they can, so that no one gets completely unnecessarily tied down. If the old person is bedridden, the burden may be heavy indeed, perhaps for a long period of time. If the elderly one is able to care for herself (or for himself as is less

A middleaged couple can enjoy much more social life and joint participation outside the home than has been possible before.

our house last year, and Mr. Baxter changed his position the first of the year. I don't feel it would have been possible if the children were still living at home." [1]

More than ever before the couple in the middle years of the family life cycle can contribute to community life and general welfare. These

[1] *Ibid.*, p. 340.

are the years when a woman is free to take an active part in some community project in which she has become concerned. While her children were small she did well to get to the parent-teacher meetings in their school. Now she may attend state and national meetings, she may hold a responsible office, she may go to the state capital to plea for a worthy piece of legislation. At the same time the middleaged man is taking on more responsible positions in his club, organization, or union.

The Kansas City Study of Adult Life finds that middleaged middle-class men and women may be successfully active in the community, or home-centered. The working-class middleaged are rarely community-centered, and tend to spend most of their leisure around home, or "with the boys" (lower-lower class).[1]

Success in participation within the community in the middle years is dependent on the foundations laid for it in the earlier years of marriage. As the family has tied into projects and purposes beyond its own immediate interests through the years, it has laid the track upon which may run the trains of accomplishment in the middle and later years. Some novel new activities are possible for the middleaged couple. But the likelihood is that the man and woman in their middle years continue on with extensions of their previous interests and activities. So too, the things they do now ready them for better or for worse in their sunset years that lie ahead.

REAFFIRMING THE VALUES OF LIFE THAT HAVE REAL MEANING—A SUMMATION

The couple's philosophy of life is being reaffirmed in everything they do toward the accomplishment of all the other developmental tasks of the middle years. They express their value systems as they create and maintain a pleasant and comfortable home; as they enjoy their financial peace of mind and plan for old age securities; as they carry out their household responsibilities together; as they draw closer together as a couple; as they work out warm mutually satisfying relationships with the families of their grown children; as they keep in touch with their brothers' and sisters' families, as well as with their aging parents; as they participate within the larger community and find themselves as persons, as a couple, as family members, as workers, as citizens; and in all the other roles that

[1] Robert J. Havighurst and Kenneth Feigenbaum, "Leisure and Life-Style," *The American Journal of Sociology*, Vol. LXIV, No. 4, January 1959, pp. 396–404.

By the time a husband and wife reach their middle years together, they have worked through a way of life that makes sense to them.

society expects of them, and that their personal aspirations define for them.

Few there are who have to talk long and loud about what life means to them, or what values they are living for. Most men and women speak most eloquently about what matters to them in the stand they take in current issues, in the way they are willing to be counted in a controversy, in what they do about what they believe to be right and just and good and true. By the time a husband and wife reach their middle years together they have worked through the life style that makes sense to them as a couple, so that it brings them a sense of peace and satisfaction (success), or so that it rankles as a conflict point between them (failure).

It's never too late to learn. Even in the reaffirmation of life's values, a couple can still make progress toward developing unity and integrity in the leisure of their middle years. Nothing can bring greater satisfaction than finding that life all adds up, and that together the two know who they are and where they are headed in the business of living.

In summary of the middle years, we may say that the family typically consists of husband and wife; the children are grown, married and in homes of their own. Although the parents miss the companionship and youthful gaiety of their children, they also feel a sense of relief that the responsibility of child-rearing is ended; a sense of achievement that their children are safely launched in the adult world; and a sense of relaxation in the peace of the quiet household.[1]

SUGGESTED ACTIVITIES

1) Chart the complementary nature of the developmental tasks of the middle-aged man and his wife, by indicating how the tasks of the two tend to draw them together and to operate in the same direction through the middle years. Star and discuss the exceptions that seem to be conflicting rather than mutually supportive.

2) Compare Chart 15, page 390, with the new delineations of life cycle data presented by Paul C. Glick and Robert Parke, Jr., "New Approaches in Studying the Life Cycle of the Family," *Demography*, Vol. 2, 1965, pp. 187–202. Write a paper describing the birth cohorts of women approach that Glick and Parke use, specifying the advantages inherent in this method of census analysis for family life cycle study. List briefly the data needed for using this approach, and review the continuing research being conducted at the University of Chicago, mentioned on page 202, for further developments in this type of analysis.

3) Using research references in the footnotes through this chapter and those in the *Readings*, such as Axelson, Blood and Wolfe, Deutscher, Feldman, Gurin *et al.*, Havighurst, Pineo, Rose, Sussman, etc., write a paper on marriage adjustment through the middle years.

4) Conduct a panel of women whose children have recently married on "How It Feels to Become a Mother-in-Law." Encourage the women to speak freely of the problems, confusions, and satisfactions they are finding in these new roles. Ask them what they have had to learn about taking in a new son- or daughter-in-law as a member of the family. Plumb the problems they have faced in reorganizing their relationships with their own children as they marry. Summarize their experiences briefly both for the pros and cons of mother-in-lawhood.

5) Make a call upon some family in the middle years that is known to you, and through direct questioning and informal observation, discover what developmental tasks the middleaged couple is working on most actively at the moment, what problems they seem to be facing, and what satisfactions and successes are apparent.

[1] Ruth Shonle Cavan, Ernest W. Burgess, and Robert J. Havighurst, "Section VII, The Family in the Later Years," for the Committee on the Dynamics of Family Interaction, Preliminary Report, Evelyn Millis Duvall and Reuben Hill, co-chairmen, National Conference on Family Life, Washington, D. C., February 1948, mimeographed materials.

6) List all the helps you can think of that growing and grown children could give their own parents that would be of some assistance in their achievement of the developmental tasks of the middle years. Include intangibles as well as specific practical suggestions.

7) Write a letter to yourself outlining what you recommend as an ideal program for the middle years of your own life. How will it differ from the middleage of your own parents? of other middleaged people known to you? Why? What will you have to do to pave the way for these ideal circumstances in life in the middle years?

8) Debate the proposition that middleaged parents should help their grown children's families financially. Use all the data you can find that gives statistical support to your arguments, at the same time that you give adequate weight to the social, emotional and psychological aspects of parental subsidy and young adult dependence. Use actual case excerpts to document points on both sides of the question, where possible.

9) Discuss one or more of the following situations adapted from case excerpts developed as class discussion stimuli by Dr. Hazel Ingersoll, Department of Home Life, Oklahoma A&M College, Stillwater, Oklahoma:

   a) Mrs. Flint is in her forties and still a vigorous woman. Her only child has gone away to school and now she finds herself without an interest in life. She writes to Joan daily, and urges her to come home every weekend. She complains about young people today being so "heartless." Dr. Flint, a physician is a very busy man. He married Mrs. Flint when she was a nurse in the hospital where he interned. He dislikes seeing his wife so disinterested in life and wonders what he can suggest that will help her. What developmental tasks confront Mrs. Flint? What can she do? How can Dr. Flint be of real help?

   b) Mr. Douglas is a fine man and a respectable citizen. He has been hard working and honest all his life. When he was first married he had great dreams of success in his career. But the children came along pretty rapidly, and Betsy, his wife, was often ill. He found himself, instead of following his desire to be a great musician, a music teacher in a small town high school. At middleage he realized that success had passed him by. He looked about him to see the compensations—a small home, a busy wife, and four growing children. "Well one never knows which way fate will lead! Maybe I'm luckier than I think. But I can't help regretting what might have been." How can his family members help this father overcome his sense of failure?

   c) Mr. Allison has always been a sportsman and, in his own words, "as healthy as a baby." When he goes camping with "the boys" he attempts to show them how young he still is by performing strenuous athletic feats. At parties he sometimes embarrasses his daughter by his attention to her girl friends. He prefers dancing with them to dancing with his own age group. Mrs. Allison laughs and says, "Oh, Daddy is just an overgrown boy, you know, we have to humor him."

What developmental tasks does he need to accomplish? Any suggestions for making aging more attractive?

d) Alice's mother and dad have been "jogging along" in marriage for twenty-five years. They take each other pretty much for granted. Daddy jokes about his increased girth and his bald head. Mom says, "Well, I'm no spring chicken either." Alice is a bit irked with her parents for "letting themselves go." As she puts it, "they appear to enjoy middle age! I wish they would try to stay young like other parents!" Discuss the attitudes of both parents and of Alice, evaluating the predominant attitudes and suggesting what developmental tasks they satisfy. How may Alice's attitude toward her parents be affecting their tasks of middleage? What does one do when young adults are ashamed of parents who do not look young and fashionable?

READINGS

Axelson, Leland J., "Personal Adjustment in the Postparental Period," *Marriage and Family Living*, Vol. XXII, No. 1, February 1960, pp. 66–68.

Blanton, Smiley, and Gordon, Arthur, *Now or Never, The Promise of the Middle Years* (Englewood Cliffs, N. J.: Prentice-Hall, Inc., 1959).

Blood, Robert O., Jr., and Wolfe, Donald M., *Husbands and Wives* (Glencoe, Illinois: The Free Press, 1960).

Bossard, James H. S., and Boll, Eleanor S., "Marital Unhappiness in the Life Cycle," *Marriage and Family Living*, Vol. XVII, No. 1, February 1955, pp. 10–14.

Cavan, Ruth Shonle, "Family Tensions Between the Old and the Middle-Aged," *Marriage and Family Living*, Vol. XVIII, No. 4, November 1956, pp. 323–327.

Cumming, Elaine, and Henry, William E., *Growing Old* (New York: Basic Books, 1961).

Davis, Maxine, *Get the Most out of Your Best Years* (New York: Dial Press, 1960).

Deutscher, Irwin, *Married Life in the Middle Years* (Kansas City, Missouri: Community Studies, Inc., 1959).

Duvall, Evelyn Millis, *In-Laws: Pro and Con* (New York: Association Press, 1954).

English, O. Spurgeon (M.D.), and Foster, Constance J., *Fathers Are Parents, Too* (New York: G. P. Putnam's Sons, 1951), Chapter 16.

Feldman, Harold, *Development of the Husband-Wife Relationship* (Ithaca: Cornell University, 1965).

Glick, Paul C., and Robert Parke, Jr., "New Approaches in Studying the Life Cycle of the Family," *Demography*, Vol. 2, 1965, pp. 187–202.

Gruenberg, Sidonie M., and Hilda Sidney Krech, *The Many Lives of Modern Woman* (New York: Doubleday and Company, Inc., 1952).

Gurin, Gerald; Veroff, Joseph; and Feld, Sheila, *Americans View Their Mental Health* (New York: Basic Books, Inc., 1960).

Havighurst, Robert J., and Orr, Betty, *Adult Education and Adult Needs* Chicago: Center for the Study of Liberal Education for Adults, 1956).

Havighurst, Robert J., *Human Development and Education* (New York: Longmans, Green and Company, 1953), Chapter 17.

Havighurst, Robert J., "The Social Competence of Middle-Aged People," *Genetic Psychology Monographs,* Vol. 56, 1957, pp. 297–375.

Hurlock, Elizabeth B., *Developmental Psychology* (New York: McGraw-Hill Book Company, Second Edition, 1959), Chapters 12 and 13.

Jewish Vacation Association, The, *Women in the Middle Years* (New York: 207 East 84th Street, New York 28, N. Y., 1960).

Neugarten, Bernice L., and Gutmann, David L., "Age-Sex Roles and Personality in Middle Age: A Thematic Apperception Study," *Psychological Monographs,* Vol. 72, No. 17, 1958, 33 pp.

Pineo, Peter C., "Disenchantment in the Later Years of Marriage," *Marriage and Family Living,* Vol. XXIII, No. 1, February 1961, pp. 3–11.

Rose, Arnold M., "Factors Associated with the Life Satisfactions of Middle-Class, Middle-Aged Persons," *Marriage and Family Living,* Vol. XVII, No. 1, February 1955, pp. 15–19.

Sillen, Janet, *A Memorandum on the Motivations of Middle-Aged Women in the Lower Educational Brackets to Return to Work* (New York: The Jewish Vacation Association, Inc., 1961).

Sussman, Marvin B., "Activity Patterns of Post-Parental Couples and Their Relationship to Family Continuity," *Marriage and Family Living,* Vol. XVII, No. 4, November 1955, pp. 338–341.

Sussman, Marvin B., "Family Continuity: Selective Factors Which Affect Relationships between Families at Generational Levels," *Marriage and Family Living,* Vol. XVI, No. 2, May 1954, pp. 112–120.

Tibbitts, Clark, and Donahue, Wilma, eds., *Aging in the Modern World* (Ann Arbor: University of Michigan, 1957).

Grow old along with me!
The best is yet to be,
The last of life for which the first
was made . . .
ROBERT BROWNING

CHAPTER FOURTEEN

Aging families

The final stage of the family life cycle begins with the man's retirement, goes through the loss of the first spouse, and ends with the death of the second. Because women live longer than men, and usually are younger than their husbands, they more often are widowed than are men. Currently, more than half of the married women (55 per cent) and less than one-fourth (22 per cent) of the men over 65 have been widowed in the United States.[1]

Typically the husband and wife have seven or eight years together after his retirement at 65. Then the average married woman can expect about eight years as a widow until her death.[2] The aging family stage of the family life cycle can be but a few years as happens when both husband and wife die soon after his retirement. It can continue for many years, as is the case in extreme longevity. An average of sixteen years plus or minus is spent in Stage VIII of the modern day American family life cycle.

The aging family stage begins with two positions: husband and wife, and ends with one: the surviving spouse. Beginning with one interpersonal relationship, the nuclear family ends with none. The aging couple continue to be "family" to their grown children, grandchildren and great-grandchildren, facing individual developmental tasks as aging man and woman, mates, parents, and grandparents, and family developmental tasks of the final stage of the family life cycle. The challenge of senescence is ego integrity without which despair may mark the final years. The goal of this period is successful aging through continued activity and comfortable disengagement.

[1] Edith G. Robins, *The Status of Aged Women in the United States* (Washington, D. C.: Senate Subcommittee on Problems of the Aged and Aging), mimeographed report, 1961, p. 3.
[2] *Ibid.*, p. 3.

MILLIONS OF PERSONS
65 YEARS AND OVER

CHART 17. Total Population 65 Years and Over [1]

The number of men and women over 65 in our population steadily increases through the twentieth century (Chart 17). Currently there are more than sixteen million persons 65 years of age and older in the United States, with millions more to reach retirement age in the decade to come.

Some older men and women become petulant, demanding, and difficult to please. Life becomes a burden for them, and for those who care for them. They resent the "insults of aging" as they gradually lose their physical attractiveness and powers, their jobs and status, their loved ones, and their former sources of satisfaction and fulfillment.[2]

Other aging men and women find the "golden years" of life the most fruitful of all, as they gather the harvest of a lifetime, and keep on vigorously growing to the very last. Oliver Wendell Holmes observed in his later years that being seventy years young is far better than being forty years old. Helen Keller, deaf-blind since early childhood, at 77 was traveling all over the world, writing and lecturing in humanitarian service,

[1] *Age Profile USA* (Washington, D. C.: Population Reference Bureau, Inc., 1961), p. 5, (Based upon U. S. Bureau of the Census data).
[2] See Robert J. Havighurst and Ruth Albrecht, *Older People* (New York: Longmans, Green and Company, 1953), Chapter 2.

when she said, "Joy in adventure, travel and love of service to my fellow men were stronger than physical handicaps." [1]

Out of a group of typical older people studied, half of those between the ages of 65 and 69 answered the question "How old do you feel?" by replying "middleaged" or even "young." Not until the group past 80 years was polled did everyone say that they felt "old," or "aged." [2]

Why do some people age so gracefully and continue to find life good in the later years, while others get old before their time and fail to find their latter decades as "the best is yet to be?" The simplest answer is that old age is not a disease, it is a time of life. And, just as other stages of life, it has its challenges and rewards, its tasks and responsibilities.

Three patterns of aging in the United States are seen by David Riesman: [3] (1) the autonomous—persons like Toscanini, whose essential aliveness of spirit kept the body alive too; (2) the adjusted—typified by the American executive or professional man who is not supposed to allow himself to age, but must keep himself "well-preserved"; and (3) the anomic—the fate of some men forced to retire, or suddenly widowed who die shortly thereafter in a metaphorical suttee; "such people live like cards, propped up by other cards."

All older people must learn the new roles appropriate to their stage of life, in which some do well and others fail.

The movement through adulthood and old age involves changes in role activity. As one's children grow up and move away, as one's aging parents grow old and feeble, as physical energy and attractiveness decrease, as death takes away husbands, wives, and friends, as retirement takes away work, as the fires of ambition die down—as those things happen, people must learn to get new satisfactions in place of old ones out of new activities in place of old ones. They must withdraw emotional capital from one role and invest it in another one. [5]

Aging men and women find that some of their former roles are now greatly reduced, while other roles are intensified as the years roll by. Less

[1] Helen Keller, "My Luminous Universe," *Guideposts*, June 1956, p. 2.
[2] Robert J. Havighurst and Ruth Albrecht, *op. cit.*, p. 9.
[3] David Riesman, "Some Clinical and Cultural Aspects of Aging," *The American Journal of Sociology*, Vol. LIX, No. 4, January 1954, pp. 379–383.
[4] *Ibid.*, p. 383.
[5] Robert J. Havighurst, "Flexibility and the Social Roles of the Retired," *The American Journal of Sociology*, Vol. LIX, No. 4, January, 1954, p. 311, copyright 1954 by The University of Chicago.

time may be given in the later decades to active working for money, and more to enjoying the fruits of former labors. Less emphasis is now on the responsibility for young children, and more to the companionship of grandchildren, perhaps great-grandchildren. Fewer strenuous physical activities and more time for reflective thought and emotional interaction are possible now. Less time in being tied down to one place and more freedom to travel, to pull up stakes and settle in a new location, and to go where one will, and when, and with whom, in a new freedom of choice are open to many a man and woman. The possibilities are many, the chances for growth and development continue on for the human personality as long as there is a will to assume responsibility for them, within the life span.

DEVELOPMENTAL TASKS OF THE AGING HUSBAND

The man of the house faces two crucial developmental tasks through the later years: (a) finding life meaningful after he retires, and (b) adjusting to decreasing physical health and strength. All other developmental tasks tend to stem from this primary pair, as is seen in reviewing the outlined tasks of the aging husband below.

1) *Finding life meaningful after retirement:*
   Continuing on some central interests and purposes.
   Gaining status and recognition from some ongoing activities.
   Feeling needed and creative for what he is and does.
2) *Adjusting to his income level as a retired worker:*
   Tapping resources built up in his peak years of earning power.
   Supplementing income with remunerative activities.
   Adjusting living standards to the realities of current income.
3) *Making satisfactory living arrangements with his wife:*
   Deciding where and how they will live out their later years.
   Fitting physical arrangements to health and economic situation.
   Carrying out household routines without undue burden.
4) *Keeping well and taking care of himself physically:*
   Getting regular health examinations and care.
   Eating adequate diet of well-chosen and prepared foods.
   Keeping neat, clean, and pleasantly groomed.
5) *Maintaining social contacts and responsibilities:*
   Enjoying old friends and making new ones.

Carrying some responsibilities for life outside himself.

Maintaining adequate roles as a citizen.

6) *Finding emotional satisfactions in intimate contact with his loved ones:*

Re-establishing close warm relationships with his wife.

Keeping in touch with his children and grandchildren.

Feeling he belongs to his kinfolk in warm meaningful ways.

7) *Facing the possibility of death in constructive ways:*

Working out a meaningful philosophy of life and death.

Preparing for the inevitability of a last illness and death of his wife and himself.

Adjusting to widowerhood if his wife dies before he does.

DEVELOPMENTAL TASKS OF THE AGING WIFE

The married woman faces certain developmental tasks in common with her aging husband, and others that are more peculiarly hers as wife. She has already adjusted to being stripped of her main life-work in her middle years as she released her grown children. She personally is affected by her husband's retirement, and she vicariously carries her husband's struggles to work out his retirement problems. But the task remains primarily his. She, too, faces the challenges of adjusting to decreasing physical attractiveness, strength, and health. She, too, must continue to find life meaningful, and to feel that she belongs to others in satisfying ways. She faces the task of meeting the loss of her spouse more often than does her husband, because statistically wives tend to outlive their husbands by several years (Chapter One). Some of the more universal developmental tasks of the aging married woman are:

1) *Helping her husband find life meaningful after retirement:*

Encouraging him in the pursuit of new interests and the continuation of the central purposes to which he has formerly devoted himself.

Assisting him to find recognition for his accomplishments.

Making him feel important as a person, for what he is as well as what he does.

2) *Adjusting to the retirement level of income:*

Adjusting living standards to the realities of their economic situation.

Supplementing her husband's income as is appropriate.

3) *Making a pleasant comfortable home in whatever circumstances they choose:*

Adjusting happily to the situation in which they are to live out their years.

Keeping home safe and pleasant for their lives as older people.

4) *Taking care of herself physically:*

Adjusting comfortably to aging processes [1] without undue rebellion or regret at her lost youth.

Maintaining good health practices in diet, exercise, prescribed routines and regular health check-ups and care.

Keeping fit and attractive through good grooming and healthy pride in her appearance.

5) *Keeping socially alive and active:*

Cherishing old friendships and finding joy in new friends and acquaintances.

Carrying some responsibilities for clubs and group life.

Keeping posted and active in civic life.

6) *Growing emotionally through satisfying contact with her family:*

Growing close to her husband in new intimacy patterns appropriate to the later years.

Maintaining close meaningful contacts with her children and grandchildren.

Feeling needed in some significant ways, for what she is and does.

7) *Living through the death of her husband wholesomely:*

Meeting bereavement courageously.

Going on alone in life after being a member of a wedded pair for most of her adult years.

Working out meaningful ways of living as a widow.

8) *Facing death as inevitable and as a part of life:*

Finding comfort in religion or a philosophy of life and death.

Accepting and adjusting to the realities of life and death constructively.

[1] That aging means a slowing down of the processes of life is illustrated by the rate of blood flow through the human body. At twenty it takes blood 20 seconds to reach the heart, at forty it takes twice as long, and at sixty three times as long, because the heart although beating just as fast does less and less work per beat through the years. Source: N. J. Berrill, "The Time of Our Lives," *Saturday Evening Post*, August 12, 1961, p. 42.

DEVELOPMENTAL TASKS OF AGING FAMILIES

The developmental tasks of both the aging husband and wife are intertwined with the aging family's developmental tasks, which can be simply summarized as:

1) Finding a satisfying home for the later years
2) Adjusting to retirement income
3) Establishing comfortable household routines
4) Nurturing each other as husband and wife
5) Facing bereavement and widowhood
6) Maintaining contact with children and grandchildren
7) Caring for elderly relatives
8) Keeping an interest in people outside the family
9) Finding meanings in life

FINDING A SATISFYING HOME FOR THE LATER YEARS

Research studies indicate that aging families want a number of things in their homes for their remaining years: (1) quiet, (2) privacy, (3) independence of action, (4) nearness to relatives and friends, (5) residence among their own kind of people, (6) inexpensiveness, and (7) closeness to transportation lines and community activities to be found in libraries, shops, churches, etc.[1]

Most often the aging man and his wife continue on as long as they can at the place they have been calling home. There things are familiar; they are known among the neighbors and are close to family and friends. Aging families in the middle-income brackets can remain on as usual, while the poorer third of older people are forced into shabby quarters that are cheap. The upper third of older people tend to get better housing as they grow older.[2]

Migration to warmer climates is a well-known phenomenon in the United States. In the decade between 1940 and 1950, California gained 16 to 23 per cent through migrations of persons over 65 years of age,

---

[1] Robert J. Havighurst and Ruth Albrecht, *Older People* (New York: Longmans, Green and Company, 1953), p. 162.

[2] *Ibid.*, pp. 162–163; and Charles R. Manley, Jr., "The Migration of Older People," *The American Journal of Sociology*, Vol. LIX, No. 4, January 1954, pp. 324–331. Both studies indicate the greater migration among the higher income levels of older persons.

and Florida gained over 40 per cent in migrations of the aging, according to Professor Lynn T. Smith of the University of Florida. But the flow of older persons into the South, Southeast and Southwest represents but a small percentage of men and women over 65 from any one community—only 2 per cent during the six-year period of the Prairie City study.[1]

Two-thirds of all non-farm families whose heads are over 65 own their own homes.[2] And, the Iowa Survey of Life after Sixty, in which three out of five older men and women were raised on farms, finds an even higher percentage owning and living in their own homes (83 per cent of the men and 78 per cent of the women over sixty), Table 29.

The most striking finding of the Iowa Survey is that the majority of

TABLE 29. *Living Arrangements by Sex and Age* [3]

| | Age Groups | | | | |
Living Arrangements	60–64	65–69	70–74	75 and over	Total
MEN:	%	%	%	%	%
In own home	85	84	80	77	83
With children	1	1	2	11	4
With other relatives	3	1	1	3	2
Rent room or apartment	10	9	7	10	9
Lives alone	14	20	24	25	20
With spouse only	61	56	54	39	52
Other relatives	3	3	3	5	3
Non-relative	7	8	6	6	7
WOMEN:					
In own home	87	80	76	69	78
With children	2	4	6	15	7
With other relatives	1	4	2	1	2
Rent room or apartment	7	11	12	12	10
Lives alone	28	29	41	39	35
With spouse only	49	32	21	10	28
Other relatives	4	4	6	4	4
Non-relative	4	10	10	6	7

[1] Robert J. Havighurst and Ruth Albrecht, *op. cit.*, p. 165.

[2] United States Senate Subcommittee on Problems of the Aged and Aging, Report No. 1121 (Washington, D. C.: U. S. Government Printing Office, 1960), p. 118.

[3] "A Report on the Iowa Survey of Life after Sixty," *Bulletin of the Institute of Gerontology*, State University of Iowa, Iowa City, Vol. VIII, No. 2, February 1961, Supplement No. 2.

older men and women live in their own homes together. More than half of all men over 60 live with their wives. Because of the differential widowhood rate, the percentage of older women living with their husbands declines rapidly from 32 per cent in the 65–69 age group, to 21 per cent in the 70–74 age group, to a low of 10 per cent in the 75 and over age group (Table 29).

About one out of ten older men and women in this survey sample live in a rented room or apartment. One out of five men (20 per cent), and one out of three women (35 per cent) over sixty live alone, in proportions that tend to increase slightly after the age of 70 for both sexes. Relatively few older men and women either live with their relatives, or share their living arrangements with their kinfolks, in this farm-oriented population.

The percentage of older parents living with their children is small: 4 per cent of the men, and 7 per cent of the women over sixty in the Iowa study. These are significantly smaller percentages of older parents living with their children than is current nationally. In 1957, roughly 28 per cent of the aged in the United States were living with children.[1]

Older persons sharing living arrangements with their adult children are found to feel more satisfied and more permanently settled than any other group.[2] Cavan suggests that separation of the generations may not be the best solution for the aging, their middleaged children, their grandchildren, or the stability of the family.[3]

Nevertheless, the long-term trend appears to be toward a declining percentage of aged persons living with their grown children.[4] Summarizing recent research on filial relations with aging parents, Schorr says,

Living together is frequently a situation in which *both* parties benefit, though a set of scales would tip one way or the other. And whatever the material balance, the receiver often renders service or repays with fondness, an important coin in itself. Conflict between such drives as advancement of one's own family and ties to the older generation is not necessarily intergenerational

---

[1] Ethel Shanas, *The Living Arrangements of Older People in the United States,* paper prepared for the Fifth Congress, International Association of Gerontology, August 1960.

[2] Carol L. Stone, "Living Arrangements and Social Adjustment of the Aged," *The Coordinator,* Vol. VI, No. 1, September 1957, p. 13.

[3] Ruth Shonle Cavan, "The Old and the Middle-Aged," unpublished paper, pp. 6–7.

[4] Alvin L. Schorr, *Filial Responsibility in the Modern American Family* (Washington, D. C.: U. S. Government Printing Office, 1960), p. 8.

conflict; parents are as much wedded to their children's advancement as are the children. Though to the onlooker, on occasion, adult children may be living disproportionally well compared with their parents, it may be that the parents would not have it otherwise and take pleasure in their children's success.[1]

Living with married children can be a hardship to members of all three generations. One study highlights some of the bases for the general belief that "no roof is big enough for two families," especially when one is the aging mother-in-law:

The three-generation household was recognized by most of the informants as a hazardous type of family living in which the combined virtues of diplomat, statesman, and saint are needed. The elders have had considerable authority in the past and they do not find it easy to relinquish power to their own children. The husband and wife have just begun to live their lives independently and somewhat resent the intrusion of a threat to this newly found authority. The youngest generation, in turn, are baffled by the splitting of authority among their elders and their own desires to be "grown up." [2]

As in so many other decisions in family life, there is no one best answer to the question of aging parents making their home with their married children. What works well for one family, would not be suitable for another. What would be appropriate at one period in the life of the family would not fit at another. "The task before us is to learn when this may be sound and when it may be disastrous, and the techniques that work in living together, so that we may equip our families to make sound choices." [3]

Hundreds of cases of husbands and wives who have found ways of making a home for their aging parents that worked out happily for all concerned, volunteer their recommendations for harmonious three-generational living along the following lines.

WHEN YOU LIVE WITH YOUR IN-LAWS

1. Develop together a clear understanding of financial, household, and other responsibilities so that each one may know just what is expected of him or her.
2. Be reasonable in your expectations of one another. No one is perfect.

---

[1] *Ibid.*, p. 17.
[2] Marvin R. Koller, "Studies in Three-Generation Households," *Marriage and Family Living*, Vol. XVI, No. 3, August 1954, p. 206.
[3] Alvin Schorr, *op. cit.*, p. 18.

Many husbands and wives make a home for their aging parents in ways that work out well for everyone in the family.

Everyone makes mistakes from time to time. Perfectionists are hard to live with in any family.

3. Make some provision for protecting the personal property of each member of the family. It may be little more than a closet or a bureau of his or her own, but everyone welcomes some place for his things that will be respected as his alone.

4. Respect each person's need for privacy. It is not only the great who need their "islands of solitude," as Adlai Stevenson suggests. The elderly, the adolescent, and all the rest of us from time to time desire undisturbed privacy. We have the right to open our own mail, answer

Lighting the bathroom upon entering and wearing glasses when opening the medicine cabinet are recommended safety practices for older persons.

   our own phone calls, and make our own friends with some sense of privacy.

5. Encourage each member of the household to develop his own talents and to pursue his own interests in his own way. This means you, too.

6. Jointly plan for whole-family activities so that each may have a share in deciding what is to be done and what part he or she will play in the affair.

7. As disagreements arise, and they will from time to time, take the time to hear the other(s) out. Listen well enough to get what the situation means to those who differ from you. Respond to their feelings as well as to the "sense" of the situation.

8. Unify the larger family unit sharing the household by celebrations and rituals that bring the family closer together in its own most meaningful ways.
9. Take a positive attitude toward your joint living arrangement by being appreciative of the benefits derived from sharing the household, rather than merely bemoaning the sacrifices involved.
10. Gain some perspective by realizing that through the ages, families have lived more often together than in the little separate family units more popular today.[1]

Wherever home is, there are certain desirables in good housing that make home pleasant at any time, but are particularly important for the later years. Henry Churchill, architect, includes features such as these:

One floor layout. This is desirable for any age—for the creeper, the housewife, the sick, and cardiac.
If not a one-floor home, the stairs should be easy and the hand-rails solid; the stairs should be well lighted. . . .
Floors should be warm and resilient. . . .
The possibility of reasonable privacy. . . .
Convenient arrangement of space, such as easy access to the bathroom, kitchen, entrances, and minimum laundry facility. That is to say, good planning.
Sunlight, of course.
Good lighting, no dark halls, closets or corners; plenty of switches.
Safe cooking equipment. . . .
Non-slip bathtubs, strong grab-bars. . . .
No drafts—sensible and easy-opening windows, perhaps louvred sub-sill ventilation.
Reduction of transmitted noise wherever possible. . . .
Outside sitting space, sunny and sheltered from the wind. . . .
Well-planned and accessible closet and storage space.
Doors wide enough for wheel-chairs. . . .[2]

Within the framework of good housing, there are specific practices suggested as sensible for aging persons' homes by the National Safety Council: putting a light near the bed, tacking down or removing throw rugs, lighting the bathroom upon entering, wearing glasses when opening the medicine cabinet, taking it easy on hot days, wearing a hat when working in the sun, carrying loads that are not too heavy, and holding the

---

[1] Evelyn Millis Duvall, *In-Laws: Pro and Con* (New York: Association Press, 1954), pp. 323–324.
[2] Julietta K. Arthur, *How to Help Older People* (Philadelphia: J. B. Lippincott Company, 1954), pp. 118–119.

handrail in going downstairs. Since accidents increase greatly through the latter decades of life (Chart 16, Chapter Thirteen), such precautions are important preventives for aging family members who want to remain active and independent as long as they can.

There comes a time in the life of some older men and women when it may be no longer possible to stay on at home. The very old, the critically or chronically ill, the infirm and the socially isolated older person frequently needs care that cannot be given within his or her home. These are the people who need some kind of institutional or foster home care, for which adequate provisions must yet be made in many communities.[1] Fortunately, the percentage of older persons who are completely disabled is relatively small, as we see from the health survey in Prairie City, summarized in Table 30.

TABLE 30. *Percentage of Persons over 65 Years of Age in Prairie City in Four Categories of Physical Well-Being or Disability* [2]

Physical State	Percentage of Men and Women Reporting
No obvious disability (Able to be out and around the city	79
Up and about but ill (Limited activity because of obvious defect or illness)	13
Homebound Not confined to bed, but cannot leave their homes)	6
Bedridden (Permanently bedfast and ill a long time)	2
Total	100

In this representative sample of older people eight out of ten are fairly well and vigorous, and not more than two out of ten are so ill or feeble as to need nursing care. One specialist in problems of the aging points out that the extension into the home of hospital, home management, housekeeping services, social case work, food, and visiting nurse services is enabling many infirm and ill to remain at home where they seem best satisfied.[3]

[1] Specific, practical helps are found in detail in Julietta Arthur, *ibid.*, Chapters 8–14, and in their related appendices.

[2] Data from Robert J. Havighurst and Ruth Albrecht, *op. cit.*, p. 65.

[3] Clark Tibbitts, "Retirement Problems in American Society," *The American Journal of Sociology,* Vol. LIX, No. 4, January 1954, pp. 301–308.

Whatever the situation, whatever the decisions that have to be made, the developmental tasks of the aging man and his wife must be accomplished as a team. Together they make their home where it suits them best, for as long as it meets their needs. As they accomplish this task successfully, they are content in their surroundings, and happy in their physical setting. As they fail to work out the fundamental responsibilities of finding a satisfactory and satisfying home for their later years, they face the unhappiness that so often accompanies failure in any of the developmental tasks at any stage of the life cycle.

ADJUSTING TO RETIREMENT INCOME

In the United States, it is generally assumed that a man retires at or about age 65. This is true particularly of men employed in industry and in some professions such as teaching, where policies for retirement are fixed. In general, fewer men are employed now after age 65 than was true in earlier decades as we see in Table 31.

TABLE 31. *Labor Force Participation Rates of Men over 65, 1900–1950, and Projections, 1955–1975* [1]

Year	Percentage Men Over 65 Employed
1900	63.2
1920	57.1
1930	55.5
1940	43.3
1950	45.0
1955	42.9
1960	41.2
1965	39.6
1970	38.0
1975	36.5

More than half of all men over 65 retire, as we see in Table 30. In 1955, of all husbands over 65 living with their wives, 35.9 per cent of the

[1] Philip M. Hauser, "Changes in Labor-Force Participation of the Older Worker," *American Journal of Sociology*, Vol. LIX, No. 4, January 1954, p. 315, Copyright 1954 by The University of Chicago; data drawn from Bureau of the Census, "A Projected Growth of the Labor Force in the United States under conditions of High Employment: 1950 to 1975." *Current Population Reports, Labor Force* (Series P–50, No. 42, Washington D. C., December 1952), and from John Durand, *The Labor Force in the United States, 1890–1960* (New York: Social Science Research Council, 1948), p. 208 ff.

"husbands only" were working, 8.3 of the families had both husband and wife in the labor force, 5.6 had the wife only working, and 50.2 of the couples had neither husband or wife at work.[1] These percentages of husbands working after age 65 contrast sharply with the 95 per cent of all married men under age 65 who are in the labor force.

There is nothing mandatory about retirement for many men. A good many self-employed men continue to work on through their later years for a variety of satisfactions: (1) a basis for self-respect and a sense of worth, (2) a source of prestige and recognition by others, (3) an avenue of social participation, (4) a source of intrinsic enjoyment and of creative satisfaction and self-expression, (5) a way of being of service to others, and (6) a continuation of pleasant routines and habits.[2] The doctor, the lawyer, the writer, the farmer, the artist, the carpenter, and the businessman who is not retired under company policy often continue to work long after retirement age, thus postponing the problems of retirement for themselves and their families.

One of the most immediate retirement adjustments is the sharp curtailment of family income. In general, the period after retirement is characterized by a lower income than for any other period in the family, as is seen in Table 32.

TABLE 32. *Income by Age of Family Head, in the United States, 1964* [3]

| | Percentage of Families in Four Income Groups | | | |
| | Under | $3,000 to | $5,000 to | $10,000 |
Age of Family Head	$3,000	$4,999	$9,999	and over
Under 25 years	25%	28%	43%	4%
25 to 34 years	12	19	54	16
35 to 44 years	11	13	49	28
45 to 54 years	11	13	43	33
55 to 64 years	18	17	40	26
65 years and over	44	23	22	11

Men over 65 have significantly lower incomes than other age groups. A decade ago most older Americans earned less than $1,000 a year, and

---

[1] "The American Husband," *Statistical Bulletin,* Metropolitan Life Insurance Company, Vol. 37, April 1956, p. 5.

[2] Robert J. Havighurst and Ruth Albrecht, *op. cit.,* p. 109.

[3] *Americans at Mid-Decade,* Series P-23, No. 16, Bureau of the Census, 1966, page 29; and *Current Population Reports,* Series P-60, No. 47.

11 per cent had an annual income between $1,000 and $2,000. Only 15 per cent of those over 65 then received more than $2,000. These incomes often had to support the husband or wife and other members of the family.[1]

The income of many of the aged is below that considered adequate for Americans living in the mid-twentieth century. Of course, there are significant variations. Some of the aged have very adequate incomes, but most do not. Some receive private pensions, but most do not. Some older people do not receive social security benefits, but most do, and the number is increasing. Those with private pension income along with social security benefits are more favorably situated than those with but one of these forms of income. Married women are better off than widows. And, most important, older men and women who are fully employed are better off than those who work part-time, or not at all.[2]

Postponement of retirement as long as possible makes sense, for the worker, the family, and for industry itself, as Robert K. Burns points out,

In the absence of widespread and prolonged unemployment, economic forces are likely to discourage earlier retirement and to encourage later retirement. The cost per dollar of benefit is 40–50 per cent greater to retire an employee at age 60 than at age 65. It is unlikely that Social Security or industry can bear such a substantial cost. By postponing retirement from age 65 to 68 or 70, pension costs could be reduced by one-third, assuming no less in the level of productive efficiency. Moreover, each year of continued employment after 65 makes possible a substantial increase in the amount of the retirement benefit. Using a straight life annuity basis, without death benefit, a pension of $100 per month at age 65 is the actuarial equivalent of $108 at age 66 or $130 at age 68. Economic forces may be expected to exert a powerful influence, together with other factors—medical, psychological, and social—to raise normal retirement age and to modify its compulsory character.[3]

Several studies indicate that while older workers tend to slow up, their steadiness on the job, their efficiency, and their regular attendance are

[1] John J. Corson and John W. McConnell, *Economic Needs of Older People* (Twentieth Century Fund, 330 West 42nd St., New York 36, N. Y., 1956).

[2] Senate Subcommittee on Problems of the Aged and Aging, *op. cit.*, p. 65.

[3] Robert K. Burns, "Economic Aspects of Aging and Retirement," *American Journal of Sociology*, Vol. LIX, No. 4, January 1954, p. 390, copyright 1954 by The University of Chicago.

quite as good as among workers at younger age levels.[1] The thinking of students on the problem leans toward a general recommendation of more flexible retirement ages, with more opportunities for creative activity for the man or woman who wants to continue active production than are now available.

Retirement means not only sharply reduced family income, but losses of a psychological and social nature as well. Work means an emotional investment for many middle-class persons who generally assume that the more experience one has the more valuable one is on the job. Such basic feelings of security are derived from one's job that one study indicates the retirement for many people "is like walking over a cliff, not only depriving the person of emotional security of work and work colleagues, but also because it is a complete undermining of the seniority system on which they have counted."[2]

Age for age, retired persons think of themselves as older than do men and women who are still actively at work. Data from the series of studies in social gerontology being conducted by the Department of Sociology and Anthropology at Cornell University disclose significantly larger percentages of retired as compared with employed persons at all age levels under 70, and at 70 and over, who think of themselves as "old." As one of the retirants in these studies says,

> When did I start to feel old? Why when I stopped working. I was always real proud that I'd come to Chicago and got a job and supported myself. Then when I couldn't work anymore, why I wasn't good for anything.[3]

Adjusting to retirement is a complex task, involving as it does not only getting along on a sharply reduced income for many aging families, but also finding life meaningful after active participation as worker has stopped. Personal and social supports are being encouraged to ease the economic burden of the aging. Age at retirement, now relatively rigid for many millions, could be much more personally adapted to the abilities and interests of the individual to the benefit of all concerned. Until more flexible practices in retirement are general, millions of aging families must

[1] Sidney L. Pressey, "Employment Potentialities in Age, and Means for Their Possible Increase," New York State Joint Legislative Committee on Problems of the Aging, *Growing with the Years*, Albany, Legislative Document No. 32, 1954, pp. 92–94.

[2] Martin B. Loeb, "The Social Factors in the Study of Aging" Part II, unpublished research paper, September 1955, pp. 5–6.

[3] Zena Smith Blau, "Changes in Status and Age Identification," *American Sociological Review*, Vol. 21, No. 2, April 1956, p. 200.

tighten their belts, rely on relatives, accept private or public assistance, or do what they can to make ends meet during the later years of life.

ESTABLISHING COMFORTABLE HOUSEHOLD ROUTINES

One of the most baffling tasks facing the aging couple involves getting used to having both husband and wife home together all day. Always before, except for brief periods of illness or lay-offs, the husband has been away at work through the working day, leaving the home and its care in the hands of the wife. Now that both of the pair are at home all day, every day, the man may "rattle around like a pebble in a pail" as one older man puts it, with nothing to do except get in his wife's way and feel that he is a nuisance around the place.[1]

The problem is quite different for the wife. She, in a sense, "retired" some years ago when the last child was launched and by now has made her adjustment to life. In another sense she never really "retires" as long as there are meals to prepare, beds to make, and household routines to see to. In her later years, she will taper off in the amount of heavy physical work she undertakes. She may get some additional equipment to carry some of the load that now is too burdensome for her failing strength. She may hire some of the heavy work done on a regular or a seasonal basis. But fundamentally her job continues as housekeeper and homemaker.

In many a family today, patterns of working jointly as homemakers have been established through the years, so that now, in the post-retirement period, the two continue on in the double harness to which they have become accustomed. Responsibilities are assumed on the basis of interest, ability, and strength, with the husband routinely assuming some chores, the wife others, and both tackling together the jobs that they enjoy doing as a team. As illness strikes, or one of the partners is out of the home for a time, the other then can take over, because he or she is already familiar with the processes involved. Decisions are jointly made, authority is assumed by the couple as a unit, and each is accountable to the other, and to the realities of the situation, in the family that has already laid a foundation for joint homemaking responsibilities through the various stages of the family.

[1] Florence Vickery, Director, Senior Recreation Center, San Francisco, California, reports that as she visits centers for older people across the country, she is impressed with the number of retired men who leave home early in the morning, taking their sandwich with them, and after spending the day at the center, return home in the late afternoon, much as they always did when they were at work.

NURTURING EACH OTHER AS OLDER HUSBAND AND WIFE

With the processes of aging comes a variety of human needs that husband and wife mutually can meet for each other and for themselves as a couple. Their active sexual life gradually diminishes as the years go by. Physical vitality declines. Eyes, ears, and perhaps teeth need mechanical assistance in the form of glasses, hearing aids, and dentures. In time they find they do not get around as much or as far or as easily as they did. All these things are normal and to be expected in the later years. Even more disconcerting is the accident or the illness that incapacitates one or the other and throws the burden of the household and the personal nursing on the able member of the pair.

Illnesses and accidents of old age are more costly,[1] critical, and chronic than at earlier ages through the life cycle. Since women tend to live longer than men, on the average, it is usually the woman who nurses her husband through the illnesses that beset him in the later years. At first she may consider his condition as temporary. In time comes the realization that the husband cannot recover and that the disease causes death, and only after a long period of disability. The wife's acceptance of the chronic nature of her husband's illness is made easier by the fact that many of the illnesses of the aging begin with mild disabilities and progress very slowly toward complete helplessness; so she adjusts slowly, taking each change as it comes. One by one she takes over responsibilities new to her. She may have to make decisions in which she has had little practice or previous experience, such as taking charge of the finances of the household. She may have to give physical care and at times even protect her husband from the results of his mental wanderings. Care of a chronically ill husband is one of the most difficult tasks that the older wife meets.

The husband faced with the illness of his wife may have an even greater task, in that much of what is now expected of him is unfamiliar to him as the man of the house. His wife who has always provided for his needs, now helplessly awaits him to serve her. He must know how to cook an edible meal, care for a disabled patient, keep the house reasonably neat and clean, and function in what traditionally is the woman's sphere of the home.

Traditionally-oriented men who have never learned to be at home in

[1] Odin Anderson, Patricia Collette and Jacob Feldman, *Family Expenditure Patterns for Personal Health Services* (New York: Health Information Foundation, 1960), p. 11.

There is nothing mandatory about retirement for many men who continue to work on through their later years.

the house are apt to be uncomfortably awkward when the burden of home-making falls upon them. Men who define their roles as males more flexibly, who have always been at home within the intimate everyday routines of family living, find these tasks much easier and far more comfortable.

Husbands and wives who have maintained healthful routines through the years fare better in their mutual nurturance of each other as an aging pair than those who have neglected their common health in the earlier stages of life together as a married couple. A good example is found in nutrition, so closely related to the well-being of the older person. The family that has existed for thirty or forty or more years on a meat-and-potato-and-gravy diet may find it difficult to switch to the high protein, fresh fruit, and vegetable regimes recommended as adequate for the aging.

Chart 18 outlines the dietary needs of the man at 60 as contrasted with

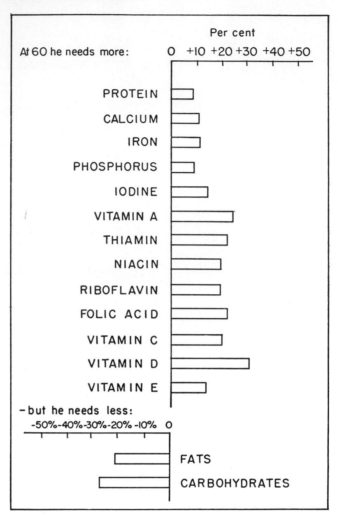

CHART 18.   Dietary Needs of Normal Man of 60 Compared to Standard Diet at Age 30 [1]

the standard diet at 30. We note that after age 60 the man or woman needs considerably less fat and carbohydrate, and more of the protective foods: vitamins, minerals, and proteins. Reasons for nutritional differences between age 30 and 60 are (1) the decrease in physical ac-

[1] C. Ward Crampton, *Live Long and Like It* (New York: Public Affairs Committee, 1948), p. 19.

Mutual encouragement and appreciation expressed in their relationship through the years give an aging husband and wife emotional support.

tivity between the active thirties and the slowing down of the post-60 period, and (2) the body building-blocks needed more by the aging to keep physically fit than was necessary at the peak of adulthood.

Further preventive regimens such as healthful balance of rest and activity; regular medical, dental and ocular checkups; wholesome acceptance of whatever aids and supplements may be prescribed, a variety of absorbing interests; and good mental hygiene go a long way toward assuring both husband and wife of maximum well-being during their later years together.

Less tangible, but quite as important is the emotional building up that each gives the other through their everyday life together. Too frequent is the soured embittered couple bent on belittling and tearing each other down in the myriad assaults upon ego and self that only the intimate can inflict. More successful is the support of one another by husbands and wives who have built up patterns of mutual encouragement and appreciation upon which they both can lean as other faculties fail. The wife who can bolster up her husband's sagging ego as he adjusts himself to retirement and a sense of diminished usefulness is often a key factor in his eagerness to start fresh in some other line, or find a place for himself in some single facet of older pursuits that now can pay off in fulfillment and satisfaction. The husband who can make his wife feel his devotion and appreciation for all she has done and all she is, helps her feel desired and desirable, more important than ever now in the sunset years. One explicit example of this is given in a report of a man who on his 55th wedding anniversary, inserted the following advertisement in his local paper:

To my sweetheart, Sophie Hensel, I wish to thank you publicly for your love and devotion and for 55 years of wedded happiness made possible by your unmatched qualities as wife, mother, mother-in-law, grandmother and great grandmother. We all revere you. Your husband, Henry Hensel.[1]

FACING BEREAVEMENT AND WIDOWHOOD

Facing the loss of loved ones is a sad task at any time. In the aging family, as dear friends drop off one by one, the sorrow is compounded by the realization, "It might have been I." Then, when inevitably the family undergoes its final break with the death of one of the original partners, the task of facing bereavement may be difficult indeed. Since women characteristically marry men older than they, and tend to live longer by several years, there are more widows than widowers. One out of four women between 55 and 64 years of age is a widow; after 65 more than half of all women (55 per cent) are widows.[2]

Bereavement is a compound crisis. It is a painful emotional shock, a sharp change in social status, often an economic catastrophe, and usually a philosophical challenge. It calls for reorganizing the habits and routines and ways of a lifetime of married living. It means the breaking of the identification that has made the marriage a good one through the years. If there have been some problems in the relationship, feelings of guilt and shame over what-I-might-have-done are often as painful as is the acute sense of loss of the familiar beloved companion.

Thomas D. Eliot has plotted the immediate effects and the secondary reactions to bereavement and outlines the various patterns found in his studies from total failure to readjust to conspicuous success in the task of facing bereavement, as follows:

[1] Associated Press release, February 28, 1953.
[2] "Marital Status and Household Characteristics: March 1950," *Current Population Reports, Population Characteristics*, Series P–20, No. 33, February 12, 1951, p. 10.

INDIVIDUAL EFFECTS OF BEREAVEMENT

A. *Total failure to readjust*
 (1) Suicide
 (2) Early death
 (3) Insanity
 (4) Moral disintegration
 (5) Obsession
B. *Partial failure*
 (1) Eccentricities
 (2) Physical illness or prostration
 (3) Aboulia, purposelessness
 (4) Isolation
 (5) Embitterment, misanthropy, cynicism
 (6) Reversion to or recurrence of griefs
 (7) Self-blame or personal hates
 (8) Fears
 (9) Loneliness
C. *Partial success*
 (1) Resignation, "God's will," etc.
 (2) Stoicism
 (3) Stereotyped formulae of immortality, misery escaped, etc.
 (4) Sentimental memorials
 (5) Effective repression of memories
 (6) Intensification of affections
 (7) Extension of affections
 (8) Deliberate absorption in distractions or duties
 (9) New or fantasied love objects
D. *Conspicuous success*
 (1) New love object
 (2) Thoroughgoing religious rationalization
 (3) Spontaneous forgetting, relaxation of tensions
 (4) Devotion to life work
 (5) Identification with role of deceased
 (6) Creation of constructive memorials
 (7) Transmutation of the experience into a productive reintegration of the personality.[1]

Even before the first shock has been fully felt, there are the funeral arrangements to see to, with all that is involved in balancing the love for the lost one with the economic considerations of the costs to be borne. The funeral usually comes on top of the expenses incurred for the last

[1] Thomas D. Eliot, "The Bereaved Family," *The Annals of the American Academy of Political and Social Science,* March 1932, p. 4.

illness. If that illness has been long, savings have possibly already been spent for doctors and nurses, hospital, and medication costs. If a sudden accident has eventuated in death, then the unexpected bills for ambulance service, hospital, doctors, mortician, and all the other costs come tumbling in simultaneously.

Even if there still is money enough for all these final services rendered the deceased spouse, the choice must be made as to the kind of funeral it shall be, and how much should justifiably be spent for it. Taboos on the discussion of death in our society keep many a husband and wife from discussing these things while they both live, and so the bereaved one is often unprepared for decisions revolving around the choice of a mortician, a casket, the burial place, and funeral service. The softly whispered, "Of course you want the best for your loved one," is too often answered with a numb nod that results in extravagant funeral costs far beyond the family resources or the standard of living represented. Even when a socially sensitive mortician attempts to help the family avoid ostentation, some "adviser" who comes to the aid of the bereaved too often runs the budget into the red in his or her efforts to be helpful.[1]

Remarriage is a likelihood for widowers more often than for widows in the United States.[2] Twice as many widowed men as widows remarry.[3] Actually the probability of remarriage for the widow over 65 is very small, only 2 for every 1,000 in the early 1950's.[4] One reason may be the smaller number of men of her age group, and the tendency for men to marry women younger than themselves that holds even for the older age groups. Another reason may be the greater self-sufficiency of the woman to maintain a household alone than is general among men.

Even though the widow may be relatively capable of living alone after her husband's death, she very probably will be lonely. Almost two-thirds of widowed persons report their single life unsatisfactory in the lonesomeness of living without a mate, even ten years after widowhood.[5] The widow may find herself socially marooned in a community

---

[1] Ernest Havemann, "Are Funerals Barbaric?" *McCall's*, May, 1956, pp. 33, 96–99.

[2] Jessie Bernard, *Remarriage, A Study of Marriage* (New York: The Dryden Press, 1956), p. 58.

[3] Paul C. Glick, "First Marriages and Remarriages," *American Sociological Review*, Vol. 14, No. 6, December 1949, pp. 726–734.

[4] *Current Population Survey* as of March 1950, April 1951 and 1952.

[5] E. G. Fried and K. Stern, "The Situation of the Aged within the Family," *American Journal of Orthopsychiatry*, Vol. 18, No. 1, January 1948, pp. 31–54.

COURTESY OF DANIEL J. RANSOHOFF: "FAMILY OF MAN"

Even though a widow may be relatively capable of living alone after her husband's death, she very probably will be lonely.

organized on a couple basis. Middle-class widows have more friends and more financial resources than do working-class widows,[1] but both face drastic changes, and each must come to terms with death, not only of her loved one(s), but within the foreseeable future for herself.

Most of these readjustments hold for the widower as well as for the widow. The tasks of facing death as a personal reality are real and urgent whenever they come. At the aging family stage, after years of couple and family living, they require rapid, flexible role changes on the part of both men and women.

[1] Zena Smith Blau, "Structural Constraints on Friendship in Old Age," *American Sociological Review*, Vol. 26, No. 3, June 1961, pp. 429–439.

The older family member left alone after the death of the spouse seems to accomplish this task best when he or she has already built some autonomy of personality, some ongoing personal interests, some backlog of economic security, a comforting philosophy of life, and a real investment in friendships. Maintaining active work and avocational interests prolongs interest in life, even after the original family has been irrevocably broken by death. Reintegration of life around remaining values is a real task involving courage, and imagination. The task is frequently made easier, especially by women, by success in relationships with grown children and grandchildren.

MAINTAINING MEANINGFUL CONTACT WITH CHILDREN AND GRANDCHILDREN

Some years ago, Dinkel pointed out some of the conflicts between the grandparent generation and those of grown children and grandchildren that arise out of contrasts and conflicts in the cultures of the three generations in a rapidly changing social scene. The grandparents in the fifty families that were studied in this research had grown up in and still held to rural ways of a pioneer culture, which to the members of the younger generations were irritatingly old-fashioned, dictatorial, and authoritarian.[1] Out of this sample's experience, Dr. Dinkel recommends the practice of mutual avoidance for those families in which there is intergenerational conflict,

When parents and children do not get along, I would not try to promote family harmony, but would rather try to decrease the dependence of one generation on the other and to lessen the number of their contacts. By all means, I would not try to force children to give economic support to their parents. In such cases there are too many potential conflicts that would be brought into being by a common residence, and I assume that support by children most often involves the parent's going to live with a child.[2]

A decade later, another study of older people in a Midwestern town of about 7,000 population, yielded more hopeful results. In this research only 15 per cent of the parents over 65 years of age were characterized by dependence and neglect, while 85 per cent were seen as relatively in-

[1] Robert M. Dinkel, "Parent-Child Conflict in Minnesota Families," *American Sociological Review*, August 1943, pp. 412–419.
[2] Robert M. Dinkel, "Social and Economic Adjustments of the Aged," *Public Welfare in Indiana*, January 1942, p. 6.

dependent, as we see in Table 33 in which the items are ranked from most independent to most dependent and neglectful.

TABLE 33. *Relative Independence of Parents over 65 Years of Age* [1]

Independence	Per Cent	Dependence and Neglect	Per Cent
Parents and children are mutually independent but maintain a close social and affectional relationship	27	Parents share child's home but are somewhat burdensome	1
Parents and children are considered as independent adults but may share home or advice with each other	44	Parents live alone but children come in regularly to give care	5
Parents are responsible for children full or part time	1	Children are distant and seldom see parents	8
Parents have some responsibility for children	5	Parents have no interest in the children	1
Parents share home of children and are a help to them	8	Parents are completely neglected by children	0
	85		15

Albrecht's study finds that independent parents have certain characteristics in common: they are proud of their children, they brag about their children to strangers, they are realistic about them and treat them as adults, they can accept and give favors and suggestions without feeling threatened. Furthermore,

A basic security in loving and feeling loved removes any threat of authority or dominance of either generation. In fact, they enjoy working and playing with members of the second generation, actually like them as people, and maintain interests and a mode of life that keep some common bonds. But they also have interests outside of the family that help maintain their own self-hood. In addition, they accept the in-laws as members of the family and are not threatened by sharing or by extending parental warmth to include the spouse of the son or daughter.[2]

These qualities are those of developmental parents (Chapter Five) who have through the years encouraged their children's autonomy and

---

[1] Taken from, Ruth Albrecht, "Relationships of Older Parents with Their Children," *Marriage and Family Living,* Vol. XVI, No. 1, February 1954, excerpts from Table 1, p. 33.

[2] *Ibid.,* p. 33.

growth at the same time that they as members of the older generation found satisfaction in their own continued development. These are the older persons who find in-law relationships harmonious, with few complaints of meddlesomeness and intrusion, and a large measure of the mutual acceptance and respect.[1]

The Cornell Study of Occupational Retirement found that the great majority of the older parents in their sample of 2,300 maintain frequent contact with their children's families. Three out of four see their children often, and 70 per cent see their grandchildren often. Other relatives are considerably less often in touch with these older persons. Only one third see their brothers and sisters often, a fourth see their nieces and nephews often, and but 12 per cent are in frequent touch with their cousins.[2]

Finding joy in grandparenthood seems to be something that is learned through the years in incorporating the knowledges, skills, and attitudes that make one an older person who is loving and lovable, interested and interesting. Many older men and women report that they find more satisfaction in their grandchildren and great-grandchildren than they ever did with their own children when the pressures of young parenthood weighed too heavily upon them. Maintaining close and meaningful contact with married children and grandchildren can be a most rewarding task of the later years. It can warm the sunset years with the steady glow of two-way affection and belonging that is well-worth achieving.

AS AGING FAMILIES, CARING FOR ELDERLY RELATIVES

As more individuals live out their full life span, with greater vigor than in earlier times, it occasionally falls to aging family members to care for elderly relatives. Ruth Albrecht's study of parent-child relationships of people over 65 years of age shows that care of aged parents was a responsibility of about 11 per cent of those whose parents were in this country, with the task falling to single and widowed women more often than to married ones, and only occasionally to men.

Memories of pleasant and unpleasant experiences with parents that took place in adolescence 50 to 70 years before color the relationships

[1] Evelyn Millis Duvall, *In-Laws: Pro and Con* (New York: Association Press, 1954), Chapter 16.

[2] Gordon F. Streib and Wayne E. Thompson, "The Older Person in a Family Context," in Clark Tibbitts, ed., *Handbook of Social Gerontology* (Chicago: University of Chicago Press, 1960), p. 476.

between aging adults and their own parents. While most men and women remember strong attachment to their fathers, and even more to their mothers, somewhat more than one in eight report disliking their parents in adolescence because they felt rejected, or they felt they were made to work too hard, or because they were ashamed of the parent's occupation or behavior.[1]

Such evidence helps interpret Dinkel's findings [2] of conflict between the generations when the older is rooted in a rural culture that believes in strict obedience, hard work, and other pioneer virtues, while the grown children rebel and establish themselves in the new ways of life that emerge in city and town in repudiation of the parents' way of life.

We would expect relationships between aging family members and their own parents, to be related to the amount and the nature of social change that has occurred in the lifetime of the individuals, and how well the various family members had been able to keep up to date as times change both in the social scene and in the shifting scene within the family life cycle. Upwardly mobile family members may be expected to have less in common with their aging parents than more conforming individuals. Persons who marry within their own group usually experience less conflict with their own parents than do those whose marriages have been less homogamous. Some family members love, revere, and welcome a chance to serve aging relatives, even in a culture that calls for individualism and independence of family members. Other families find older parents a burden assumed only reluctantly and as a last resort.

The problem is especially acute when the elderly one is blind, crippled, bedridden, or so senile that he or she needs protective supervision. If the family must provide the constant supervision that such care entails it can become a severe mental and physical strain unless a companion or nurse is employed to share the load. In cases where institutionalization is indicated, the family has not only to carefully select the most suitable resource, and prepare the senile one for it, but also must cope effectively with the feelings of guilt and implied rejection that "putting a loved one away" has meant in our culture.

Fortunately, this dark side of the picture is but a small part of the relationships between aging families and their extended family mem-

[1] Ruth Albrecht, "Relationships of Older People to Their Own Parents," *Marriage and Family Living*, Vol. XV, No. 4, November 1953, pp. 296–298.

[2] Dinkel, *op. cit.*, pp. 412–419.

bers. Only a small percentage of older persons are helplessly disabled, as we have already seen. Most families find that the later years are the harvest years in family warmth and closeness. As the older family members get into the latter decades, the differences between parents and children often level out in the sheer fact of all being retired together, able to relax and enjoy life, and to plan together for present and future pleasures. Success in this task is often closely related to effectiveness in the developmental task of keeping alive and interested in the world around in active participation through the years.

KEEPING A LIVELY INTEREST IN THINGS AND PEOPLE OUTSIDE THE FAMILY

Aging husbands and wives tend to become less active than they may once have been in community activities. Some are not physically able to get about as they used to do. Others lack transportation for getting places. Many have lost interest as time goes by, and spend more and more time by themselves at home.

A study of men and women over 65 years of age in rural New York found physical inability, lack of interest, and lack of transportation the three most frequently given reasons by the aging for letting up in organizational participation, as we see in Table 34.

Over one half of these rural aged belonged to no organization. It may

TABLE 34. *Reasons Given for Less Time Given to Organizations by 143 Men and Women over 65 Years of Age in Rural New York* [1]

Reasons for Less Organizational Participation	Number of Times Mentioned
Not physically able	51
Lack of interest	41
Lack of transportation	24
Not enough time	17
Can't afford it	14
Moved to a new neighborhood	7
Other	9

[1] Roland L. Warren, "Old Age in a Rural Township," *Age Is No Barrier* (Albany, New York: New York State Joint Legislative Committee on Problems of the Aging, 1952), p. 156.

be that being rural, limits the community activities of older persons in that there are fewer recreational and commercial facilities in rural than in urban communities, fewer public and private agencies, and less available transportation than is found in most towns and cities.

The Prairie City study of older persons in a community of 7,000 population describes 37 per cent of the men and women over 65 whose days are "spotted with wasted hours, during which they merely exist, with more or less feeling of the dreariness of life." [1]

Survey of the leisure time activities of older persons indicates that the most frequent are solitary, passive, and require no advance planning: radio-listening, reading, and visiting. Gardening falls in fourth place for men and in seventh place for older women, with sewing and crocheting ranking fourth for female family members; both gardening and handiwork are relatively solitary and but slightly more active than the most frequent activities. Next in rank comes taking auto rides, letter-writing, movies, and playing cards. Clubs, lodges, and community and church work fall in tenth and eleventh places respectively among men (Table 35).

TABLE 35. *Percentage of Older Men and Women Participating in Leisure-Time Activities, Prairie City Study* [2]

Activity	Men (N = 45)	Women (N = 55)
Radio-listening	82	82
Reading	73	71
Visiting	56	73
Gardening	51	40
Sewing, crocheting, etc.	0	60
Taking auto rides	42	45
Letter-writing	18	45
Movies	16	31
Playing cards, etc.	20	25
Clubs and lodges	11	33
Community and Church work	11	31
Travel	9	14
Golf, other sports	20	4
Woodworking, etc.	13	0

[1] Robert J. Havighurst and Ruth Albrecht, *op. cit.*, p. 136.
[2] Excerpted from Robert J. Havighurst and Ruth Albrecht, *op. cit.*, p. 138.

A much higher percentage of men and women at the higher social class levels are active in clubs and lodges, community and church work, and travel than is found at the lower social class levels. At every social class level, more women than men are active in the community; and more men engage in golf, woodworking, etc., than do women.

Older people who are active socially tend to be conspicuously happier than more solitary individuals. A study of the older men in a community of retired members of a fraternal order, finds that "men with the highest happiness scores participate nine times as much in group recreational activities (cards, shuffle-board, pool, horseshoe pitching, and bingo) than do those with the lowest happiness scores." [1]

There are two theories of successful aging: (1) the activity theory implied in the above discussion, and (2) the disengagement theory in which life space, quality and rate of interaction are seen to lessen with age. [2]

Living examples of continued activity into and through the later years, make it hard to believe that disengagement is inevitable. For instance, according to a recent United Nations report, a 68-year-old engineer re cruited for the technical assistance program in Turkey was asked, "But are you going way off there and leave your wife, at your age?" "Not a chance," replied the enthusiastic recruit, "My wife is a former nurse, and she's as eager as I am to get over there and see what she can do."

It may be that successful aging is through continued activity for some types of people, and in disengagement for others. "Persons with an active, achieving, and outward-directed life style will be best satisfied with a continuation of this style into old age with only slight diminution. Other persons with a passive, dependent, home-centered life style will be best satisfied with disengagement," suggests Robert Havinghurst. [3]

Decrease in social activities may account for the decline in happiness in the later years reported by several researchers. [4] Another study of fathers and mothers of college students concludes that social participation is definitely associated with life satisfaction for both men and

[1] Ernest W. Burgess, "Social Relations, Activities, and Personal Adjustment," *American Journal of Sociology*, Vol. LIX, No. 4, January 1954, p. 360.

[2] Elaine Cumming, Lois Dean, David Newell, and Isabel McCaffrey, "Disengagement—A Tentative Theory of Aging," *Sociometry*, Vol. 23, No. 1, March 1960, pp. 23–35.

[3] Robert J. Havighurst, "Successful Aging—Definition and Measurement," paper prepared for the International Research Seminar on the Social and Psychological Aspects of Aging, August 1960, mimeographed, p. 15.

[4] From R. G. Kuhlen, "Age Differences in Personality during Adult Years," *Psychological Bulletin*, Vol. 42, 1945, page 343; and Roland L. Warren, *op. cit.*, p. 157.

women.[1] These trends are in line with other studies at various age and class levels in which social participation and happiness are usually closely associated. Remaining actively related to life outside oneself is a developmental task necessary for the happiness of the aging person.

When men and women over 65 are asked what things in life give them the greatest satisfaction, the largest number of them report their children and grandchildren as their greatest satisfaction. Hobbies, pastimes, and housework or employment claim the next largest number, with all others (gardening, visiting, reading, etc.) mentioned much less often.[2] Since these less satisfying activities are those most frequently engaged in, the indications are that many older persons follow the line of least resistance, rather than pursuing their own real interests through the latter decades. Here again, as at other stages of the life cycle, satisfactions come from working effectively on the developmental tasks of the period, while dissatisfaction and unhappiness accrue to those who fail the tasks of the period.

The attitudes and the practices developed in childhood are related to the adjustment to aging. One study finds 11 per cent of the over-65 population of a Midwestern community, living from day to day with interests chiefly in the past. These people were hard to live with and gave little or no attention to their appearance. Another 54 per cent had little interest beyond their immediate families. While 35 per cent were altruistic, objective about their problems and tended to project their thoughts into the future. This group of men and women enjoyed social life, met people well, and took pride in their appearance. Some subjects in their eighties were so trim and alert that special questioning had to be done to establish the fact that they were over 65. These were the people who had learned social, job, and recreational skills earlier in life; they had made a good adjustment in life from childhood on; they had good relationships with other people; were able to make decisions and face problems as they came along; and had developed wholesome attitudes toward life and themselves during childhood.[3]

It is never too late to learn. Many individuals who have not pre-

[1] Arnold M. Rose, "Factors Associated with the Life Satisfaction of Middle-Class, Middle-Aged Persons," *Marriage and Family Living*, Vol. XVII, No. 1, February 1955, p. 19.

[2] Roland L. Warren, *op. cit.*, p. 157.

[3] Ruth Albrecht, "Social Roles in the Prevention of Senility," *Journal of Gerontology*, Vol. 4, No. 4, October 1951, pp. 380–386.

viously had a chance to learn special skills and to develop interests find in their later years new joys in new pursuits. A neighbor learned to drive a car at 72, preparatory to a cross-country tour. Grandma Moses learned to paint late in life. Thousands of older men and women in hundreds of towns and cities are playing in community orchestras. One Chicago manufacturer, upon retirement at 65, decided to study the violin. Over 70 now, he plays in a suburban amateur string quartet. The sixteenth-century flute-like instrument, the recorder, is enjoying a revival with many older persons actively involved in recorder groups and concerts.[1] A physician over 80 bought a boat and passed the Coast Guard course in navigation. Illustrations are numerous and as varied as older people themselves.

Golden Age Clubs, Senior Recreational Centers, and other special programs especially for older people are proving their value in helping many men and women to find life full and meaningful during the later years. Professionally trained staff, pleasant surroundings, a varied program built to challenge and meet many interests of older people, yield high dividends in such programs whose worth has been well established.

Courses like the one offered by the University of Michigan on "Living in the Later Years" explicitly deal with the challenges of aging and stimulate many an older man or woman to get involved in enough of life so that his or her final years may indeed be the fullest and best yet.

FINDING MEANINGS IN LIFE

Working out a philosophy of life is a life-long task. Through the later years its importance is heightened, as the aging person reviews his experiences and comes to terms with what life means to him. It is not surprising to find that religion means more to the aging person than it has before. One study of responses that persons over 65 make to the question, "Do God and religion hold more, the same, or less meaning for you now than formerly?," finds only four who report less meaning in religion now, in contrast to 71, who report more meaning in God and religion now, as is summarized in Table 36.

---

[1] American Music Conference, 332 South Michigan, Chicago 4, Illinois, mimeographed release.

TABLE 36. *Meaning of God and Religion Now as Compared with Formerly by 143 Older Persons* [1]

Aging Persons' Responses	Number of Persons
Much more	46
Somewhat more	25
About the same	59
Somewhat less	3
Much less	1
No answer	9
	143

A study of the religious attitudes and practices of men and women during the later years in a midwestern community similarly shows that favorable attitudes toward religion and certainty of an afterlife tend to increase with age for both men and women. Among the over-95 age group 100 per cent of both men and women polled were certain of an afterlife. Some decline in church attendance among the very elderly was more than matched by listening to church services regularly on the radio. Reading the Bible at least once a week increased from 50 per cent among women in the 60–64 year old group to 100 per cent among the 95–99 year olds.[2]

The aging family stage is rather like a period of fall housecleaning, of putting one's house in order. One reviews one's possessions and weeds out many an object that is no longer useful, with the realization that "You Can't Take It with You." Things that have been admired by grown children or friends are given to them while they can get pleasure from their use now while the aging ones are still alive to get the satisfaction of giving and sharing. Through the earlier decades of life, all sorts of things are accumulated with the thought that "some day they will come in handy." The aging years are the weighing years when the froth and the frills are discarded and only the really important things are held close.

Some say that the aging years are "second childhood." And in a sense they are. In the years of striving through adolescence and the first

[1] Roland L. Warren, *op. cit.*, p. 158.
[2] Ruth S. Cavan, Ernest W. Burgess, and Herbert Goldhamer, *Personal Adjustment in Old Age* (Chicago: Science Research Associates, 1949), p. 58.

decades of full adulthood, the true mystery of life may escape one. Competition and struggle overshadow love and tenderness. A man or woman loses touch with nature in the hustle to get ahead on the job or get a meal on the table. A raise in pay once seemed more important than a sunset. But as one grows older, although the sight is dimmed, one sees more—the glint of dew on the iris, the glory of a storm, the sweet peace of the woods at dusk, as one did as a child.

The real bond between the generations is the insights they share, the appreciation they have in common, the moments of inner experience in which they meet . . .
Old men need a vision, not only recreation.
Old men need a dream, not only a memory.
It takes three things to attain a sense of significant being:
God
A Soul
And a Moment.
And the three are always here.
Just to be is a blessing. Just to live is holy.[1]

SUGGESTED ACTIVITIES

1) Insurance company statisticians have worked out a simple formula by which any person can estimate his or her life expectancy. All you do is subtract your present age from 80 and take ⅔ of the difference as the number of years still left to you. According to this scheme, plot your own life expectancy, and write a letter to yourself to be opened in the last decade of your life, outlining the program you recommend for yourself. Include items covering health, family, work, leisure, civic interests, and anything else you feel would be valuable in making your own aging years more meaningful.

2) Write a paper on the topic "More People Rust Out than Wear Out." Document your points with research findings, as well as from your readings generally. Illustrate with cases known to you as fully as you can.

3) Invite a panel of persons over 65 in your neighborhood to participate in a group interview in which you and other members of your class question them as to their activities, their work, their personal and family interests, their satisfactions with life now as compared with

[1] Abraham J. Heschel, "The Older Person and the Family in the Perspective of Jewish Tradition," paper delivered at the White House Conference on Aging, January 9, 1961, pp. 15 and 16.

earlier in life, and their plans for the future. Ask them especially what they feel the community might do to make life better for older persons. Summarize these data, giving rough evaluations of the relative success in the developmental tasks of the various members of the panel of older persons. Tell what you feel might help more of them find their maximum success in the developmental tasks of the period.

4) Produce the play "The Room Upstairs" portraying some of the typical problems arising between older people and their grown children. Ask various members of the class to identify with specific characters during the performance: Mrs. Johnson, her daughter Fran, and her son-in-law Robert, and be prepared to discuss what the various situations portrayed meant to this particular person, as well as to the family as a whole. Order the play from Human Relations Aids, 1790 Broadway, New York 19, N. Y.

5) Refute the arguments that "You Can't Teach an Old Dog New Tricks," by quoting research findings on the ability of adults to learn, and reviewing the most frequent reasons why persons of any age tend to slow up in their learning (fear of ridicule, fear of failure, laziness, a rigid self concept, feeling "out of step," or that one doesn't belong). Summarize your findings by outlining a program of adult education for persons over 65 years of age.

6) Show the film, *The Steps of Age* (25 minutes, black and white, from International Film Bureau), looking especially for the factors that make life difficult for older persons in the family. Comment on ways in which younger persons so often thoughtlessly ignore or hurt their older relatives, and suggest some of the reasons why the generations sometimes find it difficult to live together.

7) Make a financial plan for a hypothetical married couple whose children are in college that will assure them of security in their later years, without too great sacrifice in the years that lie immediately ahead. Plot their probable income and expenditures for three decades as a middleaged and aging couple. Then compute anticipated income from investments, pensions, part-time earnings, annuities, insurance and/or other potential sources of income that will keep the aging family members free from dependence upon either their children or other assistance in their later years.

8) Review the recommendations being made in the literature for housing for the older person, summarizing your findings in an outline of suggestions for aging families.

9) Review issues of *The Journal of Gerontology* and of *Geriatrics* for the past several years, tabulating the number of articles devoted to the various aspects of aging in our society. Interpret your findings in the light of what you know about the aging family in our society.

10) Write a critical review of one or more of the following novels dealing with situations faced by older persons:

Bennett, Arnold, *Old Wives' Tale* (New York: Harper & Brothers, 1953).

Bromfield, Louis, *Mrs. Parkington* (New York: Harper & Brothers, 1943).

Chase, Mary Ellen, *Mary Peters* (New York: Macmillan Company, 1934).

Lawrence, Josephine, *Web of Time* (New York: Harcourt, Brace and Co., 1953).

11) Discuss the following situation developed as a case excerpt for classroom discussion by Dr. Hazel Ingersoll, Department of Home Life, Oklahoma A&M College, Stillwater, Oklahoma:

Jane's father is old, and she is the youngest and only unmarried child of a large family. Jane feels she must take care of her father. Now that she and Bob are ready to marry, they are concerned about what to do with her father. He has a little savings but he is infirm. He is very forgetful and often childish. They are afraid he cannot live by himself, yet they are reluctant to have him live with them. What are the various alternatives that Jane and Bob face, and what are the difficulties and advantages inherent in each?

READINGS

Albrecht, Ruth, "The Parental Responsibilities of Grandparents," *Marriage and Family Living*, Vol. XVI, No. 3, August 1954, pp. 201–204.

Allport, Gordon W., *Becoming* (New Haven: Yale University Press, 1955).

Anderson, John E., ed., *Psychological Aspects of Aging* (Washington, D. C.: American Psychological Association, 1956).

Birren, James E., ed., *Handbook of Aging and the Individual* (Chicago: University of Chicago Press, 1959).

Blau, Zena Smith, "Structural Constraints on Friendship in Old Age," *American Sociological Review*, Vol. 26, No. 3, June 1961, pp. 429–439.

Brown, Muriel W., "The Growth of Values in Childhood and Old Age," *Journal of Home Economics*, Vol. 52, No. 6, June 1960, pp. 407–413.

Burgess, Ernest W., ed., *Aging in Western Societies* (Chicago: University of Chicago Press, 1960).

Burgess, Ernest W., *Retirement Villages* (Ann Arbor: University of Michigan, 1961).

Cavan, Ruth Shonle, *The American Family* (New York: Thomas Y. Crowell Company, 1953), "Family Life of the Old," pp. 588–612.

Crook, G. Hamilton, and Heinstein, Martin, *The Older Worker in Industry* (Berkeley: University of California Institute of Industrial Relations, 1958).

Cumming, Elaine, Dean, Lois R., Newell, David S., and McCaffrey, Isabel, "Disengagement—A Tentative Theory of Aging," *Sociometry*, Vol. 23, No. 1, March 1960, pp. 23–35.

Donahue, Wilma, and Tibbitts, Clark, eds., *New Frontiers of Aging* (Ann Arbor: University of Michigan, 1957).

Donahue, Wilma, *et al.*, *Free Time: Challenge to Later Maturity* (Ann Arbor: University of Michigan, 1958).

Drake, Joseph T., *The Aged in American Society* (New York: Ronald Press, 1958).

Duvall, Evelyn Millis, *In-Laws: Pro and Con* (New York: Association Press, 1954).

Ebeling, Maloa, and Rosencranz, Mary Lou, "Social and Personal Aspects of Clothing for Older Women," *Journal of Home Economics*, Vol. 53, No. 6, June 1961, pp. 464–465.

Eisenstadt, S. N., *From Generation to Generation: Age Groups and Social Structure* (Glencoe, Illinois: The Free Press, 1956).

Feifel, Herman, *The Meaning of Death* (New York: McGraw-Hill Book Company, 1959).

Fulton, Robert, ed., *Death and Identity* (New York: John Wiley & Sons, 1965).

Gleason, George, *Horizons for Older People* (New York: Macmillan Company, 1956).

Havighurst, Robert J., *Human Development and Education* (New York: Longmans, Green and Company, 1953), Chapter 18, "Developmental Tasks of Later Maturity," pp. 277–283.

Havighurst, Robert J., "The Social Competence of Middle-Aged People," *Genetic Psychology Monographs*, Vol. 56, 1957, pp. 297–375.

Havighurst, Robert J., and Albrecht, Ruth, *Older People* (New York: Longmans, Green and Company, 1953).

Hughes, Everett C., *Men and Their Work* (Glencoe, Illinois: The Free Press, 1958).

Jacobs, H. Lee, "Spiritual Resources for the Aged in Facing the Problem of Death," *Bulletin of the Institute of Gerontology*, State University of Iowa, Iowa City, Iowa, Vol. VI, No. 3, March 1959, Supplement No. 3, pp. 3–8.

Jacobs, H. Lee, *Youth Looks at Aging* (Iowa City: The University of Iowa, 1964).

Kaighn, Raymond P., *How to Reitre and Like It* (New York: Association Press, 1954).

Kish, Henriette, *Questions Older People Ask* (New York: E. P. Dutton & Company, 1955).

Kleemeier, Robert W., *Aging and Leisure—a Research Perspective into the Meaningful Use of Time* (Fair Lawn, N. J.: Oxford University Press, Inc., 1961).

Koller, Marvin R., "Studies of Three-Generation Households," *Marriage and Family Living*, Vol. XVI, No. 3, August 1954, pp. 205–206.

Kutner, Bernard, *Five Hundred Over Sixty* (New York: Russell Sage Foundation, 1956).

Langer, Marion, *Learning to Live as a Widow* (New York: Julian Messner, Inc., 1957).

Mitford, Jessica, *The American Way of Death* (New York: Simon and Schuster, 1963).

Neugarten, Bernice L., and Garron, David, "Attitudes of Middle-Aged Persons toward Growing Older," *Geriatrics*, Vol. 14, 1959, pp. 21–24.

Pollock, Josephine, *Cooperative Extension Service Work with Low Income Families: The Aging* (Washington, D. C.: U. S. Department of Agriculture, 1963).

Pressey, Sidney L., and Kuhlen, Raymond G., *Psychological Development through the Life Span* (New York: Harper & Brothers, 1957).

Rainwater, Lee, *et al.*, *Workingman's Wife* (New York: Oceana, 1959).

Schorr, Alvin L., *Filial Responsibility in the Modern American Family* (Washington, D. C.: U. S. Department of Health, Education, and Welfare, 1960).

Sheldon, Henry D., *The Older Population of the United States* (New York: John Wiley & Sons, 1958).

Stern, Edith M., *A Full Life after 65* (New York: Public Affairs Pamphlets, 1963).

Stewart, Maxwell S., ed., *Problems of Family Life* (New York: Harper & Brothers, 1956), Chapters 7, 8, 9, 10.

Streib, Gordon F., *The Nature of Retirement* (New York: The Macmillan Company, 1959).

Streib, Gordon F., and Thompson, Wayne E., eds., "Adjustment in Retirement," *Journal of Social Issues*, Vol. 14, No. 2 (entire issue), 1958.

Strauss, Anselm L., and Barney G. Glaser, *Awareness of Dying* (Chicago: Aldine, 1965).

Tibbitts, Clark, ed., *Handbook of Social Gerontology* (Chicago: University of Chicago Press, 1960).

Townsend, Peter, *The Family Life of Old People* (Glencoe, Illinois: The Free Press, 1957).

United States Government Printing Office, Superintendent of Documents, Washington, D. C.: Federal Council on Aging, *Programs for Older People— 1960 Report to the President*

United States Senate Subcommittee on Problems of the Aged and Aging: *Action for the Aged and Aging*, 1961.

Health and Economic Conditions of the American Aged—A Chart Book, 1961.

Health Needs of the Aged, 1960.

The Aged and Aging in the United States: A National Problem, 1960.

White House Conference on Aging, Reports: *Aging with a Future*, 1961.

Education for Aging, 1961.

Employment Security and Retirement of the Older Worker, 1961.

Impact of Inflation on Retired Persons, 1961.

Free Time Activities: Recreation, Voluntary Services, Citizenship Participation, 1961.

Religion and Aging, 1961.

All the world's a stage,
And all the men and women merely
    players:
They have their exits and their
    entrances,
And one man in his time plays
    many parts, . . .
        WILLIAM SHAKESPEARE,
        As You Like It

CHAPTER FIFTEEN

What to expect through the family life cycle

The stages of the family life cycle differ in length, in activity, in intensity of family interaction, and in relative difficulty of their family development tasks. During the establishment phase the new husband and wife are building their marriage out of the dreams and realities each brings to their union. Since no two people ever grow up in identical families, each brings to marriage his or her own conceptions of what is appropriate behavior, what should and should not be done, how roles are conceived, and what a family should be like. These differences may be assimilated, they may partially coexist, one may dominate over the others, or they may remain in conflict. The channeling of the forces that bring the two persons together in marriage is powerfully motivated, making this stage not only important but potentially an explosive one in marriage. With the expectant phase of the beginning family comes the realization of imminently becoming a family with the creative thrusts toward preparing for the expected child.

The childbearing family is a busy bustling stage with things strewn about, jobs never quite done, baby's demands, and parents' crises and confusions in becoming father and mother for the first time. When one child follows another in quick succession, this stage may continue to be strenuous for some time, with little of the lull that comes in the one-child family as soon as the youngster trots off to preschool for at least part of the day. In time all of the children are in school, the family enjoys an interval of solidarity and fulfillment, and the parents are plunged into community programs—PTA, scouts, religious school, sports programs, and many etceteras—along with their children.

With the coming of the teen years, the family is atomized, with the teenagers forming peer-group loyalties, establishing their autonomy, and pushing away from their parents in the urgent tasks that must be accomplished if they are to become full-fledged adults. All this makes for emotionally charged relationships at home with parents concerned about the safety of their adolescents, the good name of the family, and their own peace of mind.

The day comes when even the most active teenager settles down and comes home with stars in eyes to announce that wedding bells are soon to ring. The busy expensive years of the launching stage, in which young adults leave home for marriage, for work, for military service, or for college, leave middle-class parents financially and emotionally spent, usually quite ready to enjoy the relative peace and quiet that is theirs in the middle and later years.

The latter half of marriage is typically spent as a couple in America today. The grown children come home only at intervals with the grandchildren. The middleaged and aging husband and wife now are relatively free to come and go as they wish. These are the harvest years of family living, when the big job of raising a family is done and the man and wife can again think of themselves and what they want out of life. If they have developed a variety of satisfying interests, if they have warm friendships and close contact with their grown children and grandchildren, these are indeed the "Golden Years." When aging family members are impoverished, jobless, useless, isolated, homeless, neglected, or incapacitated, these final years can be insufferably bleak and barren, "sans everything," as Shakespeare describes them.

FAMILY DEVELOPMENTAL TASKS THROUGH THE LIFE CYCLE

Life history profiles of today's American families can be seen through the probable difficulties of each family developmental task throughout the family life cycle. At certain stages families feel the pinch of particular pressures more keenly than at others. Through some life-cycle stages, families tend to be more vulnerable to problems, disruption, or disenchantment than others. Probabilities apply to a particular family much as growth norms for individuals serve as guide lines of what to expect—not as prescriptions for what has to be. A longitudinal look at the basic tasks of family life through the years highlights points of predictable vulnerability, and suggests positive measures for helping families achieve success throughout their development.

HOME OWNERSHIP INCREASES THROUGH THE FAMILY CYCLE

Getting married and raising a family provides powerful incentives for buying a house today. Young couples typically rent their dwelling place until the first baby comes. In a central New York study, 92 per cent of the early married childless couples rent an apartment.[1] With the arrival of children, home ownership increases rapidly and continues to rise throughout most of the rest of the marriage.[2]

Feldman finds (Chart 19) that only 4 per cent of the childless couples in early marriage own their own homes. Practically one-third (32 per cent) of the couples with oldest child an infant; more than one-half (56 per cent) of the couples with oldest child at preschool age; four out of five (82 per cent) of the couples with all children school age; 86 per cent of the couples with oldest child a teenager; and 94 per cent of the couples with one or more children at home and one or more out of the home (equivalent to what we are calling the launching stage) own their own homes—a steady rise in home ownership as children come and grow up. Then come the middle years (Stage VII) when the children have gone, there is no longer so much need for the house, and home ownership drops from a high of 94 per cent to 76 per cent. By the time the couple is aging (Stage VIII) the majority own a retirement home (86 per cent).

For most families, buying a house means assuming debts which continue through the years. Continuing housing payments closely parallel home ownership as you see comparing Chart 19 with Table 37 below. That house payments are closely related to other family indebtedness

[1] Harold Feldman, "The Development of Husband-Wife Relationships," paper delivered at the International Conference on the Family, August 1960, mimeographed appendix, Table 10, p. 5.

[2] *Ibid.;* John B. Lansing and Leslie Kish, "Family Life Cycle as an Independent Variable," *American Sociological Review,* Vol. 22, No. 5, October 1957, p. 514; and John B. Lansing and James N. Morgan, "Consumer Finances over the Life Cycle," in Lincoln Clark, ed., *Consumer Behavior,* Vol. II *The Life Cycle and Consumer Behavior* (New York: New York University Press, 1955), p. 42.

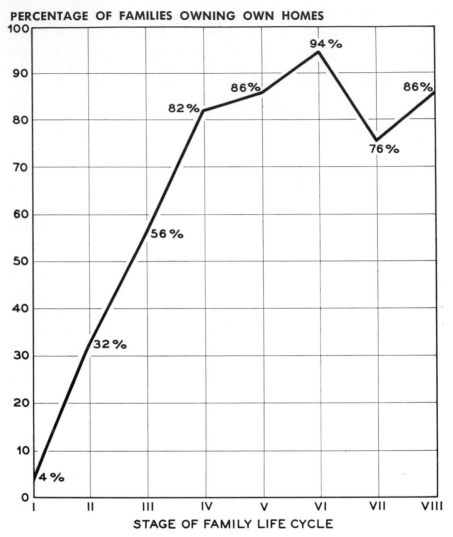

PERCENTAGE OF FAMILIES OWNING OWN HOMES

CHART 19. Families Owning Own Homes by Stage of the Family Life Cycle [1]

(for durable goods, etc.) is observed by comparing the two items stage by stage through the life cycle. In a real sense it is not just the initial cost of a home, it's the upkeep that comes dear. Having a house means filling it with all the equipment, furniture and furnishings that a modern

[1] SOURCE: Harold Feldman *op. cit.*, p. 5.

TABLE 37. *Housing Payments and Indebtedness at Different Stages in the Life Cycle*

			Young Married		Older Married 45 Plus	
	Young Single	Childless	Youngest Child Under Six	Youngest Child Six or Over	With Children	No Children under 18
Proportion of nonfarm units making any housing payments *	39%	88%	94%	95%	96%	94%
Proportion with debts of any kind †	43%	71%	88%	83%	77%	49%

° Data from John B. Lansing and James N. Morgan, *op. cit.*, p. 44.
† *Ibid.*, p. 48.

home seems to require. "Planned obsolescence" whereby an item is designed for a limited life, operates throughout the life cycle in the majority of families.[1]

Even for those who do not own their own homes, there are the ongoing tasks of finding, furnishing and settling into a place which meets the family requirements at a given life cycle stage within the time and money available. This basic family task is related in many ways to all other developmental tasks—especially to that having to do with paying the bills.

COSTS ARE HIGH WHEN INCOME IS LOW

The economic pinch is greatest during the early and the final stages of the family life cycle when costs are high and income low. Aging families have disproportionally high expenditures for health and medical care, through the period when retirement forces them into low income brackets (Chapter 14). Costs are high during the early years of marriage, partly because durable goods and equipment for the household tend to be regarded as necessities by the newly married.[2] During the establishment phase of the family life cycle, the husband's earnings are at the lowest point they will be until he nears retirement age. With each succeeding decade the college graduate husband's wages and salary income increase until he reaches a peak in his mid-fifties. Then, presumably his

[1] *Ibid.*
[2] James N. Morgan, "Consumer Investment Expenditures," *The American Economic Review*, Vol. XLVIII, No. 5, December 1958, p. 890.

children are raised and his home is equipped and paid for as shown in Table 38 comparing workers' income with amount of education and age. In general, income increases with education and with age up to the middle years.

Financial pressures remain high during the years in which children are being raised. More families with young children buy television sets, for instance, than at any other stage in the family life cycle. Similarly, percentages of families buying new cars are high in the childrearing stages, exceeded only by couples in the establishment phase.[1]

To fill the gap between her husband's income and her family's needs,

TABLE 38. *Income by Education of Family Head, in the United States, 1964* [2]

| Education of Family Head | Percentage of Families in Four Income Groups | | | |
	Under $3,000	*$3,000 to $4,999*	*$5,000 to $9,999*	*$10,000 and over*
Elementary (8 years)	26%	22%	40%	13%
High School (4 years)	9	16	52	23
College (1–3 years)	8	12	49	32
College (4 years or more)	4	6	36	54

today's wife and mother often gets a job. Three out of every ten married women are now working. At least nine out of ten women are likely to work outside the home in the course of their lives, in the United States.[3] Typically, the young wife works until her first child arrives when she drops out of the labor force until her children are in school. Then she may return to work to help meet family costs, assure the children of adequate schooling, and the family of the standard of living to which she and her husband aspire. Somewhat more wives of husbands with low incomes work than do wives of men earning more than $5,000 a year, but the pattern of wives' gainful employment is similar in both income brackets, as you see in Chart 20.

[1] Lansing and Kish, *op. cit.*, p. 514.

[2] Derived from *Americans at Mid-Decade* (Washington, D. C.: U. S. Department of Commerce, Bureau of the Census, Series P-23, No. 16, 1966, p. 29; and *Current Population Reports*, Series P-60, No. 47.

[3] National Manpower Council, *Womanpower,* New York: Columbia University Press, 1957, page 10.

PERCENTAGE OF WIVES
CURRENTLY EMPLOYED

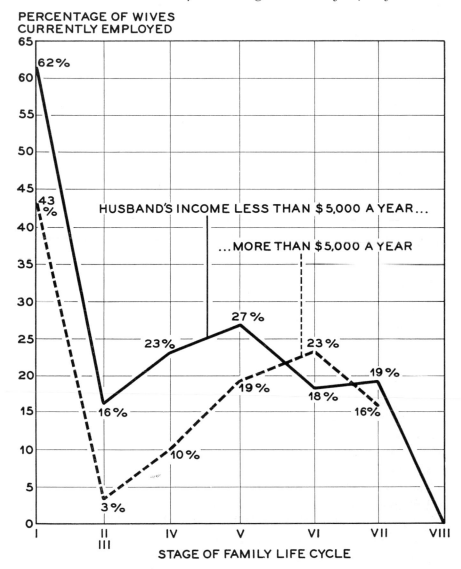

CHART 20. **Percentage of Working Wives by Stage in the Family Life Cycle** [1]

Note that during the launching stage (VI), wives of men with higher incomes tend to work in larger percentages than do women in humbler

[1] SOURCE: Robert O. Blood, Jr. and Donald M. Wolfe, *Husbands and Wives* (Glencoe, Illinois: The Free Press, 1960), p. 105.

circumstances—very possibly to help pay for the college education, ward-robes, weddings, and other costs of "suitably" launching their children into adulthood.

While there are children in the home, as many mothers work part-time as are employed full-time as Table 39 clearly shows. Thus even at the teenage stage (Stage V), of the family life cycle, although 40 per cent of the mothers are working, only 18 per cent work full-time.

What "price" does the family pay for the earnings of its wife and mother? It depends on the mother's health, ability, and liking for her job. It depends upon her husband's attitude toward her working and toward

TABLE 39. *Percentage of Working Wives by Stage of the Family Life Cycle* [1]

Employment Status	Stage of the Family Life Cycle							
	1	2	3	4	5	6	7	8
Not working	48%	84%	82%	72%	60%	64%	64%	82%
Part-time job	8	8	8	20	22	10	8	8
Full-time job	44	8	10	8	18	26	28	10
Total per cent	100	100	100	100	100	100	100	100

his role in the family. And, it depends upon the age and number of children as well as on their care when their mother is away. A recent analysis of more than fifty studies on the effect of maternal employment on children concludes, "After reading these studies, it looks as if the fact of the mother being employed or staying at home is not such an important factor in determining the behavior of the child as we have been led to think." [2]

There is mounting evidence that a family's satisfaction with its standard of living declines as children come and decreases still further as they grow up and need more and more of this world's goods.[3] Low-income families may improve financially as soon as their children are old enough to work. But the teenage and launching periods are a further strain on middle-class families who aspire to do well by their children, support them through college and into homes of their own in the style to which they would like to become accustomed.

[1] Harold Feldman, *op. cit.,* p. 6.
[2] Lois Meek Stolz, "Effects of Maternal Employment on Children: Evidence from Research," *Child Development,* Vol. 31, No. 4, December 1960, p. 779.
[3] See Blood and Wolfe, *op. cit.,* p. 112; and Lansing and Morgan, *op. cit.,* p. 49.

Disagreements about money lead all others throughout the family life cycle.[1] They rise sharply from 10 per cent of honeymooner's squabbles, to 28 per cent in families with preschoolers. From then on they come close to one-quarter of all family disagreements until the children have been launched. High levels of disagreements over money coupled with decline in satisfaction with standard of living while children are being raised may be evidence that too many American families today are aspiring for material wellbeing beyond what they comfortably can afford.

SHARED DECISIONS DECREASE WITH TIME

Husbands usually make decisions regarding their work, and buying a car.[2] Wives generally make the decisions about their work outside the home, as well as within the family, in such areas as food, and gardening. Other decisions: medical and dental care, insurance, vacations, and the purchase of such items as radio or television sets, both husband and wife tend to share, in both rural and urban families in varying sections of the country in both low and middle income groups.[3]

Studies agree that in early marriage husband and wife share jointly many more decisions than they do in the later stages of the family life cycle. There is increasing role differentiation as the marriage continues. By the launching and middle years families tend to assign decisions to one family member or the other rather than to make them jointly.[4] As parents get busier with the many tasks of raising, supporting, and releasing their children, time and energy are depleted, and it becomes easier to divide their responsibilities. Then, as they become increasingly expert each in areas where experience has proven their ability, it is understandable that they agree to allocate to the more competent and available individual the decisions that are involved in various family tasks. For instance, the Detroit Area Study finds that wives assume an increasing share of household tasks and decisions through the family life cycle. As the wife's responsibilities in the family increase, the husband's decision-

---

[1] Blood and Wolfe, *ibid.*, p. 247.

[2] Blood and Wolfe, *ibid.*, p. 21; and Glenn C. McCann, "Consumer Decisions in the Rural Farm Family in the South," paper read at the American Sociological Association meetings, New York City, August 1960.

[3] Blood and Wolfe, *ibid.*; Glenn C. McCann, *ibid.*; Elizabeth H. Wolgast, "Do Husbands or Wives Make the Purchasing Decisions?" *The Journal of Marketing,* Vol. XXIII, October 1958, pp. 151–158.

[4] *Ibid.*

making decreases sharply from a peak at the childbearing and preschool stages to a low at the aging family stage.[1]

Although production of goods in the family has decreased rapidly through recent decades, there still are a great many things that have to be done in the home if the family is to live well. Even though home

TABLE 40. *Factors Determining Time Required for Homemaking Responsibilities in a Given Family* [2]

1. Stage of the family life cycle
2. Number of persons in the home
3. Number and ages of the children
4. Special expectations and interests of the members of the household
5. Responsibilities undertaken by the homemaker in relation to the other members of the family because of their physical, emotional, educational, social and personal needs
6. Duties undertaken by the homemaker in behalf of the children's school and organizational demands
7. Functions of the homemaker as wife, hostess, companion, partner and helpmate
8. Out-of-the-home responsibilities of the homemaker in gainful employment, volunteer work, and individual enrichment activities
9. Size and nature of the home that must be maintained
10. Standard of living the family aspires to maintain
11. Levels of competence the homemaker expects of herself in the performance of the various homemaking tasks she undertakes
12. Home management skills and abilities to plan, administer and run the menage
13. Number and qualifications of other persons helping in the performance of the various household tasks
14. Type of assistance others give the homemaker and with what frequency
15. Availability of emergency resources for special services from time to time
16. Number and efficiency of the various labor-saving devices and equipment available and relative ease of keeping them in good working order
17. Location of the household in terms of time and distances required for utilizing needed resources, i.e., shopping areas, medical, dental and cultural facilities, etc.
18. Flexibility of family and personal routines allowing for simplified methods of care of the household and its members as the situation changes

production levels have decreased, standards of living have appreciably increased.

Home production of goods increases sharply through the family life cycle. The newly married wife typically is too busy working outside the

---

[1] Blood and Wolfe, *ibid.*

[2] An elaboration and adaptation of a paper delivered by Helena Znaniecki Lopata, "The Life Cycle of Social Roles of Housewife," Midwest Sociological Society meetings, Spring 1965, mimeographed, page 7.

home to engage in much home production. The young mother has her hands full in child care activities. By the time children reach the teen and launching years home production increases sharply, and by the time the children have left home it reaches a high peak.[1] The homemaker in the middle and later years has the time, the know-how, and a ready market for her homemade clothing and foodstuffs in her children's growing families. So she uses her creative energies in making more things than ever before in the life of her family.

CONFLICTING ROLES AND LOYALTIES

Conflicting roles and shifting loyalties through the life cycle inevitably bring some anxiety and guilt feelings to various members of the family at different times. During the establishment phase, the young bride often faces conflicting loyalties between her parents and her husband and may feel guilty about neglecting her mother. At the pregnant phase it is the young husband who is apt to feel guilty at having "gotten her that way" especially if she has unpleasant symptoms at the onset of her pregnancy. During the childbearing stage when the young mother is engrossed in childcare procedures that are new and demanding, she may feel guilty and her husband may be resentful at her neglect of him. As children get into the preschool stage they normally disobey their parents from time to time with subsequent feelings of guilt, while their parents departing from their parents' practices in some ways, may experience periods of anxiety, insecurity, and doubt about their parental competence.

As the children go to school and proceed through adolescence, divided loyalties appear as children form close relationships with their peers and pull away from earlier dependence upon their parents. Youthful sex practices so often hidden from their parents add further to the burden of guilt schoolagers and adolescents carry. The father, engrossed in earning a living for his expanding household, may feel guilty that he does not spend more time with his wife and children. It is when older children reach the launching stage that the mother is most apt to feel "letdown," neglected, and misunderstood as she finds herself taken for granted in meeting the many needs and demands of the family. The emancipation of the older teenagers and young adults must be accomplished, but it often is a painful and anxious period for both parents.

[1] Blood and Wolfe, *op. cit.*, p. 85.

All this is quite normal, albeit central as storm centers in the emotional climate of the family.

SEX THROUGH THE LIFE OF THE FAMILY

Both husbands and wives agree that sex relationships are important throughout a satisfying marriage. However, sex expression declines in importance through the life cycle from a peak in the preschool stage when both spouses rate it somewhere between "very important" and "quite important" to the aging family period when it still is rated midway between "quite important" and "somewhat important." [1]

TABLE 41. *Mean Weekly Frequency of Marital Coitus Reported by Wives and Husbands* [2]

Age Group	Wives	Husbands
16–20	3.7	3.7
21–25	3.0	3.2
26–30	2.6	2.7
31–35	2.3	2.2
36–40	2.0	2.0
41–45	1.7	1.6
46–50	1.4	1.4
51–55	1.2	1.2
56–60	0.8	0.8

The frequency of coitus in marriage declines gradually from three to four times a week for husbands and wives under twenty years of age to something less than once a week for both men and women approaching sixty, as you see from Table 41.

Men and women who have not graduated from high school report more frequent marital coitus in each age group than do the college educated.[3] This suggests that better educated couples may have other avenues of mutual interest and sharing besides that of physical union. As the couple proceed through the family life cycle both husband and wife become immersed in various other responsibilities. Fatigue pays a toll in decreasing interest in or vitality for sexual activity. The first preg-

[1] Harold Feldman, *ibid.*, page 11.
[2] SOURCE: Alfred C. Kinsey, Wardell B. Pomeroy, Clyde E. Martin, and Paul H. Gebhard, *Sex Behavior in the Human Female* (Philadelphia: W. B. Saunders Company, 1953), page 77.
[3] *Ibid.*

nancy has unfavorable effects on the marital sexual adjustment of one out of four husbands (23 per cent) and wives (25 per cent).[1] Most couples are advised to discontinue intercourse for a number of weeks before and after childbirth—the exact period dependent upon the individual case. Although many women report they lose most of their sexual urge while pregnant, others maintain their desire for their husbands at the usual level.[2]

After menopause, women often have a greater sexual appetite than do their husbands.[3] This may be due to the feeling of freedom that comes when the former possibility of pregnancy is gone; to the vitality modern women in their middle years enjoy; and to the fact that the husband is usually older and ages more rapidly than his wife. Orgasm ability in the wife increases with the duration of the marriage. One out of four wives (25 per cent) fails to achieve orgasm by the end of the first year of marriage. With duration of marriage, the percentage of wives yet to experience orgasm drops to 17 per cent in the fifth year, to 14 per cent the tenth year, 12 per cent the fifteenth year, and 11 per cent in the twentieth year of marriage. By the thirtieth year of marriage nine out of ten wives are fully sexually responsive.[4] For most married couples, the frequency of sexual expression decreases through the life cycle, while the level of satisfaction continues to increase up through the middle years.

The sex interests of children, teenagers, and young adults add their dimension to the family task of channeling sex expression through the family life cycle. In early childhood sex play, masturbation, the erotic implications of soiling, messing, and oedipal attachments, as well as sex questions challenge parental understanding and management. With school days comes an increase in "dirty" stories, "naughty" words, and the rash of "little sweethearts" whose kissing, note-passing, and "understandings" are recognized by classmates and parents of both families.[5]

---

[1] Judson T. Landis, Thomas Poffenberger, and Shirley Poffenberger, "The Effects of First Pregnancy upon the Sexual Adjustment of 212 Couples," *American Sociological Review*, Vol. 15, No. 6, December 1950, pp. 767–772.

[2] Bernard R. Greenblat, *A Doctor's Marital Guide for Patients* (Chicago: The Budlong Press, 1959), page 48.

[3] *Ibid.*, page 46.

[4] Kinsey *et al.*, *op. cit.*, page 408.

[5] Carlfred Broderick, and Stanley Fowler, "New Patterns of Relationships between the Sexes Among Preadolescents," *Marriage and Family Living*, Volume XXIII, No. 1, February 1961, pp. 27–30.

Teenagers coping with their maturing bodies, deepening interests in the other sex, and emancipation thrusts from their families may confide less in their parents, ask fewer questions, and avoid family discussions of the very areas that most concern both themselves and their parents; sex, petting, and marriage.[1] By the time the launching stage arrives parents may make a last-ditch effort to make sure that their daughters know what to expect in marriage, but their sons more usually are expected to work things out for themselves in the sexual areas of life.[2]

Some families are more comfortable than others in dealing with sex throughout the life cycle. These parents tend to have wholesome accepting attitudes about the sex side of life. They answer their children's questions easily. They don't get too excited about youngsters' sex play or language. They accept their teenagers' developing interests with understanding and respect. They provide helpful materials for their children's sex education. They release their young adults into full maturity without too much of a personal sense of loss. Their reward is in more mutually meaningful relationships with their children and with each other throughout the entire life cycle.

BEARING, REARING AND RELATING TO CHILDREN

Most married couples want children, and the number of children in the typical American family is increasing. The proportion of families with children under 18 increased from 52 to 56 per cent between 1948 and 1958. The proportion with 2, 3, and 4 or more children has increased while the percentage with only one child has decreased—so that 58 per cent of the nation's children are now in families of 3 or more children.[3]

Some couples, especially in the working class, find themselves overburdened with more children than they can care for, even in areas where contraceptive aid is available. According to one exploratory study, "The lack of effective contraception so common in this group is not due sim-

---

[1] Marvin Dubbé, "What Young People Can't Talk Over with Their Parents," *National Parent-Teacher,* Volume 52, Number 2, October 1957, pp. 18–20.

[2] Irving Tebor, "Male Virgins: Conflicts and Group Support in American Culture," *The Family Life Coordinator,* Vol. IX, No. 3–4, March–June 1961, pp. 40–42.

[3] Interdepartmental Committee on Children and Youth, *Children in a Changing World,* Golden Anniversary White House Conference on Children and Youth, 1960, chart 3, page 5; see also such reports as Ronald Freedman, David Goldberg, and Harry Sharp, " 'Ideals' about Family Size in the Detroit Metropolitan Areas 1954," *The Milbank Memorial Fund Quarterly,* Vol. XXXIII, No. 2, April 1955, pp. 187–197; and Blood and Wolfe, *op. cit.,* pp. 124–136.

ply to ignorance or misunderstanding; it is embodied in particular personalities, world views, and ways of life which have consistency and stability and which do not readily admit such foreign elements as conscious planning and emotion-laden contraceptive practices." [1]

Married college students often find themselves with their first baby before they had planned to have it.[2] Even though the first baby has been planned and very much wanted, its arrival is apt to be a crisis for a number of reasons: (1) inadequate preparation—as one mother put it, "We knew where babies came from, but we didn't know *what they were like;*" (2) fatigue resulting from loss of sleep; (3) confinement in home-based childcare; (4) curtailment of social life; (5) loss of income and satisfactions of wife's employment; (6) guilt in not being a better parent; (7) decline in housekeeping standards; (8) neglect of the young mother's appearance; (9) decline in wife's sexual response; (10) increased costs in having a child at time when wife's income is cut off; (11) worry about a second pregnancy in the near future; and (12) a general disenchantment with the parental role.[3] Not all pregnancies come to term. About one in ten spontaneously miscarry; and there are at least 200 to 250 induced abortions for each 1,000 pregnancies in this country [4]—bringing another kind of crisis with possible emotional and physical toll.

Problems of raising and relating to children change from stage to stage of their development. Longitudinal studies show that wetting, soiling, thumbsucking, and speech problems tend to be general in the first two years. Temper tantrums, fears, and negativism reach their peaks among preschool children. Disturbing dreams, and mood swings appear often among both boys and girls of ten and eleven.[5]

One of the first signs of the onset of adolescence is the young teen-

[1] Lee Rainwater, *And the Poor Get Children* (Chicago: Quadrangle Books, 1960), pp. 167–168.

[2] Kate Hevner Mueller in Opal D. David, ed., *The Education of Women* (Washington, D. C.: American Council on Education, 1959, p. 78, reports, "Many of these wives are able and talented, with one or two college years to their credit, but now they are dropping out of school to do typing, to have a child—either intentionally (33 per cent) or inadvertently (67 per cent) . . ."

[3] E. E. LeMasters, "Parenthood as Crisis," *Marriage and Family Living,* Vol. XIX, No. 4, November 1957, pp. 352–355.

[4] Alan F. Guttmacher, "Abortions—Medical and Social Review" in Evelyn M. and Sylvanus M. Duvall, eds., *Sex Ways—in Fact and Faith* (New York: Association Press, 1961), pp. 211–226.

[5] Jean W. Macfarlane, Lucile Allen, and Marjorie P. Honzik, *A Developmental Study of the Behavior Problems of Normal Children between Twenty-one Months and Fourteen Years* (Berkeley: University of California Press, 1954), pp. 147–160.

Courses for married couples and expectant mothers' and fathers' classes are good ways of relieving anxiety and preparing families for childbearing.

ager's critical attitude toward the physical features of his home. By middle adolescence, teenage girls criticize their mothers as homemakers, and boys challenge their fathers in disturbing ways. As a Harvard longitudinal study reports, "Adolescents in this phase criticize every aspect of their parents' personalities but it would appear that the criticisms most difficult for the parents to bear are those directed toward personal traits, mannerisms, or idiosyncrasies about which the parents have long been sensitive." [1] Parental disagreement about childrearing reaches a high point in the second decade of marriage,[2] during the children's teen years; when so many family squabbles occur. The launching stage brings problems of love affairs, mate selection, marriage, educational and vocational choices that often disturb parents who are emotionally involved in, yet with little voice in their youngsters' plans.

With the marriage of a family's sons and daughters, comes the challenge (especially for the mother) of working out new relationships

[1] Ruth M. Butler, "Mothers' Attitudes Toward the Social Development of Their Adolescents," *Social Casework*, May–June 1956, 16 pages.

[2] Charles Bowerman, "Adjustment in Marriage: Over-All and in Specific Areas," *Sociology and Social Research*, Volume 41, Number 4, March–April 1957, pages 257–263; and Blood and Wolfe, *op. cit.*, p. 247.

with daughters- and sons-in-law. By the time a woman has begun to find out what it means to be a mother-in-law, the grandchildren arrive and she becomes a grandmother. Fortunately, feelings of inadequacy as parents drop through the years. By the time mothers and fathers reach 55, and presumably have launched their children, fewer ever feel inadequate (41 per cent) than at any previous time, as parents.[1]

INTERACTION DECLINES THROUGH THE MARRIAGE

Children sharply curtail marital communication. Young married couples without children talk together more frequently on an average day than at any other stage of the family life cycle. Husband-wife conversations diminish sharply with the coming of children, and continue at low levels of frequency until the teen years. Then, apparently, adolescents are out of the home enough to give their parents a chance to communicate as a couple somewhat more. From then on through the marriage, there is a gradual increase in the amount of time husband and wife spend talking together, to a second peak in the aging family stage that still is lower than at Stage I.[2]

During the childrearing years, husbands and wives tend to become absorbed in their separate roles as fathers and mothers. They stop doing things together, and grow apart. Then when the children have grown and the couple might enjoy each other's company, they have become strangers under a common roof, with little to share with one another. This is not inevitable. Among older wives, one in four is still enthusiastic about her husband's companionship, and another one in four is quite satisfied. But fully half eventually become so dissatisfied that they either look elsewhere for companionship, or they become resigned to loneliness.[3]

It makes a woman feel better to tell her husband about her day. But the percentage of wives reporting this satisfaction declines with the coming of children—from 40 per cent of those without children to 25 per cent with schoolagers, to a low of 17 per cent at the launching stage, recovering only slightly to 20 per cent of those whose children have been launched.[4] It is as though many a mother learns to cope with her problems alone during the bustling years when there are children in the

---

[1] Gerald Gurin, Joseph Veroff, and Sheila Feld, *Americans View Their Mental Health* (New York: Basic Books, 1960), p. 137.
[2] Harold Feldman, *op. cit.*, p. 11.
[3] Blood and Wolfe, *op. cit.*, Chapter 6.
[4] *Ibid.*, p. 202.

WIFE'S MEAN SATISFACTION WITH HUSBAND'S LOVE

CHART 21. Wives' Decreasing Satisfaction with Love through the
Family Life Cycle [1]

home, and never fully regains the intimate sharing with her husband she once found satisfying.

A wife's satisfaction with her husband's love declines steadily from a peak when the babies are small to a low at the later stages of the marriage, as is seen in Chart 21. Studies agree that there tends to be disenchantment, disillusionment, and unhappiness in the later years of marriage. Reporting a follow-up study of the Burgess-Wallin couples married up to twenty years, Pineo finds a general drop in marital satisfac-

[1] SOURCE: Blood and Wolfe, *op. cit.*, p. 232. Stage VI has been omitted after consultation with Dr. Blood.

tion. "There is a loss of a certain intimacy. Confiding, kissing, and reciprocal settlement of disagreements become less frequent; more individuals report loneliness. This loss of intimacy appears to be an aspect of disenchantment."[1]

During engagement, adjustment scores of men and women are about the same. Men become disenchanted earlier in the marriage, but the drop in adjustment scores between the early and middle years of marriage is greater for women than for men, so that by the middle years the marital adjustment scores of both husbands and wives are again about equal. There is some evidence that men are premaritally more romantic than women and so become disillusioned earlier in marriage than do their wives.[2] There are indications too that wives tend to be most unhappy in their late forties and early fifties [3] when their children no longer need them, their husbands are less adequate as mates than previously, and they have not yet found a second career for themselves.[4]

Further light is shown on the decline in marital communication with age by the nationwide interview study conducted by the Joint Commission on Mental Illness and Health. They find that although marital happiness and adjustment tend to decrease with age, the percentages of husbands and wives who say they feel inadequate and have marital problems decline even more sharply as men and women grow older. The suggestion is that maturity and age bring increasing acceptance of one's lot rather than increasing positive gratifications.[5]

IN-LAW PROBLEMS DROP SHARPLY

Difficulties with relatives decline through the family life cycle. In the early years of marriage husband and wife are getting used to their roles as members of each other's families. Then they are leaving their parents in favor of their mates as first loyalties. In-law problems loom larger in the first stage than they ever will again in the family life cycle, (Chart 22).

[1] Peter C. Pineo, "Disenchantment in the Later Years of Marriage," *Marriage and Family Living*, Vol. XXIII, No. 1, February 1961, pp. 3–11.

[2] Charles W. Hobart, "Disillusionment in Marriage, and Romanticism," *Marriage and Family Living*, Vol. XX, No. 2, May 1958, pp. 156–162.

[3] James H. S. Bossard and Eleanor S. Boll, "Marital Unhappiness in the Life Cycle," *Marriage and Family Living*, Vol. XVII, No. 1, February 1955, pp. 10–14.

[4] Arnold M. Rose, "Factors Associated with the Life Satisfaction of Middle-Class, Middle-Aged Persons," *Marriage and Family Living*, Vol. XVII, No. 1, February, 1955, pp. 15–19.

[5] Gurin *et al.*, *op. cit.*, pp. 103–104.

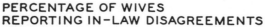

PERCENTAGE OF WIVES
REPORTING IN-LAW DISAGREEMENTS

**CHART 22.   Decline in In-Law Disagreements through the Family
Life Cycle** [1]

Several reasons are advanced for the rapid decline of in-law problems
after the first stage of the family life cycle. One is the softening effect
that becoming a grandmother has on the mother-in-law relationship,
which is found to be the most difficult, in families with in-law problems.[2]
A second closely related factor is the maturing of husband and wife, so
that their parents-in-law are more esteemed as they themselves become
parents. A third is the wearing off of the stereotype of trouble with in-
laws; and fourth, growing appreciation for the help that the older families

---

[1] SOURCE: Blood and Wolfe, *op. cit.*, p. 247.
[2] Evelyn Millis Duvall, *In-Laws: Pro and Con* (New York: Association Press,
1954), pp. 141–160 and 187–220.

give the younger.[1] Fifth is the gradual acceptance of the marriage by parents who have previously disapproved. This may be particularly true of the mixed marriage.[2]

Difficulties with relatives are best worked out early in the marriage,[3] or before. Some couples continue to cope with in-law troubles through the years. One study of supposedly successful marriages found nearly one in ten (9.6 per cent) of the husbands and wives agreeing that they never had made a satisfactory adjustment in their in-law relationships. A similar percentage (10.9 per cent) disagreed on whether they had worked out a satisfactory adjustment from the beginning, and another 7 per cent said that it had taken them from one to twenty years of marriage to make satisfactory adjustments to their relatives.[4]

Analysis of what husbands and wives say is effective in working out harmonious relationships with their in-laws finds two significant factors: (1) acceptance ("They accept me, they are friendly, close, understanding . . ."), and (2) mutual respect ("We respect each other's personalities"). Out of 748 reasons why their in-law relationships had worked out harmoniously, items involving either acceptance or mutual respect were mentioned spontaneously 563 times, or in 75.2 per cent of the cases involving 345 married persons.[5] Acceptance and mutual respect call for emotional maturity on the part of all the family members. They further indicate the successful accomplishment of the family developmental task of relating to relatives on both sides of the family.

SETTLING DOWN IN A COMMUNITY

American families today typically live in not one but several communities over time. About 9 out of every 10 persons in the United States move at least once in their lifetimes. Each year, approximately one out of every

[1] *Ibid.* pp. 37–51; and Marvin Sussman, "The Help Pattern in the Middle Class Family," *American Sociological Review,* Vol. XVIII, No. 1, February 1953, pp. 22–28.

[2] Evelyn Millis Duvall, *In-Laws: Pro and Con, op. cit.,* pp. 70–88; M. L. Barron, *People Who Intermarry* (Syracuse University Press, 1946); Judson T. Landis, "Marriages of Mixed and Non-Mixed Religious Faith," *American Sociological Review,* Vol. 14, No. 3. June 1949, pp. 401–407; Murray Lieffer, as reported in *Time,* January 31, 1949, and others.

[3] John L. Thomas, *The American Catholic Family* (New York: Prentice-Hall, 1956), p. 234.

[4] Judson T. Landis, "Length of Time Required to Achieve Adjustment in Marriage," *American Sociological Review,* Vol. 11, No. 6, December 1946, p. 668.

[5] Evelyn Millis Duvall, *op. cit.,* pp. 331–336.

PERCENTAGE OF THE CIVILIAN POPULATION
MOVING INTO A DIFFERENT HOUSE IN A GIVEN YEAR

CHART 23.   Decreasing Percentages of Persons Moving into a
Different House, by Age Groups [1]

five moves into a different house.[2] The chances of a family's moving is
four times greater in the early stages of the life cycle than in the middle and later years, as you see in Chart 23. Although these data are for

[1] SOURCE: U. S. Bureau of the Census, *Mobility of the Population of the United
States* (Civilian Population only), April 1958–1959.
[2] United States Bureau of the Census, *Mobility of the Population of the United
States, April 1958 to 1959.* Series P-20, No. 104, September 1960.

persons by age groups in the civilian population, evidence that more families with young children move than during school or teen-age stages is clear: 28 per cent of children 1–4 years of age in contrast to 18 per cent of children 5–13 years, and 15 per cent of teenagers 14–17 years old move in a given year.[1]

Young husbands have few seniority rights and other advantages to keep them from moving to a different locale when a better opportunity comes along.[2] Job shifts, aspirations for a home of their own where children may have play space, good schools, and other advantages, combine to push more and more families into the suburban areas that circle our cities.[3]

Until a family gets settled into a new community, they have more visits from their relatives than after they have lived in the new place nine months or more. By that time they typically have joined one or more clubs, and know more of their neighbors.[4]

Family members tend to follow their interests out into community activities—often by age groups. Families with young children find other young families congenial in "sitter-swaps," but otherwise are not as active in the community as are those with older children.[5] School-age children involve their parents in Parent-Teacher Associations, scout programs, Campfire Girls, as well as a variety of sports, dramatic and musical activities sponsored by church, the local "Y" and other agencies. By the time the family reaches the teenage stage the parents are drawn into

[1] *Ibid.*

[2] Paul C. Glick, *American Families* (New York: John Wiley & Sons, 1957), page 90.

[3] Factors related to the move to the suburbs are discussed in: Ernest R. Mowrer, "The Family in Suburbia," pp. 147–164; Wendell Bell, "Social Choice, Life Styles, and Suburban Residence," pp. 225–247; and Sylvia F. Fava, "Contrasts in Neighboring: New York City and a Suburban Community," pp. 122–131, in William A. Dobriner, ed., *The Suburban Community* (New York: G. P. Putnam's Sons, 1958). See also such related studies as Peter H. Rossi, *Why Families Move: A Study in the Social Psychology of Urban Mobility* (Glencoe, Illinois: The Free Press, 1955), William H. Whyte, Jr., *The Organization Man* (Garden City: Doubleday Anchor Books, 1957), and Gerald R. Leslie and Arthur H. Richardson, "Life-Cycle, Career Pattern, and the Decision to Move," paper presented at the International Conference on the Family, New York City, August 1960.

[4] Eugene Litwak, "Differential Functions of Family and Neighborhood Primary Groups for Social Succor," paper presented at the International Conference on the Family, New York City, August 1960.

[5] Kenneth R. Cunningham and Theodore B. Johannis, Jr., "Research on the Family and Leisure: A Review and Critique of Selected Studies," *The Family Life Coordinator*, Volume IX, Nos. 1 and 2, September–December, 1960, pp. 25–32.

various chaperoning, chauffeuring, and sponsoring arrangements which bring them in touch with other families with teenagers, and a variety of community activities on their own.

When the children have grown up and left home, husband and wife are free to choose either (1) disengagement and curtailment of their activities, or (2) continued activity through their developing interests and friendships (Chapters 13 and 14). Studies agree that one way to avoid loneliness and dispair in the later years of marriage is to continue to be active in pursuits that are personally meaningful.[1]

RELATIVE VULNERABILITY AND PHILOSOPHY OF LIFE

Families are most vulnerable to disruption in their early stages. Husband and wife start off with a multitude of developmental tasks that must be accomplished early in their marriage, if the union is to succeed. The man must learn what it means to be a husband in the midst of confusions and contradictions in his contemporary roles. Concurrently, the wife is tackling the complexities of life as a married woman at a time when personal and societal expectations are not clearly defined. Simultaneously, the couple grapple with the tasks of establishing the most intimate and demanding relationship of a lifetime. Before they have established mutually comfortable patterns for living together, they may be under strains too great to weather.

Divorces and annulments are more frequent during the early years of marriage than at any other time in the family life cycle. The number of divorces rises rapidly after the first few months of marriage, reaches a peak during the third year and declines thereafter through the later years of marriage. In one recent year, for example (Chart 24), the number of divorces per 1,000 marriages decreased from a high of 25.4 for couples married two years, to 9.6 for those married ten years, to 4.1 for couples married 25 years, to 1.2 for marriages of forty years duration, decreasing still further to .3 for couples married long enough to celebrate their Golden Wedding anniversaries.[2]

Aside from the fact that most of the marriages which ultimately termi-

---

[1] Harvey J. Locke, *Predicting Adjustment in Marriage* (New York: Henry Holt and Company, 1951), pp. 256–258; and Robert J. Havighurst, "The Social Competence of Middle-Aged People," *Genetic Psychology Monographs*, Vol. 56, 1957, pp. 297–375.

[2] Paul H. Jacobson, *American Marriage and Divorce* (New York: Rinehart & Company, 1959), p. 144.

DIVORCES PER 1,000 MARRIAGES

NUMBER OF YEARS MARRIED

CHART 24. **Divorces per 1,000 Marriages by Duration of Marriage, United States, 1955** [1]

nate break down in the early years, divorces are by no means a random sample of all marriages. Divorce is more likely to be of:

Non-whites than of whites
Lower than of higher socio-economic and educational status
Urban than of rural backgrounds
Residents in the West than of the East, and of the South than of the North
Childless marriages than of those with children
Persons in some occupations than of those in others.[2]

Another factor distinguishing between those who tend to divorce and those who remain married is religion. Numerous studies (Table 42) concur that married couples with no religious affiliation divorce much more frequently than do religious pairs. Of the three major faiths, the Jewish marriage is the most stable, the Roman Catholic union is intermediate, and the Protestant family is somewhat more likely to break up in divorce or separation.

Fewer devoutly religious couples divorce or separate than do those who take their religion lightly. A recent representative student sample

[1] SOURCE: Paul H. Jacobson, *American Marriage and Divorce* (New York: Rinehart & Company, 1959), pp. 145 and 147.
[2] Jessie Bernard in Evelyn M. and Sylvanus M. Duvall, eds., *Sex Ways—in Fact and Faith* (New York: Association Press, 1961), p. 95.

TABLE 42. *Percentage of Young People's Homes Broken by Divorce or Separation by Religious Affiliation of the Parents*

	Jewish	Roman Catholic	Protestant	No Faith
Bell study, 1938 *	4.6%	6.4%	6.8%	16.7%
Landis ", 1960 #	3.3	7.7	10.0	18.2

° Howard M. Bell, *Youth Tell Their Story* (Washington, D. C.: American Council on Education, 1938), p. 21.

Judson T. Landis, "Religiousness, Family Relationships, and Family Values in Protestant, Catholic and Jewish Families," *Marriage and Family Living*, November 1960, Vol. XXII, No. 4, p. 342.

reported the following percentages of divorced or separated parents: 5.5 per cent of the devout, 8.9 per cent of the religious, and 19.8 per cent of the indifferent. Significantly more devout than slightly religious, indifferent, or anti-religious parents were happily married, according to their college-age children.[1] All evidence to date is that responsible individuals with religious roots are significantly less divorce-prone and more likely to be happily married.[2]

As children arrive, the danger of disruption lessens, and other strains increase. During the childbearing and rearing stages of the family life cycle, resources of time, money, and energy are most limited. While the couple is busy establishing their home, they probably face the crisis of parenthood for the first time. The wife quits her job with the coming of children, thereby reducing the family income while its costs soar. The husband works hard to make ends meet, leaving the wife home alone most of the day, in charge of the household, the infant, and young children. Now there is rarely enough money to go around, or time and strength enough to do everything that should be done. Heavy responsibilities carried for long periods of time build up fatigue in busy parents. Energy depletion is to be expected during the years when husband and wife separately and together answer the demands of the young and growing family.

During the latter half of marriage, the couple is most vulnerable to

[1] Landis, *ibid.*, p. 342

[2] See for instance, Ernest W. Burgess and Leonard S. Cottrell, *Predicting Success or Failure in Marriage* (New York: Prentice-Hall, 1939); Ernest W. Burgess and Paul Wallin, *Engagement and Marriage* (Philadelphia: J. B. Lippincott Company, 1953); and Harvey J. Locke, *Predicting Adjustment in Marriage* (New York: Henry Holt and Company, 1951).

unhappiness, and dissatisfaction. With their children grown and gone, the middle aged and older couple no longer feel needed. They have grown apart during the busy years of parenting and now may or may not be able to re-establish their companionship in mutually satisfying ways. By now they have either attained their goals and aspirations, or they have become resigned to the realities of their lives. Vocationally the husband faces retirement, and the wife lost her major job of motherhood when the last child was launched. The excitement, vitality and challenge of the early years now often give way to disenchantment in the later years of marriage.[1]

Family living does not always dwindle away in its later stages. There are some couples who face little of life's isolation, loneliness and barrenness after their children have been launched. They do not become disengaged from life. They find themselves as individuals, as a married pair, as citizens, and as members of the larger family with new depths and dimensions in their interaction. Husbands and wives who find satisfaction in "the last of life for which the first was made" have a number of distinctive characteristics: (1) they have a religious faith or a philosophy of life that gives meaning to their being, (2) they value wisdom more than physical prowess, (3) they enjoy emotional expansion more than constriction, (4) they encourage mental flexibility rather than rigidity, and (5) they expand their interests beyond their earlier work roles.[2]

Married couples who continue to assume responsibility for achieving their developmental tasks at each stage of the family life cycle avoid many of the difficulties, hazards, and crises that threaten many another family. A sound philosophy of life makes family members less vulnerable to crisis than are those less well established within a value system.

A study of families subjected to the stresses of living in a rapidly urbanizing southern community finds good family adjustment associated highly with family philosophy and outlook, family policies and practices, and the personal resources of individual family members. Of high statistical significance in accounting for good family adjustment were the following factors:

---

[1] Peter C. Pineo, "Disenchantment in the Later Years of Marriage," *Marriage and Family Living*, Vol. XXIII, No. 1, February 1961, pp. 3–11, and other research summarized in Chapters 13 and 14.

[2] Robert J. Havighurst and Betty Orr, *Adult Education and Adult Needs* (Chicago: Center for the Study of Liberal Education for Adults, 1956), pp. 1–4.

Hobbies, community activities, and projects help the mature man meet the challenge of social isolation in the middle and later years.

1) Nonmaterialistic philosophy of life
2) Family orientation to trouble
3) Developmental conceptions of parenthood
4) Number of tasks shared by husband and wife
5) Family adaptability
6) Accuracy of family perception of problems
7) Perception of emotional problems as family concern
8) Diffusion of leadership in family problem solving
9) Problem-solving skill of wife
10) Personal adjustment of husband and wife [1]

The good family is not a family without problems; it is rather one that uses its resources to weather the storms of life that strike from time to time. Even the most successful family faces certain inevitable crises.

---

[1] Reuben Hill, Joel Moss, and Claudine Wirths, *Eddyville's Families* (Chapel Hill: Institute for Research in Social Science, University of North Carolina, 1953), mimeographed report.

Knowing what to expect, and preparing for what lies ahead is part of the challenge of effective family living.

FAMILY CRISES

A family crisis is any situation for which the usual patterns of family living are inadequate. Family crises may be classified as those resulting from loss of a member (dismemberment), those resulting from loss of status and of face (demoralization), those resulting from the addition of a member (accession), and those resulting from a combination of demoralization and dismemberment or accession, as follows:

TYPES OF FAMILY CRISES [1]

Dismemberment	Hospitalization
	Loss of child
	Loss of spouse
	Orphanhood
	Separation (military service, work, etc.)
Demoralization	Disgrace (alcoholism, crime, delinquency, drug addiction, etc.)
	Infidelity
	Nonsupport
	Progressive dissension
Accession	Adoption
	Birth (and possibly pregnancy)
	Deserter returns
	Relative moves in
	Reunion after separation
	Stepmother, stepfather marries in
Demoralization plus Dismemberment or Accession	Annulment
	Desertion
	Divorce
	Illegitimacy
	Imprisonment
	Institutionalization
	Runaway
	Suicide or homicide

[1] Adapted from Evelyn Duvall and Reuben Hill, *Being Married* (Boston: D. C. Heath and Company, 1960), pp. 298–299, from a classification originally suggested by T. D. Eliot.

Crises can be precipitated by conflicting developmental tasks of family members who fail to complement each other, temporarily or permanently. Parent-child differences contribute to tension and conflict, especially when the child repudiates his parents, and rebels from their control. Conflicting conceptions of role on the part of husband and wife can lead to conflicts in the sexual, economic, homemaking, childrearing, and many other relationships of the family. Cultural differences in incomplete assimilation of two different backgrounds in a marriage can cause trouble. Differences in aspiration are common in our society where so many family members are upwardly mobile while others remain socially conforming in their life goals. Social class conflicts precipitated by opposing class membership pressures seethe beneath the surface or are fought out in the open in many a home.

Usually, there is no one inadequacy. There is an initial cause which tends to create tensions in other areas of family life, which in turn may become critical in themselves. For example, cultural disparity may cause a lack of sexual satisfaction because of differing ideas and standards of sex behavior, which in turn may lead to suspicion of the mate and lack of cooperation as breadwinner or homemaker, which in turn may create crises in reciprocal roles in the family and draw some family members into new positions of power and responsibility at the expense of other members. All this may so weaken the affectional relationships and integration of the family as to render it unable to meet even a simple departure from its ordinary life patterns. The result, when an out-of-the-ordinary event occurs, is a crisis.

Family crises range from the birth of the first child,[1] or the reunion of war-separated fathers and families,[2] to such final disruptions as death, desertion, or divorce.[3] Families who have but incompletely achieved their previous developmental tasks, are more susceptible to trouble in those areas at later stages of the life cycle. Thus, a first pregnancy that comes before the young husband and wife have soundly established their relationship as a married couple may be a real crisis; whereas the pregnancy

[1] E. E. LeMasters, "Parenthood as Crisis," *Marriage and Family Living*, Vol. XIX, No. 4, November 1957, pp. 352–355.

[2] Reuben Hill, *Families Under Stress* (New York: Harper & Brothers, 1949).

[3] William Goode, *After Divorce* (Glencoe, Illinois: The Free Press, 1956); Earl L. Koos, *Families in Trouble* (New York: King's Crown Press, 1946); and Thomas D. Eliot, "Handling Family Strains and Shocks," in Howard Becker and Reuben Hill, eds., *Family, Marriage, and Parenthood* (Boston: D. C. Heath and Company, 1948), pp. 616–668.

and birth of the first child to a mature couple whose marriage is already soundly based and ready for its childbearing functions is taken more in stride.

PREDICTABLY VULNERABLE FAMILIES

Some families are more vulnerable to stress and strains than are others. Numerous studies indicate clearly that lower-class, less well-educated, newcomers in a community, and racial and ethnic minorities have more severe family crises, and weather them less well than do more comfortably situated families with financial and educational supports, and status to help cushion the shocks that come their way.

To the low-income family, living up to and beyond its income, there is a quality of desperation that is less frequent in the middle-class family, with reserves upon which it can draw. Conversely, the low-status family has less to lose in prestige and therefore sees as critical fewer problem situations than does a middle-class family whose position and pride are at stake.[1] One family may have a rigid family organization, with a firm adherence to a certain pattern of action in all family situations, while another may have more flexible family ways, with quite different attitudes toward what constitutes a crisis and what to do about it.

National interview surveys of mental health find differences of symptoms and of ways of handling unhappy periods by levels of income:

High income is associated with greater happiness, fewer worries, more frequent anticipation of future happiness, fewer physical symptoms, and more symptoms of energy immobilization. Low income implies current unhappiness and worries, a lack of confidence in the future, and the expression of anxiety through physical symptoms. Middle-income groups, who worry the most about money matters, are least likely to show symptoms of psychological anxiety and are most optimistic about the future.[2]

Fewer low-income families seek help with their problems or cope with them directly than do family members with more adequate incomes.[3] Low-status groups have least access to professional help, because they

[1] Earl L. Koos, "Class Differences in Reactions to Crisis," *Marriage and Family Living*, Vol. XII, No. 3, Summer, 1950, pp. 77, 78, 90; and Carson McGuire, "Family Backgrounds and Community Patterns," *Marriage and Family Living*, Vol. XIII, No. 4, November 1951, pp. 160–164.

[2] Gurin *et al.*, *op. cit.*, p. 218.

[3] *Ibid.*, pp. 374–376.

It is the unexpected quality of much in family living that makes it hazardous.

are less able to recognize their problems, they do not know where to look for help, and because help is not so readily available to them.[1]

Surveys reveal a high concentration of problems of dependency, ill-health, and maladjustment in relatively small numbers of families. In one city, 1 per cent of the city's families were responsible for 75 per cent of its juvenile delinquency in 1956. In all areas studied to date, a small percentage of hard core families account for the great majority of family problems and crises requiring attention.[2]

Studies of multi-problem families have established criteria for adequacy of family functioning as a guide for community intervention at critical points:

CRITERIA FOR LEVELS OF SOCIAL FUNCTIONING OF FAMILIES [3]

Inadequate Community Has a Right to Intervene	*Marginal* Behavior Not Sufficiently Harmful to Justify Intervention	*Adequate* Behavior Is in Line with Community Expectations
Laws and/or mores are clearly violated. Behavior of family members is a threat to the community.	No violation of major laws although behavior of family members is contrary to what is accepted for status group.	Laws obeyed and mores are observed. Behavior is acceptable to status group.
Children in clear and present danger because of extreme conflict or imminent disruption of family life, serious neglect of children or other types of behavior inimical to their welfare.	Children in no immediate danger, but family life marked by conflict or apathy which is potential threat to welfare of children	Children are being raised in an atmosphere conducive to healthy physical and emotional development. Socialization process carried out affirmatively. Adequate training in social skills.

Three serious problems confronting community organizations are (1) locating vulnerable families, (2) developing suitable institutional

[1] A. B. Hollingshead, and F. C. Redlich, *Social Class and Mental Illness* (New York: Wiley, 1958).
[2] 1960 White House Conference on Children and Youth, *Children in a Changing World*, 1960, page 23.
[3] L. L. Geismar and Beverly Ayres, *Measuring Family Functioning* (St. Paul, Minn.: Family Centered Project, 1960), page 19.

aids for families, and (3) finding ways of getting families in need of help to use these aids where they do exist. The relative "aloneness" of the American family presents both a serious problem and a distinct challenge to the family-helping professions. Effective ways of making institutional aids more acceptable and usable to families are needed. New approaches must be planned and put into effect if our families are to function at levels that insure the wellbeing of the nation's children.

ALL FAMILIES ARE VULNERABLE TODAY [1]

Every family is, to a greater or lesser extent, harassed, anxious or guilty, beset with complexities and burdened with conflicts, both within the family and within its larger relationships. Modern families are under the growing pressure of various agencies, industries, professions, and programs to modify, change and reorganize one or more of their living habits in accordance with new knowledges, norms, and values. Traditional patterns of family living and childrearing, derived from an earlier way of life now largely passed, no longer are adequate today.

The breakdown of traditional definitions of masculine and feminine roles, by which men and women were guided in the performance ot their obligations and the enjoyment of their privileges, has brought confusion and conflict within the family. Men and women are coming to marriage today with divergent expectations and needs, which frequently clash with those of the spouse. These conflicting beliefs and conceptions hamper and often frustrate both men and women in achieving their developmental tasks as husband and wife and as father and mother.

Children today grow up in a social situation in which changes in beliefs, expectations, and conduct are taking place so rapidly that parents often are unable to understand, let alone accept, what their adolescents think and do. Thus the more or less normal cleavages between the generations has been enlarged and accentuated; sometimes becoming bitter conflicts and resentful rivalries at the time when both parents and children are acutely in need of reassurance and support.

Overshadowing these family-focused difficulties are the larger social, economic, and political situations in which the needs and interests of families are not only ignored but frequently are sacrificed to the varied

[1] Adapted from Lawrence K. Frank, "Foreword of the Committee on Dynamics of Family Interaction," Evelyn Duvall and Reuben Hill, co-chairmen, National Conference on Family Life, Washington, D. C., 1948, mimeographed materials pp. 3, 4.

objectives of business, and numerous vested interests within the modern world.

Family developmental tasks are difficult under the most favorable circumstances. Meeting the demanding requirements of a growing family and encouraging the development of family members of differing ages, sexes, interests, and personalities are ongoing responsibilities of exacting magnitude. Yet the strength and fate of the entire society depend, in large measure, upon how well families fulfill their central task of raising creative men and women able to solve their personal and family problems.

SOLVING PERSONAL-FAMILY PROBLEMS

Interviews with 2,460 representative Americans over the age of twenty-one living at home provide a picture of what relatively normal, stable, adults are concerned about today. That most of their problems are family-connected is obvious from Table 43:

TABLE 43. *Types of Personal Problems for Which People Sought Professional Help* [1]

Problem Area	Percentage
Spouse, marriage	42%
Child, relationship with child	12
Other family relationships—parents, in-laws, etc.	5
Other relationship problems, type of relationship problem unspecified	4
Job or school problems, vocational choice	6
Non-job adjustment problems in the self (general adjustment, specific symptoms)	18
Situational problems involving other people (e.g. death or illness of a loved one) causing extreme psychological reaction	6
Nonpsychological situational problems	8
Nothing specific, a lot of little things, can't remember	2
Not ascertained	1
(Percentages total more than 100 per cent because some respondents gave more than one response)	

This nation-wide survey of the way Americans are facing their problems finds:

First, they have more chance for dealing with their troubles when they approach them subjectively, when they see them in internal-psychological, rather

[1] Gurin *et al., op. cit.,* p. 305.

than external-physical terms, and at the same time wrestle with them actively instead of accepting them with apathy.

Second, their ability to adopt this attitude of "healthful worry" is more than any other factor dependent upon education. The higher their education, the greater their self-awareness, the greater their knowledge of channels for help, and, as a corollary to education, the more they can afford to spend on expert, effective help.

Third, most people have to rely on their own inner resources as they face their problems. When they do obtain help, it is usually informal, expedient, and temporary.

Fourth, the problem of obtaining adequate professional help is particularly important in the lower status groups of the population.[1]

EDUCATION FOR FAMILY LIVING THROUGH THE LIFE CYCLE

There is no stage of the family life cycle when family members do not need some explicit education in what to expect, how to wholesomely satisfy their needs, fill their roles, and achieve their developmental tasks, both as individuals and as whole families. Education for family living throughout the family life cycle has been recommended by many people in recent years.[2] Years ago, the American Association of School Administrators published a yearbook on *Education for Family Life,* in which, "A plea is made for educators to rethink school activities with the needs and aspirations of home life in mind."[3]

Family life education has made real advances in the twentieth century, but it still faces real problems which greatly limit its present-day effectiveness in equipping families to carry on their multifold tasks. Some of the more common difficulties family life education confronts are: (1) knowledge about interpersonal and intrafamily relationships is not definite, explicit, or tangible. There are no pat answers in the back of the book as in mathematics, no recipes as in cooking, nothing tangible to

---

[1] Joint Commission on Mental Illness and Health, *Action for Mental Health* (New York: Basic Books, Inc., 1961), page 107.

[2] Review for instance, *Education for Personal and Family Living: A Working Guide for Colleges* (New York: American Social Health Association, 1955), pp. 20–46; 1960 White House Conference on Children and Youth, *Recommendations; Composite Report of Forum Findings* (Washington, D. C.: United States Government Printing Office, 1960), especially pp. 12, 13; Roy W. Fairchild and John Charles Wynn, *Families in the Church: A Protestant Survey* (New York: Association Press, 1961), especially pp. 241–247; John L. Thomas, *The American Catholic Family,* (Englewood Cliffs, N. J.: Prentice-Hall, 1956), Chapter 15; and Joint Commission on Mental Illness and Health, *Action for Mental Health* (New York: Basic Books, 1961), 338 pp.

[3] American Association of School Administrators, *Education for Family Life* (Washington, D. C.: National Education Association, 1941), page 6.

carry home as from a sewing class; (2) sound principles of child guidance, marriage and family relationships compete with multimillion-dollar mass media which tend to repeat outmoded superstitions, taboos, stereotypes, and old wives' tales and to exploit the love-hungry needs of individuals and of families; (3) relatively few well-trained professional persons are as yet available to fill the rapidly growing number of posts for teachers, supervisors, counselors, and consultants in family life education; (4) curricula are already so overcrowded, it is administratively difficult to add anything as all-pervasive as family life education to existing programs; (5) highly articulate critics speak for small minorities who resist elements of family life education and overrule the vast majority of American men and women, boys and girls who favor such programs; (6) progress in the knowledge, skills, attitudes, and values acquired in family life education is difficult to appraise, to grade, and to evaluate.

No one of the challenges family life education faces in present-day United States is overwhelming. Each one is effectively being met in many programs, too numerous to list, too varied to catalogue completely. Where once school administrators hesitated to consider family life education emphasis in their schools, now those who are not making some efforts in this direction are on the defensive at national, regional, and state meetings of their profession. At one time very few schools, colleges, and universities offered courses of a functional or pre-professional nature in family life education. Now most institutions of higher learning offer something which may range from a single course or two to an entire curriculum in the field of marriage and family life. Churches and youth-serving agencies, such as the YMCA, have greatly expanded their offerings in recent years. Books, pamphlets, films, skits, and teaching aids of all kinds have been developed in greater quantity and quality. Basic research is being carried on in every area of family life throughout the life cycle with findings that challenge the educator at every level.

PROFESSIONAL FOCUS ON FAMILIES

Dramatic too is the increased awareness of the various professions of their interdependence with families and their need to become more family-centered. Physicians are beginning to realize they must see the family-as-a-whole if they are effectively to treat an individual family member. Medical school students are beginning to get professional training in family-centered medical practice. Theological students increasingly

Nurses' classes on needs of childbearing families prepare them for making the birth and lying-in periods creative family experiences.

are exposed to basic materials on the nature of family life, the processes of courtship, marriage, childbearing and living as family members, as well as in the skills of group interviewing, marriage and family counseling and family life education for family members of all ages in their parishes. So too, lawyers, home economists, social workers, nurses, guidance personnel, science educators, human development students, teachers of humanities, religious educators, health and physical educators, mental health specialists, and human relations experts, as well as marriage counselors and family life specialists are devoting more and more time and attention to the family aspects of their work.

WHAT IS FAMILY SUCCESS THROUGH THE FAMILY LIFE CYCLE?

A valid measure of family success is how well the essential family tasks are being accomplished. It is agreed that the central tasks of American families today are: bearing, rearing, socializing, and educating children; assuring physical, mental, economic, and spiritual nurture of each family member; allocating responsibilities, opportunities, and resources according to the needs, readinesses, and potentialities of every member of the family; and maintaining family morale and motivation for carrying out its family functions, tasks and goals.[1]

Families' success in finding happiness and satisfaction in any one of the stages of life is dependent primarily upon how well they achieve the developmental tasks of the period. Failure tends to predispose future frustration, while success is built upon previous success. Every individual, every family, is doing well or not so well in the developmental tasks of the moment. Doing well, the person or the family-as-a-whole is happy, well-adjusted, competent, and relatively self-assured. The challenge to families, and to those who care about them, is to increase the incidence of success and diminish the frequencies of failure in the developmental tasks of life, throughout the entire family life cycle.

Family interaction in a dynamic world calls for good relationships between family members and with other aspects of the entire culture. Throughout the entire life cycle, families face certain inevitable, urgent developmental tasks necessary for their survival, continuation, and development. At every stage of the life cycle, there are challenges and hazards that call for the extension of programs of proven worth and for creative innovations that will assist families to carry more effectively the burdens of twentieth-century living. Family development as a frame of reference may provide a tool which can explore the human frontiers of interpersonal and family interrelationships with the research, education, counseling, and community services urgently needed. Today we push our way through the wilderness of family confusion but tomorrow our children's children may experience smooth, established ways of family life. Road-building is strenuous work. But the dream of a nation of vital happy families producing generation after generation of strong, creative persons is a worthy one, and a goal worth the struggle.

SUGGESTED ACTIVITIES

1) Prepare a case history of a family crisis including the precipitating factor(s), the elements contributing to its build-up, the developmental tasks of each family member involved, and the family-as-a-whole, which were

---

[1] Emily H. Mudd and Reuben Hill, *Memorandum on Strengthening Family Life in the United States,* prepared for Commissioners Charles I. Schottland and William L. Mitchell of the United States Department of Health, Education, and Welfare, the Social Security Administration, 1956, mimeographed report.

halted or blocked during the critical period. List the resources that were available, both within the family and in the larger community. Indicate which resources the family found most helpful, and give a documented appraisal of how the family weathered the crisis. Footnote your material with references to recent research and clinical findings, using some of the sources cited in this chapter as guides.

2) Prepare a paper on the relative vulnerability of the various life cycle stages of present-day American families to (a) disruption, (b) energy depletion, (c) economic strains, (d) disillusionment, and (e) disengagement. Document your material with relevant data from recent research.

3) Using one of the studies with family life cycle data (such as Blood and Wolfe, *Husbands and Wives;* Harold Feldman's contemporary research; Gurin *et al., Americans View Their Mental Health;* or various studies from one or more volumes of *Consumer Behavior,* and similar research reports, listed in your Readings, and elsewhere), plot on graph paper the curves for various variables through the family life cycle. Discuss, interpret and document the trends that are apparent as families move from stage to stage through their life cycles.

4) Choose one stage of the family life cycle and elaborate its challenges, hazards, and services needed. Document with data from research reports, and with illustrations from one or more families at this stage of development known to you.

5) Make a directory of services for families at various stages of the family life cycle and in several areas (i.e. economic, educational, religious, social work, etc.) of life, in your community at the present time. Interview the key personnel in as many as possible in an effort to get information on how many families use their services in a given year, which families in the community make most use of them, how effective their work with family members is, and what elaborations of the type of service rendered they recommend.

6) Invite one or more members of the Board of Education of a nearby school system to discuss with you current attitudes and practices in family life education within both public and private schools in your area. Interview him on the extent of community support for or criticism of courses for boys and girls in family living in the schools. Write up the interview with documentation from nation-wide reports.

7) Collect a variety of catalogues of college and university curricula and review their offerings in the field of marriage and family life for a) functional courses related to students' personal needs and interests, and b) professional and preprofessional courses and courses in the various specialties. Prepare a report on your investigation.

8) Review recent issues of *Marriage and Family Living* for 1) descriptions of educational programs in marriage and family living, 2) research reports on various aspects of courtship, mate selection, marriage and family life, and 3) practice in premarital, marital and family counseling. Report your

findings in a paper on current trends in family life education, research, and counseling.

READINGS

Allport, Gordon W., *Becoming: Basic Considerations for a Psychology of Personality* (New Haven: Yale University Press, 1955).

American Social Health Association, *Education for Personal and Family Living: A Working Guide for Colleges*, New York, 1955.

American Social Health Association, *Suggestions for Preparing Teachers in Education for Personal and Family Living*, New York, 1954.

American Social Health Association, *Strengthening Family Life Education in Our Schools*, New York, 1955.

Blood, Robert O., Jr., and Wolfe, Donald M., *Husbands and Wives: The Dynamics of Married Living* (Glencoe, Illinois: The Free Press, 1960).

Clark, Lincoln II., ed., *Consumer Behavior, Vol. II The Life Cycle and Consumer Behavior* (New York: New York University Press, 1955).

Crow, Lester D., and Crow, Alice, *Human Development and Learning* (New York: American Book Company, 1955).

Duvall, Evelyn Millis, *Family Living* (New York: The Macmillan Company, 1961 Revision), Unit VI, "Growing American Families."

Duvall, Evelyn Millis, "Implications for Education Through the Family Life Cycle," *Marriage and Family Living*, Vol. XX, No. 4, November 1958, pp. 334–342.

Duvall, Evelyn Millis, and Hill, Reuben, *Being Married* (Boston: D. C. Heath and Company, 1960 Revision), Chapters 15, 16, and 17.

Fairchild, Roy W., and Wynn, John Charles, *Families in the Church: A Protestant Survey* (New York: Association Press, 1961).

Feldman, Harold, "The Development of Husband-Wife Relationships," paper delivered at the International Conference on the Family, August, 1960, mimeographed.

Foote, Nelson N., and Cottrell, Leonard S., *Identity and Interpersonal Competence* (Chicago: The University of Chicago Press, 1955).

Geismar, L. L., and Ayres, Beverly, *Measuring Family Functioning* (St. Paul, Minnesota: Family Centered Project, Greater St. Paul Community Chest and Councils, Inc., 1960).

Gurin, Gerald; Veroff, Joseph; and Feld, Sheila, *Americans View Their Mental Health: A Nationwide Interview Study* (New York: Basic Books, Inc., 1960).

Hurlock, Elizabeth B., *Developmental Psychology* (New York: McGraw-Hill Book Company, Second Edition, 1959).

Jacobson, Paul H., *American Marriage and Divorce* (New York: Rinehart & Company, Inc., 1959).

Joint Commission on Mental Illness and Health, *Action for Mental Health* (New York: Basic Books, Inc., 1961).

Koos, Earl Lomon, *Families in Trouble* (New York: King's Crown Press, 1946).

Kuhlen, R. G., and Thompson, G. G., eds., *Psychological Studies of Human Development* (New York: Appleton-Century-Crofts, 1952).

Lansing, John B., and Kish, Leslie, "Family Life Cycle as an Independent Variable," *American Sociological Review*, Vol. 22, No. 5, October 1957, pages 512–519.

Mayer, John E., *The Disclosure of Marital Problems* (New York: Community Service Society of New York, 1966).

Morgan, Janes N., "Consumer Investment Expenditures," *The American Economic Review*, Volume XLVIII, Number 5, December 1958, pages 874–902.

Paget, Norman W., *Family Life Education Program Profiles* (San Bernardino: Kendal Pubublishing Company, 1961).

Pressey, Sidney L., and Kuhlen, Raymond G., *Psychological Development through the Life Span* (New York: Harper & Brothers, 1957).

Symposium on Recent Findings in Human Nutrition, "The Life Cycle and Its Diet," *Journal of Home Economics*, Vol. 49, No. 2, February 1957, pp. 101–115.

Toman, Walter, *Family Constellation* (New York: Springer Publishing Company, Inc., 1961).

United States Department of Health, Education, and Welfare, Social Security Administration, *Memorandum on Strengthening Family Life in the United States*, mimeographed materials, 1956.

White House Conference on Children and Youth, *Children in a Changing World: A Book of Charts* (Washington, D. C.: Golden Anniversary White House Conference on Children and Youth, 1960).

White House Conference on Children and Youth, *Recommendations: Composite Report of Forum Findings* (Washington, D. C.: U. S. Government Printing Office, 1960).

List of Charts and Tables

Index